Embodiment

Embodiment
Essays on Gender and Identity

Edited by
MEENAKSHI THAPAN

Nehru Memorial Museum & Library
New Delhi

DELHI
OXFORD UNIVERSITY PRESS
CALCUTTA   CHENNAI   MUMBAI
1997

Oxford University Press, Great Clarendon Street, Oxford OX2 6DP

Oxford New York
Athens Auckland Bangkok Calcutta
Cape Town Chennai Dar es Salaam Delhi
Florence Hong Kong Istanbul Karachi
Kuala Lumpur Madrid Melbourne Mexico City
Mumbai Nairobi Paris Singapore
Taipei Tokyo Toronto

and associates in

Berlin Ibadan

ISBN 0 19 564179 5

Typeset by S.J.I. Services, New Delhi 110 024
Printed in India at A P Offset, Delhi 110 032
and published by Manzar Khan, Oxford University Press
YMCA Library Building, Jai Singh Road, New Delhi 110 001

For my children
Jyotsna and Ayushya

Acknowledgements

This volume is an outcome of an international workshop on 'Femininity, the female body and sexuality in contemporary society' organized at the Nehru Memorial Museum and Library, New Delhi in November 1994. There were participants from all over India, and one each from France and The Netherlands and about seventy-five people participated in the discussions spread over four days. The paper writers included sociologists, historians, political scientists, psychologists, literary theorists, a medical doctor and activists. This eclectic combination is reflected in the essays selected for this volume which cover a range of issues focusing on human embodiment in one way or another. Embodiment, especially in the context of gender identity, is now a much discussed area but it is relatively new in the Indian setting where it has been somewhat obliquely addressed. This collection is a contribution to understanding a relatively unexplored domain: human embodiment and its implications for the constitution of gender identity in everyday life.

The Workshop was organized with the encouragement and support of Professor Ravinder Kumar, Director, Nehru Memorial Museum and Library. I am grateful to him for allowing me the opportunity to organize such an event during the time I was a Fellow at the Centre for Contemporary Studies. I am indebted to Professor Kumar for his unstinting intellectual and material support at every stage. My intellectual life has been deeply enriched at the Nehru Memorial Museum and Library in terms of the new avenues for research and methodology in the social sciences that have been opened up to me. It has been a most rewarding and intellectually satisfying experience.

All the organizational and administrative work for the Workshop was done by Dr N. Balakrishnan, Mrs Aruna Tandon, Mrs Vatsala Gulati, Mrs Deepa Bhatnagar and Miss Amrit Varsha Gandhi. I am grateful to them for the hard work and effort they put in for the Workshop. I would also like to take this opportunity to thank

Ms Sutinder Kaur of the Library and all the other library staff who have never hesitated to help me in locating books and journals. I must also thank Mr Mandal and the photostat team for doing superb work for me even at short notice.

I am thankful to Professor Susanne Rudolph who invited me to the University of Chicago to teach courses in Sociology for one quarter in 1995. I benefited enormously from my discussions with students and colleagues and also from the faculty seminar organized by Professor Gilbert Herdt of the Committee on Human Development. I also had the opportunity to use the well-stocked Regenstein Library (and get to know James Nye, its Bibliographer for Southern Asia) where I found material that has provided me with a unique understanding of embodiment and gender in relation to social structures and practices as well as individual experiences and perspectives.

I must also acknowledge Patricia Uberoi whose comments and suggestions have been most useful and who has been supportive at every stage. I would like to thank Neera Chandoke, Vidya Rao, Amrit Srinivasan and Vidhu Verma for their interest in this volume and their useful suggestions. At home, I would like to thank my husband, George. I have been able to pursue my academic and research interests only because of his continuous encouragement, support, and enduring love. This book is dedicated to our children who often have had to put up with my irritability and impatience. My parents have unhesitatingly helped me tide over various minor domestic crises with love and care. Many thanks to them.

June 1996   Meenakshi Thapan

Contents

Notes on Contributors

Anna AALTEN teaches feminist anthropology at the Department of Social and Cultural Anthropology of the University of Amsterdam, The Netherlands. Her published work includes *Zakenvrouwen. Over de grenzen van vrouwelijkheid in Nederland sinkds 1945* (Businesswomen. Crossing the boundaries of femininity in The Netherlands since 1945). She has also published widely on women's studies in anthropology and feminist methodology. Her current interest is in the relationship between dance, culture and cultural constructions of the female body.

Jasodhara BAGCHI is Professor of English and Director, School of Women's Studies, Jadavpur University. An activist in *Sachetana*, a Calcutta-based women's organization, she has edited *Indian Women: Myth and Reality* (Orient Longman, 1995) and contributed many articles in edited volumes, journals and newspapers.

Urvashi BUTALIA is co-founder of Kali for Women, India's first and only feminist publishing house. She has been actively involved in the women's movement and has written widely on communication, media, women, publishing and politics. She has co-edited a volume: *Women and the Hindu Right: A Collection of Essays,* and is currently engaged in completing work on an oral history of the partition of India, with specific focus on gender.

Jean D'CUNHA teaches Sociology at St Xavier's College, Bombay. Her specific area of research concern over the last thirteen years, has been the issue of prostitution, on which she has published several papers in academic journals. Significant among her published works are, *The Suppression of Immoral Traffic in Women and Girls Act 1956: A Critical Review* (SNDT Research Centre on Women's Studies, Bombay, 1986) and *Legalization of Prostitution: A Sociological Inquiry into the Laws in India and the West* (Wordmakers, Bangalore, 1991).

Seemanthini NIRANJANA has been teaching off and on in the Department of Sociology, Goa University. Gender issues and questions of an Indian Sociology are among her preoccupations. She is currently working on a manuscript elaborating a spatial axis for gender relations in India.

Tanika SARKAR is Senior Lecturer in History, St Stephen's College, University of Delhi. She has published *Bengal 1928–1934: The Politics of Protest* (Oxford University Press, Delhi, 1987), *Women and the Hindu Right* (co-edited) (Kali for Women and Zed Press, 1985) and *Khaki Shorts and Saffron Flags: A Critique of the Hindu Right* (co-authored) (Orient Longman, 1993).

Meenakshi THAPAN teaches at the Department of Education, University of Delhi. She has also taught at the Department of Sociology at the Delhi School of Economics and at the University of Chicago, Illinois. She was Fellow, Centre for Contemporary Studies, Nehru Memorial Museum and Library, New Delhi from 1993–95. Her publications include *Life at School* (Oxford University Press, 1991) and *Anthropological Journeys* (edited) Orient Longman (forthcoming).

Susie THARU, currently Jawaharlal Nehru Fellow, is a Reader in the Department of English at the Central Institute of English and Foreign Languages, Hyderabad. Her research interests are in cultural history/theory and feminism. Among her publications are: *Women Writing in India: 600 B.C. to the Present* (in two volumes; Oxford University Press, New Delhi); *The Sense of Performance in the Post Artaud Theatre* (Arnold Heinemann, New Delhi, 1984) and co-authored with others in the Stree Shakti Sanghatana Working Group on the Telengana Struggle, *We were Making History: Women in the Telengana People's Struggle* (Kali for Women, Delhi, 1988; Zed Press, London, 1988). She is a founder member of Anveshi, Research Centre for Women's Studies, Hyderabad.

Patricia UBEROI is a sociologist, working at the Institute of Economic Growth, Delhi. She has taught Sociology at the Department of Sociology, Delhi School of Economics, and the Centre for the Study of Social Systems, Jawaharlal Nehru University, New Delhi. She has edited *Family, Kinship and Marriage in India* (Oxford University Press, Delhi, 1993) and *Social Reform, Sexuality and the State* (special issue of *Contributions to Indian Sociology,* Sage Publications, New

Delhi, 1995), and published widely on questions of family, kinship and gender with reference to both India and China.

Vidhu VERMA is Senior Lecturer in Political Science and teaches Political Theory and Western Political Thought at Gargi College, University of Delhi. She has completed an M.Phil. degree from Oxford University and has recently received her doctoral degree from the University of Delhi. She has contributed to various journals and newspapers. Her current work is on citizenship, rights and feminist theory.

Susan VISVANATHAN is Senior Lecturer in Sociology at Hindu College, Delhi. She has held fellowships with the Nehru Memorial Museum and Library, Delhi (at the Centre for Contemporary Studies) and the Indian Institute of Advanced Study, Shimla. She is Charles Wallace India Trust Fellow at Queen's University, Belfast for 1997. She is the author of *The Christians of Kerala* (Oxford University Press, Madras, 1993).

Kalpana VISWANATH is working on a Ph.D. on the contemporary women's movement in India from the University of Delhi. She is also currently working on issues of women's reproductive choices and new contraceptive technologies, looking specifically at anti-fertility vaccines.

Punam ZUTSHI has taught at the Department of Sociology, Jamia Millia Islamia, Delhi. She has earlier worked at the Centre for the Study of Developing Societies, Delhi and was a Visiting Fellow, Department of Social Medicine, Harvard Medical School for the two-year duration of her fieldwork in USA (1986–7). She is currently a Faculty Member, Design Foundation Studies, at the National Institute of Design, Ahmedabad.

Introduction
Gender and Embodiment in Everyday Life

Meenakshi Thapan

I

THE SIGNIFICANCE OF HUMAN EMBODIMENT

All humans are embodied creatures and not mere Cartesian minds that happen to be located in some biological matter. It follows that female embodiment is dissimilar to male embodiment and it is therefore important to know the implications of that different embodiment for social relations in everyday life.[1] At one level, women menstruate, give birth, nurse babies, experience menopause—experiences which are unavailable to men. At another level, women and men are located in cultural settings that shape their experience of embodiment differently depending on class, ethnic, religious and caste factors. These sociospatial and other historical and political factors are therefore equally important in the experience of embodiment in everyday life.

The significance of the human body in everyday life was seriously considered by Marcel Mauss who in 1934 delivered a pioneering lecture at a meeting of the Society of Psychology in Paris on 'Techniques of the body' (Mauss 1973). He draws attention to the use of the body in different societies through modes of action, viz., techniques of the body, which essentially have to be 'effective and *traditional*' (i.e., having 'symbolic, ritual and magical value').[2] Durkheim's influence is apparent in Mauss's emphasis on tradition, the symbolic, the ritualistic and the magical import of the body in everyday life. In contemporary times, the body is also seen as being constitutive of self, i.e., the body is related to a person's sense of self-identity. It is through the lived body in everyday life that a person's sense of identity is constituted. The body has symbolic and cultural value, which may differ across cultures, and it is also defined, shaped and constrained by society. Both values and practice are therefore crucial to a person's embodiment. However, a person is also an agential body, in communication, and negotiation, with significant others in everyday life. The focus of this book is on both the socially and culturally constructed body as well as on the lived body in everyday life.

In 1984, Bryan Turner commented that 'few social theorists have taken the embodiment of persons seriously' (1984: 1). The last dozen years have seen commentaries on every possible aspect of embodiment especially in relation to the female body[3]—to the extent that we now have scholars asking the question 'Why all the fuss about the body?' (Bynum 1995). In sociology, certainly, the body, both in its material aspects and social relatedness, was not taken serious note of until the work of Erving Goffman appeared in social theory. Goffman was concerned with the techniques of the body in social relationships, such as 'face-work', gestures, and other nuances in 'the presentation of self' and maintenance of appearances as a form of public display in everyday life. For Goffman, the body is important for identifying the links between people's self-identity and social identity. He was also concerned with deviant or stigmatized bodies and their social acceptability. In an important, but less cited work, Goffman examines the use of the gendered body in commercial advertisements (see Goffman 1971, 1979).

Pierre Bourdieu's inclusion of the body in understanding and explaining social life has also proved to be very influential. He has been concerned with the body as bearer of symbolic value as well as of physical capital. His argument about the development of 'cultural capital' which is embodied in children when they acquire certain dispositions, tastes and abilities has enhanced our understanding of how education both contributes to, and is a victim of, the reproduction of dominant values, norms and social processes. It is however Bourdieu's work on the symbolic value of the body as a material phenomenon which both constitutes, and is constituted by society, which is arguably the most influential contribution to contemporary work on the body (see Bourdieu 1977, 1979; Bourdieu and Passeron 1977).[4]

In the Indian context, an important work on the body in contemporary times is David Arnold's *Colonizing the Body* (1993) in which he emphasizes the importance of 'the body as a site of colonizing power and of contestation between the colonized and the colonizers' (ibid.: 7). Vandana Shiva's work shows us the crucial links between the body and nature, between the 'earth body and the human body through the processes that maintain life' (Shiva 1994: 3).[5] Anthropologists have commented on the marked nature of woman's body by caste, religious belief, social norms and practices, and on how woman's embodiment and her sexuality serve as important boundary markers. Such work has, among other things, shown us the significance of embodiment in the cultural and religious lives of different communities.[6] Feminist activists have, perhaps more consciously than others, addressed the *gendered* aspects of social behaviour, exploitation and violence in relation to the female body in the context of, for example, rape, domestic violence, sexual abuse, and the health of women in India.[7] To the extent that woman's body is the foundation on which gender equality is built, established and legitimized, understanding the female body in different contexts, settings, and situations none the less remains an urgent research prerogative.

II

WOMEN AND THEIR EMBODIMENT

This volume seeks to understand and explicate the woman's body, in both its material and representational aspects, in the context of different social, cultural, and historical settings in contemporary society. All the essays address, in one way or another, questions relating to gendered inequalities which are revealed in the complex interplay between society, gender and body in everyday life. Woman's body is therefore central to understanding unequal gender relations; it is the site of violence, exclusion, and abuse; it also has its celebratory aspects which are revealed in imagery through artistic or aesthetic modes, or in the consciousness of women; it is the site also for agency which allows for the possibilities of negotiation, intervention, contestation and transformation.

Central to the debate on the female body in academic discourse is the preoccupation with the sex/gender distinction. A woman's identity is sought to be fixed and understood in terms of her gendered being defined essentially by her sexuality and her reproductive value. In his treatise on *Femininity*, Sigmund Freud sought to explain the 'riddle of femininity' in terms of a woman's sexual anatomy arguing that 'the

discovery that she is castrated is a turning-point in a girl's growth'
(1990: 103). Freud's limited understanding of womanhood is undoubtedly caused by his excessive interest in the *sexual* underpinnings of
gender identity which he never sees in itself but always in counter-
position to male sexuality. Feminist theory has examined sexual identity and sought to place it centrestage by drawing attention to, and
challenging, the inherent bipolarity in the debate. Feminists argue that
traditional scholarship has viewed women as placed in the Cartesian
framework of bodily need and individual experience far removed from
the rationality and objectivity of the mind which is associated with
man. Such a view has resulted in additional masculine/feminine
dualities, primarily culture/nature, objective/subjective, order/disorder,
reason/emotion, and so on. Woman, in every attribute, is rated lower
than the corresponding male attribute and it has been argued that
western society has subordinated the feminine principle to the masculine in the interests of patriarchy.

In the Indian context, woman has not been so neatly defined: she
is made up of many attributes, some of which may dominate in different contexts and settings and others in other contexts. This is the
ambivalent persona of the Indian woman, located in myth and popular
culture, as both goddess and dangerous power (*shakti*), as virtuous
wife and dangerous evil, both pure and impure in her embodiment, to
be revered and worshipped but also to be controlled through a direct
regulation of her sexuality (Das 1976; Nandy 1976).[8]

More recently, Kalpana Ram (1992) has examined Catholicism as
a field of value and of action within which the contradictory construction of femininity, the female body and sexuality takes place in a fishing community in Tamil Nadu. She argues that there is an ambivalent
view of female sexuality where, on the one hand, there is a festive
celebration of female sexuality, for example, in rituals relating to
menarche, and on the other hand, there is the 'containment of the
female body' evident in the 'metaphors and social practices of cooling,
binding and secluding the female body' (1992: 85). The ambivalent
nature of feminine identity, as perceived and represented, in popular
culture, religious beliefs and social practices therefore strengthens our
argument that woman's identity in a culturally diverse and religiously
plural Indian society is far more obscure than as represented in other
cultures.

The purpose of the western argument of highlighting the possible
differences between the masculine and the feminine was essentially to
focus on a male superiority and a female lack, as it were, grounded

in the biological and sexual difference between male and female. It is clear how the female body becomes the edifice on which gender inequality is built and legitimized. The traditional, male dominated or influenced, position which sought to emphasize sexual difference is therefore unacceptable to contemporary feminists who seek to liberate women from their identification with physical embodiment and the functions and roles associated with it. The biological female body is not therefore important in itself but only in a social context. It then follows that woman in fact is socially constructed and the concept of *gender* becomes central to our understanding of the nature of women's embodiment in the everyday world.

III

THE SOCIALLY CONSTRUCTED FEMALE BODY

Simone de Beauvoir's classic statement that 'one is not born, but rather becomes, a woman' (1953: 295) is indicative of the view that a woman's biological, psychological and social location are not as significant as the influence of 'civilization' which produces woman.[9] The social constructionist position on the woman's body emphasizes the view that a woman experiences her body, sexuality and feminine identity as a social being located in a particular cultural setting with its dominant values and norms. This view takes the physicality of the body, as matter or stuff, as given and moves on to consider the constitution of identity in gendered terms in its social context. There are certain presuppositions of this position, viz., that power is all-pervasive and all-encompassing so that we are influenced to think, act and interact in ways which are conducive to maintaining the existing unequal relations in society.

The influence of Foucault's explanation of how power works in social processes is central to the theoretical underpinnings of this perspective. Foucault's analysis of the discursive body examines its capacity to be manipulated, moulded, shaped, constructed, and changed and explains the manner in which the body is invested with different and changing forms of power. His perspective has been particularly useful for feminist analyses which take account of the socially constructed body but has vexed other feminists who have found his related theory of resistance weak and unable to offer agency to the subject who remains, in Foucault's terminology, very much a 'docile body'.[10] Foucault's influence on contemporary feminist work on the woman's body is however central to understanding the concern with the nature of the socially constructed body.

In the Indian context, the social and historical settings in which women are located undoubtedly affect the nature of their embodied experience as well as their articulation of it. It may thus be argued that Indian situational discourse has generated a different construction of woman's body and sexuality located in the specific issues of caste, communalism, the trauma of partition at the time of political independence, the socialization practices common to different cultures, the social practices of dowry related deaths, female foeticide and infanticide, rape of women belonging to particular communities, child marriage, widow immolation (*sati*), and so on.[11] In this context, Sangari and Vaid reiterate an important point, viz., that 'the lives of women lie at the interface of caste and class inequality, especially since the description and management of gender and female sexuality is involved in the maintenance and reproduction of social inequality' (1989: 5).[12] That female sexuality is controlled by caste and class factors is an indisputable fact. A woman's body and sexuality are in any case under the controlling purview of men; but men of higher castes and classes appear to have special privileges which may be coercively asserted. It is an assertion not only of patriarchal power but also of social control.

The essays in Section I emphasize the role of the community, of both men and women, in different times in contributing to the construction of woman's identity through exercising control over her body and sexuality. Woman is allowed little or no space for an independent, self-perceived articulation, definition or expression of her sexuality. Her body becomes an instrument and a symbol for the community's expression of caste, class and communal honour. Chastity, virtue and, above all, purity are extolled as great feminine virtues embodying the honour of the family, community and the nation.[13] A woman's experience of her body is largely that of shame (*lajja*) as she is seen as transgressing family and social *moral* norms in one way or another. The moral domain for woman is therefore always defined and policed by the Other. In a sense, woman's body is often no longer *her* body but has been taken over by the community, of both men and women, to establish and legitimize its image in society.[14]

Socialization practices in different cultures reflect the care and concern that goes into the upbringing of girls so that we are in fact trained to conduct ourselves according to social norms, values and practices.[15] Later, women absorb social expectations, and in fact experience them as their own, so that power, in a sense, does not operate coercively but from within. The possibility for resistance through woman's agency is none the less ever present as women use, manipulate and strategize to construct an identity that is their own. Of course it is always possible that such a feminine identity may be constructed within a prevailing and influential social discourse so that women's efforts at self-expression may not amount to any significant transformation of the social code. The socially constructed body is none the less always mediated by individual agency, individual perceptions and, above all, individual experience.

IV

THE LIVED BODY

This brings us to the crucial problematic of woman's experience of her body as a lived body in everyday life. It is only when we view the female body as a lived or communicative body, that we can begin to understand the implications of both the social construction of lived experience as well as women's own perceptions and articulations of their embodiment.

The essays in Section II focus on the lived body, that is, the body grounded in experience, in everyday life, as opposed to, for example, the objectified body of science. The lived body is located in culture and, as Iris Young has pointed out, 'culture and meaning (are) inscribed in its habits, in its specific forms of perception and comportment' (1990: 14). In her recent work on 'difference', Henrietta Moore suggests the notion of 'the "lived anatomy" and of bodily praxis as a mode of knowledge that draws on an understanding of experience as a form of embodied intersubjectivity'. Experience, then, is 'intersubjective and embodied; it is not individual and fixed but irredeemably social and processual' (1994: 3). Experience is not a collective phenomenon but varies across cultures, races and within a culture, according to class, caste and regional orientations. Yet, experience cannot be described merely as an individual's limited perspective located in a specific milieu that defines a particular woman's existence. It is common to women belonging to a particular group of similar social status located in a defined cultural and social setting.[16]

The concern then of all the papers in this section is with how gender is inscribed on woman in everyday life both socially as well as through her life experiences, perceptions, desires, fantasies. It is in this sense that gender identity is truly, as Moore has pointed out, 'both constructed and lived' (1994: 49).

Three themes emerge as the focus of this section of the book, i.e., women's embodiment in the context of space, performance and intimate relationships. Woman's experience of her embodiment in everyday life is undoubtedly linked to her location in different settings and contexts whether these are the community, the family, the workplace, or other spaces she inhabits or frequents. An explicitly spatial dimension has perhaps earlier formed the content of feminist anthropological analyses (for example, Ardener 1981, Ganesh 1993, Bennett 1983) in terms of its presence in the ethnographic material but has probably not been directly addressed as a major axis for the formation of gender identity.[17] The first paper in this section does just that.

The representation of female embodiment, especially through the visual media of dance and film, is problematic for the constitution of gender identity. The essay on ballet dancers in this section comments on some of the agential elements of shaping and moulding the body in a dancer's lived relationship to her body. Dance constructs the body as *performance*. It has been suggested that film does this even more distinctively. Performance is an activity, argues Annette Kuhn, 'that connotes pretence, dissimulation, "putting on an act", assuming a role.... Performance, in other words, poses the possibility of a mutable self, of a fluid subjectivity' (Kuhn 1988: 17). The possibilities for the constitution of gender identity in film as ever-changing, fluid and mutable, very much in Judith Butler's mode, become endless.[18] The problem however lies in *representation*.[19] Representation is a form of regulation to the extent that it reflects the social relations of power; female embodiment tends to be located in a very specific kind of imagery which mirrors social relations in a particular culture. In the Indian context, these would obviously not be very conducive to the portrayal of women, their bodies and their relationships in a manner that goes against the grain of social relations in everyday life.

The intimacy of everyday life within marriage and its experience for women has been examined in urban settings in India. Such work (for example, that of Kapur 1970, 1973; Singh 1990) has provided us with narratives of largely urban and middle and upper class women in terms of their experience of conjugal relations, their sexuality, and their relationships with significant members of the extended family, such as the mother-in-law. The analysis gives primacy to experience without grounding experience in a specific domain of inquiry. The complexities of heterosexual intimate relationships, and the problematic body imagery that is constructed and played out through these relationships, has certain definite implications for the constitution of gender identity. Two essays in this section directly examine some of these complex issues.

V

THE CONSTRAINED AND REGULATED BODY

The woman's body is socially and culturally disciplined to 'fit in' and 'adjust' to tradition and practice in different ways. Women also consciously, and unconsciously, discipline themselves to be the bearers of tradition, harmony and familial and social honour. If we seek to examine the 'scientific' discourses of social life, we might also find an element of control in biological descriptions and definitions of the female body, its organs, its functions, its processes, especially in relation to the male body. Emily Martin has argued that culture possibly plays an important role in shaping biological scientists' descriptions of what they find in the natural world. As an illustration she states that 'the picture of the egg and the sperm drawn in popular as well as scientific accounts of reproductive biology relies on stereotypes central to our cultural definitions of male and female' (1991: 485). Elsewhere, Martin has drawn our attention to the manner in which menstruation is described in standard medical texts (1990). She suggests that there is an element of negativity in the descriptions so that menstruation is seen as a 'failure to produce' so that women are really 'out of control' when they menstruate instead of getting pregnant (ibid.: 75). By contrast, male reproductive physiology, Martin argues, is portrayed in terms of 'the *remarkable* cellular transformation ..., the most *amazing* characteristic of spermatogenesis is its *sheer magnitude* ...', and so on (ibid.: 76). There is no doubt that cultural ideology influences 'scientific' definitions, descriptions, and analyses.[20] The aim appears to be a denigration of the female body in its biological aspects so that it is portrayed as less capable, less efficient and on the whole less 'together' than the male body. The implications of such descriptions are only too apparent. As a result, woman's position in the work place and at home is affected. She becomes the incompetent and belligerent colleague and partner at least for some days every month.[21] In the Indian classical tradition, she also becomes impure and her movements are restricted to certain spaces and domains. In a sense then scientific descriptions and social practice come together to discipline the female body which is out of tune, as it were, for a certain period every month.

Cultural constraints also operate in the work and life of the female sex-worker who is under constant social scrutiny and reform. The attempts to sanitize sex during the colonial period in India are too well known to bear repetition except to comment on the compelling colonial need for safe sex with exotic but perhaps disease-ridden Indians. Their own men remained above the law whereas Indian women's bodies and sexuality were to be regulated and controlled to prevent them from spreading filth and disease. Women of course sought to exercise some control over their bodies by evading the mandatory medical check-ups, thereby circumventing the imposed social regulation.[22]

VI

RESISTANCE THROUGH EMBODIMENT IN EVERYDAY LIFE

Individual agency and the possibilities for change have been present, both implicitly and more directly, in the discussion so far but we now move more wholeheartedly into a consideration of the question of resistance and subversion in direct relation to embodiment. While it is essential to present and emphasize the agential role of women in both the social and lived aspects of their embodiment, it is obvious that one needs to be careful, as Rajeshwari Sunder Rajan cautions in another context, to avoid stressing the 'romantic fiction' of resistance, however politically well-intentioned it might be (1993: 12). It is in this sense that it is important to argue that the possibilities for transformation are always constrained by the restricting nature of the dominant constructions based on gender, class, caste and regional factors. It is not necessary, moreover, that these constraints are located

The Socially Constructed Body: Caste, Community and National Identity

Tanika Sarkar examines the question of the 'chastity' of a 'good Hindu woman', as defined by the community, in her discussion of a sexual scandal in nineteenth-century Bengal. The scandal and its later representation in popular cultural modes, such as painting and drama, had an enormous impact on middle-class Bengali society in the last quarter of the previous century. Sarkar's analysis fleshes out the manner in which a sexual event takes on the tone of a scandal, becomes a dramatic event in the lives of people across society, acquires representative value in popular culture and reinforces cultural perceptions of the 'good' Hindu woman in late nineteenth-century Bengal. At the centre of the storm, created around the sexual seduction of a young middle-class wife, is the notion of a woman's chastity that is particularly sacrosanct in the confines of marriage. If this chastity becomes questionable, it is indicative of the crumbling of the conjugal order that is central to the moral code of middle-class lives.

In the entire debate, focused in one way or another on the scandal and its ramifications, the body of woman as social spectacle is symbolic of the inner spiritual essence whose purity and honour are at stake in a caste and class based society. Sarkar locates the centrality of the chaste Hindu woman in the interlocking domains of caste, class and public events and links it to the Hindu nationalism that was prevalent at the time. The Hindu moral domain was superior and the Hindu woman's 'uncompromising monogamy' was in fact a celebrated sign that, Sarkar claims, 'constituted the Hindu claim to nationhood'. She argues therefore that it was the Hindu woman (the inner spiritual being) who had to maintain this difference as the Hindu man (the outer material force) had already surrendered to a western colonial power. The body of woman, at this point, is no more than a socially constructed body, legitimized in marriage, victim of a scandal, bandied about as spectacle in public discourse, upholder of caste, religious and even national identity, and eventually socially ostracized and dismissed for her 'sins'.

A contemporary Bengali woman writer, Jyotirmoyee Devi, places woman's experience at the centre of her novel *Epar Ganga, Opar Ganga* (On both sides flows the Ganges). Jasodhara Bagchi's paper narrates the experience of the novel's protagonist, Sutara, in which the state and the community use woman's body as the site for the defilement of communal honour. This is only one aspect of the problem, within the movement today, ideological, class or community based, rural or urban, spread out all over India. These may have arisen in response to specific issues or as part of a political process seeking a change in women's consciousness and in their everyday lives. The context in which they evolve strategies for women to cope with and change aspects of their everyday lives is examined in the last paper in this collection. We also need to take stock of the movement, not only in India, to see how far we have progressed in the restoration of women's rights, the extent to which women have control of their bodies and their lives, and the possibilities that remain for a transformation of women's lives through their embodiment.

VII

THE ESSAYS IN THE BOOK

Feminist scholarship in India is less concerned with the refinement of theoretical nuances and more with the immediacy of women's experience in the everyday and with the urgency of contemporary issues that need to be addressed, questioned and resolved. The essays in this volume examine aspects of the embodied and gendered existence of women in contemporary society in different contexts, spaces and situations. Underlying all the papers is a concern for understanding the nature of the embodied existence both from the point of view of women's experience as well as from its social representations, imagery, and relatedness in everyday life.

The book has been divided into four parts, viz., those essays dealing more specifically with the constructed nature of embodiment and gender identity (Sarkar, Bagchi and Butalia); those concerned with understanding the lived or the communicative body in everyday life (Niranjana, Aalten, Uberoi and Thapan); those examining the discipline and constraint imposed on woman's body through science and social regulation in specific contexts (Zutshi and D'Cunha), and those which present the 'politics of the possible' (to borrow Kumkum Sangari's evocative phrase) and examine the place of resistance and subversion in everyday life (Tharu, Verma, Visvanathan and Viswanath).

Niranjana's use of space as an important con
not view it as only a passive and unchanging s
interaction but more to highlight space and soci
stitutive. Such space is also characterized by flui
olage/horage does not represent merely the pr
with the former subordinate to the latter. In fact
represents 'a novel configuration of relations'
constituted in each context whether it relates t
village or the caste group. What remains constant
ner in which women's bodies inhabit space ar
negotiation of spaces and identities. This also al
for women's agency provided by a spatial dimer
count of their multiple identities.

The possibilities for agency in women's nego
endless. If we are consciously aware of wome
relationship to their bodies, we can see how age
embodied existence. Anna Aalten undertakes
women very much as 'embodied subjects', as ac
construction and reconstruction of their bodi
(1990), she sees gender as a 'performative act' i
cal sense that social agents constitute reality th
of acting. Aalten views this approach to gender,
experience of the lived body, as offering infin
strained however by existing social and historica
on western dance in The Netherlands, viz., class
amines gender reality as 'it is created through
formances' in which, she argues, 'the body is
gender directives and/or to produce new ones'.

Examining the case of Olga de Haas, a you
present times, Aalten discusses the manner in
classical ballet demand a tremendous change i
example, she raises the problem of the stylizatio
in order to perform the role of a nymph: 'What
act of a sylph mean for the body of a performe
the basic principles of classical ballet tend to
movements of the human body and the dancer ha
both in the sense of how she uses her body as
resents it in performance.

The demands of classical ballet are met b
shaping and changing the contours of the body
through both repetition and manipulation. A da

the other being the manner in which the body is used by the community to preserve its own caste-class identity. Bagchi shows us how a Hindu girl merely by seeking shelter in a Muslim household, during a period of communal turbulence, is rendered impure and physically defiled in her own community. Her errant body, simply by inhabiting culturally 'wrong' spaces, therefore ensures that she is unworthy of maintaining her own caste-class identity. There is now a mark on her sexuality, a caste and communal mark, that sets her apart from her own community and also from other 'pure' women. She has to be abandoned in a women's hostel, in the quest for education, that is, a neutral space divested of caste or communal markers. Even here, however, the nuances of a contaminated body are not absent as she becomes part of a group of unknown and identity-less female bodies.

'The panopticist gaze of the community', as Bagchi argues with Foucauldian resonances, controls and regulates the girl's body, allowing her no space for seeking an alternative that might in fact liberate her from her misery. Sutara is thus robbed of agency and is unable to evolve any subversive strategies. Bagchi links the private and social crisis of the protagonist with the larger social crises and their outcome such as the cause of political independence which has its own agenda and unhesitatingly uses woman's body as a symbol of family, caste and community honour. Bagchi also emphasizes the linkages with the social and political ambience in which middle-class Bengali society is located so that we can understand the social moorings of this regulatory gaze. It is the community which glorifies chastity and raises it to an unreal and ephemeral pedestal, thus making the chaste Hindu wife 'the central icon of the glory of Hindu India'.

Moving to more recent times, Urvashi Butalia examines the implications of the partition of India in 1947 for abducted and widowed women. She focuses on the experience of abandonment, abduction, destitution and loneliness by women at that time. She also looks at the relationship of these 'unattached' women with the State which became their protector in the absence of their men. On the part of the State, it was a relationship, Butalia tells us, 'of deep benevolence and a profound patriarchy' established largely through its operation for the recovery and rehabilitation of women. The State also resumed responsibility for the 'moral well-being' of these women. Butalia argues that this concern for woman is linked to the nationalist image of the body of the nation as a pure, undefiled, sacred female body. This body had to be protected against the communal Other much more than against the colonial Other, and its defilement and loss meant a slur on national

identity dependent as it was on the pristi
feminine being. Contrarily, the loss of hono
'manhood' so that woman's body and mascu
tied up in an all-encompassing national identi
protective mantle of the guardian of women'
an effort to control women's sexuality whic
and indisciplined as the women had lost the
protectors. In addition, although the State d
cupations to the widowed women, their righ
violated so that in the end the State could no
benevolence in relationship to these women.

The Lived Body in Everyday Life: Sp
and Intimate Relationships

Anthropological discourse on woman's bo
Niranjana in her essay in this collection, ta
value of the body without addressing the m
not only as they are culturally constructed
lived realities of persons. She instead se
considers the two major axes which define
historical contexts, viz., 'femininity (as an a
grounding in the female body'. By thereby s
both the biological and the cultural in the fo
Niranjana examines the 'situated' female b
culture'. Niranjana therefore brings a differe
of gender identity in speaking of the 'body
femininity that is not simply internalized or
how we live our lives as women through our

The spatial register is central to Nir
women's lives in a village community in
southern India. This is based on the locally
horage (literally, inside/outside) which de
parameters of women's lives in the village.
mediated through their relationship to t
household, the village, and caste relationshi
underlying morality which seeks to regulate
imposing restrictions on their use of particu
has also been internalized by women who
value for their own moral good.

resolve the weight problem through dieting and Aalten draws out the
manner in which this becomes almost an obsession with all ballerinas,
even those who are at the pre-pubertal stage. After all, it was Olga de
Haas's determination, and her conscious effort to shape her body,
which resulted in her diminished thighs and more harmoniously
proportioned body. In relation to her own goals of being a first-rate
classical dancer, she therefore achieved perfection both in embodiment
and performance.

In her essay, Patricia Uberoi examines the most intimate of social
relationships, the heterosexual man-woman relationship, in popular
Hindi cinema and uses the immensely popular classic film *Sahib, Bibi
aur Ghulam* as her ethnographic text. She comments on the film's
preoccupation with 'feet' as 'the most condensed of corporeal
signifiers' both in the sense of their being objects of the male gaze
and of male desire as well as signifying social status for the male
protagonist in the film.

Uberoi recognizes and uses the 'podosemiotic' idiom of the film
to interpret its central message and main theme. She perceives the
theme of 'love', in its many forms and manifestations, as being crucial
to the film's narrative structure. It is, as Uberoi tells us, a 'treatise on
love', about love in marriage, outside marriage, as duty, passion and
also as unconsummated love. She sees all these elements of love
present in one way or another in the four man-woman relationships
present in the film which she examines in terms of two major conceptual oppositions 'duty and desire' and 'freedom and destiny'. These
oppositions remain central to the particular genre of popular Hindi
cinema in contemporary times that seek to reconcile, in one way or
another, the conflict between these oppositions in intimate relationships in everyday life. Classical Hindu thought suggests that conjugal
relations are to be governed by duty over desire, which is why sexual
passion is seldom characteristic of married life, either socially or in
the privacy of intimate seclusion. Sexuality, however, has an ambiguous status to the extent that it can be both enabling as well as
restricting for a woman whose fertility is seen as being auspicious but
her sexuality could be potentially dangerous. The tension in *Sahib,
Bibi aur Ghulam*, as indeed in other popular films of the same genre,
then is between 'wifeliness' in conformity with duty and 'sexuality'
as desire (as expressed through the courtesan seen in contradistinction
to the wife). The second opposition, of freedom and destiny, argues
Uberoi, is even more difficult to resolve, in film, especially in the
context of mate selection for purposes of marriage. Eventually, destiny

overrules freedom and this theme is amply portrayed in popular cinema as it conforms to social prescriptions as well as signals commercial success. Evidently, passion, as it is experienced by women in intimate relationships, remains regulated by a social morality that controls 'excess of passion' in relationships both outside and within marriage. Fulfilment is scarcely achieved and excessive passion can only result in tragedy and the experience of shame for women at their loss of virtue and social honour. The moral message is loud and clear: containment of female sexuality exemplified by restraint in intimate relationships. The ever-watchful 'male' (and female) gaze of the spectator says it all: the eroticism of the feet as objects of bodily display and as symbols of an erotic sexuality is to be allowed as imagery but when it is a question of *intimate relationships*, transgression is not permitted, even in representation. It would break all moral barriers and social norms and, commercially speaking, be a complete disaster.

Meenakshi Thapan examines middle and upper class women's experience of 'oppression' in intimate relationships in urban Delhi by relating such experience to women's notions of femininity, to their perceptions of their bodies and sexuality in everyday life. Central to Thapan's paper is the question: how does power take root in our minds so that we are ruled by it, from within, in our relationships in everyday life? The oppression that women experience can then be examined from the viewpoint of their understanding of their bodies and sexuality. Such a perspective allows us to see the interlinkages between patriarchal constructions of female embodiment, women's internalization of the images created by these constructions, and the extent to which these images inform their own understanding of their bodies and sexuality. 'Oppression', in its psychological form, is then an experience of a disjunction between a woman's body-image and male constructions of it. In its heightened form, this becomes 'mental torture' for women, who experience the entire relationship as oppressive and worthless. Women's experience of physical violence, added to their experience of psychological oppression, influences and even shapes their own body images in particular directions. The dimension of the nuclear and the extended family (or 'joint') households adds another perspective to their experience of their embodiment in intimate relationships. Thapan examines four case studies, and in each case, she considers the construction of body-image, its demolition by the male partner, the resultant impact on the woman's perception of her embodiment, and on the relationship itself. It is obvious, concludes Thapan, that women tend to collude with their oppressors by accepting

prevailing notions of femininity and by submitting their bodies to the discipline and maintenance techniques required for meeting ideal norms. The question Thapan raises at the end of her paper is whether there is the possibility of an alternative or an autonomous construction of femininity that is grounded more on women's own notions of presentation of bodily self in everyday life. She does not however argue for a feminist utopia and instead concludes that the body is engaged in a continuous making and remaking of the complexities of gender identity in everyday life through communication, negotiation and contestation.

Disciplining the Woman's Body: The Discourse of Medical 'Science' and the Social Regulation of Prostitution

Medical knowledge rests on socio-cultural classifications and in fact builds on this to itself become part of, as Punam Zutshi puts it in her paper on menstrual symptomatology, the 'collective representations of a society'. However, in order to understand how certain medical categories take root and are transformed, Zutshi suggests, we need to take recourse to 'the materiality of signs and symptoms'. Zutshi examines the pre-menstrual syndrome as it is important in understanding menstrual-cycle related experience and disease categories. She also takes into account the related category of menopause. Based on fieldwork conducted on the east coast of the United States, Zutshi presents her case material in which women describe, at length and in intimate detail, their experience of pre-menstrual tension. The women emphasize the experience of irritability, depression, physical pain, loss of control, lack of tolerance and the use of the analogy of 'turning into the witch' with reference to their symptomatic behaviour as someone who is 'naggy, bitchy, witchy'.

The category of the pre-menstrual syndrome is obtained, it emerges, at the intersection of two domains of knowledge, viz., that of the knowledge of hysteria and melancholy and the knowledge of the symptoms associated with the menstrual cycle. Zutshi concludes that the figure of the witch 'serves as a vehicle to convey the feeling of anger, of being out of control, having an altered consciousness or sense of self'. She then relates the symptoms obtained from the case material with medical profiles of melancholy and hysteria to understand the implications of this aspect of disease and transgression for the nature of womanhood and sexuality. Zutshi finally argues that the medical establishment is in fact instrumental in 'fixing' bodies, making them

fit for the demands of the work space, to the extent that the medicalization of the pre-menstrual syndrome is designed to deal with 'incapacity', with failure and with a flawed body. In attempting 'to iron out the flaws of women's bodies', medical science therefore seeks to impose social order and to discipline, as it were, errant bodies.

* * *

Nowhere is the social regulation of female sexuality more explicit than in the context of prostitution or 'sex-work', as it is more commonly defined. The uneven regulation and control over women's, as opposed to men's, bodies has been significant especially in the legal discourse related to it. Jean D'Cunha examines the implications of the Contagious Diseases Acts of 1868 on the popular debate on prostitution and the trafficking of women for the purposes of prostitution. These Acts legalized prostitution and at the same time gained control over women's bodies. D'Cunha argues that male sexuality was untrammelled and men were allowed endless pleasure with women being set apart for this purpose to provide 'sanitized sex'. There was some resistance to these Acts which emerged in the form of the Repeal Campaign and the Social Purity Crusades in England but this movement, argues D'Cunha, was located in a moralistic and 'victimology' perspective. Its emphasis was on virtue and charity as eminent feminine virtues and it viewed prostitutes as the embodiment of promiscuity. This perspective is unable to distinguish between the social institution of prostitution and the individual woman in prostitution, thereby concealing the vested interests in the economic and ideological systems underlying prostitution. Similarly, the other views that D'Cunha examines, viz., that of sexual politics and of relative autonomy and self-determination, are considered inadequate primarily because of their focus on single issues, such as patriarchy or basic rights, and their failure to consider the political economy dimension of gender discrimination.

D'Cunha's suggestion is that prostitution needs in fact to be considered and understood in the context of the political economy of women's reproductive labour and sexuality and North/South relations. She argues that the commodification of every aspect of human life implies also the commodification of women's bodies and that the internationalization of capital has had deep implications for the sex service industry. It is women, and children, from countries of the southern

part of the world who cater to men from the richer countries for all kinds and varieties of sexual pleasure. In addition, the perpetuation of prostitution is aided by the institutions of patriarchy, religion and racism. D'Cunha draws out the racist elements of sexual imagery and construction of woman's sexuality in the specific context of countries of the North and the South. She concludes by discussing the possibilities of drawing out women from their portrayal as victims and helping them take on an agential role without in any way legitimizing the institution of prostitution.

Subversive Voices and Resisting Bodies: Individual and Collective Strategies

Susie Tharu takes as her point of departure the extraordinarily subversive voice of the Hindu widow who plays a central role in the Hindu imaginary from the nineteenth century onwards. In her paper in this volume, Tharu examines two contemporary Indian short stories in which the widow is the chief protagonist. She sees the widow, in the context of caste, gender and citizenship, as a figure in need of both regulation and protection. Tharu equates the subject, a brahman and a dalit widow, with embodiment so that clearly Tharu is looking at woman's lived relationship with her body. The subject is the 'body-person' for Tharu and the brahman widow's subversive mode is one in which the body shrugs off discipline, and therefore exclusion and regulation, through laughter, wit, indecorous behaviour and, above all, a 'grossly irreverent appetite'. It is striking that the body of the brahman widow becomes the site for feminist struggle and Tharu comments that it is not widowhood that is presented in the story as gender oppression. Instead, the emphasis appears to be on society in its failure to sustain 'fleshly nature itself, not women'.

The second story is about a dalit widow and her young son, a school boy, who is tormented by his mother's embodiment as reflected in her whoring activities. It is not just poverty but also unsatiated sexual desire that drives the widow into the arms of a rich overseer much to the disgust and despair of her son. This widow has therefore to die as a mother before her body-person attains 'bodily life'. Tharu also draws out the caste politics and the implications of the many intricate and interwoven relationships between widow and child, the boy and his peers, the husband and wife, the widow and her lover. It is a complex whole characterized by 'untouchable' bodies, as Tharu puts it, 'that shuttle, always deficient, always in excess'. Tharu's

widows represent a moment in changing times wherein woman's embodiment takes on transformative potential, not without some problems, in a contemporary feminist quest for change. I might add that it is Tharu's reading of the two stories, and of the feminist potential in them, that brings alive to us the possibilities of a feminist consciousness within them.

Vidhu Verma's paper explores the important work of Helene Cixous focusing on the relationship she seeks to establish between sexuality and writing. Verma examines the complexities in such relationship especially in terms of its implications for the identity of women, which is then seen as being established in more or less its biological aspects.

Verma argues that the nature of the female body and sexuality is neither fixed nor universal. She raises questions regarding its validity in the Indian context where there has been a different historical context and where a very different view of the feminine has prevailed in Hindu thought. Verma also examines the sexual difference and equality debate and suggests that Cixous attempts to move beyond these arguments to the extent that she sees sexual difference as being squarely located in a structure of power where 'difference or otherness is tolerated only when repressed'. For Cixous, it is important that women do not seek equality within the system but explore other possibilities for transformation. The alternative posed by Cixous is that of feminine writing; she urges women to write with their bodies so that subjectivity can be reconstituted in new ways. Verma then asks a pertinent question, 'What is a feminine text?' Undoubtedly, it is one which is infused with facility and has voice 'close to the flesh of language'. In other words, it is a 'female libidinal economy' that stands for the Other's freedom and takes the Other into oneself instead of repressing the Other. Verma concludes however that Cixous does not take a definite stand *vis-à-vis* sexual difference although she has challenged the masculine monopoly on the construction of femininity. But to what extent feminine writing can succeed in 'constructing an alternative symbolic order', as Verma puts it, is a question that cannot be answered.

*　　*　　*

Susan Visvanathan takes us into the domain of work and seeks to understand the concept of androgyny as a positive quality of breaking down sex-role stereotypes. She uses Jung's notion of androgyny and argues that the cultural stereotyping of emotions and behaviour would end if one could become a partner to 'that contrasexual side of our nature'. The interplay of the masculine and the feminine aspects of the individual psyche are then consciously accepted. Although ·Visvanathan does not address the complexities of androgyny at great length, her use of the concept focuses on two major characteristics: its negation of gender neutrality (rather, a complementarity) as well as its flexibility so that it does not *fix* gender attributes in one way or another.

Visvanathan attempts to examine and understand the androgynous figure of a nun, Sr. Philomena-Marie (PM), who leads the fisherfolk's struggle against the ravaging of the sea in Kerala. Visvanathan comments on PM's life-history and her commitment to the fisherfolk both spiritually and in their struggle against poverty and illiteracy. She then presents PM as an androgynous figure as one in whom, following Jung, the fusion of the masculine and the feminine has taken place in such a manner that a 'whole' being is created. PM, argues Visvanathan, in her leadership of the fisherfolk, could be either male or female, nun or priest, Hindu or Christian. It is in this sense that androgyny overcomes the cultural markers of being a man or a woman and is really about, what Visvanathan calls, a 'common humanity'. Celibacy (viewed as a transcending of one's biological, psychological and social drives) and androgyny combine as much in the case of PM as in another androgynous figure, Joan of Arc, so powerfully that both women are noticed only for the 'power of their vision'. Visvanathan's view of the androgynous figure (in PM or in Joan of Arc) is very much defined in terms of the gender-less-ness, as it were, of their roles in the work they have set out to do. She is emphatic that, in using the trope of androgyny, she is not arguing for gender neutralization but for the mitigation of gender, for the transcendence of gender.

* * *

Kalpana Viswanath examines one aspect of the contemporary movement in India that takes up issues relating to women's bodies and sexuality and views the emerging strategies in this context. Anthropological literature has shown us how shame and honour are principles central to social organization but has failed, argues Viswanath, to examine women's *experience* of shame in their everyday lives. She therefore turns to the contemporary feminist movement in

India and shows how in fact the movement begins from women's experience of their bodies and sexuality in order to understand and explain their sexuality as well as the social relations of power. For example, feminists have taken up issues relating to rape beginning with the Mathura rape case. Rape is one area, argues Viswanath, 'where sexuality, violence and danger' are seen as having direct linkages to one another as well as to gender, class and caste. Feminists have tried to show the link between shame and sexual violence, i.e., a woman's experience of shame is a form of patriarchal control as a man can violate a woman's body and then throw the blame back on her. A woman who has been raped is seen as having lost her honour, that of the family, and even the community. In that lies the power of shame.

Strategies to challenge the sexual vulnerability of women have focused on women's rights to live without danger and to freely occupy public spaces. Another strategy used by feminists is to organize women to share their experiences of their bodies and, through discussion, help them to understand the nature of power and to question the functioning of this power in their own lives. There is also a concerted attempt by feminist groups to provide information to women about their bodies which is done through workshops and through illustrative material. Constantly, the strategy is to locate women's bodies, their health, notions of shame and honour within the framework of how their lives are structured by and located in different social settings and practices. Ultimately, concludes Viswanath, it is a question of how the self and identity are defined and the discourse of shame is central to this self-definition. A sexual assault therefore violates a woman's sense of personhood and if the *meaning* of a sexual assault in their own lives can be challenged by women, then, perhaps new ways of creating relationships between the body and identity can be evolved.

VIII

CONCLUDING COMMENTS

This volume provides analyses of everyday life, in different contexts, spaces, locations and historical settings, all seeking to articulate nuanced understandings of the relationship between embodiment, gender and the constitution of identity. The thrust of the essays is on both the socially constructed body as well as the lived body in everyday life grounded in the discourse of women's experience of their embodiment. The emphasis, generally speaking, is on the nature of containment, regulation, manipulation, control and agency that women experience, from both external as well as inner sources, in relation to their embodiment. Woman's body is very much a disciplined body whether this is done through social practices or through individual intervention. Social and cultural practices through, for example, certain ritual behaviour in the girl's life cycle, prepare woman for a life of compulsory heterosexuality and motherhood. In the end, a woman's destiny triumphs over her desire and possible freedom. Her subjectivity and experiential truth are formed in her movement through a socially defined, and possibly individually contested, trajectory. This is the lived truth of her embodiment.

This collection of essays takes the work on gender and identity in India forward to the extent that it takes the crucial dimension of embodiment into account. The experience of women is as important as is their position in society; the interlinkages between caste, class, community and gender intermesh in important ways so that every woman's experience of her embodiment may be different but also contains many commonalities; agency is as central to her life as is conflict; she manœuvres and strategizes, giving in a little bit here, taking a bit there, using her body for gains, privileges and gratification. The woman's body does not ever become a source of total despair for it is also the material through which she can manipulate, shape, transform her identity either in relation to her own expectations, professional demands or social practices. She emerges from the imposed discipline of her body and restriction of her space and movements, not always successful, but struggling anyhow for a voice and an agential role. It is therefore always a movement between freedom and constraint, restriction and rebellion, submission and subversion. The crucial point is that the possibilities are always open and infinite.

This volume also shows us that gender identity is not something fixed and immutable; it is both constructed and lived; and sometimes can also be transcended. It is therefore always in the making, continuously in the process of communication and exchange, evolving through the everyday life experiences of women. It is in this sense that the body becomes a vehicle for the human making and remaking of the world, always shifting sites, empowered with the potential for opening up new possibilities of being in this world.

NOTES

1. This volume does not examine male embodiment which is essential for understanding social relations in their entirety but is outside the scope of this collection of essays.

2. In this important paper, Mauss develops a classification of the techniques of the body, lists the different body techniques used by individuals in their life cycle, and places these techniques in a larger framework that includes biology, psychology and social relations. See Mauss (1973).

3. These include the work of Das (1988), Dube (1986), Thapan (1995), Featherstone, Hepworth and Turner (1991), Bartky (1990), Bordo (1993), Butler (1990, 1993), Grosz (1994), Martin (1987), Irigaray (1985a and 1985b).

4. For a good overview of the different social theories on the body, see Shilling (1993).

5. For an anthropological account of the male wrestler's body, see Alter (1993).

6. See, for example, Bennett (1983), Fruzetti (1982), Mandelbaum (1988), Ganesh (1993).

7. I am here referring to the work of feminist groups like *Jagori* and *Sakshi* in New Delhi, and other such groups or organizations in India, who are actively involved in the documentation and dissemination of knowledge and issues relating to women's embodiment in very many different ways. Also see Gandhi and Shah (1992, chs. 3 and 4) and Dietrich (1992, esp. ch. 3).

8. For anthropological perspectives on the ambivalent Hindu view of woman, see also Gatwood (1985), Wadley (1977). For a variation on the psychological perspective on Indian womanhood, see Kakar (1978).

9. I am aware that de Beauvoir's position cannot perhaps be stated in such simplistic terms. Her work has been critically examined by feminists across disciplines. See for example Mackenzie (1986).

10. For feminist discussion and criticism of Foucault, see, for example, Diamond and Quinby (1988), Sawicki (1991, 1994), Harstock (1990), Ramazanoglu (1993), McNay (1994), Cooper (1994). I have elsewhere critically examined Foucault's notions of power and resistance. See Thapan (1995).

11. In this context, Tharu and Niranjana (1994) have argued that the tension for feminist politics and gender analysis in India is set up by events, such as the Mandal issue and the rise of the Hindu Right, which emerge in the process of 'a rapidly globalizing economy, and the refiguring of the nation and its dominant classes' (p.114). There is therefore the alliance of feminism with the structures of domination shaped by gender, class, caste and community but also the possibilities of forging new alliances (ibid.). The contemporary is in a moment of flux and the articulation and definition of gender identity is part of this fluid present.

12. The Sangari and Vaid volume (1989) contains some path-breaking work on the intersection between gender, caste and nation. See also Tharu and Lalita (1993, Introduction).

13. An important consideration in this context is the definition of womanhood in the nationalist discourse in nineteenth-century India. Partha Chatterjee has argued that nationalism was not only about a political struggle for power; more importantly, 'it related the question of political independence of the nation to virtually every aspect of the material and spiritual life of the people' (1989: 238). This material/spiritual distinction, argues Chatterjee, was linked to an ideologically superior dichotomy: the outer and the inner leading in social space to *ghar* and *bahir*, the home and world (ibid.). The nationalists sought to protect the spiritual life of Indians, the inner world, the home, and this included the women in it, from the onslaught of western culture and civilization. The signs of femininity were clearly marked and included virtues such as religiosity, submission, self-sacrifice, along with elements of education which contributed to good housekeeping, and so on. In their effort to preserve and safeguard their pristine inner essence, nationalists however set up 'Woman as victim and goddess simultaneously' (Radhakrishnan 1992: 85). In this process, 'the inner self is effectively written out of history altogether in the name of a repressive and essentialist indigeny' (ibid.). Be that as it may, an important virtue emphasized during the period was 'chastity' which related directly to the regulation of women's sexuality in their everyday lives. See also Chatterjee (1993: 116–57), Chakrabarty (1993), Bannerji (1995), Sarkar (1995).

14. Cf. Sunder Rajan (1994) who has examined the recent case of the child-bride Ameena and argues that:

the subaltern female subject becomes the object of conflict between community (as Muslim) and State (as citizen), and is therefore perceived as a putative social responsibility; she is invested with agency, all the same, in being called upon to exercise her 'choice' and express her desires; she is then 'restored' to the family which is treated as the appropriate final location for the errant woman...; in the process, she becomes a 'national' cause or issue. (p. 154)

15. See for example Bagchi (1993), Dube (1988), Jeffrey (1979).

16. 'Personal politics', emerging from experience, undoubtedly contributes to the intellectual understanding of women's lives in different cultures, classes, and strata of society. The question may then be posed, what could possibly be more personal than the life of the body? Merleau-Ponty, a philosopher committed to the primacy of experience, cautions us that experience cannot be considered truth as it is coloured by 'social, political, historical, and cultural forces and in this sense cannot provide an outside vantage point from which to judge them' (Grosz 1994: 94). He none the less remains committed to understanding and explaining 'the body as I live it, as I experience it, and as it shapes my experience' (ibid.).

17. In a delightful paper, C.S. Lakshmi (1992) explores the relationship between physical space and interior space in the context of women's writings.

18. In this context, Judith Butler has argued that gender is 'the repeated stylization of the body, a set of repeated acts within a highly rigid regulatory frame that congeal over time to produce the appearance of substance, of a natural sort of being' (1990: 33). It is in the process of stylization that the possibilities for agency emerge and, as Butler points out, agency 'is to be located within the possibility of a variation on that repetition' (ibid.: 145). It is therefore imperative to participate in those very acts of repetition that serve to constitute our identities and then contest them through intervention from within. Construction then does not deny agency; it is the 'necessary scene of agency, the very terms in which agency is articulated and becomes culturally intelligible' (ibid.).

19. The politics of representation suggest that woman's body is always portrayed through the male gaze. The significance of the spectator's 'gaze' and its impact on film imagery cannot be underplayed. According to the psychoanalytic theory of 'the gaze', the observer 'objectifies the subject of the gaze in the pursuit of scopophilic and voyeuristic pleasures' so that women are always represented as the object of male heterosexual desire (Craik 1994: 12–13; see also Mulvey 1988). The problem however is that such a view presumes the link between sexuality and 'the look' as essential and ignores other important ways of representation which do not derive from normative heterosexual desire such as 'autoeroticism, homoeroticism, sensual pleasure and fantasy' (ibid.). See also John Berger's classic work on representation (1972).

20. See also Martin (1987).

21. In a recent paper, Susan Markens (1996) argues that accounts of women's experiences of the pre-menstrual syndrome (PMS) pre-eminently figure in the 'rhetorical legitimation' of PMS as a medical phenomenon in the popular press and self-help books which take on a negative tone. The negative symptoms define women as either normal or abnormal (those suffering from PMS) and present a model of women as 'deficient'. Markens therefore concludes that women have been active participants in the creation and shaping of the discourse on PMS through their experiences and accounts, based on their 'social location' (race and class), of PMS.

22. Judy Whitehead (1995) has argued that the 'nationalist mother image' in colonial North India was opposed to that of the prostitute 'defined in sanitary terms' and who was culturally excluded. The disciplinary aspect of 'sanitary regulation' was especially obvious in the control of sexual relations with Indian prostitutes who were seen as 'the epitome of dangerous contagion and exotic sensuality' (p. 41). Sundara Raj (1993) discusses the growth of prostitution in southern India in the same period and suggests that it was difficult to implement the Contagious Diseases Act due to administrative shortcomings and the unwillingness to cooperate on the part of the prostitutes and the public. For a brief discussion of this Act in the Indian context, see also Kalpagam (1992).

23. Bourdieu uses the concept of 'symbolic violence' to explain how power is internalized and operates through individuals. Symbolic violence 'accomplishes itself through an act of cognition and miscognition that lies beyond—or beneath—the controls of consciousness and will, in the obscurities

of the schemata of habitus that are at once gendered and gendering' (Bourdieu and Wacquant 1992: 172). It is in this sense that gender domination consists 'in an imprisonment effected via the body' (ibid.). For a critical discussion of Bourdieu's concept of *habitus*, see Thapan (1988).

24. In this paper, Sangari focuses on the problematics of 'consent' which often is a major impediment to organized resistance. See Sangari (1992). For examples of contemporary feminist work on resistance in different contexts, see Bachetta (1994), Oldenburg Talwar (1990), Hart (1991), O'Hanlon (1988, 1991).

25. For a review of French feminist work in this area, see Marks and de Courtivron (1980), Moi (1985), Fraser and Bartky (1992).

26. Grieve however (1981) contends that the notion of androgyny appealed to psychologists but clearly it no longer is 'an ideal which can transcend sexism' (p. 256). She is also of the view that as women, more than men, report that androgyny is their personal ideal, there is an inherent or intrinsic sexism in the term (ibid.).

27. See, for more detailed analyses, Gandhi and Shah (1992), Dietrich (1992), Kumar (1993).

REFERENCES

Alter, Joseph, 1993, *The Wrestler's Body*, Oxford University Press, Delhi.

Ardener, Shirley (ed.), 1981, *Woman and Space. Ground rules and social maps*, Croom Helm, London.

Arnold, David, 1993, *Colonizing the Body. State, medicine and epidemic disease in nineteenth century India*, Oxford University Press, New Delhi.

Bacchetta, Paola, 1994, 'All our goddesses are armed': religion, resistance and revenge in the life of a militant Hindu nationalist woman, in Kamla Bhasin, Ritu Menon and Nighat S. Khan (eds.), *Against All Odds. Essays on Women, Religion and Development from India and Pakistan*, Isis International and Kali for Women, Delhi.

Bagchi, Jasodhara, 1993, Socializing the girl child in colonial Bengal, *Economic and Political Weekly*, 9 October, 2214–19.

Bannerji, Himani, 1995, Attired in virtue: the discourse on shame (*lajja*) and clothing of the *bhadramahila* in colonial Bengal, in Bharati Ray (ed.), *From the Seams of History. Essays on Indian women*, Oxford University Press, New Delhi.

Bartky, Sandra L., 1990, *Femininity and Domination. Studies in the phenomenology of oppression*, Routledge, London.

Bennett, Lynn, 1983, *Dangerous wives and sacred sisters. Social and symbolic roles of high caste women in Nepal*, Columbia University Press, New York.

Berger, John, 1972, *Ways of Seeing*, BBC and Penguin Books, Harmondsworth.

Bordo, Susan, 1993, *Unbearable Weight. Feminism, Western Culture and the Body*, University of California Press, Berkeley.

Bourdieu, Pierre, 1977, *Outline of a Theory of Practice*, trans. by Richard Nice, Cambridge University Press, Cambridge.

—— and Jean-Claude Passeron, 1977, *Reproduction in Education, Society and Culture*, trans. by Richard Nice, Sage, London.

——, 1979, *Distinction. A social critique of the judgement of taste*, trans. by R. Nice, Routledge, London.

—— and L.W.D. Wacquant, 1992, *An Invitation to Reflexive Sociology*, University of Chicago Press, Chicago.

Butler, Judith, 1990, *Gender Trouble. Feminism and the subversion of identity*, Routledge, London.

——, 1993, *Bodies that Matter. On the discursive limits of 'sex'*, Routledge, New York.

Chakrabarty, Dipesh, 1993, The difference-deferral of (a) colonial modernity; public debates on domesticity in British Bengal, *History Workshop Journal* 36: 1–33.

Chatterjee, Partha, 1989, The nationalist resolution of the woman's question, in Kumkum Sangari and Sudesh Vaid (eds.): 233–53.

——, 1995, (orig. 1993), *The Nation and its Fragments. Colonial and post colonial histories*, Oxford University Press, Delhi.

Cooper, Davina, 1994, Productive, relational and everywhere? Conceptualising power and resistance within Foucauldian feminism, *Sociology* 28(2): 435–54.

Craik, Jennifer, 1994, *The Face of Fashion. Cultural Studies in Fashion*, Routledge, London.

Das, Veena, 1976, Masks and faces: an essay on Punjabi kinship, *Contributions to Indian Sociology* 10(1): 1–30.

——, 1988 Femininity and orientation to the body, in K. Chanana (ed.), *Socialization, education and women. Explorations in gender identity*, Orient Longman, New Delhi.

De Beauvoir, Simone, 1953, *The Second Sex*, trans. and ed. by H.B. Parshley Picador, London.

Dietrich, Gabrielle, 1992, Discussing Sexuality, in *Reflections on the Women's Movement. Religion, ecology, development*, Horizon, New Delhi.

Dube, Leela, 1986, Seed and Earth: The symbolism of biological reproduction and sexual relations of production, in L. Dube, E. Leacock and S. Ardener (eds.), *Visibility and Power. Essays on Women in Society and Development*, Oxford University Press, Delhi.

——, 1988, On the construction of gender. Hindu girls in patrilineal India, in Karuna Chanana (ed.), *Socialization, education and women*, Orient Longman, New Delhi.

Faith, Karlene, 1994, Resistance. Lessons from Foucault and feminism, in H. Loraine Radtke and H. J. Stam (eds.), *Power/Gender. Social Relations in Theory and Practice*, Sage, London.

Featherstone, M., *et al.*, 1991, *The Body. Social Process and Cultural Theory*, Sage, London.

Fraser, Nancy and S.L. Bartky (eds.), 1992, *Revaluing French Feminisms. Critical essays on difference, agency, and culture*, Indiana University Press, Bloomington and Indianapolis.

Freud, Sigmund, 1990 (Orig. 1933), Femininity, in Shiela Ruth (ed.) *Issues in Feminism. An introduction to women's studies*, Mayfield, California.

Fruzetti, L.M., 1982, *The Gift of a Virgin. Women, marriage and ritual in Bengali society*, Rutgers University Press, New Brunswick.

Ganesh, Kamala, 1993, *Boundary Walls. Caste and women in a Tamil community*, Hindustan, Delhi.

Gandhi, Nandita and Nandita Shah, 1992, *The Issues at Stake. Theory and practice in the contemporary women's movement in India*, Kali for Women, Delhi.

Gatwood, Lynne, 1985, *Devi and the Spouse Goddess. Women, sexuality and marriage in India*, Manohar, New Delhi.

Goffman, Erving, 1971, *The Presentation of Self in Everyday Life*, Pelican, Harmondsworth.

——, 1979, *Gender Advertisements*, Harvard University Press, Cambridge.

Grieve, Norma, 1981, Beyond sexual stereotypes. Androgyny: a model or an ideal, in N. Grieve and P. Grimshaw (eds.), *Australian Women. Feminist perspectives*, Oxford University Press, Melbourne.

Grosz, Elizabeth, 1994. *Volatile Bodies. Toward a corporeal feminism*, Indiana University Press, Bloomington.

Harstock, Nancy, 1990, Foucault on power. A theory for women? in Linda Nicholson (ed.), *Feminism/Postmodernism*, Routledge, London.

Hart, Gillian, 1991, Engendering everyday resistance: Gender, patronage and production politics in rural Malaysia, *Journal of Peasant Studies*, (19)1: 93–121.

Irigaray, Luce, 1985a, *This Sex which is not One*, Cornell Press, Ithaca.

——, 1985b, *Speculum of the Other Woman*, Cornell University Press, Ithaca.

Jeffery, Patricia, 1979, *Frogs in a Well. Indian women in purdah*, Zed Books, London.

Kakar, Sudhir, 1978, *The Inner World. A psycho-analytic study of childhood and society in India*, Oxford University Press, Delhi.

Kalpagam, U., 1992, Colonializing power and colonialized bodies, *The Indian Journal of Social Science* V(1): 61–80.

Kapur, Promilla, 1970, *Marriage and the Working Woman in India*, Vikas, New Delhi.

——, 1973, *Love, marriage and sex*, Vikas, New Delhi.

Kuhn, Annette, 1988, The body and cinema: some problems for feminism, in Susan Sheridan (ed.), *Grafts. Feminist cultural criticism*, Verso, London.

Kumar, Radha, 1993, *A History of Doing*, Kali for Women, New Delhi.

Lakshmi, C.S., 1992, Dealing with silence, space and everyday life, in *The Indian Journal of Social Science*, 5(1): 93–104.

Mackenzie, Catriona., 1986, Simone de Beauvoir: Philosophy and/or the female body, in C. Pateman and E. Gross (eds.) *Feminist Challenges*, Allen and Unwin, Sydney.

Mandelbaum, David, 1988, *Women's seclusion and Men's Honour*, The University of Arizona Press, Tuscon.

Markens, Susan, 1996, The problematic of 'experience'. A political and cultural critique of PMS, in *Gender and Society* 10(1): 42–58.

Marks, Elaine and Isabelle de Courtivron (eds.), 1980, *New French Feminisms* University of Massachusetts Press, Amherst.

Martin, Emily, 1987, *The Woman in the Body*, Beacon, Boston.

——, 1990, Science and women's bodies: forms of anthropological knowledge, in Mary Jacobus *et al.* (eds.), *Body/Politics. Women and the discourse of science*, Routledge, New York.

——, 1991, The egg and the sperm: how science has constructed a romance based on stereotypical male-female roles, in *Signs* 16(3): 485–501.

Mauss, 1973 (orig. 1935), Techniques of the body, in *Economy and Society* 2(1): 70–88.

McNay, Lois, 1994, *Foucault. A critical introduction*, Continuum, New York.

Merleau-Ponty, Maurice, 1962, *Phenomenology of Perception*, trans. by Colin Smith, Routledge and Kegan Paul, London.

Moi, Toril, 1985, *Sexual/Textual Politics*, Methuen, London.

Moore, Henrietta L., 1994, *A Passion for Difference*, Polity Press, Cambridge.

Mulvey, Laura, 1988, Visual pleasure and narrative cinema, in C. Penley (ed.), *Feminism and Film Theory*, Routledge, London.

Nandy, Ashis, 1976, Woman versus womanliness: an essay in speculative psychology, in B.R. Nanda (ed.), *Indian Women: From purdah to modernity*, Vikas, New Delhi.

O'Hanlon, Rosalind, 1988, Recovering the Subject, Subaltern Studies and histories of resistance in colonial South Asia, *Modern Asian Studies*, 22(1): 189–224.

——, 1991, Issues of Widowhood. Gender and resistance in colonial western India, in Douglas Haynes and Gyan Prakash (eds.), *Contesting Power. Resistance and everyday social relations in South Asia*, Oxford University Press, Delhi.

Oldenburg Talwar, Veena, 1990, Lifestyle as resistance: The case of the courtesans of Lucknow, India, *Feminist Studies* 16(2): 259–87.

Radhakrishnan, R., 1992, Nationalism, gender and the narrative of identity, in Andrew Parker *et al.* (eds.), *Nationalisms and Sexualities*, Routledge, New York.

Ramazanoglu, Caroline, 1993, *Up Against Foucault. Explorations of some tensions between Foucault and feminism,* Routledge, London.

Rich, Adrienne, 1976, *Of Woman Born. Motherhood as an experience and as an institution*, Norton, New York.

Ram, Kalpana, 1992, *Mukkuvar Women*, Kali for Women, New Delhi.

Sangari, Kumkum, 1992, Consent, agency and rhetorics of incitement, *Occasional Papers on History and Society* (Second Series, No. LIX), Nehru Memorial Museum and Library, New Delhi.

—— and Sudesh Vaid (eds.), 1989, *Recasting Women. Essays in colonial history*, Kali for Women, New Delhi.

Sarkar, Tanika, 1995, Hindu conjugality and nationalism in late nineteenth century Bengal, in J. Bagchi (ed.), *Indian Women. Myth and reality*, Sangam Books, Hyderabad.

Sawicki, Jana, 1991, *Disciplining Foucault: Feminism, power and the body*, Routledge, New York.

——, 1994, Foucault, feminism and questions of identity, in Gary Gutting (ed.), *The Cambridge Companion to Foucault*, Cambridge University Press, Cambridge.

Shilling, Chris, 1993, *The Body and Social Theory*, Sage, London.

Shiva, Vandana, (ed.), 1994, *Close to Home. Women reconnect ecology, health and development*, Earthscan Publications, London.

Sundara Raj, M., 1993, *Prostitution in Madras. A study in historical perspective*, Konark, New Delhi.

Sunder Rajan, Rajeshwari, 1993, *Real and Imagined Women. Gender, culture and postcolonialism*, Routledge and Kegan Paul, London.

——, 1994, Ameena: gender, crisis and national identity, *The Oxford Literary Review*. 16(1–2): 147–76.

Thapan, Meenakshi, 1988, Some aspects of cultural reproduction and pedagogic communication, *Economic and Political Weekly* (19 March): 592–6.

——, 1995, Gender, body and everyday life, *Social Scientist* 23(7–9): 32–58.

Tharu, Susie and K. Lalita, 1991, Introduction, *Women Writing in India. 600 B.C. to the Present. Vol. I. 600 B.C. to the early 20th Century*, Oxford University Press, New Delhi.

——, 1993, Introduction. *Women Writing in India. 600 B.C. to the Present. Vol. II. The 20th Century*, Oxford University Press, New Delhi.

Tharu, Susie and Tejaswini Niranjana, 1994, Problems for a contemporary theory of gender, *Social Scientist* 22(3–4): 93–117.

Wadley, Susan, 1977, Women and the Hindu tradition, in *Women in India. Two perspectives*, Manohar, Delhi.

Whitehead, Judy, 1995, Bodies clean and unclean: prostitution, sanitary legislation, and respectable femininity in colonial North India, *Gender and History*, 7(1): 41–63.

Young, Iris Marion, 1990, *Throwing like a girl and other essays in feminist philosophy and social theory*, Indiana University Press, Bloomington.

Scandal in High Places
Discourses on the Chaste Hindu Woman in Late Nineteenth Century Bengal

Tanika Sarkar

I

WHY TALK OF SCANDALS?

I plan to explore the social history of a scandalous event that rocked Bengal in 1873.[1] The stories that circulated around it were narrated in farces, in newspaper editorials and reports and in journals. They were also told through bazaar paintings, woodcut prints, street songs and on the stages of the new public theatre. They belong, therefore, to processes that constituted an emerging public sphere where private people argued about their intimate concerns through novel modes of public communication.[2]

Habermas has been criticized for restricting his conception of the public sphere too narrowly to the higher reaches of the European bourgeoisie, whereas other more subordinated classes had parallel exchanges of their own in public.[3] When we look at late nineteenth-century Bengal through the prism of this scandalous event, we find that our prevailing notion of a middle class that is perfectly set in the mould of a rich, successful and extremely erudite intelligentsia, begins to curdle and to separate into a lower section, with its low life of literature in sensational reportage, obscene farces and popular theatre.[4] We find that this level further shades off into prostitutes, artisans and minor theatre persons. We even see that the comments of peasants and songs of street beggars are picked up and woven into the more erudite representations of the event. It is true that these voices are neither transparent nor authentic, but are mimetically recreated. It is still important to think why the representations need to incorporate them, to refer to them in public discussion. It is, therefore, not enough to indicate the existence of multiple levels within a class often assumed to be seamless and which is conceptualized on the basis of its dominant expressions on a few preselected themes. It is important to reconnect the levels through their mutual arguments and exchanges, to locate and describe the sites where they occurred.

Since it is somewhat unusual for Indian historians to look at public events that do not directly flow from or into nationalism and nation-making processes, it is necessary to say a few words to defend the project.[5] In order to locate an occurrence that would make a cut into intermingled social worlds, we need a particular kind of event. Ideally, it should be one that would involve itself with the 'ordinary' and the everyday, as well as include dimensions that compelled serious, wide ranging discussions on themes of general interest. In other words, we need the quotidian and the domesticated at a moment of rupture, at a point of their eruption into public affairs. And herein lies the value of a sensational event, a *cause célèbre*. It straddles the customary as much as the transgressive, it knits up the everyday with the grand themes of a historical period, illuminating points of interweaving and elements of mediations, as also revealing unsuspected meanings in known historical developments.

There is a major archive for reconstituting events of this category—the archive of criminal cases. It is true that the repositories of old case documents are seriously incomplete or kept in unusable conditions, or have simply disappeared for the most part. Nor did we have, unlike the *ancien régime* in France, the custom of publishing *mémoirs judiciares* or trial briefs by lawyers, or *remonstrances* or court's objections to royal decrees.[6] For the more notorious trials, that deal with scandalous themes, none the less, we do have reports and representations in other kinds of texts as well.[7] The chasing up of a legal offence through a courtroom trial and through reports on its public reception[8] immediately brings us closer to legal and judicial processes as well as to the various components of the modern public sphere—the press, the theatre or popular printed literature which have always fed avidly on crime. Sometimes, as in the present case, we may even find parts of this sphere in the making, as was the case with the new public theatre of Bengal which extensively worked on this scandal. The institutionalization of the public sphere takes us into the realm of market forces which condition the representations and their forms. They also lead us to social histories of the creators of representations.

We need therefore, a scandalous crime. The coupling of the two terms is not fortuitous. Rajeswari Sunder Rajan, in an unpublished paper, has drawn our attention to the changing definitions of the word scandal. Whereas in 1582 it denoted a 'moral lapse', and in 1590, a 'damage to reputation' or a 'disgraceful reputation' (1622), by 1814 it also comes to mean 'slander'. By 1838 it means both 'offence to moral feeling or decency', and 'injurious report published concerning another which may be the foundation of legal action'.[9] Whereas the older meaning of a violation of norms is carried into early nineteenth-century usage, a new meaning also develops additionally, which moves from slander to legal offence, shifting the onus of definition from the moral community to the lawcourt. It is interesting that the 1838 definition also includes 'published report' as a criterion, indicating both the consolidation of a public sphere and its constitution through the print medium.

The Bengali counterpart to the word is *ketchha* which is taken from the Persian *kissa*. While the Persian original referred to stories, mostly of fabulous romances, the Bengali derivation changed its meaning to one of scandalous stories, thus obliquely affirming the potentially transgressive character of romances. In the representations of the scandal that concern us, however, we find the English term frequently in use, even in Bengali texts.

A trial makes scandalous disclosures, publicizes intimate transgressions. Its reception has the same function as enlarging the scope of gossip, pulling it out of hidden, intimate, familiar circles into the realm of public concern and argument. An event is something that creates a shared field of discussion, and thereby sets up an interpretative community that reads the text of the event. An event of a 'gossipable' kind adds a peculiarly intimate twist to it. If gossip flourishes within an intimate group and draws its discussants into a tighter circle of acquaintances and concerns, a scandal has the same function within an anonymous, abstract public: it draws an unseen community of concerned people closer together by focusing on intimate issues about its constituents. The range of its reception defines the space of the public sphere.

II

THE EVENT AT TARAKESWAR: REPRESENTATIONS

In 1873 a sensational murder case came up before the Hooghly Sessions Court at Serampore in South West Bengal. The powerful Mohunt Madhavchandra Giri of Tarakeswar, the manager-cum-guru of the rich and popular Saivite temple and pilgrimage centre in Hooghly, was accused of seducing and raping Elokeshi, the young wife of Nobinchandra Banerji who worked as an employee at a military press in Calcutta. He then established a liaison with the connivance of Elokeshi's parents with whom she had been staying while her husband worked in Calcutta. On a visit to his wife, Nobin came to know of this through village gossip and he angrily confronted his wife. A frightened and repentant Elokeshi told him all and Nobin decided to forgive her and take her away from Tarakeswar. The Mohunt, however, ordered his musclemen to bar their way. In a fit of blind rage, Nobin severed Elokeshi's throat with a fish knife, and then full of horror at his own deed, turned himself in at the local police station with an unequivocal confession. An Indian jury acquitted him on grounds of insanity but the European judge demurred, and the case was sent up to the Calcutta High Court. Nobin was sentenced to life transportation but in 1875 he received a pardon because of the massive public petitions for mercy. The Mohunt was sentenced to three years of rigorous imprisonment and a fine of three thousand rupees, but Bengali public opinion generally considered the punishment to be grossly lenient.[10]

It is evident from the summary that both the event and the trials were of a sensational nature. The Mohunt and his English lawyer were mobbed outside the court and the trial was frequently interrupted by excited crowds of spectators who demanded either clemency for Nobin or a harsher sentence for the Mohunt.[11] Calcutta and district town notables got up petitions and subscriptions to help Nobin.[12] A plea for mercy got over ten thousand signatures, revealing an involvement of the lesser middle class folk as well.[13]

Six months after the event, the *Bengalee* newspaper commented on its continued publicity:

No case in our generation has excited such a deep, enduring and widespread interest as the case of Nobinchandra Banerji and the Mohunt of Tarakeswar .... Groups of peasants who may not have heard of the Road Cess ... may be seen discussing some subject with great solemnity. Approach them, and you will find the burden of their talk to be Nobin and the Mohunt.[14]

Plays written as late as 1924 referred to the Elokeshi episode in such a way as to assume that it would still be public knowledge.[15]

Tarakeswar had been a centre of great scandals, at least from the early nineteenth century. In 1824, Mohunt Shrimanta Giri was executed for murdering the lover of his mistress.[16] In 1912 Negendrabala Debi accused the Mohunt of raping her daughter.[17] In 1924, the Swarajists organized a satyagraha campaign against Mohunt Satish Giri's alleged sexual and financial misconduct and managed to achieve a measure of public control over the temple funds.[18] We find that it is from the second decade of the nineteenth century that such scandals became a focus of public attention. Certainly, the focus owes a lot to the new possibilities of publicity—the new lawcourts and trial procedure which at times were something of a public spectacle and that followed the tropes of a suspense drama, the press which repeated the trial events at length and commented on them and the growth of dissident religious sects among Hindus who agitated over the legal redefinition of norms of Hindu conjugality. Yet, despite its highly sensational nature, the 1824 scandal had not created waves of representations, nor did it have as tenuous a grip on public memory. Whereas the 1873 events are vividly remembered and recalled during the 1924 satyagraha, in 1873 itself I found barely a reference to 1824. The growing expansion in the range of apparatus that made up the public sphere, the relative downward reach that was developing at this time, would partly account for the longer lease of life that the 1873 scandal enjoyed.

The talk ranged over an astonishing variety of subjects.[19] Missionaries speculated on the possible disenchantment of Hindus with their leadership and institutions. English-owned newspapers debated on the morals of native society, British justice and on whether or not the Government should embark on a more intrusive course of action *vis-à-vis* Hindu institutions. Bengali newspapers gave elaborate, often verbatim reports of trial proceedings and critically discussed the stances of European judges, Hindu lawyers and jury, as well as public responses to the events and to the trials. There were passionate debates about the precise degree of culpability of each of the characters involved in the scandal, as well as about whether the various judgements fairly and correctly interpreted and applied the laws. Finally, as the last level in the spiral, there were arguments about the nature of colonial law and of Hindu religious norms. It is evident then, that the interest in the scandal itself spilled into and encompassed the trials which constituted a subsidiary set of events or a subplot, and that continued, supplemented and interpreted the events of the scandal. It is also clear that a larger Bengali public tribunal organized itself around the Hooghly Sessions and Calcutta High Courts that judged the conduct of the trials.

Popular presses brought out a series of farces on the rape, the murder and the trials. I have worked on twenty-five major ones,[20] certainly the largest corpus among nineteenth-century farces related to a single contemporary event. At least four of them were reprinted several times and one had a prolonged run as a play that made the fortunes of a new public theatre company and which was enacted by several other aspiring ones in Calcutta, Dacca and district towns.[21] One of the printed plays was the first Bengali publication that displayed a two-toned, coloured woodcut print.[22] Collections of popular songs on the event were compiled and printed.[23] Bazaar painters at Kalighat, another major pilgrimage centre at Calcutta, produced a whole series of paintings or *pats* on the theme, and the woodcut printers of the cheap publishing concerns at Battala, in north Calcutta duplicated them in large quantities.[24] A brisk market developed over the production and sale of objects commemorating the event—saris and betel leaf boxes were inscribed with Elokeshi's name, fish knives had it scored into the iron since Nobin had decapitated her with such a knife. A balm for headache—specially effective, it claimed, for headaches brought on by hard study for examinations,[25] that allegedly used the oil that the Mohunt had produced inside the gaol as part of the prison labour, sold at exorbitant prices.[26] A report on the variety of metal objects in use in Bengal that was written in 1894, referred to the sale of these commemorative objects even then. Interestingly, this was the only group of objects mentioned in the report that clustered around the event.[27]

While debates on sexual morality are to be expected from such a scandal, richly spiced as it was with adultery, murder and an exciting trial, it is remarkable how wide ranging and deeply political the cast of the debates was. It was as if the event provided an occasion to all Hindus to ponder on themes that involved the very constitution of Hindu 'society' or 'public.' These were terms far more in use in contemporary Bengali writings than community or nation and they should be explored, therefore, independently rather than be subsumed under the latter largely attributed categories.[28] The Bengali equivalent for the word society was *samaj*, a word that used to refer to a caste or a sub-caste in earlier, pre-colonial times. Now it had come to encompass the entire Hindu community, at least in Bengal. The new usage probably drew life from the early nineteenth-century discussions about the social and religious reform movements that eventually established distinctions between the Hindu Samaj and the Brahmo Samaj. Interestingly, the word 'public' acquired no Bengali equivalent, but was retained as such Bengali texts, where it was very frequently in use. It came to be used interchangeably with people. It split off from the word *samaj*: while the latter would now refer to a religious sect or community, 'public' would be a more open, diffused and non-denominational category, which constitutes itself by openly publicizing its opinions on themes of general and shared interest.[29]

Investigations into the moral health of Hindu religious leadership had started on a large scale from the early 1860s by reformist journalists who began to report on the sexual corruption of the immensely powerful Ballabhacharya sect in Western India.[30] *Hutom Penchar Naksha*, the first major Bengali book of satirical fictional prose, made much of sexual escapades of religious gurus and mendicants.[31] The new education, reform and the development of modern, dissident religious sects scrutinized the power of traditional sacred authorities to rule over Hindu society. They would especially be concerned about the ability of traditional sacred norms and institutions to protect the life and the spiritual and intellectual growth of Hindu women. Obviously, the Elokeshi scandal fed into both reformist and orthodox anxieties powerfully since they related directly to the relationship between Hindu norms, leaders and women. At the same time, it went beyond reformist-orthodoxy lines of debate. As we shall see later, the discussions did not simply reduce the protagonists into a site for contested constructions of tradition, nationhood or community. The intimate sexual-emotional configurations, the many possible and conflicting lines of their interpretation, remained of crucial overwhelming significance to the discussants, beyond their symbolic or signifying aspects.

This becomes clearer through a contrast. In 1890, a ten-year-old child, Phulmonee, was killed when her husband raped her. The event forced a rather unwilling colonial government to acquiesce in reformist demands to penalize cohabitation with wives below the age of twelve—the Age of Consent Act of 1891. Bengali revivalist-nationalists, with few exceptions launched a massive protest campaign against colonial interference into Hindu sacred interiority, while a small and besieged minority of reformers heaped up scriptural and medical evidence in support of the new law. In public discussions, Phulmonee and the conditions of her murder practically disappeared. I am told that there is a single play entitled *Phulmonee*,[32] but I have not found any evidence that it was enacted. There are some farces on the Age of Consent issue, one of them by the famous playwright-cum-actor Amritalal Basu,[33] which satirizes reformism. The incident, however, does not at all feature in the play. The only vivid descriptions of Phulmonee's death are available in the court depositions made by her mother, grandmother and aunt.[34] Clearly, it was the behaviour of the colonial government that was the scandal, not the rape and death of a little girl. In the failure of that case to attain the status of a scandal, in the displacement of arguments from the event to themes of colonialism and indigenous patriarchy, lies the distance that measures out the space between a more fluid and open interpretative community of the 1870s and a monolithic nationalist-indigenist inter-pretative perspective at the turn of the century.

III

A TIME FOR SCANDALS: POLITICS IN THE 1870s

What made the 1870s a good vantage point for an interest in the stories of Nobin, Elokeshi and Madhavgiri before they could be subsumed and obliterated by discussions of Hinduism and colonialism? I shall reflect on several conditions here. The 1870s were, in many ways, an interesting transitional moment in Bengal. Broad, generalized formal political institutions had not yet fully articulated themselves and the politics of associations and congresses would come into their own only from the next decade. Nor had the limited local self-government arenas and the narrow electoral facilities that Viceroy Ripon would make available from the 1880s, yet made their appearance. So, certain forms of a participatory politics had not entirely taken shape as yet. Exercise of critical reason by private individuals in public was articulated through the new vernacular prose; editorials in the mainstream newspapers or journals coming out of Calcutta, the theatre, the satirical plays, the new novel and discursive essays whose themes would im-mediately be translated into simpler polemic in the farces, pamphlets and racy news items in the more marginal newspapers. As Habermas states for Enlightenment Europe, a public domain, in its early phase, is dominantly constituted by intimate matters within a literary mode.[35] A literary mode is eminently hospitable to themes of love, violence and betrayal.

The making of the public sphere in Bengal in the 1870s saw a remarkable downward reach. Theatre escaped the exclusive control of upper-class patrons and their private, amateur shows. It form the first public companies and stages under the initiative of middle-class young men of north Calcutta. Tickets were priced so as to allow, at least occasionally, the lower middle classes into the new public halls.[36] The great Bengali newspaper, The *Amrita Bazar Patrika*, was founded by a district town middle-class family that was not renowned for great educational or cultural achievements.[37] In less than a decade, another important newspaper, *Bangabashi*, would innovate a novel marketing strategy to target a readership of the lower middle class commuting clerks from district towns and villages.[38] Farces, pamphlets, tracts and lyrics were written and published by men and even a few women without the knowledge of English, Persian or Sanskrit, who began to wield the everyday language of the new vernacular prose as soon as they thought they had an interesting story to tell. Stories—whether in newspaper reports or in the great domestic novels of Bankim or in the pulp Battala farces and fiction—were also largely about everyday domestic dramas.[39] Kalighat paintings and woodcut prints from Battala were no longer the enormous folded scrolls that painters displayed with songs, dances and narrations as part of a composite cultural event, nor were they great art objects commissioned and owned by courtly patrons alone. They were small, portable commodities that could be sold to individuals, piece by piece, at generally affordable prices, and could be put up on walls in ordinary homes for continuous display. Battala metal engraved and woodcut prints, often reproducing Kalighat paintings, flooded the market between the 1850s and 1870s. These were much cheaper, being a paisa each when plain, and two paise each when tinted with red, blue and green. Kalighat paintings, on the other hand, cost an anna each. Both kinds were purchased by all sorts of people. Mrs Belnos' painting of a crowded, meagre, single-room family hut of a poor woman that was printed in 1832, shows a Kalighat painting against the wall.[40] On the other hand, a rich man's drawing room was described as decorated with a Battala print.[41] The pictures were biting satires on modern life, sparing neither the traditional holy men nor the new middle class.

The new public theatre was especially a space that was shared between the highbrow connoisseurs and a *petit bourgeoisie* of skilled

artisans, clerks and hackwriters who patronized the theatre enthusiastically, and who sometimes managed to dictate terms of its survival
and success. The newly formed Bengal Theatre had opened with two
erudite plays by the great playwright Michael Madhusudan Dutt on
classical themes. Both were miserable flops. In despair, the management experimented with a play by an unknown playwright,
Lakshminarayan Das. His scandal play, *Mohunter Ei Ki Kaj !* (Is This
Worthy of a Mohunt?) seems to be the only thing that he ever wrote
that made a name. Nothing else is known about him except that, unlike
most authors of Battala pulp, he belonged to a low Shudra caste. In
fact, quite a few of the authors of these farces were men of relatively
low castes.[42] A later play refers to Das' parlour at Panchanantala at
Howrah, where street beggars go and pick up songs on the scandal.
For a brief moment, then, he had become a well-known figure in the
city, a point of reference, although it seems that the fame did not
survive the play.[43] Another play was priced at one anna, which, like
the price of a Kalighat painting, was reasonable and likely to command
a wide readership.[44] The fortunes of the Bengal Theatre were made
from the proceeds of this one play (*Mohunter Ei Ki Kaj*!), the
phenomenal theatre run was remembered in the next century by a
major playwright-cum-actor of those days,[45] and the play was picked
up by a host of other companies and taken out of Calcutta. It also left
a trail of scandal plays in its wake, many of whom fondly or enviously
recalled its vast success in their scripts. So 'common' had theatre become that the great men of the theatre were already bemoaning the
downgrading of a noble art form which would now lower its tone to
accommodate the lower orders. Interestingly, Girish Ghose, the giant
of the theatre world, wrote a doggerel on this note, which focused on
the low caste composition of the new audience as a measure of its
corruption.[46]

The early 1870s were a transitional moment in yet another sense.
They intervened between the passing of the trauma of post-1857
colonial reprisals and brutality, and the beginning of a new round of
repression and racial discrimination under Viceroy Lytton from the
late 1870s. Lord Northbrooke's viceroyalty constituted a brief, relatively mild interlude, with no costly wars or entanglements with
foreign affairs.[47] The trouble over the Income Tax proposals had died
down and there was some space to look beyond the doings of the
State, though, of course, these remained important. With the decline
of indigo, a major arena of blatant racial outrage was no longer so
much in public view. Critical reason and reflections could now turn

inward, within structures of social and religious institutions, towards the family and the intimate domestic domain. This was the time when Bankimchandra wrote his great domestic novels, when proposals for Hindu marriage reforms by dissident Brahmos constituted the most significant political controversy for Bengali Hindus. It was a moment of relatively frank and open introspection. An appropriate language for the literary discussion of such themes had reached a point of great refinement by that time. The 1870s were the golden age of Bengali satire, as well as of a subtle and delicate combination of tones of irony and romanticism that pervades Bankim Chandra's literary essays and novels as much as sections of the Battala farces and the scandal plays. The upsurge of white racism, first in Lytton's policies and then during the Ilbert Bill agitation, would soon delegitimize self-criticism and impulses for change, would lead to a fierce status-quoism *vis-à-vis* social and religious institutions and norms, and would ground an emergent nationalistic spirit squarely on the defence of Hindu patriarchy as the last remaining, autonomous, non-colonized space.

There were other, class/caste related reasons for the resonance that such a scandal acquired in the 1870s. A bourgeois public sphere is bound up with the confirmation of its autonomy within civil society which necessitates the simultaneous existence and acknowledgement of an intimate sphere of domestic affect where the bourgeoisie established its claim to an essentially human identity. In colonial Bengal, however, the emergence of a bourgeois—or, simply a Hindu middle class—public sphere related in a strikingly different way to the intimate sphere. Far from being a bourgeoisie in the established sense of the term, the connections of this middle class with productive forces and relations were markedly passive. The Permanent Settlement had generated a parasitic class of rent receiving landowners. After the 1840s, most of the major Bengali financial and commercial ventures had collapsed. By the end of the century, trade, manufacturing and industry, of any significant scale, had come to be controlled by Europeans and non-Bengalis.[48] The classes that had some surplus capital to invest had been traumatized by the fluctuations in business cycles that wiped out their ventures and investments between the 1820s and the 1840s. They had, therefore, turned to land as the most secure field of investment, and a few of the major zamindars were experimenting with improving measures that might have turned them into the first generation of capitalist landlords.[49] Large possibilities of profitable investment lay in the untrammelled 'rent offensive' by the gentry, its absolute control over tenants, that the Permanent Settlement had allowed. Any pro-tenant departures in State policy, therefore, would threaten the last avenues for entrepreneurship as much as they would make parasitic landlordism a little less comfortable. The highly organized protest movement by Pabna tenants in the early 1870s against illegal extraction of cesses by landlords was for them, a challenge of a new kind.[50] They also inclined the government a little towards granting a measure of security to an upper category of tenants.[51] From the 1870s, too, there were the beginnings of some official classification of lower castes with the intention of reserving for them some kind of affirmative action in the future. They coincided with a widespread self-respect movement among the low caste Namasudra peasants.[52]

The developments were deeply threatening for the class/caste hegemony of the educated, largely upper caste Hindu gentry. They also threw into sharp relief the pretensions of its paternalist self-image. In the agitation against white indigo planters in the previous decade, the landlords had occasionally confronted the planters and had supported the peasant refusal to cultivate indigo.[53] With the Pabna agrarian uprising, the notion of a symbiotic relationship collapsed.[54] The fragility of the paternalist claims of an upper caste orthodox patriarchy had similarly become evident through reformist agitation and colonial legislation to partially alter gender relations within Hindu conjugality. We find, therefore, the makings of a profound and comprehensive crisis here for an upper caste, landowning middle class. Colonial rule had entirely deprived the upper caste gentry of any possibility of politico/military powers. Activism, whether in rural land relations, or in trade, finance and manufacture, was definitively eroded by the 1870s. Since an autonomous sphere did not develop within civil society where the middle class could dictate its terms to production forces and relations, its social privileges, its claims for autonomy and political power in the future could only be legitimized in the realm of human relations and religious belief. And, given the highly problematic reflections of both in the Elokeshi-Mohunt cases, at a time when social privileges in civil society had been threatened significantly, the political meaning of the scandal becomes evident. Hindu conjugal sexuality and its other—adultery and/or rape—became an important register to test the morality of fundamental social and religious institutions.

This very significance, however, would soon turn into a burden. Introspection and self-criticism would appear to be slippery forms of self-indulgence that seemed to be very inadequately marked off from harsh and racist stereotypings. The scandal, therefore, marks a point of culmination as well as a point of departure.

IV

A TIME FOR SCANDALS: HINDU LAW AND HINDU CONJUGALITY IN THE 1870S

The times were right for a major preoccupation with intimate conjugal matters. From the early decades of the nineteenth century, there were a number of proposed legal changes within the Hindu conjugal order. The suggestions combined to problematize the foundations of Hindu domestic norms. Upper caste domestic practices had long conditioned the living patterns of most upwardly mobile agrarian, artisanal and trading castes. While Brahmanical norms were widely generalized— for example, the ban on widow remarriage and the custom of infant marriage prevailed among girls from lower castes whose caste customs did not originally prescribe that, and even Shudra castes practised *sati*—there had been a corresponding long-term hardening of gender norms for women. Within *Dayabhaga*, the neo-*Smarta* legal school that was prevalent in Bengal, a progressive whittling away of women's rights to property had been going on for several centuries. Raghunandan, the influential sixteenth-century authority of the *Dayabhaga* school of law, had made pre-pubertal marriage obligatory for brahman girls,[55] and from the eighteenth century, the *Krishnagar Raj*, a seat of *Smarta* orthodoxy, had tightened up the discipline of austere widowhood.[56] The process got invariably reflected and generalized at aspiring power caste levels.[57] Reformist projects, therefore, threatened not simply upper caste rigidity from which lower caste custom was exempted: they put at risk a larger structure of brahmanical hegemonic domestic practices.

The deep involvement of Hindu public opinion with legal changes and processes indicated a relatively autonomous area of initiative that had been reserved for it within colonial rule. It is important to recognize that colonial law itself had upheld the right of indigenous religious systems to exercise control over the realm of belief and personal relationships. Personal laws were made identical with religious norms, and changes would be allowed only on grounds of a more precise procedural interpretation. The very legal identity of the person, consequently, created a sharper sense of belonging to a religious community which, in its turn, was closely tied to a control of the intimate sphere. Such an understanding of Hindu and Muslim personal laws, that now could refer to Hindus and Muslims as monolithic wholes, instead of to the customary practices of castes and sub-castes as in earlier times—though there was never a sharp or complete displacement of the latter by the former—helped to lead on to a notion of homogeneous, sharply bounded religious community identities.

In the 'Company' period, this operation of personal laws had meant a dependence on rulings by *pundits*. Later, by the 1860s, their services in the law courts were dispensed with since the compilation and codification of a sizable body of Hindu legal texts had already been finalized. The displacement of living, embodied legal authorities with textualized ones, however, remained incomplete, and the opinion of Hindu lawyers and judges was deferred to up to Privy Council levels.[58] The *Amrita Bazar Patrika* made an interesting case for extending judicial powers to a Bengali Deputy Magistrate:

Bengalis are sure to make much better use of the powers ... than Europeans ... the fear of society and relatives and friends as well as other considerations will keep them back from doing anything likely to produce lamentations among their own people.[59]

The ideal legal and judicial operation, according to this construction, was the obverse of a universality that had been evacuated of all particularity. It was expected that the law dispenser was accountable to the opinion of his community and its norms which overrode claims of neutrality. The institution of a native jury system in seven Bengal districts by the 1860s—including Hooghly where the Tarakeswar cases were first lodged—expanded the scope of Hindu public opinion. English judges deferred to Hindu custom in reaching their verdict. The Sessions Court Judge, Mr Field, said that he was assuming the fact of adultery because Elokeshi had been found 'joking and flirting' with the Mohunt, an unrelated male. While this would not count as evidence in the case of Europeans, in Hindu society such behaviour would surely signify an adulterous connection. Hearing the appeal lodged by the Mohunt at the High Court, Judge Markby made a similar point.[60] In the 1890s, the jury was withdrawn from a lot of categories of cases but marriage-related disputes remained within their purview.[61] In fact, in the 1870s there were strident demands for an extension of the jury system. Over the Tarakeswar cases, heated debates followed the decision of the European judge who had overruled the juridical decision that Nobin was insane, and hence not culpable.[62] Given the larger context of judicial changes, the Tarakeswar cases tied into a contestation of the European judge's right to rescind an Indian juridical opinion in matters of domestic disputes. They also reinforced middle-class allegations about Lt Governor Campbell's offensive against the Hindu gentry that manifested itself in the new educational plans, the Road Cess, the arbitrary new Criminal Law Procedure Code and an antipathy towards Hindu lawyers.[63]

So the crowds that besieged the Mohunt and his lawyers and who interrupted the court proceedings, the petitions that asked for a reversal of the court judgement, the preoccupation of the Bengali press with the course of the trial, stemmed from an awareness of this informal right and function that had been claimed in the name of Hindu public opinion. The Kalighat paintings that usually depicted scenes from Indian domestic life and mythological events, made a rare departure in the Mohunt cases. The courtroom scene, where the European judge sentences the Mohunt, spawned a series of paintings and prints.[64] Public trials linked up the intimate sphere with the public domain, the everyday with the extraordinary event, through the mediation of crime.

Popular imagination was so saturated with courtroom images that quite a few of the scandal plays were simply a duplication of the trials and of the subsequent disciplinary proceedings. The divine world corresponded to the procedures of earthly justice. Elokeshi and her parents are tried in the courts of the gods where the prison guard and the police constables are Muslim spirits—'Mamdo bhoots'—since in descriptions of the actual events the same personnel are shown as Muslim characters.[65] The considerations at the divine trial are no more exalted than they are on earth: Elokeshi is chastised for throwing the Shaivite family name into disgrace by 'tempting' the Mohunt. The Mohunt is punished for squandering the family properties of Baba Taraknath by his indiscreet lust and for using the temple funds for his own defence.[66] The title of a farce was a couplet: *The Mohunt is at the end of his tether/He has developed dysentery, so hard he has to work at the oil press.*[67] The oil press refers to the hard labour sentence under which the Mohunt was supposed to work as a human substitute for the bullock that normally drives the press.

The inherent suspense associated with an unfolding trial establishes a particularly lively affinity with the nature of drama and lends itself to effective dramatization in any case. Simultaneously, if drama closely followed and modelled itself on trial scenes, the trial itself was theatrical enough to be consumed as drama. Newspapers remarked on this: 'People flock to the Sessions Court as they would flock to the Lewis' Theatre to watch *Othello* being performed.'[68] It is interesting to note that the Hooghly Sessions courts became so overcrowded during the trials that an entrance fee was charged and only those who followed

English were allowed entry, since much of the proceedings—the Mohunt's English counsel's speeches and the European judge's summing up and verdict—would be in English.[69] In a sense, this can explain the popular hunger for Bengali plays that duplicated the court proceedings. They would render the trials—partly conducted in a foreign language—into a comprehensible vernacular.

How does one explain the popular involvement with scrutinizing the operations of law? Law was something that was being made and remade in everybody's view for virtually the entire century. It was possible to follow from newspapers and from published reports, not only what laws were passed, but also what people were saying about them. Moreover, the laws related to the most intimate aspects of life. From the early nineteenth century, along with the new laws on sati and widow remarriage, a continuous process of compilation of custom and codification of legal texts had been going on. This was accompanied by the printing, translation and popularization of major texts at accessible prices. An informed and wide ranging public discussion followed the processes of compilation as well as that of the proposed reforms and changes. Law lectures and professorships were instituted by Calcutta notables, newspapers monitored the functioning of western legal experts and Hindu lawyers and scholars were prolific with alternative interpretations and rulings.[70]

The most important feature of the process was its visibility, its 'publicness'. Structures governing one's innermost beliefs, intimate relationships as well as everyday practices are necessarily imbricated within visible or invisible legal processes. These structures were now being dragged out, debated and contested before public eyes. In the process, the ideological basis of prescription and of common sense was demystified and made transparent. Simultaneously, legality clashed with religious prescription in unprecedented ways: *sati*, the universally accepted sign of womanly virtue, was now classified as a crime. Widow remarriage, an entirely illegitimate desire, was made legal. Not that the laws inverted the actual pattern of patriarchal practices. They did, however, open up a gap, a tension between what was normatively illicit and what was legally permissible. It produced arguments about what had always been largely unquestioned. What used to exercise power as sacred prescription, as eternal norms, or had been embedded within an unself-conscious common sense, was opened up for frontal interrogation. This greatly worried those who were vested with power over Hindu society. Nobin Chandra Sen, upper caste poet and senior civil servant, opposed Bengali translation of sacred legal texts that the Bangabashi Press had sponsored, since they were not meant to be exposed to low caste eyes.[71]

V

OTHER SCANDALS IN THE 1870s

The 1870s were a great time for other sexual scandals as well. In 1873 itself, there was the Hogg vs. Hogg case. The director of the Postal Department, Mr Hogg, suspected a liaison between his wife and Mr Cordery, an official in the department of education. He intercepted their letters and brought charges of adultery. The *Englishman* demanded that instead of Mr Cordery, Hogg himself should be punished for the violation of professional ethic.[72] Bengali newspapers would often turn to this case from the Elokeshi episode with some relief.[73] They would contrast Bengali sympathy for Nobin who had killed an adulterous wife, with the dry legal sterility of English papers where professional ethic was privileged over true husbandly responsibility.[74]

In 1875, the widowed daughter of Ishwarchandra Napit, barber to the Lt Governor of Bengal, was found missing. Since she was having affairs with two police constables, they suspected the barber of murdering his daughter. With the connivance of the European Police Commissioner, the family was tortured and a confession was forced. While the final scene was going on at the Alipore Court, and a skull, reportedly of the dead girl's, had been produced to clinch the case, the girl dramatically walked in to announce that she had eloped with another lover.[75] The case became a byword for police tyranny and corruption, occasionally also for British misrule and the hollowness of colonial forensic and judicial procedures.

In 1878, the so-called Great Adultery Case reached the Calcutta High Court when Jogen Bose accused Upendranath Bose of adultery with his wife Kshetramoni and fathering her child. His wife made spirited rebuttal of the charges in court and accused the husband of being an unworthy partner. The case was further complicated since Upendranath was an uncle of Kshetramoni. There were especially scurrilous depositions by neighbours and servants, reporting on bedroom scenes with graphic vividness. Both the parties were upper caste, educated and rich middle-class people.[76]

Most of the cases dealt with the crumbling of the conjugal order among important people. All the comments evoked dystopic images of a society where the conjugal relationship no longer counted for anything. Yet, representations of these other cases were largely restricted to newspaper reporting. The Napit case produced a single farce of very high quality,[77] and the Great Adultery Case inspired two farces that were nowhere as well-known. I have no evidence that they were ever enacted.[78] A minor farce on the Hogg Case, *The Police of Pig and Sheep*, was enacted on 1 March 1876 at the Indian National Theatre. It does not seem to have been repeated elsewhere.[79] Obviously, the Elokeshi-Mohunt case tapped a more dense and formidable structure of anxieties.

VI

THE BAD MOHUNT AND THE TAINTED PILGRIMAGE: RELIGIOUS WORRIES

At a time when traditional Hindu sacred authorities were facing a series of defections and challenges from reformers and Christian missionaries, even the orthodox faithful were finding it troublesome to defend or argue for their continued leadership. While the sexual and financial corruption of holy men in control of sacred places had long been common knowledge, the new challenges made their continued acceptance embarrassing. Around the time that the Tarakeswar cases exploded, there were similar charges of sexual exploitation by women pilgrims about other mohunts, especially the Mohunt of Sitakundu and the Mohunt of Chandranath at Chittagong.[80] In 1873, the wealthy Mohunt of Begusarai in Monghyr was killed by the local peasants for misconduct and for oppression of tenants. The Bengali press observed that Madhavchandra Giri had escaped lightly.[81] It is significant that farce after farce appealed to the Sanatan Dharmarakshini Sabha to come to the rescue of Hindu society.[82] This was an obviously new and modern organization that developed as a response to Christian proselytization and Brahmoism. Traditional hegemonic authorities were obviously in a state of crisis and such disclosures helped to generate a cluster of a new kind of religious leadership that would play a large role in the revivalist movements from the next decade.

More significant was the doubt about whether the colonial State should not revise the non-interventionist Religious Endowments Act of 1863 and intercede positively in preserving the sanctity of holy places. The doubt hinted at affirming the State as a better guardian of religious life than indigenous authorities. In fact, much of the criticism of the colonial authorities was directed at suspected connivance between the mohunts and the government, at too little interference and control.[83]

An interesting fact about the cases was the widespread and immediate consensus that the Mohunt was guilty—a conviction that did not wait to be confirmed by the court decisions. The trials were celebrated in the farces and in the paintings primarily as a great social leveller. Nobin was the poor and helpless Brahmin youth who managed, finally, with the aid of law and justice, to expose the mighty, overpowerful Mohunt. He was, incidentally, a purer, *Kulin* Brahmin, more exalted in caste terms than the Mohunt whose precise caste status in his preascetic life was in some doubt. Some thought that the unquestioned public sympathy for Nobin derived from this.[84] The Mohunt's prison sentence, his hard labour, his humiliation at the hands of the judges, the prison guard and the police, were the exclusive themes of several farces and of many songs. A large number of plays have titles that refer to his woes—that is, they have the punishment as their central theme.[85] We have already referred to the immense popularity of the oil which the Mohunt had allegedly manufactured during his prison sentence. In fact, this form of hard labour was a relatively new one and its novelty perhaps partly explains the ubiquity of this motif in the farces and paintings, as well as in the marketplace. In 1838, a report was published by a committee appointed from the principal members and secretary of the law commission. It suggested that the earlier custom of engaging criminals in outdoor labour like road building should be changed into the indoor work of prison manufacture whose products would be sold outside to set up a fund for public works. In 1858, a public exhibition of such items was held in the Calcutta Town Hall and the sale profits amounted to Rs 111,582, accruing from the fifty-five prisons in Lower Bengal in the year 1855–6.[86] There was thus a new and heightened consciousness about the transformed nature of prison labour, much publicized by official sales promotion techniques, which must have gathered major profits from the Mohunt case. The high price of the supposedly Mohunt-made oil was also partly a celebration of the demonstrated superiority of the power of law to the power of the social leadership. Similarly, when the great estate holder Jayakrishna Mukherjee was tried and imprisoned for fraud, *Hutom Penchar Naksha* recorded (or invented them itself) the street songs that celebrated his fall.[87] A scandal play joyfully observes a case involving the Maharaja of Burdwan: 'Even Maharaja Tejchandra Bahadur is forced to make a daily appearance in the courtroom. ... English judges do not differentiate between the high and the low.'[88] I found only one play that criticized the humiliation of a holy man by unbelievers, and that concluded that Durga had sent the famine of 1873 to visit Bengal to avenge the troubles of her favourite son.[89] Another play depicted the seduction of Elokeshi as a result of the genuine love that the Mohunt had conceived for her. At the end, he is deeply repentant.[90] His immoral ways are, otherwise, nowhere in question. The bazaar paintings and the woodcut prints generally show him as a weak, dissolute womanizer and the temple as a haven for pimps.[91]

The pilgrimage at Tarakeswar had boomed largely because of the fame of its miracle cures for several diseases, especially barrenness.[92] A large number of young women therefore flocked to the place and undertook the necessary penances in mixed crowds and in complete lack of privacy in highly congested space. In a number of the scandal plays Elokeshi visits the Mohunt the first time to receive cure for barrenness and the Mohunt, attracted by her, plans to seduce her. There were rumours that the Mohunt used to select his victims from young women pilgrims and then his musclemen would procure them for him.[93] The women could not then return to their families and could only find sanctuary in the growing brothels of Tarakeswar. Newspapers in 1873 were full of lurid descriptions of the licentiousness of the temple *pandas* or touts at Puri and Tarakeswar.[94] Much earlier, a satirical verse narrative had depicted Tarakeswar as a place for illicit assignations.[95] There were many reports on the proliferation of brothels at pilgrimages.[96] The Elokeshi episode was a massive public confirmation of all these fears. The unholy ambience of holy places spilled into wider suspicions about religious occasions and ceremonies in general. These were seen as licensed misconduct in public places which might also be used by pious women—the bathing ghats for instance.[97] Missionary criticism of Hindu practices was often based on horrified reports of the sexualized nature of Hindu religious beliefs and rites, and they could have shaped the self-critical or self-purificatory mood among worried Hindus. Yet a purely mimetic motivation would be too slight an explanation that simply substitutes influence for cause; we need to seek the roots of a positive reception of this strand of missionary criticism among Bengali Hindus more in their own experiences and problems. The larger reformist critique about the place of woman in the Hindu social order was translated at a more immediate and palpable level as the vulnerability of women at the hands of their social guardians and superiors. Much of the reporting in vernacular newspapers focused on abduction or attacks on women by zamindars, policemen, upper caste superiors and holy men.[98] The Elokeshi scandal made the family—natal as well as marital—complicit with the structure of violence. That perhaps, was the most powerful source of anxiety. All prescriptive texts—religious as well as modern legal—consign woman to the domestic space under a protectionist ideology. The myth of the domestic sanctuary now stood decisively exposed.

There were other standard patriarchal worries about the pilgrimage journeys by women, especially their enhanced mobility in an age of safer roads and modern transportation. The new railways carried much larger numbers of women into such ambiguous holy places. The journey itself exposed 'respectable' women of ordinary means, who would normally be secluded within the domestic space, to male contact and male gaze in highly mixed crowds. The journey and the act of pilgrimage therefore, aroused deep male fears about boundary erosion, about exposure to men and different castes. The railway carriage became the sign of a dangerous modernity, of Kaliyug, of the loss of gender and caste anchorage. A contemporary satirist brilliantly evoked images of the socio-sexual chaos in the overcrowded carriage: 'The *hari* [the lowest of untouchables] on top of the *babu*, woman on top of man, man on top of woman, the bum against the mouth, and the mouth behind the bum.'[99]

Reformists argued that the scandal had made pilgrimages redundant, since the sacredness of the spots had been disproved by the immorality of its custodians. The orthodoxy, on the other hand, insisted that woman's holiest space lay within the family, in devoted service to the household and the family deity. It was only an immoral woman who uses a religious pretext to wander outside the home. Scandal plays lectured young women who wanted a son by the grace of Baba Taraknath: while the preservation of the line was a sacred duty, barrenness could best be cured by pleasing the gods at the domestic shrine. It is more important to be a good woman than even to be the mother of sons.[100]

VII

WHO IS THE GOOD WOMAN? LEGAL AND MORAL DEBATES

But who is the *good* woman? Where does her goodness lie, and what destroys it? Up to the 1870s, the questions remained remarkably open and troubled. I think that with these questions, we come to the heart of the puzzle, to the waves that the scandals made.

The *good* woman—whether in reformist or in orthodox rhetoric—would primarily be the good wife although the terms of description would differ. But how would the laws of the land define the *good* wife? Here, we enter into radical uncertainties about legal definitions and their consequences, as well as about the more basic question: what are the laws for the Hindus?

The nineteenth century in Bengal was the century *par excellence* for the review of conjugality. The century had more or less started with the *sati* issue which split Hindu society right down the middle. The agitation in support of widow remarriage strengthened the cleavages. Around the time of the Elokeshi scandal, huge controversies were going on over the Brahmo Marriage Bill of 1872 which had initially proposed a radical package of reformed marriage laws for all Hindus. Since at this point Brahmos insisted on classifying themselves as Hindus, the reforms threatened to revolutionize marriage laws for all Hindus. Eventually, Law Member Henry Maine agreed with an enraged Hindu orthodoxy that Brahmos constituted a separate sect and that Manu's prescriptions remained canonical for Hindus. The aborted prospects of a fairly revolutionized conjugality still rolled onto a thorough review of marriage norms and practices that preoccupied Hindus for the rest of the century.[101]

What was on trial were the foundational texts of Bengali Hindu conjugality, *Manusmriti* and the *Dayabhaga* modifications made by Raghunandan. The core of the system was the notion that the *good* woman is the chaste wife who remains faithful to the husband even if the marriage is not consummated, even if the husband dies—for marriage is not a contract but a sacrament. Such a wife alone is the true *ardhangini*—half the body of her husband, and it is on that understanding that she is granted a limited usufruct right to the husband's property under *Dayabhaga*.[102]

Upon this finished structure of an asymmetrical conjugal order, the law allowing widow remarriage dealt a massive blow, the full normative implications of which were being worked out in case after case even beyond the century. Its progenitor had seen it as a way of saving infant widows. He was bitterly disillusioned by its meagre results.[103] Yet, the significance of the Act should really be traced in its long-term normative contestation of the fundamental assumptions of Hindu conjugality. Whatever the intentions of Vidyasagar, the law itself had not stipulated that only *akshatayoni* or virgin child widows would be covered under it. It, therefore, enabled a situation where adult widows, having experienced a full-fledged sexual relationship with their husbands, could still remarry and still count as *good* women—legally, if not under sacred norms. The legal redefinition, however, put enormous strains on the foundational moral concept that the good woman is one who has sexual contact with only one man in her entire lifetime, and if the husband's other marital obligations or death precludes even that, she remains untouched by anybody else. The core notion of the *ardhangini* goes for a massive toss.

A legal loophole emerged in the 'Great Unchastity Case' or the Kerry Kolitani vs. Moniram Kolita case of 1873 that unwittingly further complicated matters. A widow who does not remarry and whose chastity is beyond doubt at the time her widowhood commences, is allowed a limited share of the husband's property under *Dayabhaga*. In 1873, a widow was accused of 'subsequent adultery' (adultery, since the marriage bond continues beyond the husband's death as long as the wife is his half-body)—a charge that was proved in court. The High Court decision allowed her continued access to property since she was chaste when she came into property, and after that, the right became an absolute one.[104] It tore open the system that had made woman's property right conditional on her chastity and it fractured the supreme importance of chastity itself. A bourgeois notion of the absolute nature of property rights, then, clashed with scriptural and customary insistence that without absolute chastity, a woman has no right to anything.[105]

The Widow Remarriage Act of 1856 had stipulated that widows about to remarry would forfeit their husband's property. In the next century, judges and lawyers would perplexedly consider if it was fair to allow an 'adulterous' widow to enjoy full rights to property while a respectable woman, who decently plans to remarry, would have to forfeit that. Would this be more or less conducive to the moral health of Hindu society?[106]

Completely unforeseen consequences of judicial application of legal provisions, then, combined with a new attitude towards individual property rights and new reformist agitations to loosen up the system of Hindu patriarchy which had so far exercised absolute control over social mores. Reformist patriarchal norms, on the other hand, never really acquired that hegemonic power. Nor were new laws grounded on any strong or coherent notion about individual right, far less of gender justice. Their most significant historical function was then, not so much the creation of a full-fledged alternative order as of being contestatory, destabilizing and problematizing. They certainly created the conditions for public dialogues, and made way for at least the idea of counter-norms. In 1873, the National Theatre staged the highly successful play, *Swarnalata*, which put various aspects of the Hindu conjugal order on the dock. Newspapers provided lengthy reviews of the plot, characters, message and possible social implications of each aspect of the play. They reported at equal length on audience reactions. The audience was the mirror to public opinion, and public opinion was the *de facto* jury.[107]

VIII

WHO IS THE GOOD WIFE? DEBATES IN THE THEATRE

Other, secondary aspects of Hindu conjugality were taken up energetically in the interpretations of the scandals and in the scandal plays. Elokeshi's father was an old man who, apparently, had been cruelly manipulated by the young and greedy stepmother. Unable to satisfy her sexually, he promised to buy her jewellery instead, and for that he had allegedly sold off his own daughter to the Mohunt. This theme dominated nearly all the scandal plays. The helpless lust of old men was a motif in many popular satires and farces, as was the husband's subordination to a young wife which added a new bite to the highly popular 'henpecked man' and the 'domineering woman on top' theme. More upmarket contemporary satires on the subject were Dinabandhu Mitra's *Biye Pagla Bruo* and Michael Madhusudan Dutt's *Buro Salik-her Ghare Ron*.[108] They not only influenced the representation of the motif in the scandal plays, but their popularity also shaped the reception and treatment of that aspect of the scandal itself in the public mind.[109] Such an inversion of the regular conjugal hierarchy was shown as the cause of familial disorder, of abdication of the father's sceptre, of a collapse of moral regulations.[110] Characteristically, in the popular, semi-obscene bazaar literature, the more mortal sin was not an old man's possession of a young woman against her will, but the latter's power over the man. In the Elokeshi episode, where male guardians in the Hindu family and society emerge as decisively unworthy, and where the culpability of the unchaste woman is somewhat undone through the acts of rape and murder; the focus on a greedy and corrupt woman relocated the story on a more familiar and acceptable register of misogyny and restored the trope of a female folk devil who gives the wrong twist within the social order.

Another theme that was very popular with the bazaar folk literature—a trend that the Elokeshi scandal confirmed—was the fear of the wife's prolonged sojourn at her natal home. Forced transplantation of a very young girl on the totally unfamiliar soil of the patrilocal family was a traumatic process that remained incomplete in most cases; the girl would never entirely identify with the new family within her heart and a permanent sense of homelessness would continue to besiege her. A patrilocal patriarchy, therefore, retained deep suspicions about the natal home, about her incomplete emotional integration with her new family. Visits to the parental home were a rare pleasure, dependent upon the whim of the new authorities and mostly withheld, since the bride soon became the source of the hardest domestic labour within the new household. The wife who spends a large slice of her time with her own parents is a woman who is depriving the new masters of valuable labour time. However, control over labour is a concept that needs to be masked and mystified, whether in political or in domestic economy. Control over the wife's sexuality, the other argument against long absences from the new home, on the other hand, was a more familiar one, securely grounded in sacred prescription, and, therefore, possible to articulate more openly. Elokeshi's crisis, in most plays was explicitly linked to her long stay with her parents where she had escaped the discipline of her husband's control. Sympathetic older relatives advised her that fidelity to her husband was a more urgent and superior need than obedience to parents, that the married woman has no second master other than her husband.[111] In these ways, Hindu patriarchy was appropriating some new turns that colonial laws had given to the structure of disciplinary mechanisms that ruled over woman, transferring the jurisdiction and execution from the hands of a large kin group to that of the husband.[112]

The central problem, however, was what to make of Elokeshi. The plays are dialogic, multiphonal on the point, even though on the secondary aspects they have a more conventionally patriarchal answer. On the other hand, the bazaar paintings and prints are less ambiguous. In the series on the first meeting between the Mohunt and Elokeshi, they all show three figures; a completely captivated Mohunt, an older woman go-between who is a low caste person (*tili-bou*), and Elokeshi, dressed in a dancing girl's costume, and casting an immensely experienced, 'come-hither' look at the Mohunt.[113] Clearly, she is seducing him. Equally clearly, since in other scenes she is dressed in a sari, its absence in this one points at her innate non-wifely tendencies, her illicit desires, her status as a public woman at heart.

Given the condemnation so explicitly made in this group of popular representations, the ambivalence of the scandal plays is striking. Elokeshi was unchaste, she also had a fairly longstanding affair with the Mohunt, even if she had been raped in the first instance. She certainly could be no simple victim figure here, despite her rape and her murder. That would constitute a total, clear break with Hindu conjugal norms.

The problem of representation is often managed by a double voicedness. Two sets of women talk about Elokeshi, one the village wives, and the other, the village prostitutes. On the whole, the wives condemn her, they doubt her love for Nobin, they allege that she was only too happy to be raped, they confidently and proudly assert that no one can rape a woman against her will. Elokeshi presents them with a sudden access to worth and moral superiority.

In contrast, prostitutes are compassionate, full of criticism of male lust and weakness. They believe in Elokeshi's innocence since they know how easy it is to be misjudged. Their comments, counterposed to those of the wives', make the boundaries between the two hermetically sealed worlds of wives and prostitutes open and porous, the properties of both interpenetrating: prostitutes bemoan the loss of Elokeshi's wifely status and Elokeshi's fall shows up how fragile the status of the wife is and how narrow the gap between her and her Other. These dialogues, therefore, ironize the dialogues of the wives. They also draw in prostitutes within the play as part of the interpenetrative community.[114]

The inclusion is not accidental or fortuitous; they are a sign of new times within the theatre, a *double entendre*. The Bengal Theatre, which staged the first scandal plays, was also the first to employ prostitutes in female roles, replacing earlier conventions where young boys played female roles.[115] It did so in the teeth of both reformist and orthodox opposition, the former objecting to the entry of bad women into a noble cultural form, the exposure of young men to evil influence, and the latter disapproving of the new resources and opportunities that prostitutes would now enjoy as artists, resenting their elevation.[116] Girish Ghosh later would try to disarm both kinds of opposition by composing plays on sacred themes where actresses enacted holy characters, thereby turning theatre into a moral-pedagogical space and redeeming prostitutes by the aura of the characters they enacted.[117] It is important to note that the great actress who enacted the sacred roles and who sent off the saint Ramakrishna into a trance, denied at the end of her life that theatre had thereby turned into an act of religion. She insisted that it was pure entertainment that really served no religious purpose. In Vaishnavite devotion, identification with a holy character leads one closer to God, hence devotion itself is a form of theatre.

The Bengal Theatre also employed an intensive advertising campaign to make theatre a family entertainment. It did so both by secluding special spaces for respectable women viewers and by focusing on domestic dramas. The scandal plays were among the first of such ventures.[118] For the first time, then, the two poles could be contained within the same space and a larger drama unfolded beyond the stage as the respectable female gaze was turned on its erotic Other. Also, for the first time, prostitutes played both the wife and the prostitute, as well as the dangerous middle term—the fallen wife. The *double entendre* was extended and enriched. In a very perceptive essay, Sudipta Kaviraj has talked about a spiralling ironical confusion between the wife and the mistress in Bankim's novel *Indira*, leading to a dizzying interpenetration of identities.[119] That kind of ironical comedy of errors is, perhaps, a perception of the age of theatre. It is also a perception of a time when the basic anchors of conjugality have started to waver.

For the wives in the audience, the situation would come to evoke curious responses, creating complicated circuits of desire. There would be the horror of meeting the Other in the flesh; there would also be the sting of seeing her as a successful woman in public. A number of contemporary plays dealt with themes of the abandoned wife, with the errant husband who pursues an actress/mistress. In fact, several of the scandal plays surmised that Elokeshi was left at her father's place for similar reasons. The wife-viewer would be simultaneously exposed to a dramatization of her condition, and to its transcendence by a glamorous rival. The spectacle of her goodness is thus rendered infinitely more problematic by the simultaneous spectacle of a glorious alternative—both transgressively dissolved within the same, unchaste woman's body. Visually, therefore, chastity was both problematized and continuously polluted, even while it was formally celebrated.

IX

ELOKESHI

In 1873, the colonial government was deliberating on new laws for the compulsory registration of Muslim marriages and divorces. In its perception, Muslim men and women walked in and out of marriages far too easily and errant wives returned to husbands they had left as if the marriage was still on.[120] While colonial lawmakers saw in this a sign of Muslim moral immaturity, sections of the Hindu press were more sympathetic, especially towards wives who desired to return to husbands despite an earlier divorce. The *Bengalee* made an immensely significant statement in this connection: 'You say my conduct in taking back my wife is dishonourable, I, myself am frail.'[121] May be the Hindu middle class found it easier to be more tolerant of the problems of Muslim women than those of its own, but there were some signs of change, at least in ethical approaches. The limits of the sacred significance of woman's chastity were being probed, and the probings were carried a little beyond the expected limits. A daring assertion is made when the paper says: 'I, myself am frail'. That is, for woman, too, fidelity may not be the only test of love. Also, that the sexual conduct of men can be judged by the same rules as those that apply to women.

It is here that the scandal gains its most powerful resonance. All the accounts agreed that Nobin had always been a loving husband—a fact that was proved when, on coming to know of the scandal, his first impulse was not to leave or kill her, but to run away with her and retrieve their lost happiness. Yet, Elokeshi had lived for some time with the Mohunt, most of the time fairly acquiescently. Whether or not she was still loyal to Nobin emotionally, she had certainly surrendered her sexual chastity decisively.

Woman's chastity had become a keyword in the political vocabulary of Hindu nationalism which had begun to develop at about this time. The Hindu woman's unique steadfastness to the husband in the face of gross double standards, her unconditional, uncompromising monogamy, were celebrated as the sign that marked Hindus off from the rest of the world and that constituted the Hindu claim to nation-hood. The chaste body of the Hindu woman was thus made to carry an unusual political weight since she had maintained this difference in the face of foreign rule. The Hindu man, in contrast, had allowed himself to be colonized and had surrendered his autonomy before the assaults of western power—knowledge.[122]

It was in this highly charged political context that the scandal was being reviewed. According to newspapers, for a fairly wide segment of middle-class and popular opinion, Nobin was morally wrong in taking back his guilty wife. Such love conceals a lapse from moral duties of the husband and of the Hindu man's dharma. Abandonment would have been both morally right and prudent, but even killing for such a crime was not excessive. The murder, to be justifiable, however, should have preceded the escape attempt. Less judgemental and more sympathetic songs still criticize him for trying to rescue an unworthy wife and thereby putting his own life in danger.[123]

At the same time, Nobin's passionate love for an unfaithful wife powerfully captured popular imagination. According to police reports, he had rushed to the police station after the murder with these words on his lips: 'Hang me quick. This world is a wilderness to me. I am impatient to join my wife in the next.'[124] The words were reported verbatim in all newspapers and plays, and songs were woven around them.[125] There was no one given way of relating to them. People very confident of the Hindu husband's dharma, still responded to their emo-tional pull and at least wondered about the sources of such love. We have already noted the reference to the Lewis Theatre where *Othello* was being played. The popularity of the play was enormous. Perhaps, the theme of tragic sexual jealousy at least partly structured the recep-tion of the event by the theatre going and reading public and lifted it from the domain of unconditional assent to the act of murder. Con-versely, a growing unwillingness to live by prescriptive gender judge-ments alone, an ability to see love as an unresolved social problem, conditioned the reception of *Othello* as well as of the scandal plays.

On the whole, however, a fairly moderate version of conjugal duties prevailed. Nobin's words were celebrated not as the sign of unreason and weakness, but of noble and strong love.[126] The incorporation of this love within the given boundaries of Hindu conjugality was at-tempted through a narrative move. In most of the plays, Elokeshi is first drugged and then raped.[127] The interval between the first rape and the confession—that is, the time when Elokeshi had lived with the Mohunt—was telescoped and virtually erased, so as to reduce her moral culpability and to legitimize Nobin's forgiveness.

A few of the plays go a little further. If all the scriptures, including the great Manu, insist that woman should be obedient to her male guardians, that she must not act or think or judge for herself, then did Elokeshi have an option beyond obeying her father and the holy man in her husband's absence? If she lived within a structure of prescriptions that left her with no option, then had she transgressed at all? In that case, should not the prescriptions be on trial rather than the woman's conduct? A number of plays make this point by focusing on the scene where Elokeshi helplessly gives in to her parents, rather than on rape or seduction. Lack of will and helplessness are identified as the source of her ruin rather than an incurably immoral female nature. Passivity, meekness, gentle obedience—that is, precisely the prescribed wifely norms—are not only portrayed as dangerous but also as repulsive traits, to reduce the entrenched aesthetic charge and emotional appeal of their figuration.[128] Soon, strong counter-images were evolved of independent, assertive and active figurations of female virtue as alternative inspirational models. Interestingly, this figuration takes place not within the domestic space so much, as within an emerging space of anti-colonial activism.[129]

A few reformist voices carry the interrogations even further. If social norms and prescriptions rather than an innately weak feminine disposition had caused the predicament, then was the woman for killing? However strong his love and bitter his temporary rage, was then Nobin not a murderer, and, hence, deserving of punishment? Was then the European judge not more correct than the Indian jury and public opinion? The petitioners who pleaded for Nobin's release had admitted that Elokeshi was more sinned against than sinning; however, given the choice of leaving her with the Mohunt and killing her, Nobin, they said, had acted as a true husband, since a life of dishonour is worse for woman than death. Plays and songs and most newspapers did not go beyond this. The *Bengalee*, a reformist newspaper, raised a lone voice to articulate an unexpected argument:

In sympathizing with the unfortunate Nobin people forget that the victim was not the man that he and all Bengal believe to be a vile seducer, nor the still worse scoundrel who bartered his daughter's virtue ... but a tender girl of 16 years. ... What had she done to forfeit her young life?[130]

She had been unchaste, but that no longer seems to suffice as an adequate reason. For, 'I, myself am frail.' Here we have—even for reformers who usually moved within patriarchal parameters of womanly purity and companionate marriage—an unusually powerful articulation of male guilt. Rammohun Roy had expressed it when he described how men ensure that ignorance would be the lot of women and then describe it as her natural condition.[131] Vidyasagar expressed it in a lament: 'Alas, the wretched women of India ... for what sins in your past lives are you born as women of this country?'[132] Couched in protectionist terms, it none the less, goes beyond the parameters of naturalizing gender differences and stipulating a protective ambience towards the 'weaker sex'.[133] It grounds the weakness of women in male prescriptions, demands and disciplinary order. Hindu nationalists of subsequent decades would displace this male self-division into guilt about surrender to western and colonial cultural domination.

The new public sphere surely did not promise anything like a coherent challenge to the divisions: male-public/female-private. None the less, that division does not act as a central, unambiguous structuring principle either. It radically questions its own presuppositions which falter even while they are being recast. I think that for a limited historical moment, the faltering was more significant and that a simple or flat notion of recasting does not capture much of what was really involved.

It is within this sense of guilt that the deepest resonances of the scandal need to be located. And the real transition to Hindu cultural nationalism lay through a suppression and displacement of this guilt. Soon public debates would decisively shift their ground and there would be little room left for looking at women like Elokeshi—a girl whose father sold her off, whose guru raped her and whose husband killed her.

NOTES

1. This is the first essay from a larger work in progress on law, family, religion and nationalism in late colonial Bengal. The essay, however, is still being broadened out. I am grateful for comments and criticisms on earlier drafts by Radhika Singha, Ravi Vasudevan, Neeladri Bhattacharya, Ratnabali Chatterjee and Sumit Sarkar. An earlier version of this paper has been published in *Studies in History*, no. 1, 1997.

2. For an understanding of the formation of a bourgeois public sphere, I have relied extensively on J. Habermas, *The Structural Transformation of the*

Public Sphere: An Enquiry into a Category of Bourgeois Society, trans. Burger and Lawrence, M.I.T. Press, Cambridge, Mass, 1989.

3. See Geoff Eley, Nations, publics and political cultures: placing Habermas in the nineteenth century, in Craig Calhoun, (ed.), *Habermas and the Public Sphere*, M.I.T. Press, Cambridge, Mass, 1993.

4. For a discussion on a layered middle class, see Sumit Sarkar, Kaliyug, Chakiri and Bhakti: Ramakrishna and his times, *Economic and Political Weekly*, 18 July 1992.

5. Notable exceptions obviously exist, and the superb study of Ranajit Guha of the abortion and death of a low caste nineteenth century widow comes readily to mind. There is again, Sumit Sarkar's exploration of a turn-of-the-century murder case involving a religious cult and a Brahmin guru and his low caste disciples in East Bengal. See Guha, 'Chandra's Death', in idem (ed.), *Subaltern Studies V: Writings on South Asian History and Society*, Oxford University, New Delhi, 1987. Also, Sarkar, The Kalki Avatar in Bikrampur: A village scandal in early twentieth century Bengal, in *Subaltern Studies VI*, 1989. As examples of histories of the former category of events connected with mainstream nationalism, see Shahid Amin's study of the Chauri Chaura events in *Event, Metaphor, Memory*, Oxford University Press, New Delhi, 1995.

6. These sources constitute the 'literature of judicial scandal' that Sarah Maza has used in her brilliant study of pre-Revolutionary sensational trials. See *Private Lives and Public Affairs: The Causes Célèbres of Prerevolutionary France*, University of California Press, Berkeley, 1993, p.1.

7. Sarkar, the Kalki Avatar in Bikrampur. Sarkar found evidence of the Doyhata case in a newspaper report and in a pamphlet.

8. For an argument in favour of a connected study of laws, the judiciary, the trial process, and public responses, see J.M. Beattie, *Crime and the Law-courts in England: 1661–1800*, Clarendon Press, Oxford, 1986, Introduction.

9. See *The Scandal of the State: Women and Institutional Protection in Contemporary India.* I am grateful to her for allowing me to use it.

10. A history of the scandal and the trials is to be found in citations from the High Court Judicaire at Fort William, Bengal 24/10/1873: Criminal Jurisdiction, Queen vs. Nobin Chandra Bannerjee. Cited in the *Bengalee*, 22/11/1873.

11. See *The Englishman*, 28/11/1873.

12. A petition signed by the 'acknowledged leaders of native society' was issued from Calcutta. A second one was signed by 'some gentlemen from Mymensingh' district of East Bengal. That had cast some aspersions on the High Court judgement on Nobin which had allegedly alienated Lt Governor Campbell and made him turn down the appeals for mercy. A third petition came from Maharani Swarnamoyee of the Cossimbazar Raj family, who was renowned for her magnificent charity, and who had received the title of Maharani in 1871; *Hindoo Patriot*, 1/12/1873.

13. *Sulabh Samachar*, 2/9/1873. Report on Native Papers (henceforth RNP), Bengal, 1873. Also, *Hindoo Patriot*, 18/8/1873.

14. *Bengalee*, 1/11/1873.

15. Pareshchandra Choudhury, *Tarakeswar Mohanto Mahatmya*, Calcutta, 1924.

16. West Bengal District Gazetteers, Hooghly, A.K. Bannerjee (ed.), Calcutta, 1972, pp. 725–6.

17. Government of Bengal, Home Political Confidential, FN 111/1912 (1–2): Conduct of the Mohunt of Tarakeswar; Petition by Nagendrabala Devi.

18. E. A. Morinis, *Pilgrimage in the Hindu Tradition: A case study of West Bengal*, Oxford University Press, Delhi, 1984, p. 92.

19. Terms such as 'talk' should be used circumspectly, however, since, unlike Habermas' public domain of cafes, salons and literary sessions, I refer to more mediated forms of representations and discussions which were not face to face. Also, John Thompson has rightly criticized Habermas for an essentially dialogic conception of the public sphere: 'His way of thinking about print was shaped by a model of communication based on the spoken word.' Thompson, The theory of the public sphere: a critical appraisal, in C. Calhoun (ed), *Habermas and the Public Sphere*, p. 97.

20. See also J. Goswami, *Samajchitre Unabingsha Shatabdir Bangla Prahashan*, Sahityashri, Calcutta, [1381], pp. 257–78. Goswami lists twenty-three farces on the topic. Shri Pantha in his *Mohanto Elokeshi Sambad* (Ananda Publishers, Calcutta, 1984) lists a total of thirty-four scandal plays on the event.

21. L. Das, *Mohanter Ei Ki Kaj!*, Calcutta, 1873 and 1874 (parts 1 and 2).

22. According to Sukumar Sen, *Uh! Mohanter Ei Ki Kaaj*, Calcutta, 1873 (published from the Bentinck Press at Battala) used a two-toned lithograph. Other farces on the scandal also had coloured illustrations. See for instance, *Ajker Bajar Bhau*, anon, Calcutta, 1873.

23. N. Ray, *Nutan Mohanta Tappa*, vol. 1, Calcutta, 1874.

24. See W.G. Archer, *Bazar Paintings of Calcutta: The Style of Kalighat* London, 1953. Also A. Paul (ed.), *Woodcut Prints of 19th Century Calcutta*, Calcutta, 1983.

25. We find here the repercussions of a new education system that now increasingly became the source of all middle-class employment, and often, of livelihood as well. The concrete features of the system are rarely taken into account in discussions of modern education: one of them being a regular and rigorous schedule of public examinations of the entire student body at a fixed point. A new pathology takes shape as a fresh form of headache comes into being. I would at some time like to explore the presumed relationship between the restorative powers of the product of the penal work of a fallen holy man and the problems of male students, along with the reasons for the special efficacy of this medicine for this category of patients. *Bangabandhu*, 5/12/1673, RNP, Bengal, 1873.

26. It sold for Rs 9 a seer, ibid.

27. T.N. Mookherjee, *A Monograph on the Brass, Bronze and Copper Manufacture of Bengal*, Calcutta, 1894. I am grateful to Nayanjot Lahiri for the reference.

28. The *Bharat Samskarak* of 26 September bitterly complained that by not taking stronger steps to clean up the pilgrimages, the government was ignoring Bengali, Hindu 'public opinion': 'The Bengalis are silent, but it does not follow that they have no ... public opinion ...'. (RNP, Bengal, 1873). The *Halishaher Patrika* of 21 November published an appeal by Nobin that was addressed 'To the People of Bengal', ibid.

29. The *Hindu Hitaishini* of 29/3/1873 complained that even though many charges had been brought against the Mohunt of Sitakundu, the government was ignoring popular opinion and taking no steps against him. This amounted to a violation of 'the rights of people'. RNP, Bengal, 1873. Note the justiciary character that is attributed to the people or public and the claim that it may dictate to the legal and judicial authorities.

30. See C.H. Heimsath, *Indian Nationalism and Hindu Social Reform*, Princeton University Press, 1964, ch. 3. Also, Amrita Shodhan, *Caste, Religion and the Law*, unpublished Ph.D. University of Chicago, 1995, ch. 4.

31. K.P. Singha, *Hutom Penchar Naksha*, Calcutta, 1862. Reprinted by Basumati Press, Calcutta, 1784, sakabda.

32. I owe this reference to Mrinalini Sinha.

33. The two plays are *Sammati Sankat* by Amritalal Basu and *Ain Bibhrat* by Harendralal Mitra See J. Goswami, *Samajchitre Unabingsha Shatabdir*

34. See T. Sarkar, 'Rhetoric against the Age of Consent: Resisting colonial reason and death of a child wife', in *Economic and Political Weekly*, 4 September 1993.

35. J. Habermas, *The Structural Transformation*.

36. The Calcutta National Theatrical Society on 10 November 1872 advertised its first class tickets as priced at Re. 1 and its second class tickets at 8 annas. These were expensive, but not prohibitively so. B.N. Bandyopadhyaya, *Bangiya Natyashalar Itihas: 1795–1876*, Calcutta, 1340, p. 97.

37. Smarajit Chakrabarti, *The Bengali Press 1818–68: A Study in the growth of public opinion*, Calcutta, 1976.

38. A.K. Sen, *Hindu Revivalism in Bengal, 1872–1905*, Oxford University Press, Delhi, 1993, p. 239.

39. In 1873, Bankim Chandra's great domestic novel *Bishabriksha* appeared. It spoke about conjugal and extra-marital love, of polygamy and widow remarriage. See *Bankim Rachanabali*, vol. 1, Sahitya Sansad, Calcutta, 1953. On the popular and pulp fiction, see S. Sen, *Battalar Chhapa O Chhabi*, Ananda Publishers, Calcutta, 1984.

40. On the *pats* and prints, see Archer, *Bazaar Paintings*, Hana Knizkova, *The Drawings of the Kalighat Style: Secular themes*, Prague, 1975; A. Paul (ed.), *Woodcut Prints of 19th Century Calcutta*, Calcutta, 1983.

41. A.C. Gupta, *Banger Guptakatha*, Calcutta, 1885.

42. The author is Lakshminarayan Das. Other low caste authors include Chandrakumar Das, Iswarchandra Das De, Upendranath Das, Tinkari Das Ghosh, Nemaichand Seal, and Maheshchandra Das, Jaharilal Seal and others.

43. Surendrachandra Bandyopadhyay, *Mohanter Karabash*, Calcutta, 1873.

44. Harimohan Chattopadhyay, *Mohanto Pakshe Bhutonandi*, Calcutta, 1873.

45. *Amritalal Basur Smritikatha*, included in B.N. Bandyopadhyaya, *Bangiya Natyashalar Itihas.*, p. 237. Incidentally, Basu wonders here whether Lakshminarayan was not a Christian. It, however, seems unlikely, for the fact would have attracted attention elsewhere.

46. B.N. Bandyopadhyaya, ibid., p. 112.

47. See A. Seal, *The Emergence of Indian Nationalism: Competition and collaboration in the later nineteenth century*, Cambridge University Press, 1968, ch. 4.

48. See A. Tripathi, *Trade and Finance in the Bengal Presidency, 1793–1833*, Oxford University Press, Calcutta, 1979, ch. 5.

49. On this, rather ignored phase, see N. Mukherjee, *A Bengal Zamindar: Jayakrishna Mukherjee of Uttarpara and his times*, Firma K.L. Mukhopadhyay, Calcutta, 1975, chs. 5 to 12.

50. See K.K. Sengupta, *Pabna Disturbances and the Politics of Rent: 1873–85*, Peoples' Publishing House, Delhi, 1974.

51. See B. Chowdhury, Agrarian economy and agrarian relations in Bengal, 1859–85, in N.K. Sinha (ed.), *The History of Bengal, 1757–1905*, Calcutta, 1967.

52. See S. Bandyopadhyay, *Caste, Politics and the Raj: Bengal 1872–1937*, K.P. Bagchi, Calcutta, 1990. Also, Social Mobility in Bengal in the Late Nineteenth and Early Twentieth Centuries, unpublished thesis, Calcutta University, 1985, ch. 5.

53. See Amiya and B.G. Rao, *The Blue Devil: Indigo and colonial Bengal*, Oxford University Press, 1992, ch. 5.

54. See K.K. Sengupta, Pabna Disturbances. An interesting point to note about the Pabna rising in this connection is how confidently the peasants used the lawcourts against the landlords.

55. See S.C. Bandyopadhyay, *Smritishastre Bangali*, A. Mukherjee, Calcutta, 1368/1961, ch 4.

56. See Shibnath Shastri, *Ramtanu Lahiri O Tatkalin Bangasamaj*, New Age Publishers, Calcutta, [1362], 1. Also R.K. Ray, *Palashir Sharajantra O Sekaler Samaj*, Ananda Publishers, Calcutta, 1994, p. 76.

57. I have discussed this in 'Rhetoric against Age of Consent'.

58. For a discussion, see ibid.

59. *Amrita Bazar Patrika*, 30/1/1873.

60. Cited in J. Goswami, *Samajchitre*, p. 268. Also Shri Pantha, Mohanto Elokeshi Sambad, p. 74.

61. S. Bannerji, *Studies in the Administrative History of Bengal*, Calcutta, 1975.

62. See *Biswadoot*, 3/11/1873, RNP, Bengal, 1873. Also, *Hindoo Patriot*, 18/8/1873 and 1/12/1873, RNP, Bengal, 1873.

63. See *Hindoo Patriot*, 1/12/1873. Also *Halishahar Patrika*, 28/11/1873.

64. Knizkova, *The Drawings of the Kalighat Style;* Archer, *Bazaar Paintings*. I think that Archer has wrongly identified the temple and the trial scenes as pictures related to general rather than to a specific theme. He seems to be unaware of the Elokeshi episode and he dates the trial scenes around 1845, going by the style of the headgear of the figures. However, in many of the other paintings and prints, the same scenes are firmly attached to this particular scandal. They are also appended in texts of the scandal plays. Their provenance is then decisively to be located within the Elokeshi episode. The paintings that Archer refers to are from the collections of Dr O.M. Samson and J. Lockyard Kipling, both of which were acquired well after the Mohunt's trials. See Archer, Plate 7, p. 35, for the courtroom scene which he describes as 'An Englishman dispensing justice', C. 1845. The picture shows the Mohunt on dock, a Brahman man as also under arrest, and the severed head of a woman. Similarly, Plate 18, p. 46, describes the temple scene and the first meeting between the Mohunt and Elokeshi as 'Women at a shrine'.

65. S.C. Bandyopadhyay, *Jamalaye Elokeshir Bichar*, Calcutta, 1873.

66. ibid.

67. Tinkari Das Ghosh, Calcutta, 1874.

68. *Bengalee*, 22/8/1873.

69. *The Englishman*, 28/11/1873.

70. See *Bengalee*, 8/7/1874, about the institution of the Tagore Law Professorship.

71. See A. Sen, *Hindu Revivalism in Bengal: 1872–1905*, Oxford University Press, Delhi, p. 140.

72. *The Englishman*, 28/11/1873.

73. *Bengalee*, 17/5/1873. Also, *Hindu Hitaishini*, 1/11/1873. RNP, Bengal, 1873.

74. *Bharat Sanskarak*, 27/11/1873, RNP, Bengal, 1873.

75. For an account of the case, see Government of Bengal, Pol 254–Progs. of the Lt Governor of Bengal, 1873: *'Case of Neemchand etc–Howrah Sessions'*. Also, *'Note on the Howrah Murder Case'*; No. 1370, Calcutta, 11/3/1873. Also, *Friend of India*, 22 May 1873.

76. For a brief mention of the case, see M. Borthwick, *The Changing Role of Bengali Women, 1849–1905*, Princeton University Press, 1984, p. 141. For a detailed and excellent study, see P. Rule, 'Who Owned Khettramoni? The Great Adultery Case', Calcutta, 1876 (unpublished paper). I am grateful to her for allowing me to use her paper.

77. *Napiteswar Natak or the Great Barber Drama*, anon, Calcutta, 1873.

78. N. Das, *Makkelnama*, Calcutta, 1878 and M.C. De, *Mama Bhagnir Natak*, Calcutta, 1878. See J. Goswami, *Samajchitre*, p. 253.

79. B.N. Bandyopadhyay, *Bangiya Natyashalar Itihas*, p. 202.

80. *Dacca Prakash*, 16/3/1873 and *Hindu Hitaishini*, 29/3/1873. RNP, Bengal, 1873.

81. *Doot*, 22/9/1873, RNP, Bengal, 1873.

82. See for instance, T. Mukhopadhyay, *Mohanter Ki Durdasha*, Calcutta, 1873. It is interesting that other ascetics did support the public demand for deposing Madhavchandra from his post as Mohunt. A Paribrajak Paramhans, for instance, had filed a case against him, asking for his removal. Yet, the newspapers and the farces do not ask the ascetic orders to come to the rescue, but they appeal to modern revivalist organizations. See *Sambad Prabhakar*, 14/10/1873, RNP, Bengal, 1873.

83. *Sahachar*, 1/12/1873, RNP, Bengal, 1873.

84. *Bengalee*, 22/7/1873. Also, *Bangabidyaprakashika*, 5/12/1873, RNP, Bengal, 1873.

85. See B.N. Mukhopadhyay, *Mohanter Chakrabhraman*, Calcutta, 1874; T. Mukhopadhyay, *Mohanter Ki Durdasha*, Calcutta, 1873; C.K. Das, *Mohanter Ki Saja*, Calcutta, 1873; S.C. Bandyopadhyay, *Mohanter Dafarafa*, Calcutta, 1873; J.C. Ghosh, *Mohanter Ei Ki Dasha*; S.C. Bandyopadhyay, *Mohanter Karabash*, Calcutta, 1873, and several others.

86. J.S. Mill, Memorandum of the improvements in the administration of India during the last thirty years. See Robson, Moir and Moir (ed.), *John Stuart Mill: Writings on India*, University of Toronto Press, Routledge, 1990, pp. 116–17.

87. *Hutom*, op. cit., p. 45.

88. J.N. Ghosh, *Mohanter Ei Ki Dasha?*, Calcutta, 1874.

89. H.M. Chattopadhyay, *Mohanto Pakshe Bhutonandi*, Calcutta, 1873.

90. S.C. Bandyopadhyay, *Mohanter Dafarafa*.

91. See Knizkova, *The Drawings of the Kalighat Style*. Paul, *Woodcut Prints*.

92. *Ajker Bajar Bhau*, anon, Calcutta, 1873.

93. M.C. Das De, *Madhavgiri Mohanto Elokeshir Panchali*, Calcutta, 1874.

94. *Halishahar Patrika* report cited in *Sulabh Samachar*, 24/5/1873. Also, *Grambarta Prakashika*, 16/8/1873, RNP, Bengal, 1873; *The Englishman*, 13/12/1873.

95. B.C. Bandyopadhyay, *Nababibibilash*, 1822. *Rachanasamagra*, Nabapatra Prakashan, Calcutta, 1987.

96. In J.C. Ghosh's scandal play, as a sign of ultimate humiliation, Muslim peasants discuss this aspect of Hindu pilgrimages. *Mohanter Ei Ki Dasha*, Calcutta, 1873. It is interesting that in another satire, the voice of the Muslim had been used as the supreme criticism of the pretensions of Hindu piety. See Michael Madhusudan Dutt, *Burro Shaliker Ghare Ron*.

97. *Amritabazar*, 20/2/1873; *Sulabh Samachar*, 18/3/1873, RNP, Bengal, 1873. See also S.N. Shastri, for the same point. Also J.C. Modak, *Stri Purushe Tirthayatra*, Calcutta, 1870.

98. See previous notes on the misconduct of pandas and other mohunts. Also, *Sahachar*, 7/7/1873, *Dacca Prakash*, 5/6/1873 and Bharat Sanskarak, 30/5/1873, RNP, Bengal, 1873.

99. Kalidas Mukhopadhyay, *Kalir Nabarang: Kalir Mahatmya*, Calcutta, 1873, p. 9. Also, *Bharat Sanskarak*, 29/8/1873, RNP, Bengal, 1873.

100. J.N. Ghosh, *Uh Mohanter Ei Ki Kaj*, Calcutta, 1874.

101. See my *Rhetoric on the Age of Consent*. See also A.K. Sen, *Hindu Revivalism*, ch. 2..

102. See L. Carroll, Law, custom and statutory social reform: the Hindu Widow Remarriage Act of 1856 in J. Krishnamurty (ed.), *Women in Colonial India: Essays on Survival, Work and the State*, Oxford University Press, Delhi, 1989.

103. See Bandyopadhyay, Caste, widow remarriage and the reform of popular culture in Bharati Ray, (ed.), *From the Seams of History: Essays on Indian women*, Oxford University Press, Delhi, 1995. Also, A. Sen, *Ishwarchandra Vidyasagar and the Elusive Milestones*, Riddhi, Calcutta, 1977.

104. See Carroll, Law, custom. See also *Murshidabad Patrika*, 18/4/1873, RNP, Bengal. Also *Bengalee*, 26/4/1873 and 17/5/1873.

105. *Dacca Prakash* argued that under *Dayabhaga*, 'when once the widow has come into possession of her husband's property, it is no longer his but hers and no one has any right to deprive her of it' 20/4/1873. *Murshidabad Patrika*, however, indignantly asserted that the High Court decision would encourage unchastity among widows, 18/4/1873, RNP, Bengal, 1873. The *Bengalee* used a different argument: 'What we object to is the arbitrary interpretation put by judges on our ancient sacred texts in the face of the opposition of the single native judge who had a seat on the court.' 17/5/1873.

106. Carroll, Law, custom.

107. *Bengalee*, 9/5/1873.

108. Mitra, *Biye Pagla Burro*, first published in 1866. *Dinabandhu Rachanabali*, Sahitya Sansad, Calcutta, 1967, pp. 97–123. It was enacted with huge success by the National Theatre in 1873, with the famous actor/playwright Ardhendushekhar Mustafi playing the main role. See B.N. Bandyopadhyaya, *Bangiya Natyashalar Itihas*, p. 120. M.M. Dutt's *Burro Shaliker Ghare Ron*, first published in 1859 and first staged in 1866, had a long stage run, well up to the 1870s. *Madhusudan Rachanabali*, Sahitya Sansad, Calcutta, 1965, pp. 255–68. See Introduction by Kshetra Gupta, pp. 52–4.

109. In 1873, the Jorasanko Nabaranga Natyashala sponsored a play on the same theme, entitled *Bridhhyasya Taruni Bharyya*. Calcutta, 1873.

110. See for instance, N.L. Ray, *Nobin—Mohanto—Elokeshi Natak*, 2nd edn., Calcutta, 1875.

111. *Uh Mohanter Ei Ki Kaj*.

112. On this see Radhika Singha, Making the domestic more domestic: criminal law and the 'head of the household'—1772–1843, in *Indian Economic and Social History Review*, (33)3, 1996.

113. See Archer, *Bazaar Paintings*; Paul, *Woodcut Prints*.

114. See for instance, Chandrakumar Das, *Mohanter Ki Saja*, Calcutta, 1873.

115. B.N. Bandyopadhyay, *Bangiya Natyashalar Itihas*, pp. 148–51. The first actresses were Jagattarini, Golap, Sukumari Datta, Elokeshi and Shyama.

116. See *Amritabazar*, 16/1/1874. Also, *The Hindoo Patriot*, 18/8/1873.

117. See Binodini Dasi, *Amar Katha Nati Binodini Rachna Samagna*, Sahitya Sangstha, Calcutta, 1934. (First published, 1912).

118. B.N. Bandyopadhyay, *Bangiya Natyeshalar Itihas*.

119. S. Kaviraj, *The Unhappy Consciousness: Bankimchandra Chattopadhyay and the formation of a nationalist discourse in India*, Oxford University Press, Delhi, 1995, ch. 1.

120. GOB, Judicial Department: Registration of Muslim Marriages, no.373, Dacca, 7 June 1873, File 506–9/12.

121. *Bengalee*, 26/4/1873.

122. Tanika Sarkar, The Hindu wife and the Hindu nation: domesticity and nationalism in nineteenth century Bengal, Studies in History 82, ns, 1993.

123. See for instance, *Bangadarshan*, 13/9/1873; *Bharatamskarak*, 6/9/1873; *Hindu Hitaishini*, 1/11/1873.

124. Reported in *Friend of India*, 5/6/1873.

125. See for instance, M.C. Das De, *Madhavgiri*.

126. *Uh! Mohanter ei ki Kaj*.

127. B.N. Mukhopadhyay, *Mohanter Chakrabhraman*, Calcutta, 1874.

128. M.C. Das De, *Madhavgini*.

129. See for instance, U.N. Das, *Surendra Binodini*, Calcutta, 1876, where a woman outwits a tyrannical *Sahib*. The play was a contributory factor behind the passage of the Dramatic Performances Act.

130. *Bengalee*, 1 November 1873.

131. Cited in Prabhatmohan Gangopadhyay, *Banglar Nari Andolan*, Calcutta, 1352, p. 15.

132. *Ishwarchandra Vidyasagar, Bidhababibaha: Dwitiya Pustak* in *Vidyasagar Rachana Sangraha*, Paschimbanga Niraksharata Durikaran Publication, Calcutta, 1972, p. 165.

133. For an elaboration of the notion of protectionism, see Kapur and Cossman, *Subversive Sites: Feminist Engagements with Law in India*, Sage, New Delhi, 1996, pp. 22–3.

Female Sexuality and Community in Jyotirmoyee Devi's *Epar Ganga Opar Ganga*

Jasodhara Bagchi

The primary attention of Europeans is on the body, the primary attention of the Hindus is on the inner nature.

Chandranath Basu, *Savitritatva*

I

MULTIPLE ASSAULTS

Written in 1968, Jyotirmoyee Devi's *Epar Ganga Opar Ganga* (on both sides flows the Ganges) is one of the rare novels about the partition of Bengal and the communal violence that preceded it. The novel focuses on violence and, possibly, rape of a Hindu girl in East Bengal and her subsequent marginalization by her own community in the post-partition 'secular' India. With restraint and daring rare in her generation Jyotirmoyee Devi (born in 1894) presents the physical trauma of the young adolescent girl. Her sexuality remains the great 'unspoken' in the novel. Yet it remains the pawn in the sinister game in which the 'community' enters with nationhood in order to keep alive the caste-class hegemony. In her angry Preface the author tries to call the bluff of the purity of female sexuality as a manipulative device in the hands of patriarchy. Her anger is directed as much against the inner as the outer forces that use the community to violate the female body and sexuality as the most vulnerable emblem:

I do not know of the historical writings in any other culture except the *Mahabharata*, which has a chapter called *Stree-Parva*.

(Jyotirmoyee Devi 1992: 125)

However, she points out, though called that, the chapter hardly deserves the name. She goes on to say,

In actual fact, even Vedavyasa could not bear to write the real *Stree-Parva* ... Cowards do not write history. There are no great poets among women. Even if there were, they would not have written about the violation of their own dignity.

Hence there is no recorded history of the real *Stree-Parva* .... The *Stree-Parva* of male humiliation? The Stree-Parva of all times? ... The chapter that remains in the control of husband, son, father and one's own community—there is no history of that ultimate humiliation, shame, that final pain ....

The *Stree-Parva* has not ended yet. The last word is not yet spoken.

(ibid.: 440–1)

Jyotirmoyee Devi is not merely a writer whose centenary we are celebrating in a ritualistic spirit. There is something about her novel of partition that calls out to me. Let me try and respond.

Defilement of communal honour through violation of female sexuality is a theme that resonates through the entire process of our nation-building act of which the popular mass media bear ample testimony. As far as I can see, the discussions and papers to which we are looking forward in this seminar will address this question in its contemporaneity. At one level, the anger in Jyotirmoyee Devi's Preface may read like yet another of the familiar *gat*. But the construction of her narrative shows that the anger is directed as much against the violent tampering with the female body to express the triumph and intimidation of one community over another, as the way it is picked up as an exclusionary boundary with which the women's own community preserves its caste-class identity. The main narrative is presented as a flashback that opens on a night when a sudden strike of communal frenzy hits the peaceful tenor of existence of a Hindu household living in East Bengal. Before they have understood anything the father disappears, the mother jumps into the pond to save her honour, the married sister disappears and the young adolescent girl Sutara loses consciousness under the assault and molestation. She is the only surviving member of her family to be nursed back to health by their Muslim neighbours. Through the haze of fear and physical pain she tries to piece out the nature of the outrage, since people are too embarrassed to answer her questions. However, those who have been involved with riots and partition will instantly catch on that the trials of Sutara do not end with the assault on her body but are about to begin.

Tameezuddin, her father's friend whose family nursed her to well-being faces threat from his own community. He reports to his own family,

I tried to tell them, why are you meddling with the women of the Hindu community, we have women in our homes too. Do you know what they said? When were the women not dragged and pulled? Read their Puran. Didn't Ravan abduct Seeta? And what about Draupadi? I said, that was not right, everyone knows. They said, let us not talk about right and wrong. It happens in every country. We know. (ibid.: 141.)

This is reiterated later in the novel by a Punjabi Hindu woman. When finally, Sutara's brother living in Calcutta does get to hear about Sutara's survival, his response is lukewarm. It is Tameez Sab's wife who, as a woman, understands the dynamics of this social situation, better than most others.

'Why not let her remain here. She can go back later. And—will they accept her if she goes back—.' (ibid.: 144.)

The fears are fully justified. After she is escorted back into the riot-torn Calcutta of 1946–7 by Tameezuddin Sab and his eldest son (taking, one should note, considerable personal risk) Sutara has to move in as a guest of her brother's father-in-law where the family has taken temporary refuge. Having been touched by a Muslim is never openly mentioned as the reason of the discrimination against her, but she is treated from the beginning as an untouchable, outside the fold of caste and community. The sites where she is most openly discriminated against, is in the kitchen and the pot of drinking water. She is excluded from the use of these spaces. She overhears the mistress of the house:

Six months in a Muslim houseold, what caste purity could such a girl be left with! All right you have brought her, but at least let her remain in a corner like Hadis and Bagdis! Instead of this you have let her enter into all the household activities. Who knows what she has eaten and done in the past few months! What are we left with!

She is sent off to a hostel run by Christian missionaries where she meets girls in similar ambiguous positions:

... yet again a fear surrounded her. Everyone unknown in this school run by memsahibs ... most of the girls were orphans. A group of girls, throw-aways, lost and mopped up in the famine of '42 [sic] or in the evil days of the partition.

Those who have no tradition, or even if they had, they have lost it now, these troupes of virgins.

The sense of being an identity-less flotsam has a hidden layer of pain at the loss of legitimacy imparted by society's stamp on their sexuality. The whispered rumour, the unspoken fear of Sutara's violated chastity, hints of a 'rape' and the physical contamination of her stay in a Muslim household are all based on communitarian taboos that need to be unpacked and historicized. It is no accident that hazy, largely muted articulations of the violation of female sexuality were so common in stories of partition (Das and Nandy 1985: 190–1). In a survey of recent studies on partition (Butalia 1993; Bhasin and Menon 1993; Das 1990) there has been a warning against invoking the 'communal identities' of South Asian women (Hardgrove 1995: 2427–30). Yet the prioritizing of community's imputed control over the female body and sexuality remain, endorsed.

In a recent, much acclaimed book by Partha Chatterjee, *The Nation and its Fragments* (1992), 'community' and 'women' are presented as two fragments of the nation. At the moment of the birth of two nation states in the place of one colonial state, the bodies of nameless women and their sexualities are brought under the control of their respective communities to complete the grand act of vivisection. The 'limit to the realm of disciplinary power' that is supposed to 'mark the idea of a community' is a gruesome chimera to the hordes of women like Sutara who watched from the margins of the community, the incomprehensible, the birth of two nation states.

Since the community's control over female sexuality lies at the centre of patriarchy (Lerner 1986), the female body becomes the pawn whenever there are crises in the social order. It is not surprising that in writing a novel about partition Jyotirmoyee Devi's mind goes back to the *Mahabharata*. The central event of the epic is Draupadi's public humiliation by disrobing and dragging her by the hair into the public arena. In the brahmanical patriarchal tradition hair is the symbol of female sexuality, so that the tonsure of the Brahman widows was a de-sexualizing ritual (Chakravarti 1995: 2252). The anguished reference to the *Mahabharata* while narrating the story of Sutara signifies Jyotirmoyee Devi's protest at the degradation that women have to face at junctures of male-engineered social crises. Female sexuality, therefore, is as much loaded with the semiosis of woman's social existence as by her private familial one.

The semiotic load, taking the garb of 'culture', called upon to contain the so-called 'natural' 'biological' 'overflowing' 'turbulent' female sexuality, was one of the chief markers of a 'class' boundary of respectability. A process of 'Otherization' is implicit in this social process. Thus uncontrollable sexuality became a sign for women of the lower classes. An odour of prostitution clings to the lower class working women (Sen 1994; Chatterjee 1993). As Uma Chakravarti formulates in the revealing title 'Whatever Happened to the Vedic Dasi?' (1989) the colonial construction of the *Bhadramahila* as the renaissance of the Vedic golden age was based on a systematic erasure of the *dasi* (the serving woman). The social order and its class division is thus interpelleted by female sexuality both in its presence and absence.

What is worth noting is that this drawing up of class boundaries is fully accommodative of identity-based communities. As I shall take up a little later, the chastity of the Hindu woman was also a way of demarcating the sensual Muslims. Popular literature and the popular plays on the Bengali stage of the late nineteenth and early twentieth centuries abound in these stereotypes. Identity-based community consciousness thus enters into an easy collusion with the so-called homogenizing modernizing nation-state.

In recent scholarship on modern India there has been a renewed celebration of 'tradition' (Borden 1989). The thrust of this revival is to critique the so-called 'modernity' of the nation-state. In the recent deployment of post-modernist theory in reading Indian society, the domain that has been privileged is the 'community', considered, according to this view, 'primordial' by the so-called 'modernizing' Nation state (Nandy 1990; Chatterjee 1992). This is supposed to have ushered a new trend in the analysis of communal violence and transformed the reading of partition from a mere 'constitutional' account (Chatterji 1995; Hardgrove 1995) to a more community-oriented one.

Post-modernist pluralism has initiated a cult of the 'fragmentary', that has tended to privilege the 'pre-modern' community over the 'modern' nation-state. As most try to show, when it comes to women, body and sexuality, the community becomes the main agent of the nation-state. The fragmentariness of communities, therefore, is illusory. At best it resembles the 'flexi-mode', much favoured by modern capitalism in its capacity to mutate, re-group and re-align.

II

SEXUALITY AND ITS DISCONTENTS

Excessive emphasis on the body was always considered to be the signifier of the morally degraded west as opposed to that on the soul that
stood for the spiritually pure east. This mainstream stereotyping was
transferred even to counter-voices like feminism. Feminist questioning
of the power hierarchy in the matter of sexuality was read as belonging
to the bourgeois decadence and was eyed with suspicion by the Left
(Snitow *et al.* 1983: 11–13). The division that this falsely conceived
opposition introduced into women's movement was also visible in the
opposition posed between women's sexual rights, seen as appropriate
to advanced capitalist countries and women's socio-economic right
considered to be more appropriate to poorer Third World countries
like India. In the ultimate analysis, however, the opposition is superficial. When Sojourner Truth lifted her work-served muscular arm and
asked 'aren't I a woman' (Rendall 1985: 253), the superficiality of the
distinction posed between labour and sexuality dissolved. Catherine
Mckinnon's famous aphorism 'What labour is to Marxism sexuality is
to feminism' remains as unsatisfactory and an unacceptable opposition.
As I have argued elsewhere, these attempts at salvaging class analyses
from the contamination of gender analysis are harmful not only for
gender analysis but for class analysis as well (Bagchi 1995). It is essentialist and denies the history of women of the Third World (See
also Sarkar 1991).

From the early days of the second wave of Anglo-American
feminist critique, sexuality has been identified as the most marked
domain of women's oppression (Millett 1969; Firestone 1970; Rubin
1975; Dworkin 1979). In two major areas of feminist intervention and
research this emphasis bore significant fruit: the ones on motherhood
that glorified women's sexual subordination in a heterosexual family
or in movements of social consolidation (Chodorow 1978; Bagchi
1990), and the ones on prostitution, that zone demarcated by society
itself for legitimizing the illicit (Walkowitz 1980; Bhattacharji 1987;
Chatterjee 1993). Feminist scholars have delved deep into the archive
of early history to trace patriarchy's need to control female sexuality
(Lerner 1986; Bhattacharji 1991, 1995; Chakravarti 1993).

Patriarchy's power over and desire of female sexuality was, therefore, not simply the post-Enlightenment regimen of rationality finding

embodiment in the 'modernizing' nation-state alone. Communities that claim pre-colonial pre-rational native wisdom are perfectly fit vehicles of this power and desire. Prioritizing communities over nation-states does not necessarily lift the veil of silence that envelops the oppressed groups. The patriarchal power wielded by the post-colonial states is an accretion from various micro-technologies of power produced by active collusion between the colonial State and the indigenous communities.

III

EAST VERSUS WEST

The experience of the colonizing west had, built into it, the element of desire that lent a special sanction to the urge to dominate. The initial 'gaze' of power that the Occident had cast over the Orient was one of desire camouflaging greed that got transmuted into the common sense of European bourgeois life-style. What was transgressive in the aspirations of Dr. Faustus (Marlowe 1591)

I'll have them fly to India for gold /
Ransack the ocean for orient pearl

(I.i. 81–2)

is taken for granted in the toiletry of Belinda (Alexander Pope 1712):

The various offerings of the world appear;
From each she nicely culls with curious toil,
And decks the goddess with the glittering spoil.
This casket India's flowing gems unlocks,
And all Arabia breathes from yonder box.
The tortoise here and elephants unite,
Transformed to combs, the speckled and the white.

(Canto I, 125–36)

Female sexuality, as embodied in the mysterious east, continues to haunt the Occidental imagery, whether as desire or power. To recall Said's classic formulation 'the metaphors of depth, secrecy and sexual promise' mark the endeavour of the Orientalist when faced with the Orient (Said 1978). Edmund Burke's recognition of darkness and fear as the central ingredient in the new aesthetics that recognized the sublime, made space for the otherwise unspeakable experience of the Empire (Suleri 1992: 39). The combination of highly charged sexuality and the self-denial of asceticism with which Hindu womanhood was presented in the Oriental tales and poems in the early years of British Romanticism, embodied the Burkean sublime. Though the names of the heroines are adaptations from the names of Hindu goddesses Kailyal in Southey's *The Curse of Kenama*, or Luxima in Lady Morgan's *Missionary*—the travails of her body and the trials of her sexuality form parts of the constellating image of the crisis-ridden meeting of east and west (Drew 1987; Leask 1993).

The body of the upper caste woman, specially in the context of her marital status was present at the heart of the three major legislations that saw to the consolidation of British rule in Bengal. In 1829 the Act banning *satidaha* or widow immolation was passed; this was followed in 1856 by the Widow Remarriage Act and in 1891 the Bill on the Age of Consent, though interpreted differently by advocates of both traditionality and modernism. The controversies generated by the three legislations helped to determine the class and gender contours of the indigenous elite in Bengal. After these, no thinking on State, civil society nor on community could bypass these contours. Wherever one addressed the gender question, in education, in health, in socialization or any other aspect of society, it would be difficult not to examine the parameters of sexuality laid down. Not only did Jyotirmoyee Devi, writing about the 1947 partition in 1968 have to negotiate it, any of us who have to engage with the gender question cannot ignore it.

Rammohun Roy, the great agitator on the occasion of the banning of *satidaha*, used arguments of egalitarianism and social justice, but even he extolled the virtues and self-restraint of Indian widows in leading lives of continence and chastity, dedicating themselves to the memory of their dead husbands. This argument created problems in the next agitation for social reform, in Vidyasagar's campaign for widow remarriage. If Vidyasagar was sceptical and dismissive of this glorification of the sexuality of Hindu widows, he was also interested in the containment of the sexuality of young widows through marriage. This was combined with his anger against traditional Hindu society in its inhuman treatment of women, and mostly child widows. They were prevented from taking nutritious food, specially protein (even lentils are prohibited to traditional Hindu widows) in case their sexual urges were roused. Vidyasagar appeals to the dangers of leaving so much sexual energy untrammelled, leading to infanticide, foeticide and prostitution (the popular word is the same for both in colloquial Bengal *ranr).* Even the great champion of women's education and autonomy worried about the cohesion of the brahmanical community.

The period that intervened between this major legislation and the next, saw a qualitative change in the social construction of gender within the precincts of the upper caste Hindu community. A process that I have called self-ethnicization of the Hindus (Bagchi, forthcoming), brings about a sharper redrawing of lines along brahmanical community-centred orthodoxy. Despite continuities in the gender thinking of the dominant community, there does occur a qualitative leap in the ideology of female chastity. While during the two enactments of laws, the agitation in favour of the passing of the laws succeeded in mobilizing a social consensus, about in the third instance the agitation was against legislation by the colonial State.

As a scholar has legitimately asked, was the debate about the age of consent, or the age of coercion? Female sexuality was debated in its most gruesome medical and Shastric details. Phulmani, a ten-year-old girl died of the first sexual intercourse in marriage. What should, therefore, be the age of marriage and the age of consent to sexual intercourse so that violence in marital sex could be legally condoned?

The controversy that ensued was a clear case of the community taking offence at the foreign intervention of the State. It is not as if the orthodoxy had not lined up against the previous legislations. What was different in the 1980s was that the community signalling its difference with the State had taken on the proportion of a nationalist consensus (Sarkar 1993, 1995). The community was seen as the great handmaiden of the incipient nationhood that was going to grow in strength in its construction of an alternate nation, wearing a distinctly Hindu look. If a spirit of Panopticism was evident in the drastic medicalization of woman's body during this controversy that raged for thirty years, who will do the reckoning of the kind of surveillance exercised by the threatening brahmanical community in their insistence that a girl must shed her first menstrual blood not in her natal home but in her marital home? In the context of colonial Bengal it seems a little simple-minded to think of the community as more woman-friendly than the nation-state. Its flexibility to enter into different power games should not be underestimated.

Legitimation through the control of female sexuality was growing as an essentializing force within the community. The more inward the community the more it needed to demarcate its identity as a principle of 'difference'. The ritual purity of identity needed a pronounced alien, the Hindu sovereignity was posed against the Muslim rule from which the British rule freed them. The chaste wife or the *patibrata* became the chief signifier in the game between the community, the colonial State and the incipient nation-state. Thus the instructions for the chaste wife went far beyond the bounds set for the 'angel in the house', the model for the Victorian wife. The *patibrata* was not only submissive but transgressive in her submission to wifely duties that was clearly not just a familial but a communal role.

The stiff opposition to the Age of Consent Bill was grounded in a field of discursive practice that centred round the image of the *patibrata*, the most fully contained of the Hindu images of feminine ideal. *Sati* (not Suttee) and *Savitri* are the two figures from the epics and *puranas* which led the catalogue of female worthies that became the commonplace of the Hindu community. The fear-spangled sublimity with which the early colonizers had perceived the Oriental woman is appropriated by the communitarian model of womanhood, privileging it in a reverse direction this time. Her sexuality, acknowledged to be potentially threatening, is made socially acceptable through the patent of wifehood, the husband being given the sole proprietorship of this potent sexuality. The relationship, we have to note, is asymmetrical, since the masculine form of the word *sati* has no sexual connotation. Thus the *patibrata* is not simply a domestic concept, an image of the 'private' or inner sphere alone. A certain rethinking of the entire scenario is called for.

Let me turn to the writings of Bhudeb Mukhopadhyay, discussed by Tapan Roy Chowdhury (1968) and Partha Chatterji (1986) to show how insurrectionary the image of the 'chaste wife' becomes. In his *Parivarik Prabandha* (Essays on the Family) Bhudeb includes a chapter entitled 'The Religion of the Sati':

In the literature of no other parts of the world will you have descriptions of heroines like Sabitri, Sati, Sita, Damayanti and others with which our Sanskrit drama (sic) is replete. The lays depicting the Sati-hood of the wives and mothers of the heroes of Rajasthan would be considered strange in any other country. Even the literature of the weak, downtrodden Bengal contains descriptions of Ranja Khullana and Behula, who provide examples of the Ideal of Sati.

What does this trend in our literature signify? It clearly indicates that this land is the holy habitat of the host of Satis. There is yet another proof in an old popular practice. Have women of any other country accompanied the husband in a funeral pyre? Leave alone accompanying could they even think of it? An Englishman witnessing such a scene confessed 'It is the Hindoos who believe in after-life, we don't.' (Mukhopadhyay 1881)

Strange thoughts for a family manual, and this too, from a law-abiding educationist! Half a century after the legislation against *satidaha*, the pure, contained sexuality of the Hindu woman guarded by 'death by fire' becomes the most pronounced talisman on the protection of the caste-class boundary of the Hindu community (Chowdhury and Sengupta 1993). It is against this image that the Muslims are figured. In a novel written in 1880 Pharichand Mitra (once of Young Bengal fame), the great satirist Teckchand Thakur wrote:

Mussalmans are more sensual, their womenfolk are trained differently; they have little faith in the other world. (Mitra 1879)

The liminal nature of the *patibrata* can be maintained with the help of a potential rapist. Just as for the white American woman the potential rapist is a poor black man, similarly the *patibrata* preserves her chastity against 'Ravana' the Muslim. Padmini is lifted from a lay by the *charans* of Rajasthan to the 'high' epic form in the hands of Rangalal Bandyopadhyay (1858). The uncontaminated sexuality of these diverse figures of Sati becomes symbolic of the sovereignity of the community in a state of siege.

As Uma Chakravarti's work brought out so perceptively, women's freedom and access to knowledge was used for constructing the argument for a Hindu golden age, discovered by the British Orientalists, by applying the cultural relativism of European Enlightenment. Similarly, if one were to adopt the findings of the gender-blind work of David Kopf on British Orientalism, to women's history, we may read an anxiety about female sexuality resulting in her confinement indoors, as a marker of the Islamic Dark Ages. Reading between the lines, this accusation cuts both ways: it helps to signal the Muslims as the perpetrators of the confinement of womenfolk indoors (through the popularized concept of 'purdah') and the occasion for it, because the Hindu women were perceived as potential victims of physical molestation by the Muslim men. Thus the triadic historiography of an Enlightenment Europe of an enlightened classical age being revived by an enlightened modern age by dispelling the intervening darkness of a medieval age, finds a very comfortable slot in the elite Hindu historiography of British India. With the slide characteristic of a class that was both hegemonized and hegemonizing, the *patibrata* or the chaste wife becomes the central icon of the glory of Hindu India. Containment of female sexuality thus gets built into the historical model of Bengal Renaissance bandied about with equal gusto by the left and right in India. It is a model that rests on the notion of the rebirth of Hindu India and effectively lubricates the passage of Hindu revivalism into the cultural nationalism of the *swadeshi* period.

The discourse of proto-nationalism as well as nationalism in Bengal is replete with images of women worthies who are preservers of the community. Ranging from Peary Chand Mitra, once a fiery member of the Young Bengal down to Chandranath Basu, who was a professed disciple of Shudeb Mukhopadhyay, and an ideologue of the conservatives in Bengal, the image of the Hindu woman, chaste and spiritual, was the badge of identity with which the Hindu community slowly marched towards aspiring nationhood. While the egalitarian impulse kindled by Derozio, is still an ingredient in Peary Chand's rhetoric— thus he extols the freedom of choice exercised by the Vedic and Puranic women in questions of marriage, in the same breath as Manu's insistence on the purity of women's lives—in Chandranath Basu the question of equal opportunities for women is conveniently eluded.

The figure of Savitri, in whom Susie Tharu had read Victorian racism (Tharu 1989) emerges as an extremely strong champion of the ideal of the *patibrata*. In a relatively unknown text the semiosis of Savitri is expounded in a domestic context:

The Patibrata wife is the road to mobility and liberty of man. Instead of making gifts of proud and destructive luxury items if we present them with the lives (*charitabali*) of Sita and Savitri, and if the followers of Annapurna, the descendants of Sita and Savitri, the women of India, follow the footsteps of Sita and Savitri, then this fallen country will become the blessed land again, greater than heaven ... Womankind, though half our existence form our complete life, the way to wholeness. The day the evil example and evil education of the foreigners made its deformed entrance in the purest of our inner domain (*antahpur*), that is the day our downfall began. Those who wish for the welfare of our country (*swadesh*) should, before everything else, purify themselves by preserving their own inner domain, (Basu 1900)

This is how the incipient nationalism is fed by the community-focal politics of identity. The author of *Savitritatva*, Chandranath Basu is also the author of *Hindutva* in which all the Hindu institutions are extolled as a pre-history of the desired nation-state. The gendered narrative of our nationalism picks on the most unorthodox of the heroines Savitri, whose story forms an episode in the *Mahabharata*. By one of the ironies of history, Savitri, who married of her own choice, at a mature age, both of which were reprehensible to the Hindu revivalists, is then picked out to stand for the essentialized image of a reified unsullied Hindu community.

IV

THE COMMUNITY AS PATRIARCHY

After such knowledge, what forgiveness? Jyotirmoyee Devi, whose pen has often lashed out against the 'purity' of the Hindu community, was an inmate of one. When she began to write she did inherit a tradition that either glorified woman or made her into a victim. Behind both, however, remained the grand appropriation of female sexuality by the community.

The 'good woman' of the popular culture was the upholder of the community and eventually became the sign of the nation. Savitri is chosen, not because she is a model wife in the Victorian pattern, but because she can challenge the god of death and bring her husband from 'the undiscovered country from whose bourne no traveller returns.' The sanction that the figure of Savitri receives from the community is due to her ability to negotiate the liminal. The strong phalanx of orthodoxy that excludes Sutara from entry into the everyday world of her own family is ultimately a fear of the body and sexuality: a body over which her own community had lost control and possession, for however brief a period: women who are riot victims or victims of holocausts like the partition are hit twice by the community-based patriarchy. The first through the male aggression of the 'Other' community, which asserts its territoriality by using her body and asserting its status of a community. The second is when the intra-community compulsions are invoked in order to reject the woman in the name of its own identity as a community. The anger in Jyotirmoyee Devi's Preface is against the reduplicating patriarchal assault: one as physical assault over her body and sexuality; the other is the prolonged panopticist gaze of the community over her body.

It is against this ideology of the purity of the community that the protagonist of Jyotirmoyee Devi's novel has transgressed. There are no histrionics of heroism woven round the act, for she is robbed of her agency. Had it not been for the outlet of 'education' Sutara would have been washed away like flotsam. Small wonder that at the formative years of the gender ideology that we have been tracing, somewhat sketchily, women's education was seen as a threat to female sexuality (Hindu girls in Bengal were threatened with widowhood in the early years of female education). The marginalization by the community persists. It is symptomatic that she is particularly unwanted at weddings and is seen as an obstruction to the marriage of the future generation. As a single girl she is free to take a job in Delhi where she meets victims of the other partition (the one of the Punjab). Somewhere Sutara begins to comprehend the game. It is bodies like hers that have got to be expunged for the community to nestle and breed in the bosom of the class-ridden nation-state. The mass media, textbooks, the family-generated socialization processes combine to keep the game alive.

Jyotirmoyee Devi is right. The last word has not been spoken yet. Women are again being pushed towards the 'community', to be repeatedly washed by bloodbaths, redeemed by violence. It is time to listen to the voice of this forgotten woman writer. Born a hundred years ago, widowed with six children at the age of twenty-six, she lived the life of an orthodox Hindu widow till she died at the age of ninety-four. Though deprived of formal schooling, she continued to call the bluff of the community as a trope of resistance, wielding a pen that Mahasweta Devi has hailed as 'cerebral'.

REFERENCES

Bagchi, Jasodhara., 1990, Representing nationalism: ideology of motherhood in colonial Bengal, *Economic and Political Weekly* xxv (42–3), WS 65–72.

—— (ed.), forthcoming, *Ethnicity and Empowerment of Women: the colonial legacy*, Kumari Jayawardena, Kali for Women, New Delhi.

——, 1995, Bartaman Biswe Nari Andolan O Nara Narir samparka, *Nandan* July 1995, NS 5(7): 31–4.

Basu, Chandranath, 1990 (orig. 1892), *Hindutva, Savitritatva*.

Bhasin, Kamala, Ritu Menon *et al.*, 1993, Recovery, rupture, resistance: Indian State and the abduction of women during partition, *Economic and Political Weekly*, April 24.

——, 1994, *Against All Odds. Essays on Women. Religion and Development from India and Pakistan*, ISIS, Kali.

Bhattacharji, Sukumari, 1987, Prostitution in ancient India, *Social Scientist* 150, February.

——, 1991, *Prachin Bharat: Samaj O Sahitya*. Ananda Publishers, Calcutta.

——, 1995, Laws against women, in J. Bagchi (ed.), *Indian Women: Myth and reality*, Orient Longman, Calcutta.

Borden, Carla (ed.) 1989, Contemporary India: Essays on the uses of tradition, Oxford University Press, Delhi.

Butalia, Urvashi, 1993, Community, State and gender: women's agency during the partition, *Economic and Political Weekly*, April 24.

Chakrabarty, Dipesh, 1990, Communal riots and labour: Bengal's jute mill-trends in the 1890s, in Veena Das (ed.), *Mirrors of Violence*, Oxford University Press, Delhi.

Chakravarti, Uma, 1989, 'Whatever happened to the Vedic *Dasi*? in Kumkum Sangari and Sudesh Vaid (ed.), Kali for Women, New Delhi.

——, 1993, Social pariahs and domestic drudges: Recasting widowhood among nineteenth century Poona Brahmins, *Social Scientist* 21(9–11, 244–6) 130–58.

——, 1995, Gender, caste and labour: Ideological and material structure of motherhood, *Economic and Political Weekly*. September 9, 2248–56.

Chatterjee, Partha, 1986, *Nationalist Thought and the Colonial World. A Derivative Discourse*? Oxford University Press, Zed Books.

——, 1989, A nationalist resolution of the women question, in Sangari and Vaid (ed.), *Recasting Women.*

——, 1992, *The Nation and its Fragments. Colonial and post colonial histories*. Oxford University Press, Delhi

Chatterjee, Roma, 1995, Communalism and violence, *Economic and Political Weekly*, 7 October, 250.

Chatterjee, Ratnabali, 1993, Prostitution in nineteenth century Bengal: construction of men and gender, *Social Scientist* 21(9–11, 244–6): 159–172.

Chodorow, Nancy, 1978, *The Reproduction of Mothering: Psychoanalysis and sociology of gender*, University of California Press, Berkeley.

Chowdhury, Sengupta, 1993, The return of the Sati: a note on heroism and domesticity in colonial Bengal, *R.F.R.*, (OISE), Toronto.

Das, Veena, 1976, Indian women: work, power and status, in B.R. Nanda (ed.), *Indian Women from Purdah to Modernity*, Nanda Radiant Publishers, New Delhi.

——, 1990, Communities, riots, survivors in the South Asian experience, in idem (ed.), *Mirrors of Violence*, Oxford University Press, Delhi. 1–36.

—— and Ashish Nandy, 1985, Violence, victimhood and the language of silence, *Contributions to Indian Sociology* (n.s.) 19(1): 177–95.

Drew, John, 1987, *India and the Romantic Imagination*, Oxford University Press, Delhi.

Dworkin, Andrea, 1979 (Paperback 1989), *Pornography: Men possessing women*, E.P. Dutton, New York.

Firestone, Shulamith, 1970, *The Dialectics of Sex: The case for feminist revolution*, Quill, New York.

Hardgrove, Anne, 1995, South Asian women's communal identities, *Economic and Political Weekly*, 30 September, 2427–30.

Jyotirmoyee Devi, *Epar Ganga Opar Ganga*, reprinted Subir Ray Chaudhury and Abhijit Sen (ed.), *Rachana Sankalan Sincerely,* School of Women's Studies and Dey's Publishing, Calcutta.

Kakar, Sudhir, 1990, Some unconscious aspects of ethnic violence in India, in Das (ed.), *Mirrors of Violence.*

Kopf, David, 1969, *British Orientalism and the Bengal Renaissance*, University Press, California.

Lerner, Gerda, 1986, *The Creation of Patriarchy*, Oxford University Press, New York.

Leask, Nigel, 1993, *British Romantic Writers and the East,* Cambridge University Press, Cambridge, Indian edn. 1993.

Millett, Kate, 1969, 1977, *Sexual Politics*, Virago.

Mitra, Pearichand, 1879, *Etaddeshiya Streelokdiger Purvavastha.*

Mukhopadhyay, Bhudeb, 1881, *Parivarik Pravandha.*

Nandy, Ashis, 1983, *The Intimate Enemy: Loss and recovery of self under colonialism*, Oxford University Press, Delhi.

——, 1990, The politics of secularism and recovery of religious tolerance, in Das (ed.), *Mirrors of Violence.*

Pandey, Gyanendra, 1990, *The Construction of Communalism in Colonial North India*, Oxford University Press, Delhi.

——, 1990, The colonial construction of communalism. British writings on Banaras in the nineteenth century, in Das (ed.), *Mirrors of Violence.*

Ray Choudhury, Tapan., 1988, *Europe Reconsidered*, Oxford University Press, Delhi.

Rendall, Jane, 1985, *The Origins of Feminism: France, U.K., U.S.A.*

Rose, Jacqueline, 1986, *Sexuality in the Field of Vision.* Verso, London.

Rubin, Gayle, 1975, The traffic in sex: a note on the political economy of sex, in Rayner M. Reiter (ed.), *Towards an Anthropology of Women*, Monthly Review Press, New York.

Said Edward, 1978, *Orientalism,* Vintage Books, New York, First Published 1978.

Sarkar, Tanika, 1991, Gender ideology in Bengal: reflections on the Birati rape case', *Economic and Political Weekly,* February.

——, 1993, Rhetoric Against the age of consent: resisting colonial reason and the death of a child wife, *Economic and Political Weekly*, September.

——, 1995, Hindu conjugality and nationalism in late nineteenth century Bengal, in J. Bagchi (ed.), *Indian Women: Myth and Reality.*

Sen, Samita, 1994, Honour and resistance: gender, community and class in Bengal 1920–40, in Serkhar Bandyopadhyay *et al.* (ed.), *Bengal: Communities, development and State*, Manohar, Delhi.

Snitow, Ann, Christine Shansell and Sharon Thompson, 1983, *Powers of Desire: The politics of sexuality*, Monthly Review Press, New York.

Suleri, Sara, 1992, *The Rhetoric of English India*, University of Chicago Press, Chicago.

Tharu, Susie, 1989, Training Savitri's pedigree: Victorian racism and the image of women in Indo-Anglian literature, in Sangari and Vaid (ed.), *Recasting Women.*

Walkowitz, Judith, 1980, *Prostitution and Victorian Society: Women, class and State*, Cambridge University Press.

Weeks, Jeffrey, 1985, (rptd.1993), *Sexuality and its Discontents* Routledge, New York.

Abducted and Widowed Women
Questions of Sexuality and Citizenship During Partition

Urvashi Butalia

I

INTRODUCTION

Partition is such a major event in India and Indian history that over this past half century it has continued to dominate collective memory, especially in north India, in a way that virtually no other event in recorded history has. 1947 is a year that is marked in India as the year of independence. At the level of popular memory however, partition often overshadows the importance of independence because of its much more direct impact on the lives of people. Virtually all fiction from northern India, whether in English, Hindu, Urdu, Punjabi (Gurmukhi), Bengali has, until recently, remained preoccupied with partition. Poetry, song, cinema, story-telling within families constantly recall the sweet and bitter memories of pre-partition India and its aftermath. Yet, despite their overwhelming presence in 'culture' these aspects remain largely absent in the recorded history of partition. Reading formal history one might, until recently, have been forgiven for thinking that partition meant only government-to-government debate, and decisions and negotiation at the political level. And indeed, one might further be forgiven for thinking that this was a history marked by the absence of any attention or focus on gender. Yet in recent years, it has become amply clear that the story of partition is a deeply gendered narrative in which women were centrally implicated in a variety of ways.[1]

There are many points from which one can approach a gendered history of partition. The violence that accompanied partition marked women and women's bodies in particular ways: we know of the rape and abduction that happened on a mass scale, of the cutting off of women's breasts, the tattooing of their bodies. We know too that in many places women were killed by their families, in others they took their own lives, and in some they also participated in the violence.[2] The dramatic changes partition brought in what was hitherto seen as the 'normal' life of communities and families—caused by the dislocation, the mass deaths, the forced migration—led to another little discussed aspect, widowhood and destitution for women. Many were unexpectedly rendered single as would-be partners died, or disappeared, and the marriageable age passed. In a curious kind of paradox, partition also threw up another unforeseen consequence: the mass influx of refugees and the consequent necessity of fulfilling their needs for shelter, jobs, food, and clothing, opened up a new career for middle-class women, social or welfare work, which, in turn, enabled their entry into the public sphere in an unprecedented way.

A gendered history of partition would thus need to focus attention on the centrality of women in changes in community and family, in the making of a 'national' identity, in the communalism that so deeply marked this particular event and in many other aspects. I am not attempting such a history here. Rather, I focus here only on two related aspects of this history: the multiple and layered strands of the experiences of abandonment and abduction on the part of thousands of women and the somewhat different, but also similar, experiences of those women whose husbands died in the 'war' that was partition. How did society and the State deal with these two sets of single—or as the State called them, 'unattached'—women who were on its margins; and further, how did the women themselves cope with this experience and what kind of relationship did they develop with the State and society? In a sense, both 'sets' (I use the word with some hesitation. The women were by no means homogeneous, and the lines of demarcation between widows and abducted women were not clear cut and distinct) became the concern of the State because, left without their men (and in the case of abducted women who had been recovered, even *rejected* by their men), they were seen as somehow 'unequal' to the task of carving out lives for themselves. Further, it was felt that because many were, in a sense, left rudderless not only by virtue of being removed from their men, but somehow because the central legitimating unit of the family (where their roles were very clearly defined) had come undone. Whatever efforts were made to restore some 'normalcy' in the lives of these women attempted therefore to relocate them within the fold of the family, whether real or simulated.

Relief and rehabilitation were the due of every citizen, male or female, rich or poor. Once people had been given the help needed, however, the State stepped out and left them to stand on their own feet. But for these women, there was a difference: those who could not be relocated inside families, whether their own, or new ones, became the long-term responsibility of the State, and in a peculiar twist, the State assumed the mantle of a surrogate family, a role that was simultaneously marked by a deep benevolence and a profound patriarchy.

II

THE ABDUCTED WOMEN

The story of partition, the uprooting and dislocation of people, was accompanied by the story of the rape, abduction and widowhood of thousands of women on both sides of the newly formed borders. The mass movement of people on foot, by bus, train, cart, left women, children, the aged and infirm, the disabled, particularly vulnerable. Little is known of the histories of these people and how they dealt with the trauma, pain and dislocation of enforced migration.

This silence is all the more surprising when one sees the dimensions of the problem. Literally thousands of women were abducted in what became two free countries. Abduction is a catchall description that has come to be used for all women (and some men) who disappeared during the confusion of partition. While it is true that many were actually abducted, it is equally possible that some may have gone of their own accord. None the less, the two countries treated all women missing or living with men of the other religion after a particular time as 'abducted' women.[3]

On the basis of complaints received from relatives the two countries compiled lists of missing women. While there is no way of ensuring that the figures were reliable (for instance a complaint about a particular woman could often be filed separately by three relatives and this might appear in a list three times at different places), some figures did find their way into public record. From these it seemed as if the number of Hindu and Sikh women abducted in Pakistan was roughly 33,000—although some estimates put this figure at 50,000—(this did not include women from Kashmir and it was felt that if these were added the figure could well have reached 50,000). Lists received from Pakistan showed the figure of Muslim women abducted in India to be around 21,000.[4] Whether or not these lists were accurate, they did serve to point to the size of the problem. It was because of this, and because of considerable pressure from the families, that the Indian State decided to mount what came to be known as the Central Recovery Operation, to locate, recover and, if necessary, 'rehabilitate' abducted women. The basic assumption of the Central Recovery Operation was that any woman found living with a man of the other religion after a certain date (and as we shall see later, there was some dispute on exactly when this cut-off point was to be located) would be presumed to have been abducted or forcibly pushed into that relationship, and she therefore had to be 'rescued'. If women protested, and said they were in one or other relationship as a matter of choice, it was assumed that such statements were being made under pressure and had therefore to be discounted.

In September 1947 the Prime Ministers of India and Pakistan met at Lahore and took a decision on the recovery of abducted women. In a joint declaration they voiced what they felt was their main responsibility:

Both the Central Governments and the Governments of West and East Punjab wish to make it clear that forced conversions and marriages will not be recognized. Further, women and girls who have been abducted must be restored to their families, and every effort must be made by the Governments and their officers concerned to trace and recover such women and girls.[5]

Later, in December of the same year, this joint appeal was given executive strength through an Inter Dominion Treaty in which both countries resolved that all women abducted or forcibly married after 1 March 1947 should be recovered and restored and that a joint organization of both dominions would be set up to carry out the rescue work. A subcommittee was set up which was to submit a report in three days on what steps needed to be taken. Between them, the governments also decided to collect particulars of abducted women, to broadcast joint appeals for recovery, to organize transit camps in every district for the abducted women while they awaited their transfer to a central camp to be set up in each dominion, exchanging weekly statements regarding the number of abducted women. A book published in 1952 by the Central Recovery Organization in India gives a district by district list of Hindu and Sikh women who went missing or were presumed abducted in Pakistan.[6] The Pakistan newspaper *Dawn* (founded by Jinnah) published regular appeals for information about abducted women, asking people to supply full details of where the woman was last seen, etc.

Bringing women out of a hostile environment was not an easy job. It was difficult, first of all, to trace the woman's whereabouts. All sorts of tactics, including subterfuge and disguise, were used by the rescue teams.[7] It was also felt that in an exercise of such a delicate nature, it was important to involve women and thus a number of women were drawn into the campaign. Indeed, the key officers charged with the recovery of abducted women were themselves women. Mridula Sarabhai was put in overall charge and assisting her were a number of women such as Premvati Thapar, Bhag Mehta, Kamlaben Patel, Damyanti Sahgal and others. It was felt that women were better placed to handle the delicacy of the situation and to 'persuade' those who were reluctant to give up their new homes, to return to the parental-national fold. Such rescue teams continued their work for several years, but as was to be expected, the work was not without problems. Almost from the beginning, it was fraught with difficulty and tension. While the two countries had agreed in principle to work together and to open up their territories to rescue teams from the other country, realistically, such openness was impossible.

In the early stages Pakistan protested against the involvement of the Military Evacuation Organization (MEO) and suggested that its duties should be confined only to the guarding of transit camps. The actual work of rescue, it suggested, should be given to the police. The Indian government was reluctant to do this claimimg that in many instances the police themselves were the abductors. Abductions by people in positions of authority happened on both sides. Kirpal Singh[8] cites several cases. In one, two assistant sub-inspectors of police went to recover an abducted woman and themselves raped her. In Montgomery, a tahsildar of Dipalpur, while participating enthusiastically in broadcasting/publicizing appeals for information about abducted women, is said to have kept an abducted woman with him for some eight months. The question was taken up at the Inter Dominion Conference in December 1947 and in January next. India's complaint against Pakistan was that it had suddenly closed off five districts of West Punjab to Indian social workers and police, claiming that they were close to the theatre of operations in Kashmir.

While the 3 September agreement quite clearly specified that abducted persons (The Act defined an abducted person as 'a male child under the age of sixteen years or a female *of whatever age* [my italics] who is, or immediately before the 1st day of March 1947, was a Muslim ...') had no real choice in the question of their recovery, and this was reiterated in the Inter Dominion Treaty, it appears from government records that this was a question of some dispute between Pakistan and India. Pakistan argued that some women were happy in their new surroundings and had offered resistance to being rescued. The Deputy High Commissioner of Pakistan is said to have written to the Chief Secretary, East Punjab, thus: 'One ... has written to say that his daughter ... aged 13 years, has been kept by one ... son of ... Jat of village Bhoma, District Amritsar. In reply to his request for the recovery of the girl he was informed by the Indian military authorities that his daughter did not wish to leave her husband.' One abducted woman is reported to have said to the District Liaison Officer, Gujranwala: 'How can I believe that your military strength of two sepoys could safely take me across to India when a hundred sepoys had failed to protect us and our people who were massacred?' Another such statement was: 'I have lost my husband and have now gone in for another. You want me to go to India where I have got nobody and of course you do not expect me to change husbands each day.' A fourth said, 'But why are you so particular to take me to India? What is left in me now of religion or chastity?'[9] Whether or not we should take these statements at face value is a question that is beyond the scope of this paper. For example, in the absence of any evidence to the contrary we can only speculate that the women may not have been coerced into saying this. None the less, these statements do testify to a certain reluctance on the part of some women to be 'recovered' and it is also clear from Indian records that many women did refuse to come back.

The recovery operation lasted several years and during this time, women had perhaps 'settled' into families, some had 'accepted' their fate, some had had children and therefore many did not want to face a second dislocation. Social workers such as Kamlaben Patel and Damyanti Sahgal who worked in the Central Recovery Operation, spoke eloquently of the women who did not want to return, of those who were torn about what to do with their children. Born of Muslim fathers, for Hindu families these children would be living symbols of the pollution of the race and therefore could not be integrated into Hindu society.[10] The fear was not unfounded. Despite the many appeals issued by Gandhi and Nehru that recovered women were to be treated as if they were sisters and were not 'polluted', when women did return, often families would not take them back. For those who had children the situation was worse, for often they were forced to choose between their children and their 'families'. Unable to support children on their own, several chose to give them up and return to their natal families. This left the State to deal with the problem of unwanted children, a factor that contributed in a major way to the winding up of the recovery operation.[11]

In support of its arguments that women did not want to return, Pakistan produced declarations—supposedly written by the women themselves—which were attested by magistrates. The Indian side viewed these with some scepticism, but eventually a compromise was worked out according to which 'women who ostensibly professed reluctance to be sent back to their original fold were to be segregated in social camps and there exposed to a process of resolute persuasion.[12] Resolute persuasion was just another word for wearing down resistance and defences, until the woman had no choice but to return to the place/family earmarked for her by the State.

The Agreement entered into by the two countries later became an ordinance (promulgated on 31 January 1949). Shortly afterwards, in the same year, the Abducted Persons Recovery and Restoration Ordinance became an Act. Interestingly, there was no parallel legislation on the Pakistan Side although there was an Ordinance under which the Pakistani State operated. The Act provided for the setting up of a joint tribunal to deal with disputed cases. By the time legislation actually came into force—1949—the bulk of the recoveries had already taken place and numbers dropped gradually after that. In addition, according to Kirpal Singh, the majority of women who were recovered were not those who had actually been lost.[13] The Act remained in force till 1957 when it was withdrawn because there was opposition to it. It was also because of this opposition that at the Indo-Pak conference held in May 1954, it was discussed that some way should be found to ensure that abducted persons were not forced to go to the other country against their will. Special homes were then set up where unwilling persons could be housed and given time to make up their minds 'without fear or pressure'. How much of a choice this actually gave women is another question. Let us turn now to look at the experiences of the other large group of women who came in for State attention, the widows.

III

THE WIDOWS

In 1989 some three hundred women sat on *dharna* and relay hunger strike outside the home of the then Home Minister, Buta Singh. The majority of them were over sixty years of age, all survivors of partition. Many among them had been forced to abandon their homes in West Pakistan and move to India; they had lost their husbands, sometimes other members of their families and several were left with small children to bring up.

The number of women who, in the years immediately after partition were categorized as 'partition widows', was not small. Reports of the Ministry of Relief and Rehabilitation put the figure somewhere in the region of 75,000 with approximately 30,000 of these being from Bengal. In a note dated December 1949, Rameshwari Nehru said that the number of women from West Punjab under the care of the government in October 1948 was 45,374. A substantial percentage of these were widows.[14] As the chart below shows, on 31 December 1953 the number of unattached women and children receiving relief from the government was 36,737. The three hundred who sat on *dharna* in 1989 then, were only a small number of this total. None the less, they were somewhat representative, coming from diverse backgrounds and histories. Some belonged to Sindh and Baluchistan, most were from Punjab and their families had been engaged in a range of occupations—from selling furniture to *kirana* (grocery) shops to petty trade of different kinds.

Eighty-year-old Veeranwali belonged to Adi Narola village (district Jhelum) and came to India in a *kafila* (foot convoy). Devi Bagya, whose husband owned a *kirana* store, came later from Karachi where migration took place after the January riots in 1948. Premvati's cultivator husband was killed in the riots in village Kana Kacha near Lahore and she came to Delhi with her three-year-old son. Sheelavati, from Toba Tek Singh, was temporarily luckier. She managed to reach Attari by train with her husband and children and spent a month in the camp there. But her husband, a chronic tuberculosis patient, soon had to be removed to hospital at Kingsway Camp and he died there after a year. Sheelavati then sent her children to a government-run home in Jullunder, and herself stayed on in Delhi. Rukman belonged to Lahore and had lived as a destitute on the pavements of Delhi for some time. Another older woman had lost virtually her entire family

Unattached Women and Children, Aged and Infirm Persons (including Dependants) from West Pakistan in Receipt of Gratuitous Relief (31 December 1953)

State	No. of homes/ infirmaries	No. of inmates in homes/ infirmaries	No. in receipt of gratuitous relief outside homes/ infirmaries	Total
1. Ajmer	1	160	48	208
2. Bhopal	1	1,704	–	1,704
3. Bombay	3	3,871	6,832	10,703
4. Delhi	1	1,281	50	1.331
5. Kutch	1	864	–	864
6. Madhya Bharat	1	128	318	446
7. Madhya Pradesh	3	328	49	377
8. Mysore	–	–	107	107
9. PEPSU	3	1,849	76	1,925
10. Punjab	11	14,330	–	14,330
11. Rajasthan	7	1,678	403	2.081
12. Saurastra	4	2,074	31	2,105
13. Uttar Pradesh	3	400	45	445
14. Vindhya Pradesh	–	–	111	111
TOTAL	40	28,667	8,070	36,737

Note: Where December 1953 reports have not been received, latest available figures have been incorporated.
Source: Report of the Ministry of Relief and Rehabilitation, 1953.

during the riots: her daughter, her sons and their wives had jumped into a well and committed suicide and she came to her new homeland, alone, and spent the rest of her life, similarly, alone working until she began to lose her eyesight and became too old to travel. In 1989 she was bed-ridden and was trying to eke out an existence on the meagre pension the State allotted to partition widows. While these are only some instances, by 1951, some 1.75 lakh (175,000) refugees had come to settle in Delhi alone, roughly 40 per cent of whom were women, and a large percentage of these, widows.[15]

In the early days, the government instituted a number of relief measures for the vast numbers of refugees that flowed in. These included transit camps, relief centres, vocational and technical training centres, housing boards, etc. Widows formed a category that required special attention—not only were they alone, or with small children, but they were unused to dealing with the public world. Once apprised of this, on 24 November 1947 India set up the women's section of the Ministry of Relief and Rehabilitation with Rameshwari Nehru as its honorary director. The section was charged with very specific responsibilities. These were:

(1) to organize relief to women and children, especially unattached women and children.
(2) to help in the rehabilitation of unattached women and children.[16]

By the end of March the following year, three women's homes had been set up in Delhi (province) and three in East Punjab (Kurukshetra, Jullunder and Amritsar). In an attempt to make them self-reliant, women in these homes were taught a variety of 'trades' including calico printing, embroidery, knitting, soap making, vegetable and fruit preservation and spinning. Apart from the government, a number of voluntary organizations also stepped in to work with women. These included the Arya Samaj, the Rashtriya Swayamsevak Sangh, a number of Gandhian and Christian missionary organizations, the Kasturba Gandhi Trust, the Central Relief Committee, the United Council for Relief and Welfare and later, the Tata Institute of Social Sciences and others. Initially, the work of the women's section in the Ministry of Relief and Rehabilitation extended to the whole country, but gradually, states took on responsibility and the women's section began to concentrate its energies more on the centre.[17]

In 1948, a number of *silai* (sewing) centres were also set up in Delhi. Initially only eight—with some 441 workers—these centres became very popular and by 1951 their number had risen to thirteen with about 1,880 workers. Women in these centres earned between 12–20 rupees a month.[18]

The rehabilitation of single women and widows was based on an interesting premise. As citizens of India, all displaced people who had been forced to flee from Pakistan had a right to claim maintenance or compensation from the State. And indeed, the massive relief and rehabilitation effort—whatever its problems—mounted by the State shows that the latter was well aware of this responsibility. As a task, however, this was something that had to be timebound. Once people's claims had been settled, and they had been provided the wherewithal to get back on to their feet, they were left to rebuild their lives. With widows, and some abducted women, this was not the case. The State accepted them as a 'permanent liability', ostensibly because, having lost their men, and therefore having become (by implication) unable to fend for themselves, these women were 'unattached' and the State had to assume the role of parent/protector to look after their interests. The following quote describes this in no uncertain terms:

The dispersal of displaced persons from West Pakistan has long been completed and there are no relief camps for them at present. There are, however, *Homes for the aged and infirm, the unattached women and children who have been accepted as the permanent or semi-permanent liability of the State.* [My emphasis.]

The Government of India have assumed responsibility for the care and maintenance of unattached women and children, the old and infirm and their descendants. Their present number is of the order of 74,000 – 38,000 from East Pakistan and 36,000 from West Pakistan. The great majority of them are being looked after in the Homes and Infirmaries specially set up for them, though a small number still continues to receive dole outside.

The aged and infirm constitute a permanent liability of the Government, but efforts are being made to train up the unattached women and children and the dependants of the aged and infirm in suitable vocations and crafts to enable them to stand on their own feet before long. Provision has also been made for their education.[19]

The women were treated as 'war widows'. As Rameshwari Nehru said, because the struggle they had inadvertently been part of could well be regarded as a war, they had to be classed in the category of war widows and war orphans and treated as such. The State, however, also assumed responsibility for their social and economic rehabilitation as well as their 'moral well-being'. Attempts were made to provide training in a variety of trades and professions so that the women could enter into jobs, or set up their own training; others were provided start-up capital as well as things such as sewing machines, employment exchanges were instructed to place women in jobs, children were taken up for adoption, schools and other educational institutions were opened up, as were marriage bureaux where younger women's marriages were arranged. A difference was made between women who were completely alone, and those who had relatives who could help them. The latter were to be supported till such time as they became self-sufficient while the former were fully the responsibility of the State.

Initially faltering, the relief and rehabilitation operation for widows and other unattached women became one of the major welfare operations undertaken by the Indian State. The purpose of all the training that was being offered was to give widowed women a chance to integrate into the economic mainstream of Indian society. Additionally, however, it was recognized that mere economic rehabilitation was not enough. In Rameshwari Nehru's words

At the very outset the Section [the women's section of the Ministry of Relief and Rehabilitation] realized that rehabilitation is an intricate process and can be achieved only if adequate attention is paid to the *psychological, educational and emotional needs of the women*. It is of utmost importance to make them self-reliant and self-supporting and *restore their sense of dignity and worth*. [My italics.][20]

Here was the first of the differences between the group we have loosely identified as 'widowed women' and those who came to be seen as 'abducted women'. While the two did sometimes overlap, what marked the difference between them was the fact that abducted women had actually been in sexual contact with men of the other community, while widowed women were in some way chaste, having had sexual contact (presumably) only with their husbands. Thus it was that to them that a sense of dignity and worth was given, and it was for them that it became important to pay attention to their psychological, educational and emotional needs. These needs too, were, on the face of it, simpler than those of abducted women—for the latter, once having been exposed to the supposedly rampant sexuality of the Muslim male, who could predict what shape their needs would take? The problem was further complicated by the fact that many women had publicly said they did not want to return to their original husbands or families, some had expressed doubts but were not certain, some articulated the dilemma but saw no real choice in returning. These dilemmas did not seem to exist for widowed women. The State was their parent, benevolent, caring, and attentive to their needs, as well as protective of their reputation.

It was this same sense of dignity and worth that led the three hundred widows to sit on *dharna* in 1989. More than four decades after partition, these women remained the responsibility of the State and indeed, saw themselves as such. After all, they said, 'we are its [the State's] children. And if the parent does not look after the child when the child needs looking after, who will?' By the time their strike took place, several had managed to build small houses from the pieces of land allocated to them, their children had grown up, some had moved out and some had done the opposite—married and brought their wives home to stay. Once the only breadwinners, these widows now found themselves in the unenviable position of being dependants, dependent on their sons, or sometimes their daughters. Their agitation therefore demanded the two things that would enable them to hold on to a sense of dignity: the non-closure of their *silai* centres (which was inevitable as their numbers had depleted and other claims were being made on the space), and an increase (marginal) in their pension. As one of them said, 'It doesn't matter that the amount is small, at least those *kambakhats* will not be able to lord it over us.' In the end, after several days of sitting on *dharna* (one of the women said, 'I walked all the way from Pakistan, I'll walk here every day if I have to until our demands are met.'), the State capitulated on the demand for an increase in the pension. In actual money terms, this amounted to an investment of a mere Rs 2.5 lakh a year on the part of the State, and that too for the few years that remained of the lives of these women. More than the money value, however, was the symbolic value. The parent-protector was fulfilling its responsibility, virtually to the end. The widows had a right to make this claim, they said, because in times of crisis, who does one turn to but one's parent. 'He is our *mai-baap*', they said, turning to the house of the then Home Minister, 'and we will place our demands before him.'

IV

SEXUALITY, CITIZENSHIP AND THE STATE

In the years immediately following partition, the sexuality of women, whether inviolate or violated, became a subject of concern for the Indian State and more specifically for the Hindu community. The concern, for example, reflected for the abducted and raped woman had little to do with her or what must surely have been her own sense of violation of her body and spirit; rather, it was a concern for male honour as it works at different levels—in the family, the community and the nation. This was reflected in many different discourses: representatives of political parties in the Legislative Assembly had extended and detailed debate on the issue. Newspapers were full of the concerns of men on the question of the abduction of women. To many writers of the *Organiser*, the weekly mouthpiece of the Rashtriya Swayamsevak Sangh, the fact of the mass rape and abduction of Hindu women (the fact that thousands of Muslim women too had suffered, was conveniently glossed over) was a 'challenge to our manhood, no less than to our *nationalism*' (my italics) It was something that made the nation 'writhe in pain and anguish—the only remedy to which was the 'Kshatriyaization' of the Hindu race, so that the men could do their expected and assigned task, to protect and defend the women, and thereby to protect and defend the nation, the community and the family. In this lay the proof of their nationhood.[21]

But how and why did widows, normally ostracized to the margins of society, come to assume such importance for the State? The Central Recovery Operation, and some of the rhetoric surrounding it, provides us with some clues to this. Of the 50,000 or so women who were said to have been abducted, or who were simply missing, the State had managed to recover only some 8,000. Rumour had it that these 8,000 were not from among those who had been reported missing. In that sense the Central Recovery Operation had been a major failure. It therefore also represented the loss of honour, of manliness, of national identity, which exercised Indian men in the aftermath of partition. Its relative failure, however, made the exercise of widow rehabilitation much more important. It is ironical that once past the crucial state of the immediate aftermath of partition, the State, parent-like, did not withdraw its support from widows (nor did they, drawing upon the same relationship, cease to make demands of the State).

Many things were responsible for the failure of the Central Recovery Operation: the difficulty of actually locating women; if they were found at all, the opposition put up by some families to their 'acceptance' into the fold; and most difficult of all, the problem of what to do with the children born of mixed unions. As is well known by now, many families who had earlier reported their women missing, now refused to take them back because they had been 'polluted' through sexual contact with men of the other race. Worse, some even had children, living symbols of the pollution which made it difficult for families to now take them in. When women who had children were recovered, they were faced with the impossible 'choice' of having to give up their children if they wished to be taken back into their families. And the State then had to take on the task of settling the children thus 'abandoned' into orphanages and homes. It was for all of these reasons that the Recovery Operation finally had to be closed down.

The post-partition Indian State was a fragile one, troubled and caught in a situation of enormous complexity and flux. On the one hand, were the expectations of its millions of citizens that the State would immediately address itself to the task of fulfilling the many promises on which it had come to power. On the other, were the immediate—and unexpected—tasks of the aftermath of partition: the mass influx of refugees, their need for food, shelter, clothing, medical attention, paying out compensation, locating missing relatives, dividing assets and so on. At the heart of all this lay the problem of women—marginal and secondary as citizens, but significant and crucial as symbols. If the State could be said to have looked after its women, it could be said to have protected its honour, and rendered itself legitimate. Widows therefore presented a much more easily identifiable constituency, and indeed one whose sexuality was not called into question, and the massive rehabilitation operation mounted for them enabled the State to regain some of its legitimacy. The attempt to recover abducted women was also part of the same exercise, although of course it met with only questionable success.

The sexuality of widows on the other hand had, in a manner of speaking, remained intact and thus they did not pose the same kind of problem as abducted women did. The death of their (the widows') husbands had left them bereft and alone, often unable to fend for themselves, but they had not, unlike abducted women, been cast into the hands of the 'Other'. Nor did they have with them the unpleasant reminders—children—of such liaisons with the 'Other'. They could thus, more easily become the recipients of State attention and largesse. Thus it was that the State lavished not only attention but also created a number of social welfare schemes designed to help widows to earn a living, acquire a permanent place to live, and have the means and wherewithal, both economic and social, to get on with their lives and be a part of society.

Where both widowed and abducted women were concerned, what could be said to have happened was that the 'normal' order of things, as reflected in the continued existence of the family, had come undone. The family was thus central to the enterprise of preserving/restoring the order of things. Women, who should have been in families, (whether their natal ones or those they had married into) were suddenly on their own, unattached, alone. Thus everything was done to help single women to bring up their own families if they had them, or to integrate into families of relatives, and failing these possibilities, to create a sort of 'family' inside welfare homes which the women could call their own. For abducted women, even though their number was small, the family was even more crucial. Having once been exposed to the 'libidinous Muslim' (it mattered little that there had been large numbers of rapes on the Indian side as well), the danger of their sexuality getting out of control was very real. Sexual chaos only reflected the chaos the nation was going through, and it was imperative that some semblance of order be restored: inside families, with women's sexuality strictly regulated, this was possible. Where real families could not be found, it fell upon the State to take this role.

Clearly, while the State instituted what was a major humanitarian operation, and one which, with all its faults, was also beneficial to large numbers of women, it none the less constructed women differentially from men. Not citizens in their own right—and this at a time when citizenship and the question of rights were key questions being debated—but mothers, sisters, wives who had both to be rehabilitated, and protected, who had to be brought into the mainstream economically, but retained within the family, whether 'real' or simulated, and whose sexuality had to be kept in check. Not surprisingly, no such concern was reflected for men.

NOTES

1. Among the recent works that have focused on partition as a gendered narrative are various essays. My own work includes an article: Community, State and women's agency: some questions on women and partition, in *Economic and Political Weekly*, Review of Women Studies, April 1993; and a somewhat expanded version of this article in Ania Loomba and Suvir Kaul (eds.), *India: Postcoloniality, Literature, Culture, special issue of the Oxford Literary Review*, January 1994; also, Hindus and Muslims: men and women: communal stereotypes and the partition of India, in T. Sarkar and U. Butalia (eds.), *Women and the Hindu Right*, Delhi, Kali for Women, 1995. See also Ritu Menon and Kamla Bhasin, Recovery, rupture, resistance, in *Economic and Political Weekly*, April 1993 and a somewhat expanded version of this article in K. Jayawardena and M. de Alwis (eds.), *Embodied Violence: Communalizing women's sexuality in South Asia*, and, Of national honour and practical kinship,' in Veena Das, *Critical Events*, Oxford University Press, Delhi, 1995.

2. See Butalia, (ed.),

3. The Act defined an 'abducted' person as:

a male child under the age of sixteen years or a female of whatever age who is, or immediately before the last day of March, 1947, was a Muslim and who, on or after that day and before the 1st day of January, 1949, had become separated from his or her family and is found to be living with or under the control of any other individual or family, and in the latter case includes a child born to any such female after the said date.

4. Figures here are taken from various sources including G.D. Khosla, *Stern Reckoning: A summary of the events leading up to and following the partition of India*, Oxford University Press, Delhi, 1949, reprint 1989; *Report on the Working of the Ministry of Rehabilitation 1951–52, and NonMuslim Abducted Women and Children in Pakistan and Pakistan side of the Cease Fire Line of*

Jammu and Kashmir State, Government of India, Ministry of External Affairs, 1952.

5. U. Bhaskar Rao, *The Story of Rehabilitation*, Government of India, Publications Division, Delhi, 1967.

6. See Government of India 1952.

7. In personal interviews both Damyanti Sahgal and Kamlaben Patel spoke of the different disguises and stratagems they used when engaged in the search for abducted women.

8. Kirpal Singh, *Partition of the Punjab*, Publications Bureau, Punjab University, Patiala.

9. Ibid.

10. Kamlaben Patel, personal interview and in her book, *Mool se Ukhda*, trans. from the original Gujarati, Delhi.

11. Damyanti Sahgal, personal interview.

12. Rao, *The story of Rehabilitation.*

13. Kirpal Singh, *Partition of the Punjab.*

14. Rameshwari Nehru, Private papers, Nehru Memorial Museum and Library, Delhi.

15. A substantial amount of this information comes from an investigative report prepared by the People's Union for Democratic Rights, *Sadda Hak Ethey Rakh.*

16. Ibid.

17. Government of India, *Report on the Working of the Ministry of Rehabilitation 1951–52* and research done by PUDR for their report *Sadda Hak.*

18. PUDR, ibid.

19. Government of India, *Report on the Working of the Ministry of Relief and Rehabilitation, 1951–52.*

20. Ibid.:, Rameshwari Nehru, Private Papers.

21. See my article, Hindus and Muslims: Men and women.

Femininity, Space and the Female Body
An Anthropological Perspective

Seemanthini Niranjana

I

SITING THE BODY

It may be useful to begin this anaysis, interlocking theory and ethnography, with a brief and selective critical appraisal of the anthropological discourse on the body. Such an account would not only indicate my own location *vis-à-vis* these questions, but would also be suggestive of an orientation we could be bringing to studies of femininity in contemporary society. It will also enable us to develop, in a vocabulary that is essentially spatial, a line of analysis that has remained unsystematized in such studies.

The most dominant model offered by the existing anthropological focus on the body has been, admittedly, a symbolic one, where the body is perceived as sign or code, important to the extent that it is speaking about a social reality other than itself. Suggestive as it may well be to speak of the body as representing encoded social meanings, as an 'image of society' or even a 'metaphor for society', the question remains whether these perspectives can acknowledge the materiality of bodies, not merely as they are formed or represented by/in a culture, but how they constitute the lived realities of persons. How we are to begin speaking of the 'materiality' of the body is doubtless a troubling question, and could do with a reminder that the reference here is not to the body 'as such' (which could steer us into the realm of philosophical discourse), but to the challenge of elaborating a more comprehensive anthropological approach to the body. This would entail a scrutiny not merely of how the body is 'coded', but also demand an attentiveness to the practices which systematically constitute and animate the body.

The recognition that the materialization of bodies is routed through certain regularized (societal) practices, taking place within definite parameters of time and space, could further serve to dislodge the dualistic terms of reference to bodies in our discourses, taking us beyond perspectives on the body as either 'given', or as somehow 'constructed'.

A substantial part of feminist anthropology, however, has hitherto sought to deal with the problem posed by the body for analysis by choosing to align itself with the constructivist axis; in the context of feminist theory this has meant taking a specific stand *vis-à-vis* the sex/gender distinction. More often than not, analysis has moved away from a grounding in sexual difference (i.e., in a biologically differentiated male and female), by arguing that this starting point, in speaking of 'woman' as a biological category, fails to recognize the innumerable differences amongst women, based on caste, class or kinship positions. Instead, studies have increasingly focused on the different ways in which femininity and masculinity are culturally constituted, across diverse socio-cultural contexts. The outcome has been a steadily growing body of work, what one may describe as a feminist symbolic anthropology (see, for instance, Ortner and Whitehead (ed.), 1981). which, in wanting to highlight the differential construction of gender and sexuality, seems to have deflected attention away from the female body itself,[1] to the layers of symbolic representation in which it gets swathed.

Though I am by no means claiming that this symbolic turn in anthropology is *the* most important genre of gender analysis, I refer to it largely because it illustrates, in so many ways, the problems of persisting with a sex/gender distinction. The reluctance within such studies, to speak about the female body other than as a symbol has also led to a focus on femininity as an acquired trait, an attribute that is socially constructed, or as a social category 'imposed on a sexed body'. As critics of the sex/gender distinction (for example, Gatens 1992) have argued, the liberative dimension of gender in an earlier phase of scholarship seems to now be actually constraining analysis, largely due to this perception of gender as attributes inscribed upon a neutral body. To be sure, to delink sexual difference from gender is to suggest, in effect, that femininity is an arbitrary form of behaviour, and that the body is irrelevant to comprehend its manifestations. Taken to their logical extreme, words like 'inscribing' or 'imposing' assume the body as a blank slate, as nothing apart from the cultural meanings constituting it, whereas, in reality, the body is not quite a receptacle, but the very medium through which meanings are produced. In order to put this misleading and distortive wave behind us, it is imperative that we re-establish connections between the two principal axes which define female subjects in specific socio-historical contexts, viz., femininity (as an acquired attribute), and its grounding in the female body. Perhaps one way in which this restoration of both biology and ideology to the constitution of female identities can be achieved is to work with a notion of the female body as 'situated', in space, time, and culture. Here, unlike in other approaches, the sexed body is neither a mere symbol, nor an inert biological foundation on to which gender ideas are written. Rather, it is as that which is imbricated in the very techniques of the body, or more broadly, the bodily practices of women, i.e., the modes in which they walk, work, talk, dress, etc., the body becomes the very medium through which femininity (in its cultural form) is constituted.

In many ways, this starting point, by blending the biological fact of womanhood with its ideological or cultural dimension, works to refuse superficial separations between sex/gender or body/mind. It also strikes a different note in relation to a range of other debates and perspectives on the body: such as, whether to postulate it as a tangible, pre-discursive entity, or whether to perceive it as an indeterminate field open to contextual definition; whether to focus on the body as an object which is constituted through numerous channels of representation, or whether to approach it as an object of varying cultural constructions; or again, to speak like Foucault (1978) of the body as the site of a range of institutional and regulatory discourses. For, despite their dissimilarity, what these viewpoints share is an inability to speak of the *body as subject*,[2] not in the sense of, for instance, how ideas of femininity are internalized or subjectively experienced, but how we actively orchestrate our lives as women through the body. To ask, instead, how we inherit, and live through, a female body can open up several levels for scrutiny, such as—how women inhabit the body, what the socio-cultural meanings invested in the female body are, how women's bodies occupy and orient themselves in space, and so on. To work, with a notion of the *body as situated* allows us to explore these questions at length, since it not only conceptualizes the body as 'subject', but, more pertinently as a *situated* subject, or a *lived body*— formulations which reveal the interface between the material body, the representational body, and the modes in which women activate these constitutive conditions. The alternative view of femininity and the female body that this can offer is grounded in a specific claim—the claim for a *spatializing* of bodily discourses and practices. Such a tracing of the spatial dimension calls attention to the contexts through which subjects live their lives, the arenas, events or qualities that mark bodies as female (or male), as well as how the body itself condenses our location in a cultural space. Spatializing our discourse on the female body could also suggest that it may be possible to speak of differences, within and across genders, along these lines, without necessarily falling back upon the binarism of the body as either culturally constituted, or as prior to its cultural inscriptions.

II

OF FEMININITY AND SPACE

The original study on which these observations are based was cast largely in the mould of a study of the construction of femininity. In its initial stages, looking for ways to map this process, I began to ask within what existing discourses had it hitherto been approached. It seemed easiest, for instance, to highlight socialization as central to the process of acquiring feminine roles, whereby women, in learning the cultural ideas and values that shape the 'female' get reproduced as gendered subjects. Clear and persuasive as this line of analysis could be, it never failed to be a source of discomfort as well, stemming from the doubt whether, since cultural scripts of femininity are outside the person (and therefore have to be learnt) women were not being reduced to passive subjects.[3] A similar doubt underlay the attempt to trace the cultural perceptions of femininity through the life stages of a woman, despite the fact that this includes a recognition of the female body, the changing perceptions of it and how these are internalized by a woman. Thinking back, it seems apparent that this sense of unease had something to do with the whole argument about the cultural 'construction' of gender, with its implicit banishment of the body and the problem of raising the question of agency within such a framework. One was also acutely conscious of the fact that most studies on femininity in India seemed to alternate between 'materialist' (where women were studied in relation to various contexts of material inequality) and 'culturalist' analyses (which involved studies of femininity and the female role in terms of marriage, kinship, religious and other practices; see Niranjana 1992). It seemed imperative to offer a fuller analysis, besides overcoming these oppositions.

It was only later, while poring over the material collected from the field, that I began to find a way of negotiating these problems, which was based on a realization that a very strong spatial narrative governed the lives of people in the village community and, more significantly, that much of what was said of femininity, the female body, or even the activities of women were all embodied in this idiom. It was this recognition, or the centrality of space and its constant negotiation through words and deeds, which provided an invaluable axis along which to speak about processes within the community. The compelling presence of the question of space in a people's daily lives also hinted at a highly complex trajectory, moving beyond a mere physical reference. Decidedly, the complexity of this dimension calls for an approach that can adequately map its traces, mediating between perspectives at once material and cultural. While such a mapping would entail a larger perspective on the question of social space and spatiality *per se*, what is being offered here is a detailing of but one aspect of this world of relations, namely, the practices and discourses of femininity and their articulation through a distinctive spatial register. The focus on women's speech and activities as a mode of tracing this relationality is intended not so much as a representation of positions and perspectives obtaining in the field, but as an attempt to discursively retrieve ongoing processes in the social world.[4] Thus the focus is something more than a methodological strategy alone, voicing also a substantive disposition towards questions of social ontology and conceptualization.

Drawing upon suggestions thrown up within the village cluster studies,[5] I will now endeavour to indicate how considerations of spatiality inform, in particular, the bodily practices of women within the community. One could also draw attention, thereby, to how the body, and the modes in which it inhabits space, itself comes to be deployed as a medium through which the 'female' is constituted. The articulations suggest that socio-spatial parameters of women's lives hinge on a delineation of what is known in the vernacular as *olage-horage*. Whether one is talking about matters as diverse as work, quarrels, the family, caste group, 'proper' behaviour, women's activities, or interaction within the village, all these are described with recourse to the vocabulary of *olage-horage*. These spatial ideas, strongly embedded in the perceptual schemes of people emerge as the principles orienting their daily practices, the axes along which the world is ordered into one's own or other, female and male, good and bad, familiar and strange, and so on.[6] The following section attempts to unravel these notions, offering an outline of the registers of spatiality and femininity.

III

SPATIAL REGISTERS

We will begin with some indications of the modes in which bodies and spaces are gender-marked through a consideration of the domains and activities of women, and place alongside this the ways women speak about their lives.

The central preoccupation of women in the village cluster studies, across differences in caste and economic standing, are the needs, even the survival, of their families. The household, in more ways than one, is located at the centre of these women's lives, being both the object of, and the locale for, a large chunk of their daily activities. Yet, in the course of their activities, these women also negotiate a variety of situations and circumstances that may even take them beyond the household as physical space. Starting with a woman's typical household activities, we can see how her movements are choreo graphed by certain implicit cultural rules governing the use of space. For instance, most of them, in the course of their household chores, rarely venture beyond certain conventional boundary markers separating *uru* (village) from *kaadu* (though literally forest, it here refers to the uncultivated wild spaces surrounding the village).[7] Even in carrying out their tasks of collecting fuel and grazing sheep or cattle, women go in small groups, and follow fixed and familiar tracks immediately around the village, always keeping the settlement in view, or within shouting distance of one another. There is also a strong reluctance to enter groves, bamboo thickets, or cross surrounding hillocks, fearing an exposure to undesirable people, spirits, or places. Such perceived dangers define what is out of bounds for women, and in doing so, reinforce the security and informality of the village/*uru* as an inner space that is one's own.

Having a telling impact on women's use of space are the variations that are introduced into the work-day patterns of women when we raise questions such as caste and the extent of women's participation in wage labour or subsistence family labour. Among economically worse-off groups (who are also largely lower castes and usually landless), a woman, in addition to domestic chores, also undertakes wage labour. Her options, however, are limited in comparison to men, and she looks for employment as either agricultural or construction worker within her village, or at most, at the brick kilns situated in the spaces bordering her village and the next. This is not only because of her domestic responsibilities, but also because, as we shall see, transgressing these spaces, even in search of subsistence work, is often seen as casting a shadow on her, and her family's moral standing.

Among better-off families belonging to the dominant castes, particularly the small and middle farmers in the village, women withdraw for wage labour, though they continue to work on family fields in addition to doing the household chores. Yet, the widespread assertion by several women like Kamalamma, a Vokkaliga woman, that they do not 'work outside' suggests that they perceive this space, i.e., the family land, and their work on that land, not as something external, but as extension of their household chores. Sowbhagya's perceptions of the nature of women's work established this continuity:

I'm not denying that a man's work is important ... but a woman's work is the main thing. We not only have to toil in the fields, but also in the house ... attend to the children, attend to the house, do the cooking, and when your man goes to the field, go there and help him too. ...

A recognition of the household as women's space and women's responsibility is an opinion that is widely expressed, whether or not this is contrasted with the activities of men. Sharadamma, a Lingayat woman, underscores this sentiment:

Who will cook, and care for the children and home if not the woman? What will happen to the household if we don't The dharma of men is different ... they only do outside work.

This identification of women's interests with the inside—*olage* in the local idiom—here the household or hearth, is most strongly expressed among women of upper castes, who do not seek wage labour, and for whom the household becomes the sole preoccupation. Their access to economic resources is limited, and their seclusion induces them to concentrate mainly on maintenance and reproductive tasks. To that extent, their mobility is restricted and their visibility also decreases, since they also confine their interaction to their caste neighbourhood. Rajamma's assertion—

Our menfolk labour outside and provide for the household; as for us, we look after work inside the house. We don't need to go out for anything. ... Besides what business have we going near places where men are?

—underlines the significance of space as structuring a woman's world, an underlying principle which is so taken for granted that it often remains invisible in analysis.

IV

CIRCUMSCRIBING THE FEMALE BODY

But what *does* it mean to highlight space as significant? What is implied in identifying it as the central axis of our investigation? For, in spite of being assumed as self-evident, the specificities of this invocation of space actually vary greatly, whether in debates on cultural identity or in attempts at conceptualizing social systems. To speak of space and femininity, as done here, is to refer not merely to geography, but also to how this patterning of physical space is interwoven with the lived practices and meanings of members of a community; it entails asking questions such as: how is space circumscribed in relation to women—in terms of their work and interests, yes, but also in terms of their bodies? Or, to pose it a little differently, how are *female* bodies circumscribed in space? And how does this operate in the daily lives of women? In what ways are these ground rules adhered to, retraced, or even circumvented? The foregoing account offered an initial two-tiered understanding of women's location in space (to which we shall soon add other dimensions). One is the perception of the village or *uru* as 'safe' for women, the other, further breaking down this space, to refer to the household or hearth as an inviolate and intimate realm for women. With these indications of how spaces are gendered and circumscribed, let me intersperse a series of random expressions of people in the village, and draw your attention to another crucial discourse folded into this process—a discourse on female morality and sexuality, indicating how rules regarding the use of space is itself constitutive of perception of the female body.

I referred earlier to the variations introduced into analysis by attending to the work dimension. The work opportunities of women outside the home are structured in definite non-economic ways, where the nature and place of work are major factors to be taken into consideration.

The work place of these female labourers is invariably near and familiar, since travelling long distances to work unaccompanied not only carried the fear of what is alien, but is also seen as 'wrong', bearing the stigma of moral suspicion. Women who transgress their habitual, 'assigned' socio-physical spaces run the risk of being labelled as of 'loose virtue', and are subject to strong censure by older members. In some cases, women were forced to discontinue going to work outside their village, since elders considered it 'unsafe' and 'immoral', a blot on both family prestige and women's honour. The opinion expressed by an elderly male, in response to women who worked all day at a seasonal fruit-pulping unit several miles away is typical of such a sentiment:

The point is not one of simply wanting to earn money. True, nothing will happen to those among them who are 'straight', and can work and earn with their wits about them. But there are others who are spoiled. It is not right, going out like that. ... Once you go out, who can say whether you are upright or not?

The concern here, which seems to be on regulating women's sexuality/morality by confining them to 'safe', legitimate places—such as inside the house, or inside the village—was questioned by Sharada, a young Vokkaliga woman who pointed out that partial transgressions of women's space were inevitable in the face of dire economic necessity:

... If we are totally confined to the house, then what will happen when there is some trouble? Now that Mahadevamma has been deserted by her husband, she is back at her mother's place with the little children. But how long can they support everybody? And can she just sit at home? It is she who has to feed her children. ...

The delineation of inner spaces, such as the household, and one's own *uru*, as safe, legitimate places for women strongly suggests that such women's spaces are also being projected as intensely moral realms. Everyday expressions as that of a mother chiding her young daughter, 'Why are you standing at the door, you slut? Get inside the house. Don't you have any work to do?', or 'Can't you come back home immediately? What work do you girls have on the street?' carry implicit references to shame, honour, chastity, female sexuality and its regulation. Yet there are exceptional voices that coexist with these ideas of the inside as an inviolable space for women, which puts the onus on one's good conduct, rather than one's surroundings, as decisive. According to Rudramma,

Girls going out is not wrong in itself. It all depends on how we conduct ourselves. If we are straight, who can do anything to us? We can even go about
our work alone, but nothing can happen. Gold will shine and be pure wherever
you throw it. But some others are not like that. However much one tries to
hide them from the public eye, they will spoil. They needn't even go out ...
for those who are bound to spoil will spoil even if sitting before the stove. ...
That inside is safe and outside is not is all false. Our honour and shame remain
in our own hands.

Though the modes of negotiating it seem to be different, the crux of
the matter remains female morality, and how it is perceived.

To the dual paths along which women's spaces and identities are
constituted, i.e., through her household and village, we may now add
another dimension—that of caste—as the other major axis along which
issues of space and female morality are addressed. There have been
several competent analyses of the centrality of the proper channeliza-
tion of women's sexuality to the maintenance of caste purity. I would
here like to pursue a slightly different line of analysis, highlighting
dimensions such as women's role as major custodians of caste values,
and indicating how the delineation of caste boundaries complicates the
ways in which women and men inhabit space. Typically, observance
of rules of interaction between castes is indicated through statements
such as 'we don't eat at their place', or 'we don't accept food at their
house', which are based on ideas regarding the superiority or in-
feriority of castes. A majority of the upper caste women, in particular,
are punctilious about pollution rules of caste in their daily lives, especially in comparison with men who at times transgressed caste codes.
These women point out that caste rules are often flouted by men as
they are not only more mobile, but required to deal with a range of
different people and situations during the course of their work—a condition which hints that pollution rules cannot be maintained
meticulously in the outside realm. This 'lapse' is seen as placing an
additional responsibility on the women to observe caste rules and conform to caste behaviour.

Underlying caste interaction as well are notions of space as one's
own and Other, or as 'inner' and 'outer'. But interestingly, the
parameters of these realms—what is called in the vernacular, *olage*
and *horage* respectively—are not necessarily the same for men and
women at all times. For women, in this context, the *olage* signified
the family and/or the caste group, whereas for men, it represented not
these alone, but the entire village (*uru*); within their village (the inner
sphere for men), they too were required to follow caste rules. In jux-

taposition, the *horage* (outside) for men, represented by the public nature of the town/city, is a space where caste rules could be suspended until the person's re-entry into his *uru*. Further, even though pollution rules are followed inside the village by men, their observance does not quite match that by women within their inner realm (here the caste group), a space which defines itself in juxtaposition with a new configuration of the outer realm (as represented by the other caste groups in the village). As Shivalingamma observed:

Actually, it is women who follow caste restrictions so much. ... If she doesn't then she is condemned outright, and people will worry about caste purity. But whenever a man neglects caste rules, he is merely reprimanded, or ridiculed as ignorant and rash. ...

V

THE FLUIDITY OF SOCIO-SPATIAL MATRICES

Such presentation of the negotiation of space and femininity—through the household, caste and village—can be invested with significant theoretical functions as well. Most importantly, it serves to counter the implicit tendency to view space as mere context or setting for interaction, as passive dimension that is determinate and unchanging. Instead, it not only highlights space and society as mutually constitutive, but goes a step further to complicate these relations by showing how femininity comes to be negotiated both spatially and socially. The point is not so much that these processes of circumscribing the female body are occurring in space, but that they are both the product of, and the medium through which, physical, moral and cultural spaces are marked.

Here, what is referred to as the *olage* is set up as a fundamentally moral realm, preoccupied with issues of women's honour and family prestige on the one hand, and caste idioms of purity and pollution on the other. This space, which coincides, by and large, with the domains inhabited by women, is never only the household, but includes the caste group and/or the village at different contextual junctures. In a dual sense, woman, and the manner in which she inhabits space, becomes a key to preserving the parameters, physical and moral, of the group: first, in that considerations of protecting female honour/sexuality not only inform the rules underlying women's use of space, but are also the hinge along which groups—whether these are households, castes or village—draw their boundaries; and second, in that women themselves are often central actors in this process of cultural reproduction. There is yet another sense (though not elaborated here) in which one can underline the importance of speaking about women and space, which is by asking whether, in demonstrating the location of women in particular socio-spatial contexts, one could re-address the question of female agency; and readdress it in a manner that highlights its fluid configurations, as it intersects with caste, region, class, and so on.

It must be reiterated, however, that the concern here has not been simply with space, and the manner in which it is structured for a group of women. For this experience of space, femininity and the female body to become possible (or available) as a form of knowledge, we would need a reorganization of our theoretico-conceptual field: regarding how we perceive space, how we read bodily practices, the modes in which bodies inhabit multiple spaces, and even a new understanding of representations. Above all, we would need to open up language to this whole new domain of seeing, talking and being. I will only hint at the magnitude of this task with reference to the socio-spatial matrix of *olage-horage*, which, as we saw, is used to describe issues ranging from work, the household, 'proper' feminine behaviour, women's activities within the village, and even caste interaction. Though it translates broadly as inside-outside, it must be emphasized that the nuances in tone and meaning are not adequately conveyed by these terms. What is even more important is to recognize that *olage-horage* are not just rhetorical usages or descriptive devices, but a substantive vocabulary charting not only physical space, but moral grounds as well. This is in clear evidence in the norms governing female conduct, perceptions of the female body, and the rules underlying women's activities, speech and movement, where the delineation of the 'inside' as women's realm is actually identifying that realm with issues of (female) morality and family honour. Yet, such a delineation is based not on any abstract principle of space, but is accomplished and lived in cultural terms. In spite of its ostensible spatial connotations, *olage-horage* incorporates within it a number of bodily references contained within its talk of danger, dishonour, safe-unsafe, proper-wrong, pure-unclean, and so on; and it is these notions which regulate one's movement within, between and beyond these spheres.

It may be necessary to clarify at this juncture that the *olage-horage* taxonomy, as a way of mapping spaces, does *not* echo the domestic-public model which has often been used to account for the productive, reproductive and social roles of the sexes. A central assumption of the latter has been that women, by virtue of belonging to a domestic domain centring around childbearing, rearing, cooking and other maintenance work defined by Rosaldo (1974: 23), 'as those minimal institutions and modes of activity that are organized ... around ... mothers and their children') are excluded from the public domain (involving political and economic activities, (Sanday 1974). Since the public realm is associated with the exercise of power and control over persons and things, the domestic, in lacking these qualities, becomes, by definition, a subordinated space. In recasting space (and its negotiation) as multiple and relational, the *olage-horage* taxonomy renders such oppositions irrelevant. There are continuous shifts and transformations in how these spaces are characterized, since they acquire and shed meanings according to context. In speaking of the *olage* as women's space, we must be careful not to miss the fluidity, the ever-changing contours of that space: it could signify the safety of one's own village when pitted against another village or town; it could refer, in the context of intercaste relations, to the shared homogeneous space of one's own caste or kin group; or it could even connote the intimacy of one's own hearth *vis-à-vis* other households. Thus, though to speak of *olage* seems to convey a fixity in space, a location for women, what must be recognized is that it represents, each time, a novel configuration of relations, where different aspects get highlighted and become definitive at different times. What is constant, however, is that woman, or more specifically, female sexuality and its regulation, remains both the target of, and the medium through which not only female identity, but also the boundaries of space come to be negotiated. At each juncture, the manner in which women, women's bodies, inhabit space, becomes the anchor through which the fluidity of realms and identities is negotiated.

The fluidity of the *olage-horage* taxonomy, which results from its boundaries being relatively unfixed, continuous and contextual, opens up to other crucial questions such as those of power and its exercise, and the possible impact this could have on forms of female agency. The indeterminacy of the taxonomy, i.e., its shifting configurations, prevent us from slotting, in a one-dimensional manner, the *olage* as subordinate (and hence women as powerless), or the *horage* as associated with dominance. Instead, it allows us to ask what implications women's identification with the shifting bases of the *olage* could have for their agential practice; how these heterogeneous bases mingle with other structures of domination or subordination, and so on. As we know, women's agency has been a widely debated issue, either along lines of resistance to victimization, direct access to structures of power, in terms of indirect agency which falls back upon manipulative strategies, or even in terms of how 'consent' to existing arrangements itself could provide a basis for resistance (see, for instance, Sangari 1993). One could perhaps work upon the preceding narrative of women and space to draw out the complexities involved in speaking of female agency in terms of the contradictory and interlinked locations of women in culture—across households, families, caste groups, class and even regions. Especially since women are often central to the delineation of group boundaries, discussions of agency must be routed through their multiple identities. Such a line of vision, in working with a notion of women as 'situated subjects', underlines the importance of providing our discussions of agency with a definite spatial grounding. Equally, by recovering a possibility of politics, such a move could be deployed in a refusal to associate space with stasis (as it has generally been cast, in oppositional relation to the dynamics of the time dimension).

VI

CONCLUDING REMARKS

Recent decades have been witness to intense debates within feminism regarding issues of equality and difference (see, for instance, Bock and James, ed., 1992). With particular reference to the latter idea, two main usages (see Rhode, 1990) have been emphasized: one, a reference to *sexual* difference, and two, a highlighting of difference *between* women, whether of colour, country, class or caste. Clearly, while the first perspective underlines the difference made by biology, the second examines the difference made by culture to our gender experience. What is striking, however, and constant across both of the above, is the tendency to tie up gender difference with inequality. It is such an exclusive binarism of biology/culture and its underlying basis in inequality that our analysis has sought to displace.

Relating femininity with space is, as we have tried to demonstrate, important in allowing us to reclaim, and situate, the female body—not as bearing certain universal, unchanging and essential qualities, but as deployed, simultaneously, at various junctures, in definitions of identities and spaces. Indeed, by asking how female subjects are situated within, or come to inhabit, various socio-spatial junctures, it seems possible to speak of 'difference' along another register altogether: not only of the differences among women (the gender axis), or between women and men (the sexual difference axis), but rather in terms of the spatiality informing these 'worlds'.[8] I believe this offers a crucial position to start from, especially in enabling us to map the heterogeneous logic of cultures, where gender, as one dimension, intersects simultaneously with several other axes of identity.

We may note again our point, that it is not necessary to turn our backs upon the biological moorings of the female body in order to be able to speak of differences among women; nor is it necessarily the case that to acknowledge the body is to fall back upon an 'essentialist' idea of the feminine, *viz.*, a perception of femininity as an innate essence, traceable quickly and finally to biology. Rather, that the tracing of spatial and gender maps by and through the female body is to infuse a heterogeneity into the discourse, while also making it more responsive to how cultures speak differently about genders, bodies and sexuality, and the various levels at which identities and differences are constituted.

ACKNOWLEDGEMENTS

Discussions with Sasheej Hegde helped me formulate the arguments here, though the implications of his suggestions may still have to be pursued.

NOTES

1. What is being indicated here is not the existence of the female body as some pre-discursive, already-given foundation, but the need to reclaim it as a sort of materiality, that is, as a force actively negotiating the bounds of normative behaviour.

2. What is the idea of the 'subject' entailed here? Notions of the subject, subjecthood, subjection, subjectivity, etc., have been the locus of wide-ranging debate, involving philosophers, political and social scientists, feminists and others. While it would be impossible to do justice to the various strands of thought here, one could underline some central and recurrent issues: (a) the conferral or assumption of subjecthood, seen as always taking place within a specific operation of power relations; (b) subjecthood as involving subjection/submission, usually 'as willing obedience, coming from inside' (Balibar,

1994: 9); and (c) subjecthood as creating the space for subjectivity, for an exercise of the liberty and creativity of a human being. To speak of the 'body as subject' is to draw on all these resonances of the term: as constituted, within a given matrix of discourses and regulatory practices, and as constituting, that is, as determining the very ground of these practices/discourses. The issues of domination—of gender domination, which, to echo Bourdieu (1992: 170), is the 'paradigmatic form of symbolic violence'—is not being pursued here, although this must constitute a recurrent dimension of the relations explored in these pages.

3. This deterministic version of gender construction, however, is not the only plausible position. Judith Butler (1990), for instance, explores other possibilities through the notion of gender performability. But as she clarifies in a subsequent work (1993), this is not to be understood as presupposing an individual who deliberately chooses a particular gender role. Rather, the subject who enacts gender, in being grounded within a materiality of the body, is always already constructed. As such, performability implies not an act of choice, but a 'reiterative and citational practice' that reproduces the regulatory norms of sex. Attempting, on the one hand, to rethink the meaning of construction itself, and on the other, to offer an account of the 'materialization' of bodies, Butler also raises several fundamental issues about the nature of the body and the subject.

4. As Bourdieu (1992: 49) maintains: '*Language is a technique of the body*, and linguistic (and especially phonological) competency is a dimension of bodily *hexis* in which the whole relation to the social world expresses itself' [emphasis in original]. Bourdieu of course is insistent that 'systems of sociologically pertinent linguistic differences' must be related to 'structured systems of social differences' [*infra,* 149]— a line I do not develop here, but indicate all the same. My work here is really preliminary to such a task of 'praxeology'. In indicating the caste locus of my informants, I am not matching their dispositional strategies, however. Also see note 5.

5. Fieldwork was conducted in a village cluster outside Bangalore city between 1988–89. A socio-material profile of the villages has been provided in my unpublished doctoral dissertation *Symbolic meaning and rural social structure: a sociological study of the construction of femininity,* Bangalore University, 1994.

The village cluster comprises two large Hindu villages (with an approximate population of 500 and 1200) and four related hamlets, lying about 30 km west of Bangalore. The villages are multi-caste, with households depending largely on agriculture, either as independent farmers or wage labourers. The major castes are Lingayat (a dominant upper caste), Harijan, Vokkaliga (a middle peasant caste, though not uniformly prosperous) and Kuruba (an impoverished, marginally landed, lower caste), with a smattering of service castes.

While the variables of caste (and class) are undoubtedly of determining significance in that they introduce certain complexities into women's use of space, it must be underlined here that across these variations is an underlying homogeneity in the modes in which the spatial idiom is persistently used to refer to issues of female morality, shame, honour and rules of movement. This raises the question of whether, and how, spatiality can be conceptualized as a quasi-determining influence on their negotiation by gender. I do not undertake this analysis here, however.

6. The axis of *olage-horage* may be roughly rendered as 'inside-outside' though the latter may not entirely capture the nuances and shifting boundaries of these spaces (See the considerations to follow).

7. This point assumes special significance, given the assertion from some quarters of women's proximity to nature, a standpoint which also folds into the tendency to persist with the nature/culture distinction in speaking of women (Ortner 1974). By attending to the actual movements of women in and around the village, the argument implicit here is that the body-space encounter is layered with references to 'nature' and 'culture' in ways that are not always strictly separable. See MacCormack and Strathern, (1980), for an examination of the cultural specificity of the nature-culture divide, and the complexities attendant on its mapping in diverse cultures.

8. Approaching the issue in a more situated manner, we could suggest a view of gender difference as *supplemental difference*. See Niranjana 1994 for a preliminary formulation. What needs to be stressed, however, is the location of this 'difference' within a larger socio-cultural whole, not as subordinate, but as incessantly renegotiating its relations with the whole.

REFERENCES

Balibar, E., 1994, Subjection and subjectivation, in J. Copjec (ed.), *Supposing the Subject*, Verso, London.

Bock, G. and Susan James (eds.), 1992, *Beyond Equality and Difference*, Routledge, London.

Bourdieu, P. and Loic J.D. Wacquant, 1992, *An Invitation to Reflexive Sociology*, Polity Press, Cambridge.

Butler, J., 1990, *Gender Trouble: Feminism and the subversion of identity*, Routledge, New York.

——, 1993, *Bodies That Matter* Routledge, New York.

Foucault, M., 1978. *History of Sexuality*. Vol. I., Vintage, New York.

Gatens, M., 1992, Power, bodies and difference, in Barrett and Phillips (eds.), *Destabilizing Theory—Contemporary feminist debates*, University Press, Stanford.

MacCormack, C.P. and M. Strathern (eds.), 1980, *Nature, Culture and Gender*, Cambridge University Press, Cambridge.

Niranjana, S., 1992, Discerning women: variations on the theme of gender—a review, *The Indian Journal of Social Science* 5(4): 393–412.

——, 1994, On gender and difference: towards a rearticulation, *Social Scientist*, 22(7–8): 28–41.

Ortner, S., 1974, Is female to male as nature is to culture?, in M.Z. Rosaldo and L. Lamphere (eds.), *Woman, Culture and Society*, Stanford University Press, Stanford.

———, S.B. and H. Whitehead (eds.), 1981, *Sexual Meanings—The cultural construction of gender and sexuality*, Cambridge University Press, Cambridge.

Rhode, D.L. (ed.), 1990, *Theoretical Perspectives on Sexual Difference*, Yale University Press, New Haven.

Rosaldo, M.Z., 1974, *Woman, culture and society: a theoretical overview*, in Rosaldo and Lambhere (eds.), *Woman, Culture and Society*.

Sanday, P., 1974, Female status in the public domain, ibid.

Sangari, K., 1993, Consent, agency and rhetorics of incitement, *Economic and Political Weekly*, 28(18), (1 May) : 867–82.

Femininity and the Body of Female Ballet Dancers in The Netherlands

Anna Aalten

I

INTRODUCTION

In 1978 the Dutch ballerina Olga de Haas, aged 33, died of the consequences of too much alcohol, too little food and a complicated kidney disease. Young, beautiful and extremely gifted, she was considered one of the great talents of the Dutch ballet. Olga de Haas started her professional career as a ballet dancer in 1960 with *Het Nederlands Ballet* (which later became *Het Nationale Ballet*, the main ballet company of The Netherlands) when she was 16 years old. In 1963 the well-known Russian ballet pedagogue Natalia Orlowskaja came to The Netherlands and artistic director Sonia Gaskell stimulated Olga to work with her. Orlowskaja was impressed by Olga's talent and gave her several major roles to dance. Olga was an instant success; both the public and the critics loved her. After that performance Olga's career bloomed. She became a principal soloist and danced all major roles of the classical repertoire. But the demands of the profession were too much for her. Her addiction to alcohol affected her work and caused her to lose roles. She found this difficult to cope with and tried to get her prominent position back by working very hard. In addition, knowing that she was chosen for her first duets because she was one of the lightest girls of the company and therefore easy to lift, she started dieting severely (Van de Weetering 1979: 99–103). The combination of alcohol and a lack of food proved fatal.

In an obituary, Rudi van Dantzig, choreographer and former artistic director of *Het Nationale Ballet*, wrote about Olga's first years with the company:

Olga de Haas and Simon André in 'Giselle'. Photograph by courtesy of *Het Nationale Ballet*

'Her line pattern was somewhat disturbed by her upper legs that were a little too heavy, and which disturbed the harmony in her, apart from that, so fragile build. ... she worked a lot, almost too much, and made tremendous progress. Not only did her technique become increasingly better and more balanced, her build also changed. The heaviness disappeared from her legs. It was as if she had demanded of herself: I must look like this. Through sheer will-power and persistence her build indeed changed. The proportions of her body became increasingly harmonious and her outward appearance fragile, while her technical and inner strength could be felt ever more clearly'. (1981: 6–7).

Van Dantzig's words are an eloquent illustration of the paradoxical relation of body and mind in the professional world of ballet. Olga de Haas's thighs were too heavy (at least for a ballet dancer), but by sheer will-power and determination she succeeded in making the surplus of thigh disappear. Olga presented herself by way of her body, but according to Van Dantzig in the end it was her mind that ruled the body.

In this article I want to look into this paradox by examining femininity in relation to the body in western classical ballet. For some time now practitioners of women's studies have been struggling to free their research on (aspects of) the female body from the Cartesian separation of mind and body which is so typical of western science and society. Contemporary feminist theory has paid considerable critical attention to the masculinist underpinnings of epistemologies which split mind from body (Jaggar and Bordo 1989). Ironically, however, women's active and lived relationship to their bodies seems to disappear in feminist accounts on the body. My research project on femininity and the body requires an approach in which women are studied as embodied subjects. The work of feminist philosopher Judith Butler offered me the first ingredients for this kind of approach. That is why I begin the article with a short introduction to Butler's ideas. I continue my search with a historical inquiry into the relationship between femininity and dance, concentrating on gender images in classical and neo-classical ballet. In the last part of the article I shall elaborate some of the questions that are central to my current research project on 'dance, femininity and the body'.

II

SEX, GENDER AND THE BODY

Anthropology as a science has always known a permanent tension between 'the physiological' and 'the cultural'. This tension is expressed, for example, in the well-known nature-nurture debate which has been going on since the 1920s. The main question there is how much human behaviour can be accounted for by biology and how much is determined by culture. It is impossible to answer this question without defining 'culture'. In the review of all the different ways in which anthropologists have defined the concept of 'culture', one thing is striking: all definitions centre around the notion of learned behaviour (Kroeber and Kluckhohn 1952). Learned behaviour is set against the instinctive behaviour animals supposedly demonstrate. The distinction between 'learned' and 'instinctive' is for most anthropologists the explicit or implicit core of their notion of culture. It is important to note here that 'learned' and 'instinctive' are seen as exclusive categories. The dichotomous way in which the physiological and the cultural are seen, fits in remarkably well with the general dualism of western science. Concepts such as objectivity and subjectivity, rationality and emotionality, body and mind, nature and culture are placed opposite to each other as exclusive and complementary categories. The opposition is also hierarchical. Objectivity is better than subjectivity, the mind is superior to the body. Anthropologists are no exception to this attitude. They tend to vigorously dismiss any biological explanations of human actions. Apart from the cultural materialist schools, the physical is not seen as something to take into account but only viewed as a static, given fact. The task of an anthropologist is to look at culture, its creativity, and its variance; people's bodies are only to be considered as the material that was already there.

In feminist anthropology the separation of the physiological and the cultural is reproduced on a conceptual level in the distinction between sex and gender. 'Sex' is everything concerned with the physiological differences between women and men, while 'gender' is about the cultural elaboration of these differences. In the past the distinction between sex and gender has been extremely useful in the battle against biological determinism that was present in so many of the analyses of female-male relationships. However, recently the distinction has been seriously questioned. The work of feminist biologists makes it clear that sex and sexual differences are far less obvious or natural than we had been assuming all along. Feminist biological research has shown how difficult it is to distinguish physiological and socio-cultural processes (Birke 1986; Bleier 1984; Hubbard 1990; Van den Wijngaard 1991). The distinction between sex and gender is also questioned on a philosophical level by Judith Butler (1990), among others.

In an attempt to develop a theory of gender identity inspired by Simone de Beauvoir's famous formulation 'one is not born, but rather becomes a woman', Judith Butler proposes to see gender as 'the corporeal locus of cultural meanings both received and innovated' (1987: 128). But when we define the body as a locus of meanings, which aspects of this body are natural or free of cultural imprint? Or to quote Butler:

Indeed, how are we to find the body that pre-exists its cultural interpretation? If gender is the corporealization of choice, and the acculturation of the corporeal, then what is left of nature, and what has become of sex? If gender is determined in the dialectic between culture and choice, then what role does 'sex' serve, and ought we to conclude that the very distinction between sex and gender is anachronistic? (ibid. 129).

To answer these questions Butler looks again at de Beauvoir's work in combination with the ideas of Wittig, Foucault and phenomenologists such as Merleau-Ponty.

On the face of it de Beauvoir's famous statement seems to adopt a Cartesian mind/body dualism, presenting the view of a disembodied agent taking on a gender. However, examining it more closely it becomes clear that in saying that one becomes a woman, de Beauvoir

...does not imply that this 'becoming' traverses a path from disembodied freedom to cultural embodiment. Indeed, one is one's body from the start, and only thereafter becomes one's gender. The movement from sex to gender is internal to embodied life, a sculpting of the original body into a cultural form. (ibid. 131)

Instead of reproducing the Cartesian view of a body that must be transcended, de Beauvoir introduces the notion of the body as a situation. There are at least two ways of interpreting this notion. The first is to see the body as a material reality: as something which is there and can be held. Yet also as a material reality a body is never just there; it always has a meaning, because it has already been defined in a social and cultural context. The second way of interpreting the notion of the body as a situation is to regard having a specific body as an obligation to take up these social and cultural definitions and to come to terms with them. The acceptance of the notion of the body as a situation poses a serious problem for the distinction between sex and gender, because

if we accept the body as a cultural situation, then the notion of a natural body and, indeed, a natural 'sex' seem increasingly suspect. The limits to gender, the range of possibilities for a lived interpretation of a sexually differentiated anatomy, seem less restricted by anatomy than by the weight of the cultural institutions that have conventionally interpreted anatomy. Indeed, it becomes unclear when we take Beauvoir's formulation to its unstated consequences, whether this linkage is itself cultural convention. If gender is a way of existing one's body, and one's body is a situation, a field of cultural possibilities both received and reinterpreted, then both gender and sex seem to be thoroughly cultural affairs. (ibid. 134)

I can only fully agree with Butler here.

But if both sex and gender are cultural affairs, what then is the relation between a female body as a material reality and different meanings of femininity? If we do not believe that the meaning of femininity can be derived from some physiological fact, if we do not regard the relation between sex and gender as a causal one, how do we view it then? If we want to study the body in relation to meanings of femininity, but without falling into the trap of causality, how do we go about it? Again I turn to Judith Butler for a possible direction. Butler criticizes the common idea that femininity and masculinity are to be seen as the cultural *expression* of a material fact, namely the female or male body. Instead of a notion of gender as expressive she proposes to see gender as a *performative* act (Butler 1990a: 279). She develops this notion of gender as a performative act using the phenomenological theory of acts as the ways in which social agents constitute reality. Butler's notion of gender as a performative act can be seen as an elaboration of her earlier thoughts on the body as a situation. In Butler's view, the body and gender are closely connected, but not as a biological facticity and as the cultural interpretation of that facticity. The body and gender are connected, because '... gender is instituted through the stylization of the body, and hence, must be understood as the mundane way in which bodily gestures, movements, and enactments of various kinds constitute the illusion of an abiding gendered self' (ibid. 270). Butler goes on to say: 'Consider gender, for instance, as a *corporeal style*, an "act", as it were, which is both intentional and performative, where "performative" itself carries the double-meaning of "dramatic" and "non-referential"' (ibid.: 272–3). The idea of gender as a performative act offers the possibility of looking at the ways in which individuals live their bodies, thereby constituting gender. This process of constituting the body, be it female or male, offers infinite possibilities, but within the confines of existing historical directives. 'As an intentionally organized materiality, the body is always an embodying of possibilities both conditioned and circumscribed by historical convention. In other words, the body *is* a historical situation, as Beauvoir has claimed, and is a manner of doing, dramatizing, and *reproducing* a historical situation' (ibid.: 272). Here Butler offers us the foundations of a research agenda that gives attention to the body in relation to the construction of femininity, while freeing itself from the 'Cartesian ghost' of a separation of mind and body.

In her proposal to see gender as a performative act which constitutes reality, Butler breaks away from the popular notion of a distinction between the reality of sex and the appearance of gender. Instead, the female body is not more 'real' than different meanings of femininity. Gender reality is created through a continuation of performances in which the body is stylized to fit existing gender directives and/or to produce new ones. In the notion of the body as 'not merely matter but a continual and incessant *materializing* of possibilities' (ibid.) lies the parallel with the diminishing thighs of ballerina Olga de Haas.

III

DANCE AND GENDER

Western academic dance, better known as 'ballet', has its roots in the French court dances of the fifteenth and sixteenth centuries. In the seventeen century under the reign of Louis XIV, a true lover of dance, dancing at the court became a real art. Every evening all members of the court performed ballets. These performances required a lot of preparation and one's place in the court's hierarchy might depend on one's knowledge of the right steps in the dance. The variation of steps was small, so the performance of complicated geometrical patterns was most important, usually ending in a solo by the king himself, for example in the role of the Sun. It was Louis XIV who gave an impetus to the development of dance as a profession by the foundation of the *Académie Royale de la Danse*, which gave the academic ballet its name. In 1670 the king stopped performing himself, thereby clearing the way for performances by professional dancers. The performing of ballet was removed from the court in favour of the theatre.

Until the beginning of the nineteenth century the ballet was a male affair, although since the beginning of the development of dance as a theatrical art women had been visiting the dancing schools and performing in the theatres. Male ballet masters travelled Europe to train dancers, male choreographers created ballets and male dancers were the stars, loved by the public. For women the fashion of those days dictated long skirts which made their possibility for dancing very limited. Men's clothing left them much freer in their movements and they earned the public's love and admiration by their complicated steps and their, in those days spectacular, *entrechats*. Female dancers were not only limited by their clothes, but also by the idea among ballet masters 'that any sort of technical *tours de force* such as pirouettes or any movements not *gracieux* or *doux* were improper for women dancers' (Daly 1987–8: 57). This was why Voltaire wrote about Marie-Anne Camargo, a successful eighteenth-century ballerina with an excellent technique, that she 'was the first ... to dance like a man' (Migel 1972: 37). Camargo was trained by her father, a well-known ballet master, and although according to the critics she was not a beauty, she earned applause because of her technical abilities. Apart from that, she was daring enough to cut her skirt a few inches to allow the public to see her excellent footwork (and her ankles). Camargo was not the only legendary woman of those days, but men kept their dominant place on stage until the beginning of the nineteenth century.

The situation changed radically during the days of the Romantic movement, which gave a new impetus to ballet. The period of reason was over. Feeling, passion and irrationality ruled not only in literature and art, but also in the theatre. Ballet changed its character; elves, witches and other fairytale figures took the place of heroes and kings. The first performance in 1832 of *La Sylphide*, in which an ethereal female creature was the leading part, marked a turning point. The story of *La Sylphide* differed considerably from the stories that were performed in the pre-Romantic era. *La Sylphide* was situated in a simple village in Scotland instead of at some high king's court or a legendary Greek battlefield. The leading parts were not kings or heroes, but village people, a witch and a sylph. The central theme of the story was love. Not a heroic or erotic love, but the pure, uncorrupted love between a human being and a supernatural creature. And the final message of the ballet was also romantic: real happiness and fulfilment cannot be reached on earth. In the first performances of *La Sylphide* the role of the sylph was danced by Marie Taglioni, the daughter of the choreographer, and this performance may be seen as the beginning of the Romantic era in ballet (Jowitt 1988: 30). Taglioni was a talented dancer with an 'extraordinary frailty', which gave her an 'ethereal appearance' (Haskell 1958: 29). Her father, a ballet master in Vienna, gave her a tough and thorough training in the technical side of dance (Migel 1972: 124). In her performances Taglioni used *pointes*, dancing shoes with a special padding to protect the toes when the dancer rises to stand several seconds on her toes. Taglioni was not the first woman to use *pointes*, but the technique had been viewed more as a feat until then. Taglioni made *pointe* work her trademark and worked hard on perfecting it by discovering ways to strengthen her feet and rise on to her toes without apparent effort. Her mastering of the art was such that a new verb was coined: *taglioniser*, that was to dance and move with the lightness of Taglioni (Migel 1972: 131). Taken together, her fragile appearance, her rapid technique and the expert use of *pointes* made Taglioni the ultimate symbol of femininity in her days.

The nineteenth-century Romantic conceptualization of femininity seems to have been full of ambivalence. In their rejection of reason and rationality the Romantics honoured women for their supposed connection to nature. Women were seen as creatures who were closer to their feelings than men; therefore they came to symbolize emotionality, one of the ideals that the Romantics strove for. On the other hand, there was the Romantic preoccupation with the dichotomy of flesh and spirit. In this dichotomy the body was seen in opposition to the soul, the physical in opposition to the spiritual. In this opposition body and soul were not seen as equals, but as hierarchically ordered, the soul or spirit being superior. Because of their presumed connection with the natural world, women were associated with the lowliness of the body. 'Hence the odd paradox that dance—the only art form whose raw material is the human body—began to idealize the image of the disembodied woman'. (Copeland 1990: 27; see also Klein 1992: 118–24). So when Marie Taglioni was worshipped not only as a dancer, but as a symbol of femininity, the admiration of the public concerned itself with a specific kind of femininity. The femininity Taglioni performed was the femininity of a celestial creature, an incorporeal nymph, a disembodied woman who had become spirit only. Taglioni's image was not that of a body put on stage, but that of purity, comparable to the immaculate Virgin Mary. Or, in the words of the author Jules Janin, one of her admirers: 'She was so pale, so chaste, so sad' (quoted in Migel 1972: 132). Lightness, purity, chastity and an inclination to fade or fly away were important features of this image.

The most popular ballet in the first half of the nineteenth century, however, was not *La Sylphide* but *Giselle*, which had its first performance at the Parisian Opera. It is the story of a farmer's daughter Giselle who falls in love with Albrecht unaware that he is an aristocrat. Albrecht seduces her. Later, when she finds out who he is, she kills herself by piercing his sword through her heart. After her death Giselle joins a group of *willis*, the revengeful ghosts of betrayed virgins. Guided by their ruthless queen Myrtha the *willis* set out to kill Albrecht, but Giselle's love reaches across the grave and she saves him from death. Both in its artistic qualities and in its theme *Giselle* can be seen as the highlight of the Romantic ballet. The leading part demands very strong technical skills and:

> ... in addition to that a great range of expression. She starts as a care-free village girl, fond of dancing and very much in love. Next we see her betrayed and driven mad, until she dies a suicide. Then, in the following act, she is a spirit who must impress upon us the fact that she is lightness itself and so make a vivid contrast with the red-cheeked villager of the first act. (Haskell 1958: 139–41.)

The ballet can also be seen as the story of a confrontation between the immorality and decadence of the aristocracy, impersonated by Albrecht, and the purity of ordinary village people like Giselle. There is a lot of emotion: passion, death and magical revenge by the *willis*. Finally it is the superior emotion—Giselle's pure love—that conquers both the evil forces of queen Myrtha and death. In 1841 Carlotta Grisi danced the first performance of *Giselle*. The ballet has been on the repertoire of every major ballet company in Europe and the United States ever since.

Lightness becomes the keyword in the ballets of the nineteenth century. 'Light as weightlessness, light as luminosity: in English the same word serves both meanings' (Jowitt 1988: 39). Dancers are seen as artists who successfully challenge the law of gravity. This is not only the consequence of taste and fashion, but also of changes in ballet technique. Through training the dancer's turn-out of the hips is increased, making it possible to raise the legs higher, to execute more beats and to change directions more rapidly and more fluidly. More and higher jumps are used, spectacular pirouettes and innovating *lifts* (whereby the male dancer lifts the female dancer and carries her across the stage) become part of the standard technique. And, of course, there is the perfection of *pointe* work for women. Nowadays dancers use blocked and stiffened *pointe* shoes that make it possible to stand on the very tip of their toes. The nineteenth century ballerina had nothing but her toe pads and the only way she could stay on tiptoe was by exertion of all her leg muscle and a tremendous lift in her body. All these technical innovations demand a strong control of the body by the dancer. The central focus of the dancing body moves up from the belly to the chest (Klein 1992: 128). Both as a consequence of the changes in technique and of the Romantic spiritual aspirations, the basic movement in classical ballet from now on was upwards, in a constant striving to disregard gravity and reach for the immortality of a heavenly creature.

Among the writers of ballet history it has become customary to say that women have dominated classical ballet ever since the Romantic period. This is probably a true statement when we limit ourselves to domination by women onstage in a numerical sense. The fairy worlds of the Romantics are, as a rule, unbalanced in their populations and the all-female *corps de ballet*—a standard part of every company for the performing of group dances between the duets and the solos by the principal dancers—does not have a male counterpart. Offstage, it is men who are in control of training programmes, work rules and company policy, because ballet masters, choreographers and company directors are mainly men. Stating that women dominate ballet can also be true when we are talking about the image of ballet as an art and as an occupation. Many young girls dream of becoming a ballerina which, as an occupation, can be considered the pinnacle of femininity. Has nothing changed since the days of the Romantics? Are *taglioniser*, and the purity and spirituality Marie Taglioni stood for, still the ideal in classical ballet?

This is not the place to go into a detailed history of ballet since the nineteenth century. But because I want to shed some light on what happened to Olga de Haas, a young Dutch ballerina of our times, I have to give at least a sketch of the body images in present-day classical and neo-classical ballet. I shall confine myself to a short description of the ideas and work of George Balanchine (1904–83), the most influential innovator of classical ballet in the western world, whose choreographies belong to the standard repertoire of *Het Nationale Ballet* in The Netherlands. Balanchine was born in Russia and trained at the famous Kirov-school in Leningrad. At the Kirov the style of late-Romantic choreographer Marius Petipa is dominant, carrying on a tradition that goes back to the French dancer and ballet master Auguste Vestris who danced with Taglioni in the 1830s. Balanchine was invited by Diaghilev to become a member of his famous Ballet Rusee, a touring ballet company that had its base in Monte Carlo. In 1933 Balanchine left for New York where he got the opportunity to form his own company, now called the New York City Ballet (NYCB). In a country that had absolutely no tradition in classical ballet NYCB became one of the major ballet companies in the world. And Balanchine is considered as one of the most important innovators of western academic dance.

Balanchine's choreographies are abstract ballets; they are pure dance without a story. The costumes are very simple, hardly anything more than a dancer's training costume, and the decor is often nothing more than a dancing floor. Although abstract, his ballets usually have a central theme that reminds us of the Romantic ballets. In most of Balanchine's choreographies women are the shining central figures. It is the women who lure the men and keep them imprisoned in their webs. The fact that women have leading parts in most of his ballets is often regarded as proof of Balanchine's adoration of women. Balanchine himself made it clear that women were his inspiration and that without his muses he could not have made his masterpieces. His proclamation that 'the ballet is a purely female thing; it is a woman' is probably quoted as often as Simone de Beauvoir's statement about becoming a woman. And the interpretation of his words appears to be just as complicated. On the one hand, Balanchine seems to have placed women in ballet at the centre of attention. He adored women and created choreographies especially for his favourite ballerinas. He married four star members of his company and was romantically involved with several others (Jowitt 1988: 266). Most of his choreographies have women in the leading parts and offer the female members of the group ample opportunity to demonstrate their technical skills. On the other hand, the remainder of Balanchine's quote states: '... it is a woman, a garden of beautiful flowers, and the man is the gardener' (quoted in Copeland 1990: 9), thereby making it clear that men are in command finally. On another occasion Balanchine stated: 'Woman is naturally inferior in matters requiring action and imagination. Woman obligingly accepts her lowly place. Woman is an object of beauty and desire. Woman is first in ballet by default, because she is more beautiful than the opposite gender' (quoted in Adair 1992: 116). Feminist analyses of his choreographies have shown that although women have the leading parts in his ballets it is the men who initiate the moves

Anna Seidi in 'La Valse.' Photograph by courtesy of *Het Nationale Ballet*

and who manipulate and control the women (Jowitt 1988: 270; Adair 1992: 116).

What kind of femininity is performed by Balanchine's ballerinas? At first sight there seems to be a great difference between the images of paleness, chastity and sadness that were put on stage by the heroines of the Romantic period, like Marie Taglioni and the performance of lady-like self-confidence and elegance by Balanchine dancers like Maria Tallchief and Suzanne Farrell. But on a closer look there are striking similarities. The Balanchine ballerina is a distant beauty, as unattainable as Taglioni's sylph. She moves about with grace and elegance, charming the men around her without being able to relate to them. She moves much faster than a nineteenth century sylph, but where the sylph can be compared to an enchanting light, Balanchine's female dancer is like lightning (Jowitt 1988: 260). The impression of lightness is strengthened by Balanchine's use of technique; its speed and swiftness and the extensive *pointe* work. Balanchine's ballerinas are like contemporary nymphs: innocent, cool and with a natural purity.

IV

DANCE, GENDER AND THE BODY OF THE BALLERINA

After this brief detour in ballet history I want to return to the original subject of this article: the story of ballerina Olga de Haas and its relation to theories on sex and gender in feminist studies. If we start from Judith Butler's proposal to see gender as a performative act and to view the body as a materializing of possibilities, and subsequently examine ballet, many questions arise. How can we relate the cultural meanings of femininity in classical ballet to the stylization of the body of the ballerina? How is the body of a female dancer used to perform the femininities that are required?

In the summer of 1993 I attended a performance of *Giselle* by *Het Nationale Ballet* in Amsterdam. In *Giselle* the specific technique of classical ballet can be seen in its purest form. The physical starting point is always the *en-dehors*, the turn-out, where dancers try to turn their legs to make their feet stand in a 180 degree corner. Originally the *en-dehors* was meant to enable the dancers to move sideward on stage, thus looking the audience in the face while they danced. But a good turn-out also enables a dancer to lift her leg higher, to jump further and to change direction faster. The spine is the centre in classical ballet. A dancer keeps her body up, letting her arms and legs do most of the work. The emphasis of the movements is always upward; the pursuit of the spiritual can be seen in the movements (Kirstein 1983). Female and male dancers use the same five positions, but they use them to make different movements. For example, until the mid-1950s American male dancers, unlike their female colleagues, were not supposed to lift their legs higher than hip level (Hanna 1988: 171). Female dancers make smaller movements, quicker and show less strength than male dancers. In *Giselle* the *willis* very often use the *sissonne*, a small, swift jump. Male dancers jump higher and further, showing off their virtuosity. Several of the dancers I interviewed told me that they were told repeatedly to minimize their jumps during their training, because they were 'jumping too masculine'. The use of *pointe* shoes also contributes to the swiftness and the impression of weightlessness of the ballerina. *Pointe* shoes are used exclusively by female dancers; they materially underline the difference between female and male dancers. Lastly, the costumes in *Giselle* express a femininity that is ethereal, not of this earth. The white *tutus* that are worn by the *willis* turn them into dazzling creatures that can fly away any moment.

How does the performance of a nymph relate to the material reality of a ballerina's body? How does a dancer stylize her body to fit the existing directives? What does the performative act of a sylph mean for the body of the performer? The role of *Giselle* is seen as the touchstone for the real ballerina. Female students at the ballet academies in The Netherlands are trained to dance this role or one of the other principal roles of the nineteenth century. Their training is aimed at learning the right technique. Because the basic principles of the classical technique go against the natural movements of the human body (human feet do not stand out in a 180 degree corner), the training process is long and arduous. A good turn-out is basic in classical ballet and since the eighteenth century dancers have gone to extremes to accomplish it. In Taglioni's days beginning dancers were sometimes put in a box with braces that could be adjusted via a series of grooves. As an anonymous dancer tells us: 'There, heel to heel, with my knees pointing outwards, my martyred feet became used to remaining in a parallel line by themselves' (quoted in Adair 1992: 87). To increase turn-out many dancers had their maids or colleagues stand on their hips and Carlotta Grisi 'said sourly that those times Jules Perrot stood on her hips while she lay face down on the floor with legs spread were the erotic high points of their liaison' (Jowitt 1988: 43). Nowadays a good turn-out is attained through extensive training starting at an age as early as possible. William Hamilton, orthopaedist and a doctor of the New York City Ballet ten years ago, states that there 'are few, if any, *absolute* contra-indications to dancing. If pressed, I would say that very poor turn-out of the hips precludes a ballet career' (1982: 83). This opinion is also voiced by a physiotherapist I interviewed at the ballet academy in Amsterdam: an auditioning student can be extremely talented, but without the required turn-out she will not be admitted. I interviewed a girl who passed all the auditions at both academies in The Netherlands, but was sent away because her turn-out wasn't good enough. She tried again the year after, but her body had not improved; now she has decided to specialize in modern dance.

But very often talent and training can overcome possible physical shortcomings and young bodies can be moulded into almost any form. Some of the dancers I interviewed talked about their bodies as being 'easy', but others suffered enormously during their training years. One dancer told me she had been in pain constantly at the academy during the first four years, but she 'had become used to that'. The same goes for dancing on *pointe* shoes. Human toes are not made to walk on and the feet of female dancers are legendary because of their ugliness. Still, *pointe* shoes are used, not only in the choreographies of the nineteenth century repertoire, but also in neo-classical ballet and even in post-modern choreographies by William Forsyth and others. Good *pointe* work demands years of training and constant practice, and even then it is never easy. But it does have its merits; a dancer moves faster and turns easier on *pointe* and, as one dancer told me 'it is the closest to flying a human being can ever get'.

Although the human body can be moulded into many forms, the basic material of a dancer has to be there. Ballet academies select their students on the basis of physical qualities. Apart from a good turn-out certain body proportions are absolutely necessary for dancers who aspire for a career in classical ballet. For female dancers having the right body proportions means having long legs, a slim body and no hips. A combination of long trunks and short legs is not acceptable for women in classical ballet and even the most talented and hardworking dancer cannot change that. On the other hand, the extent to which a dancer is thought to have the right body proportions also depends on fashion and taste. The proportions of female dancers in major American and Western European companies these days are clearly influenced by Balanchine's preference for extremely slim and tall bodies with long legs, a short torso, a long neck and a small head. As NYCB dancer Violette Verdy once said: 'These days everybody's a greyhound' (quoted in Jowitt 1988: 268). Looking at the body of the typical Balanchine ballerina one is reminded of the words of the French nineteenth century writer and ballet lover Stephane Maliarmé: 'The main point is that the ballerina is not a woman who dances' (quoted in Klein 1992: 121). A feminine body, with roundings at the hips, buttocks and breasts, is definitely not considered being well proportioned for present-day ballet. Nowadays in ballet beauty and grace for women is equated with excessive thinness. And this is something a dancer can achieve if she works at it.

Weight has been an issue in ballet since *lifts* became part of the standard repertoire. If one considers the number of times male dancers in classics such as *Giselle* and *The Sleeping Beauty* have to lift their female colleagues and carry them around the stage it is easy to see why this is so. I remember reading somewhere that once a male dancer refused to lift Fanny Elssler, who as the result of build, diet and childbearing was somewhat less ethereal than her contemporary Marie Taglioni, with the words: 'I am a dancer, not a miner.' On the other hand, the contact improvisation dancers of the 1960s have shown that weight is not the determining factor when trying to lift someone (Adair 1992: 148). Weight is obviously important, but the emphasis on thinness for female dancers has more to do with fashion and taste than with any technical demands of the profession. Portraits and photographs of nineteenth-century ballerinas show that dancers were heavier then. Even a comparison with dancers of a more recent past makes clear that while the physical demands have become greater, the bodies of female dancers tend to be thinner. In my conversations with female dancers of major companies in The Netherlands the enormous pressure that is put on female dancers to be thin came up often. Female dancers are constantly told to watch their weight by teachers, ballet masters, choreographers and directors. Some dancers experience a permanent struggle against food and the autobiographies of some present-day dancers can be read as the account of this struggle (Bentley 1983; Kirkland and Lawrence 1986). The preoccupation with weight starts at the schools where young girls on the verge of puberty are scrutinized for the first physical signs of femininity. An American former dancer, now a doctor, describes how the extreme thinness of young dancers can delay the onset of menstruation and keep them in, what he calls, a 'puberty holding pattern' (Vincent 1979: 99). As a consequence of low body fat that causes a lack of estrogen and other hormones these girls preserve the body configuration of an adolescent (Vincent 1979: 77–107). Any signs of feminine curves are met with disapproval, both at school and in the company. The aesthetic ideal of the present-day ballet world is therefore the subject of a lot of feminist criticism (Gordon 1983: 134–63; Adair 1992: 60–1; Novack 1993) and the cause of much misery in dancer's lives (Brady 1982; Kirkland and Lawrence 1986). In their attempts to conform to the ideal body many female dancers have eating disorders. As far as I know there has not been any systematic research on the eating patterns of dancers in The Netherlands or in any other country. Journalist Suzanne Gordon who spent more than a year at some prominent ballet schools in the United States estimates that at least 15 per cent of the girls at these schools suffer from *anorexia nervosa* and many more have eating disorders (1983: 140). A recent survey at the ballet academy in Amsterdam shows that 40 per cent of the female students menstruate irregularly. The majority of them have a lower weight than is normal for their age group, but 44 per cent think that losing weight would improve their dancing and 70 per cent constantly watch their weight (Procee 1991). Impersonating a sylph obviously does have its price. On the other hand, the physical demands do not lead to eating disorders for all dancers. Some are built slim; others perceive the need for a constant bodily control not as a threat, but as a challenge.

We may now ask ourselves: what happened to Olga de Haas when she worked so hard and starved herself in order to conform to the demands of her profession? Van Dantzig (1981) thinks it was Olga's will-power and determination that caused the changes in the shape of her thighs and gave her body more harmonious proportions. It is clear that in saying so he voices a Cartesian split between body and mind in which the mind rules the body. Evidently this way of thinking seems to be common among ballet masters, teachers and choreographers. Dancers are trained to control their bodies to the extreme. They control their muscles and their appetite; they are told to dance through pain and exhaustion. Assuming the Cartesian split of body and mind as the basic of ballet, my question would then be: how do dancers themselves perceive this? Do they look at their bodies as some raw material, pliable and inferior, to be moulded by a superior mind? We shall never know if Olga de Haas considered her body as 'a materializing of possibilities', completely pliable and subjected to her will-power. Her body drew its own boundaries with respect to its possibilities. But we can learn from the knowledge of present-day dancers and find out how they live and stylize their bodies to fit existing gender directives and possibly to produce new ones.

REFERENCES

Adair, Christy, 1992, *Women and Dance. Sylphs and Sirens*, Macmillan, London.

Bentley, Toni, 1983, *Winter Season: A dancer's journal*, Random House, New York.

Birke, Lynda, 1986, *Women, Feminism and Biology. The feminist challenge*, Harvester Press, Brighton.

Bleier, Ruth, 1984, *Science and Gender: A Critique of biology and its theories on women*, Pergamon Press, New York.

Brady, Joan, 1982, *The Unmaking of a Dancer. An unconventional life.* Washington Square Press, Washington.

Butler, Judith, 1987, 'Variations on sex and gender. Beauvoir, Wittig and Foucault, in S. Benhabib and D. Cornell (eds.), *Feminism as Critque. Essays on the politics of gender in late-capitalist societies*, Polity Press, Cambridge: 128–143.

——, 1990a, *Gender Trouble. Feminism and the Subversion of identity*, Routledge, London.

——, 1990b, Performative acts and gender constitution, in S.E. Case (ed.), *Performing Feminisms. Feminist Critical theory and theatre*, John Hopkins University Press, Baltimore: 270–283.

Copeland, Roger, 1990, Duncan, Graham, Rainer and sexual politics, *Dance Theatre Journal* 8 (3): 60–10 27–30.

Daly, Ann, 1987–8, Classical Ballet: a discourse of difference, *Women and Performance. A Journal of Feminist Theory* 3(2): 57–67.

Dantzig, Rudi van, 1981, *Olga de Haas. Een herinnering*, Walburg Pers, Zutphen.

Gordon, Suzanne, 1983, *Off Balance. The real world of ballet*, Pantheon Books, New York.

Hamilton, William, 1982, Nature's choice: the best body for ballet, *Dance Magazine*, October: 82–3.

Hanna, Judith Lynne, 1988, *Dance, Sex and Gender. Signs of identity, dominance, defiance, and desire*, University of Chicago Press, Chicago.

Haskell, Arnold, 1955, *Ballet*, Penguin Books, Harmondsworth.

Hubbard, Ruth, 1990, *The Politics of Women's Biology*, Rutgers University Press, New Brunswick.

Jaggar, Alison and Susan Bordo (eds.), 1989, *Gender/Body/Knowledge. Feminist Reconstructions of Being and Knowing*, Rutgers University Press, New Brunswick.

Jowitt, Deborah, 1988, *Time and the Dancing Image*, William Morrow, New York.

Kirkland, Gelsey and Greg Lawrence, 1986, *Dancing on My Grave: An autobiography*, Doubleday, New York.

Kirstein, Lincoln, 1983, Classic ballet: aria of the aerial, in R. Copeland and M. Cohen (eds.), *What is Dance? Readings in theory and criticism*, Oxford University Press, Oxford: 238–44.

Klein, Gabriel, 1992, *Frauen Körper Tanz. Eine Zivilisationsgeschichte des Tanzes,* Berlin, Quadriga.

Kroeber, Alfred and Clyde Kluckhohn, 1952, *Culture. A critical review of concepts and definitions*, Vintage Books, New York.

Migel, Parmenia, 1972, *The Ballerinas. From the court of Louis XIV to Pavlova*, Da Capo Press, New York.

Novack, Cynthia J., 1993, Ballet, gender and cultural power, in Helen Thomas (ed.), *Dance, Gender and Culture,* Macmillan, London: 34–49..

Procee, Gea, 1991, *Eetproblemen. De docent-dansopleiding als risicogebied* mimeo, opleiding docent klassieke dans, scriptie pedagogiek, Amsterdam.

Van de, Weetering, Conrad, 1979, *Over ballet. Brieven aaneen jonge ballerina* Bruna, Utrecht.

Van den Wijngaard, Marianne 1991, *Reinventing the Sexes. Feminism and biomedical construction of femininity and masculinity 1959–85*, Eburon, Delft.

Vincent, L.M., 1979, *Competing with the Sylph: Dancers and the pursuit of the ideal body form,* Andrews and McMeel, New York.

Dharma and Desire, Freedom and Destiny
Rescripting the Man-woman Relationship in Popular Hindi Cinema

Patricia Uberoi

I

PROLOGUE: ON A PERSONAL NOTE

The backstalls of Shimla's old Regal cinema, nestled against the slope of Jakko Peak; the rhythmic roar of roller-skates on the wooden floor of the adjacent skating rink; cacophonous background music of no recognizable genealogy or vintage....

Sahib, Bibi aur Ghulam (1962, producer Guru Dutt, director Abrar Alvi)[1] was one of the first 'real' Indian films I had ever seen. Of course, in my student days in Australia I had joined other *aficionados* of avant-garde and foreign cinema to watch Satyajit Ray's *Pather Panchali* (1955) and Merchant-Ivory's *The Householder* (1963). And, like my companions, I was under the impression that these were 'Indian' movies—that is, until I saw first *Sahib, Bibi aur Ghulam*, and then *Brahmachari* (1968, director Bhappi Sonie) at the Regal. Where *Pather Panchali* had seemed exotic, but somehow aesthetically familiar, the latter films (good examples of what would now be classed as 'middle' and 'popular commercial' cinema respectively) were a completely new cinematic experience—cognitively and aesthetically.

There was one particular scene in *Sahib, Bibi aur Ghulam* that left a very deep impression on me—at the time, and in subsequent recall. It is the innocence and authenticity of that moment that I attempt to recapture in this paper, against the grain of conventional anthropological good sense: 'Never trust first impressions.' The advice would seem particularly pertinent, considering how very little I had understood of the dialogue, sporadically translated, and how unprepared I was for the whole experience. 'Rather "Russian"', I remember remarking to my companions, in lieu of any more profound opinion.

Contemporary reception theories, however, have recently sought to revalorize the remembered fragments of viewers' experiences, suggesting that these condensed moments may disclose resistant readings of cinematic texts whose narrative structures tell quite different stories. Not unexpectedly, such studies are often the work of feminist critics who, rejecting both the misogynist concept of feminine masochism and the patronizing idea of 'false consciousness', seek to identify the sources of female viewers' pleasure within manifestly androcentric texts (e.g. Mash 1995; Mazumdar *et al.* 1996).[2]

Though I can claim no such elevated rationale for my own selective recall of *Sahib, Bibi aur Ghulam*, I do believe that there is a purpose to be served in affirming the authenticity of that moment when I found myself confronted by a truly exotic aesthetic, and a completely unfamiliar body language. This moment (which I will revert to later on in this paper) was the meeting of the film's chief female and male protagonists—Chhoti Bahu (Meena Kumari) and 'Bhoothnath'[3] (Guru Dutt). It was clearly a moment of *mystery*, for the film narrative unfolds in flashback from the memory of that scene: the echo of a woman's voice saying, ever so gently, 'Come, come here'. It was a moment of heightened eroticism, artfully anticipated in the preceding scenes. And it was a moment of transgression, as Bhoothnath enters the private space of the grand *haveli*, becomes party to its secrets and sorrows, and transgresses on the relationship of another man, of an 'other' class, with his wife. That this double transgression is the focus of attention and the site of desire is signalled by the film's polysemous title—*King, Queen, Knave/Jack*; *King, Queen, Slave*; or *Master, Mistress, Servant* (Rajadhyaksha and Willemen 1995: 348)—which privileges this particular love triangle over the two other three-cornered relationships that the film narrative also explores: (1) that of the husband, the wife, and the 'other woman', who is a courtesan; and (2) that of the man, the woman he is destined to marry, and the woman who is the object of his fascination. Indeed, when the film was first released, this transgression proved unacceptably explicit, and Guru Dutt felt obliged to replace the final scene, showing Chhoti Bahu resting her head on Bhoothnath's lap as they journey out of the *haveli* together, with an alternative sequence, less offensive to conservative audience sensibilities, and less morally and narratively open-ended (see Kabir 1996: 113–14; and plate illustration).

Now, follow Bhoothnath's gaze as he hesitatingly enters Chhoti Bahu's chamber—the room which, as we have come to know, her husband never deigns to visit (see illustration, p. 164):

Black and white tiled floor.
A small mat is placed for him to sit on.
Across a floral carpet, the sight of a woman's painted and ornamented feet.
Three slow steps across the carpet, and the feet come to rest.
Her face, in close-up.
Her eyes and forehead.
Her lips, smiling.
Her seated figure, beautiful, bejewelled.[4]
Her seated figure in the wider setting of the bed-chamber.
Again, the seated figure.
She leans forward, as though to confide.

That the spectacle of a woman's feet should focus this intensity of mystery, of desire and of transgression was the beginning of my awareness of the cultural 'otherness' of the body language of desire in *Sahib, Bibi aur Ghulam*. No doubt it was my own cultural otherness that had inscribed this podoerotic scene so unforgettably, but a re-viewing of the film some thirty years later only affirms and re-inscribes that first intense impression. It suggests, moreover, that the podoerotic rendering of this encounter was merely an aspect of a more complex podosemiotics, an almost obsessive focus throughout this film on feet as the most condensed of corporeal signifiers. Here (1) as already remarked, women's feet (or feet and hands together) are presented as the erotic objects of the camera's/the male gaze, a look then returned with eyes of extraordinary expressiveness;[5] (2) male as well as female feet serve as the diacritical markers of different social roles, statuses, relationships and professions; and (3) feet function as the highly condensed visual foci of dramatic moments in the unfolding of the cinematic narrative. Specifically, in the matrix of man-woman relationships that *Sahib, Bibi aur Ghulam* explores, feet present the very first objects of gaze, in one way or another: women's feet as objects of male desire, or male feet to index the man's social status and role-relationship *vis-à-vis* the woman observer, and the tensions and ambiguities inherent within their relationship. This podosemiotic rendering of first encounters throughout the film is surprisingly, almost inexplicably, consistent, and assumes special significance in the light of Guru Dutt's reputed concern, as director, with the initial images of all dramatically important scenes and songs.[6]

The foregoing account of the impact of my first viewing of *Sahib, Bibi aur Ghulam*, of my sense of wonder that an erotic encounter should be rendered so powerfully in the concentration of a man's gaze on a woman's feet, suggests the contours of a distinctively South Asian corporeal aesthetic. It illustrates Marcel Mauss's observation (1934) that the human body, though universal, is very differently understood and deployed in different cultural settings. On the other hand, it might also be possible—though this would require a closer investigation of body language throughout Guru Dutt's corpus of films—to construe the podoerotic and podosemiotic focus of *Sahib, Bibi aur Ghulam* as an 'idiolect', expressing the film-maker's personal vision/obsession.[7] Alternatively, one might point to the role of local and contextual factors—notably the notorious censorship policies of the Indian government and the self-censorship code of post-independence Indian film directors which, puritanically suppressing display of the kiss and scenes of explicit love-making, deflect the expression of sensuality into other modalities (Rangoonwalla 1979: 100–5).

But beyond the contingent, the personal and the culturally particular, one may also acknowledge the several insights of Frazerian anthropologists, clinical psychologists, Freudian psychoanalysts, scholars of comparative religion and symbolism, sexologists, and self-confessed foot fetishists[8] who, in their different ways and from different vantages, have pointed to some universals of foot imagery. Such studies have demonstrated the consistency with which, across human cultures, (1) women's feet serve as the signifiers of the female genitals in particular, and female sexuality in general; (2) the big toe serves as the signifier of the phallus (in fact, much better than that organ itself, for the toe is never flaccid) (Rossi 1977: 4); (3) the kissing and caressing of feet is simultaneously an act of homage and of sexual pleasure;[9] (4) styles of footwear convey psychosexual messages, as of sexual availability or repulsion; and (5) shoes and boots disclose, apparently with great economy, various social roles and statuses.[10] The fact that podoeroticism is often categorized as 'abnormal' sexual response—the most common form of sexual 'fetishism' in a continuum from normal to abnormal sexuality—need not detain us further here.

II

THE BODY LANGUAGE OF POPULAR CINEMA

Though a number of critics and Guru Dutt's former colleagues have testified to the importance Guru Dutt attached to the expressive qualities of eyes (e.g., Kabir 1996: 45, 71, 73), the podoerotics and podosemiotics of *Sahib, Bibi aur Ghulam* have not, so far as I know, been the subject of critical notice or comment. Thus Kabir, for instance, identifies the scene in which Chhoti Bahu and Bhoothnath first meet as a pivotal one in the film narrative, but construes Bhoothnath's gaze at Chhoti Bahu's feet—as she herself does—as merely an indication of his extreme shyness in the presence of a woman: 'this is as high as Bhoothnath's eyes dare venture', she concludes (ibid.: 112), completely discounting the complex erotic overtones of the encounter.[11]

But whatever the interpretation of the camera's gaze in films such as *Sahib, Bibi aur Ghulam*, on one matter there is very widespread public agreement—that is, that the body language of popular Indian cinema has undergone enormous change over the last generation, particularly through the last few years. For the most part, this change is deplored, and attributed to the crude tastes of the lowest common denominator of the viewing public, to the concupiscence of unscrupulous directors and producers, and lately to the seditious influence of an alien 'cultural invasion'. Countless articles and public statements condemn the body language of the song-dance items in popular cinema, particularly the simulated coitus that has now substituted the erstwhile innocence of 'running around trees', near-miss kisses, and ever-ruptured embraces. But even more than the display of aggressive masculinity, the explicit display of female sexuality, collapsing the long-established cinematic opposition of 'good girl'/vamp, wife/whore, has become the subject of widespread public outcry and indignation.[12] Of course, guardians of public morality have always warned of the corrupting influence of popular cinema—on women, on youth, and on the uneducated masses—but from today's vantage films like *Sahib, Bibi aur Ghulam* have now come to be viewed, with great nostalgia, as representing both superior histrionics and—linked to this—more controlled, less 'vulgar', body language. As some recent articles in the Indian 'men's' magazine, *Debonair*, opined, where Waheeda Rehman (the film's other female lead) could express great depths of passion simply through 'her large soft eyes', and where Meena Kumari 'could evoke deep personal grief merely by raising her eyebrows' (Khubchandani 1993: 44),[13] the heroines of today tend to express themselves almost entirely through 'their assets'; 'the bigger the better' (Gangadhar 1993: 22)![14]

There is no denying a major discontinuity between the idiom of smouldering eyes and that of heaving bosoms and gyrating bellies, between heroines counterposed against vamps and heroines who act (dance) like vamps. But before making facile judgments about the changing values of popular cinema, it might be as well to attend first to the underlying problematics that popular cinema addresses, albeit with the materials at hand and in the idiom and body language of the day. In this sense, recognizing the podosemiotic idiom of *Sahib, Bibi aur Ghulam* is not an end in itself, but merely an entry-point to interpretation of the film's message, a set of signposts to the quality of significant relationships and to critical moments in the unfolding of the film narrative.

III

THE PROBLEMATICS OF ROMANCE

What is the problematic that *Sahib, Bibi aur Ghulam* addresses? What is the film all about?

One answer to this question, very commonly suggested, is that *Sahib, Bibi aur Ghulam* is a story about the demise of a decadent feudal society which is subverted not only by its own inner corruption but by the emerging consciousness of the exploited classes, by the relocation of political power in the hands of the British colonial rulers, by the rising fortunes of the ruthless new commercial class that prospered under colonial patronage, and by movements of nationalist self-reform such as the Brahmo Samaj.[15] The set of male protagonists present these various alternatives. The zamindar and his younger brother (Rehman) represent the dissolution of the old feudal society; the rival zamindars, the equally corrupt and rapacious new moneyed class; the Brahmo factory owner, the idea of non-violent social reform towards the goal of national liberation; the nationalist revolutionary, violent opposition to foreign rule; the hero, the new India of the professional classes.[16]

The decline of feudalism is indeed the explicit backdrop of the film, whose story is told in flashback through the eyes of an engineer supervising the demolition of a ruined mansion. As an innocent and rustic young man, the engineer—Bhoothnath—had once been witness to the extravagant life-style of its owners, the Chowdhury family, and to the corruption that underlay its magnificent facade. The estate owners whiled away their time in the characteristically decadent pursuits of men of their class—in drinking and dalliance with courtesans, in celebrating with pomp and ceremony the wedding of a pet cat, and in competitive pigeon-flying[17]—equally oblivious of the sufferings of the peasantry they mercilessly exploited and their own growing indebtedness to money-lenders.

Confined within the zenana quarters, their womenfolk were unhappy and unfulfilled. The senior woman of the household, the zamindar brothers' pathetically deranged mother, was incessantly immersed in superstitious and purificatory rituals, while the elder brother's mean-mouthed wife (Bari Bahu), was preoccupied with the petty vanities that became her husband's status as the master of a great house. Forever disconsolate, the younger brother's beautiful and neglected wife, Chhoti Bahu, yearned for her husband's attention, and for someone to call her 'Mother'. But the young zamindar's desire lay elsewhere, with one of the city's most famous and beautiful courtesans. All actors in this drama of barren decadence seemed unaware that time was running out for them and for their self-destructive way of life, though the reminder was ever-present in the symbolic figure of a madman, obsessed with clockwork, who inhabited the liminal space between the public and the private quarters of the mansion. The process of self-destruction was ultimately completed with the brutal elimination of Chhoti Bahu by the elder zamindar's henchmen in their final act of loyal service to their master.

A second opinion has it that *Sahib, Bibi aur Ghulam* was a revolutionary film in so far as it allowed for the frank expression of a 'good' woman's sexual desire.[18] (Conventionally, in Hindi cinema, only the bad woman, the seductive 'vamp' figure, could openly and unashamedly call attention to her sexual needs.) The reference is to Chhoti Bahu's (ultimately unsuccessful) attempt to seduce her husband into staying away from the *kotha* (courtesans' house) by herself playing out the part of the courtesan. This observation comes somewhat closer to the line I will be pursuing here but, in valorizing Chhoti Bahu's transparent expression of sexual desire, it misses the crucial fact that her acknowledgment of desire was not emancipatory, but actually personally humiliating and deeply transgressive; conceivable only when she was intoxicated and rewarded, ultimately, with death. Thus the good wife's display of desire is merely a voyeur's delight. In the end, deviance finds its just reward and the viewer is returned, through fantasized transgression, to endorsement of the normative moral order.

Both the interpretations cited above affirm the politically and socially 'progressive' features of *Sahib, Bibi aur Ghulam* against a more general theory of the development (or maldevelopment?) of commercial Indian cinema in counterpoint to western cinema on the one hand, and to the emerging Indian art cinema on the other (see Vasudevan 1993). By the same token, however, they are perhaps more assessments of political correctness than insights into the problems that the film seeks to address, and to which it provides some fictionalized resolutions. To my mind, the story of the decline of the old feudal order in *Sahib, Bibi aur Ghulam* merely constitutes the backdrop for an elaboration through the cinematic narrative of the dynamics of the man-woman relationship and the limits of feminine desire for modern times and for the new nation (cf. Vasudevan 1995).[19] In other words, I see *Sahib, Bibi aur Ghulam* not so much as a treatise on feudalism but as a treatise on 'love'—love within marriage, love outside marriage, love as duty, love as passion, unconsummated love—set against the background of an emerging new society. The acknowledgment of feminine desire, and the plotting of its limits, is one aspect of this exploration—and undoubtedly a most important one (cf. Orsini n.d.: 1–2; Vasudevan 1995). But it is not the whole of it.

There are altogether four man-woman relationships explored in *Sahib, Bibi aur Ghulam*: (1) that of the Brahmo reformer's daughter, Jabba (Waheeda Rehman), and Bhoothnath (Guru Dutt), the chief male protagonist, from whose perspective the story unfolds; (2) that of the younger zamindar, Chhote Sarkar (Rehman) and a courtesan; (3) that of Chhoti Bahu (Meena Kumari) and her Chhote Sarkar; and (4) that of Bhoothnath and Chhoti Bahu. Taken together, I will seek to demonstrate here, this matrix of relationships presents the problematics of the man-woman relationship in terms of two dominant conceptual oppositions—of dharma (duty) and desire; and of freedom and destiny—transposed on to the world of the imaginary (cf. Jayamanne 1992: 150). And while the expressive idiom may have been transformed over the years since 1962, from feet and hands and eyes to bosoms and bellies and 'pelvic thrusts' (so-called), the problem of reconciling duty and desire, and freedom and destiny in the context of love and marriage remains a constant preoccupation of the romantic genre of popular Hindi cinema, as well as of other genres of popular (and possibly elite) culture (see e.g., Orsini 1995, esp. 11, 19; Singh and Uberoi 1994; Uberoi 1995a, b.)[20]

Before looking in greater detail at the four relationships presented and explored in the cinematic narrative of *Sahib, Bibi aur Ghulam*, it might be as well to try and identify, howsoever crudely at this point, the *sociological* referents of the conceptual oppositions that I have posited here as defining the problematics and dynamics of the man-woman relationship in popular cinema.

Dharma *and Desire*

The classical or normative Hindu understanding of conjugality enumerates the goals of marriage as: dharma ([*dharm*], duty), *praja* (progeny) and *rati* (pleasure)—in that order of importance.[21] Obviously, progeny are the outcome of sexual union, but carnality is not meant to be an independent end in itself (except, possibly, in the Tantric tradition); nor is sexual passion considered a proper and lasting basis for marriage. On the contrary, it is felt that the conjugal relation should be governed by the notion of duty: the duty of a husband to provide adequately for his wife according to his means, and to impregnate her in her proper 'season'; and of a woman to make her body available for this purpose, and to serve her husband as her 'god' with loyalty and unquestioning devotion. That is, in this conceptual scheme, the 'love' of husband and wife is ideally conceived as one of affection and respect, protection and service; but not—essentially—of sexual passion.[22]

Though this is an ideal, enshrined in rules of etiquette that require husband and wife to avoid all public displays of intimacy, and in the overall cultural valorization of sexual continence (*brahmacarya*), it is widely recognized that sexuality is a very strong bonding force which has a logic and potentially threatening dynamics of its own (cf. Das 1976; Trawick 1990). Thus, while a wife's *fertility* is highly valued (and indeed necessary to establish her position in her husband's home and to consolidate her marriage), her *sexuality* is regarded as a dangerously bewitching force: a man over-infatuated with his wife is likely to forget his primary loyalty to his parents and siblings and, if provoked, to demand the division of the joint family. As sociologist M.S. Gore has put it in the typically dry language of his discipline, 'minimising the significance of the conjugal bond' is 'a functional requirement of the joint family, as a system' (Gore 1968: 34–5).

Anthropologists, too, have consistently recorded the duality and alternation of themes of auspiciousness and danger, as well as purity and impurity, in South Asian puberty and marriage rituals (as a well-known instance, see Yalman 1963), and related this to the ambiguousness of the feminine principle as expressed in the structure of the Hindu pantheon. That is, in the role structure of the pantheon, goddesses may be benign and auspicious, when paired with and controlled by a male deity (the 'spouse' goddesses); or independent and powerful, either protective or destructive as the situation may require, or downright malevolent unless properly appeased.

Psychologists have their own explanations for the salience of this split-feminine phenomenon in South Asian cultures: they identify it as the fantasized projection of the Indian male child's intense relation with his powerfully protective/ punishing mother (e.g. Nandy 1980; Kakar 1978: ch. 3). This in turn is construed as the outcome of the mother's unfulfilled longing for an emotionally satisfying relationship with her husband, beyond the constraints imposed by the joint family structure.

Be that as it may, the conceptual separation of functions of procreativity and sexuality found an institutionalized form in some of the traditional life-styles of the aristocratic and wealthier classes of Indian society—for instance, in the leisure culture of the nobility of Awadh (see e.g., Oldenburg 1991; Rao 1996), or in the system referred to as temple dedication (e.g., Marglin 1990; Srinivasan 1988). In either case, the 'other' women were independent professionals and property owners, highly cultivated in music and the arts. They were not only considered permanently auspicious, since technically they could not be widowed, but they conferred social prestige on the powerful men who successfully won and maintained them. As Bari Bahu reminded her younger sister-in-law in *Sahib, Bibi aur Ghulam*, she ought to have been proud, and not resentful, of the fact that her husband had both the material means and the potent masculinity to attract and retain the affections of the most sought-after of the city's courtesans.

As is well-known, the conceptual and institutionalized separation of roles of wife and courtesan came under challenge in the colonial period, when efforts were made to reform or refashion the ideal of Indian marriage after the Victorian model of monogamous companionability. This created a legitimate and widened space for the expression of romance and sexuality within—rather than outside of—the marital relation. However, since the joint family remained (or now was consciously advocated as) a cultural ideal, an immense tension was created between the ideal of conjugal intimacy and the renunciation of that intimacy in the wider interests of the solidarity of the joint family.

In the Hindi cinema, as often observed, the opposed dimensions of wifehood—procreativity and sexuality, love as duty and love as sexual passion—have typically been separated into distinct social roles and assigned to different social spaces.[23] The wife is loyal, dutiful, and fulfilled through motherhood, while the 'other' woman—the bad girl, 'vamp', prostitute, courtesan—is the repository of sterile sexuality. She must be narratively kept in her separate place lest she endanger the family and the social order. The wife belongs to the home; the other woman to space outside the home— the street, the *kotha*, the night-club floor (Kazmi 1994: esp. 237–8; Kesavan 1994: 253–5).

Though ideally the categorical opposition of wife and other woman should not be blurred, popular cinema constantly plays with the challenge of bringing about a seamless fusion of wifeliness and sexuality, dharma and desire. Needless to say, this is a very dangerous game, ever-pregnant with the possibility of disaster. Dharma may negate desire, or desire overwhelm dharma, leaving nothing but the 'vulgarity' that contemporary public discourse on the deportment of screen heroines so deplores. Indeed, it normally requires an extraordinary happenstance to make the inconceivable conceivable and to engineer the reconciliation of opposed social roles and their attendant moral values. This is surely the function of many of the convoluted plots of Hindi commercial cinema, that is, to mediate the tension between social duty and individual desire.[24]

Freedom and Destiny

As problematic as the reconciliation of dharma and desire is the resolution of the opposition of freedom and destiny in the process of mate-selection. Despite a century or more of the introduction of Western liberal values and the valorization of modern individualism in other aspects of social life, marriages in India are still usually parentally arranged. Indeed, this is widely believed to be the safest and most appropriate method of mate-selection. Sexual experimentation before marriage is for the most part deeply disapproved (though differentially for boys and girls), while 'romance' is conceived not so much as a legitimate prelude to marriage as an aspect of the successful consolidation of the conjugal relation, i.e., *after* the marriage has already taken place (see Singh and Uberoi 1994). So-called 'love' (i.e., self-arranged) marriages are viewed with considerable suspicion,[25] no doubt justifiably so in the sense that (by definition) they undermine parental authority, threaten the basis of the social order of a caste society, rupture the chains of reciprocity that unite affines in relations of material/marital exchange and, in some understandings, also defy the forces of destiny that are believed to link two individuals uniquely through several successive lifetimes of partnership.

However, if romance has only a dubious and limited role in the man-woman relationship in India before, or even after, marriage, it is fulsomely celebrated in myth and fantasy—for instance, in representation of the playful passion of Radha and Krishna (Kakar 1986), in the popular theatrical traditions (see e.g., Hansen 1992: esp. chs. 6 and 7), and latterly in the mass media, especially stories, novels, popular music and films. None the less, even in the contemporary media there exists a marked tension between the value of free individual choice and social or cosmological necessity. Obviously, the best resolution—in celluloid as in real-life—is that one should freely choose as a partner the sort of person whom elders, or a procedure of horoscopic matching, would have chosen for one: this is the subcontinental meaning of the phrase, 'made for each other'. The plots of many popular films do exactly that, albeit with many devious twists and turns, and one cannot imagine a happier ending to a romantic quest. Alternatively, the aspect of sexual attraction that underlies romantic love and invests it with danger should be domesticated and transformed in the course of the film narrative into the idiom of dharma: of protection and self-sacrificing service. The exercise of unalloyed free choice, without these other mediations, is usually a prescription for doom—cognitive and commercial.

IV

A PARADIGM OF DESIRE

As might be expected, the dynamics and problematics of the four man-woman relationships explored in the cinematic narrative of *Sahib, Bibi aur Ghulam* are made evident in the very first encounter of the respective protagonists. We take up each of these encounters in turn here, focusing as a point of entry on the corporeal imagery of feet.

(1) Jabba and Bhoothnath

Bhoothnath is the pet-name of a simple but educated young Brahmin man whose brother-in-law, the tutor in a great house, finds him a job as a clerk in a workshop owned by a wealthy and cultivated Brahmo social reformer, Suvinay Babu. The workshop produces a very special *sindūr* (vermilion),[26] according to an old family formula, which claims for it the power to inspire passion; conjugal passion, that is. Bhoothnath's first worry, on learning that his future employer is a Brahmo, is that he might incur impurity in eating the food his employer provides as part of his contract, but he is reassured that a Brahmin cook will prepare his meals specially for him.

Bhoothnath's initial encounter with his employer and his employer's sophisticated daughter, Jabba (played by Waheeda Rehman), is a disconcertingly embarrassing occasion, for his entrance is presaged by the loud squeaking of his brand new leather shoes[27] (The same squeaking also precedes his first meeting—alone—with Jabba). Jabba laughingly mocks him for his comic pet-name and his rustic awkwardness; and the scene ends with Bhoothnath standing apologetically and tongue-tied in front of her, clutching the offending shoes to his breast. Despite her mocking tones, however, it is clear that Jabba is instinctively, almost inexplicably, attracted to this gauche young man. He, for his part, is completely disconcerted by her unwomanly forwardness.

Gradually, to Bhoothnath's perplexity and embarrassment, Jabba begins to take over some of the personal functions that family members perform for each other: as he later complains in confidence to Chhoti Bahu (in the course of their very first meeting), Jabba treats him as though they have some sort of 'relationship' *(sambandh)* with each other. The corrupt Brahmin cook who had been purloining his rations is sacked, and Jabba herself begins to cook for him. (His high-caste scruples are apparently overcome now by either hunger or gratitude). When he is accidentally injured in police firing in the bazaar following a bomb-throwing incident, she takes it on herself to nurse him. Significantly, too, she reveals herself as rather unreasonably suspicious and jealous of his undisguised adoration for Chhoti Bahu.

There are, however, some seemingly insurmountable obstacles to the recognition and declaration of their feelings for each other. The first is Bhoothnath's 'innocence'—his unwillingness to recognize and acknowledge the stirring of physical attraction when, in two memorable scenes, the two come into very close physical proximity to each other,[28] and his failure to understand the many hints that Jabba drops, in prose and in verse. This tongue-tied innocence is complemented by Jabba's own transformation from a forward, 'modern'-type girl, to a demure woman who shyly hides her growing love and waits patiently for its recognition and consummation.[29]

The second are the considerable religious and class differences that make the rustic and orthodox Bhoothnath a misfit in the sophisticated and westernized society of the Brahmo social reformers. The squeaking shoes index this social incompatibility with remarkable economy. As it turns out, however, the incompatibility is more apparent than real, for the two were actually already husband and wife, married in their childhood before Suvinay Babu's conversion to Brahmoism.[30] Thus, their mutual attraction was not transgressive under the circumstances, but an affirmation of their destiny with each other. They did, indeed, already have a 'relationship'.

(2) Chhote Sarkar and the Courtesan

We first see the courtesan in the *kothā* as the reclining and intoxicated zamindar himself sees her—as a pair of peremptory but alluring feet, teasingly offered for his eager grasp as she sings of her intoxication with him. Dalliance with courtesans, as we are told in the course of the film, is both a recognized aspect of the life-style of men of Chhote Sarkar's class and a natural outlet for the 'hot-blooded' masculinity that a wife could not be expected to satisfy. But his infatuation with the dancing-girl is, clearly, quite excessive and his neglect of his wife too complete, for he provides her neither sexual satisfaction, nor the satisfaction of motherhood. It is this double excess that indexes the moral corruption of this declining way of life: the system is no longer stable. Expectedly, despite her bold declaration of undying passion, the courtesan quickly switches her affections to a rival zamindar when Chhote Sarkar is persuaded to indulge himself at home with his wife. In the fight that ensues when the zamindar returns to the *kothā*, he is seriously injured. Bedridden and paralysed, he is ultimately potent neither for his wife nor for his mistress.

The zamindar's relationship with the courtesan is an elective one, based on both mutual sexual attraction and cultural compatibility. But it is asymmetrical, for the zamindar's excessive passion is not genuinely reciprocated. More to the point, it is neither endorsed by destiny, nor transformed into a quasi-conjugal relation by appropriate acts of protection, devotion and self-sacrifice. Under the circumstances, it could only have a tragic outcome.

(3) Chhoti Bahu and Chhote Sarkar

Chhoti Bahu's relationship with her husband is expressed in two contradictory registers that merge dangerously as the narrative proceeds. The first is that of the dutiful and self-sacrificing Hindu wife, who worships her husband as god and seeks to please him in every possible way. The second, as already suggested, is that of a woman who so actively desires her husband's presence and love that she dangerously exceeds the proper limits of wifely devotion and seeks instead to become the sole object of her husband's sexual desire. Blinded by her frustration, she becomes involved in a socially transgressive (if sexually innocent) relationship with the young Bhoothnath.

Two scenes in particular give expression to the ideal image of wifely devotion. In the first of these, Chhoti Bahu is represented by a proxy, the loyal and sympathetic man servant, Bansi, who goes on her behalf to the zamindar's private chamber to dip his big toe into a cup of water. Without first ritually consuming this water, the young wife refuses to eat. In fact, for this reason she has remained hungry since the previous day as her husband, unmindful, was whiling away his time as usual at the *kotha*. Bansi tries first to achieve his goal by stealth, and then by pleading, and finally succeeds in distracting the still half-intoxicated zamindar with a glass of wine, awakening his recollections of the pleasures of the previous night. Chhote Sarkar is revealed as callously indifferent to this conventional gesture of wifely devotion.

The second scene is a climactic one. Rejected and taunted by her infuriated husband, angry that she had called him back from the *kotha* on a false excuse, Chhoti Bahu recklessly accepts his malicious challenge to provide him the sort of services (*seva*) that the courtesan provides—to drink with him, and entertain him. Though their relationship is thus consummated, to the eerie echo of Chhoti Bahu's delirious and drunken laughter, Chhote Sarkar in due course feels suffocated by his wife's cloying devotion, dishonoured by her unwifely deportment, and unmanned by his new domestication. He decides to resume his old life and renew his old passion. Desperately, Chhoti Bahu tries to detain him with a song—the famous 'Na jao saiyan'—in which wifely devotion and sexual passion merge seductively:

Beloved, do not leave
the gentle embrace of my arms.
My eyes fill with tears.
I long for your embrace.

If you will not stay
What will become of me?

....

This cascade of hair
These *kohl*-darkened eyes
This glittering veil
The desire of my heart—
All this is for you alone.
Today I will not let you go.
I am devoted to you
I thirst for you
You are my love,
the light of my eyes.
I shall take the dust from beneath your feet
And powder my brow with it.
You who elude me
I implore you to heed me
I am all yours
I am at your feet.
Here I shall live, and
here I shall die.[31]

Predictably, she falls at his feet, but he is unrelenting. In the bitter exchange that follows, she defends her alcoholism as the great 'sacrifice' *(balidān)* that she has had to make for her husband's sake, but her protestations of innocence are subverted by the excess of desire that had motivated her and betrayed her wifely dharma. Resolutely, Chhote Sarkar slips on his shoes and walks out of the room, heading back to the *kothā*, where his erstwhile mistress has meanwhile found herself a new admirer.

Though Chhote Sarkar had initially found the idea of wifely sensuality transgressively exciting, he ultimately seeks to re-establish the proper separation of the wife/courtesan roles; too late, perhaps, for Chhoti Bahu (like the real-life Meena Kumari) has become an alcoholic. Finally, from his sick bed, he asks Chhoti Bahu to give up drinking. 'I began drinking for your sake; now I will give it up for you', she answers, with rather unconvincing bravado.

(4) Bhoothnath and Chhoti Bahu

The relationship of Bhoothnath and Chhoti Bahu, the last to be presented to the viewers, is one of intuitive understanding and barely sublimated eroticism.

Somewhat to his consternation, Bhoothnath is told by the man-ser-vant Bansi that Chhoti Bahu wishes to see him in her room, alone, at night. This is a most improper suggestion, but the innocent Bhooth-nath—though nonplussed—does not read it as a sexual invitation, for he has already formed a poignant image of Chhoti Bahu as a sad and pining wife, forever awaiting her husband's return from the pleasures of the *kothā*. At the outset of their first encounter, like Lakshman in the presence of Sita, Bhoothnath's gaze is first focused on her feet. With trepidation he looks up—at her face, her eyes, her soft lips, her seated figure. This vision is iconic of the cinematic image of Meena Kumari, whose beautiful aspect both conceals and discloses a life of personal sorrow and tragedy.

Unlike the haughty Jabba, Chhoti Bahu speaks kindly to Bhooth-nath. She does not mock his name: 'It's one of the many names of God', she says. Instinctively, he feels that she understands him, and he blurts out to her his embarrassment over Jabba's familiar behaviour with him. The feeling of closeness is clearly reciprocated as Chhoti Bahu reveals to him the reason why she had called him and, despite herself, discloses something of her sorrow and frustration. She asks Bhoothnath to bring her, very discreetly, a pot of the special love-in-ducing *sindūr* that is manufactured in the Brahmo's factory where he works. Bhoothnath willingly does so, and is deeply dismayed when he later hears that it has failed to enchant the neglectful zamindar.

Chhoti Bahu next sends for Bhoothnath for a very different sort of errand, to procure wine for her so that she can be her husband's drink-ing companion/lover: 'If my husband asks me to drink, I must drink', she says defiantly, overruling Bhoothnath's reluctance. In this scene, she is no longer sitting, adorned, smiling, in the light, but standing in the dark, face averted with shame.[32]

The physical effect of Chhoti Bahu's attempt to play the courtesan for her errant husband is apparent when Bhoothnath next visits to ask her to keep some money for him in safe-keeping. She is now reclining, draped carelessly over her bed. The words she had first used to him, kindly, are now uttered in slurred and seductive tones: 'Come, come here'. 'Are you afraid of me?' she asks, as he hesitates. Protesting her drunkenness, Bhoothnath momentarily takes on the disciplinary role of the proper husband: 'You can't drink in front of me', he says angrily, forgetful of his station and his relationship to her. 'You can drink in front of your husband if you like.' Snatching the bottle away from her, he grabs hold of her arm. 'What, you laid hands on me', she shouts in fury and collapses, as Bhoothnath retreats in dismay from her room.

It is only when her husband, from his sick-bed, finally requests her to stop drinking that Chhoti Bahu determines to make the effort.[33] Chhoti Bahu asks Bhoothnath to escort her to meet a famous *sadhu*—to pray for her husband's health, or perhaps for the strength to renounce liquor. Touching her head to her husband's feet in parting, Chhoti Bahu leaves the *haveli* in the company of Bhoothnath. This is yet another act of impropriety on her part, observed by the elder zamindar, who orders her execution. In the carriage, alone with Bhoothnath, she seems to have a premonition of her impending doom and asks him to see that, when she dies, her corpse is dressed in bridal attire and *sindur* put on her forehead so that everyone will know her for a virtuous wife. That her corpse is ultimately buried, secretly and ignominiously in the crumbling *haveli* suggests, perhaps, that her virtue was indeed in doubt, that she had suffered the punishment that was her due.

Chhoti Bahu and her husband were linked by destiny in sacramental marriage, and Chhoti Bahu protests the sanctity and eternity of this relation to the end. But her love was not reciprocated. On the other hand, between Chhoti Bahu and Bhoothnath there existed an instinctive and reciprocal understanding: 'You're the only one who understands me', are her last words to him. They are in so many senses kindred spirits, instinctively attracted. But their circumstances do not allow the self-recognition of the transgressive and adulterous passion that the film's title iconicized and that ultimately provokes Chhoti Bahu's assassination. The problem was that both Bhoothnath and Chhoti Bahu were linked by destiny elsewhere.

V

Happy and Unhappy Endings

Across several genres of popular culture, 'endings'—happy or tragic—index right and wrong, true and false. Only one of the four man-woman relationships of *Sahib, Bibi aur Ghulam* ends happily, and this, surely, carries an important lesson for the viewer.

The attempt to reconcile the roles of wife and seductress, husband and lover, as articulated in the tragedy of Chhoti Bahu and her husband, Chhote Sarkar, is unsuccessful. Excess of passion in a relationship *outside* marriage, with the 'other' woman, and excess of passion, asymmetrically, *within* marriage, led equally to tragedy; to paralysis, death and murder. When not endorsed by social sanction and cosmological destiny, relations of instinctive companionability and sexual attraction could lead nowhere, whether they were sexually fulfilled, as in that of the zamindar and the courtesan, or continent, as between Chhoti Bahu and Bhoothnath.

The only relationship that ended happily from the protagonists' point of view—that of Jabba and Bhoothnath—was one where the end was preempted in the beginning. They were already married, and their rediscovery of each other, despite the Brahmos' repudiation of the custom of child marriage, was almost foreordained. This was also a relation in which the slow growth of sexual attraction was firmly subordinated within the compass of normative conjugal proprieties. This is no doubt a neat solution, but it is ultimately an unsatisfactory one. Almost a sad ending to a happy-ever-after story.[34] The reason is, quite clearly, that the romance of destiny has almost eclipsed the romance of individual freedom and desire, such as Bhoothnath did indeed have with his soulmate, Chhoti Bahu. For the more satisfactory resolution of this tension, one needs to look elsewhere—for instance, to the story of *Pakeezah* (1971, director Kamal Amrohi)[35]—which plays dangerously with the same elements, dharma and desire, freedom and destiny, and arrives at a less ambivalent resolution.

Perhaps Guru Dutt was too much a realist, or too sad a person, to have indulged such a fantasy. His marriage to Geeta Dutt (the playback singer, Geeta Roy) having broken up, his affair with Waheeda Rehman ended, depressed and drinking heavily, he committed suicide not long afterwards without completing another film.

ACKNOWLEDGEMENTS

This paper originated in a presentation made under the title 'Phantasms of Desire' in the 'Indian Screen Event' held at the Australian Film, Television and Radio School, Sydney, 21–4 October 1994, accompanying the screening of Guru Dutt's *Sahib, Bibi aur Ghulam*. I am grateful to Kari Hanet, Maree Delofski and Safina Uberoi, organizers of that event; to Uma Chakravarti and Urvashi Butalia who encouraged me to take up the challenge; to Laleen Jayamanne, Ravi Vasudevan and Meenakshi Thapan who have commented on the paper in its several versions; and to Aradhya Bhardwaj for her assistance throughout.

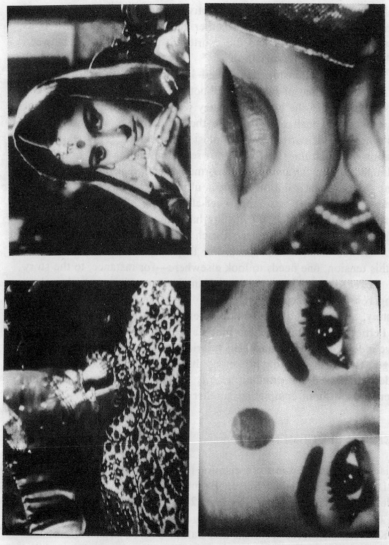

Bhoothnath's first encounter with Chhoti Bahu. From the sight of her ornamented feet across a floral carpet, Bhoothnath's gaze tracks in to her face, her eyes, her lips.

NOTES

1. After the failure of *Kaagaz ke Phool* (1959), Guru Dutt never again signed a film as director. Direction of *Sahib, Bibi aur Ghulam* was credited to his close friend and long-term lyricist and dialogue writer, Abrar Alvi, for whom it won the 1962 *Filmfare* award for direction. *(Sahib, Bibi aur Ghulam* also won the awards for best film, best actress [Meena Kumari] and best photography [V.K. Murthy]). Understandably, there has been some controversy over who is to be considered the 'real' director of the film, Guru Dutt or Abrar Alvi, especially considering Guru Dutt's depressed state of mind during the making of *Sahib, Bibi aur Ghulam*. See Kabir 1996: 120; also Rajadhyaksha and Willemen 1995: 348.

2. Cf. Kazmi's discussion (1994) of the problematics of the role of the female protagonist in Muslim 'socials'.

3. 'Bhoothnath' [Bhūtnāth], an epithet of Shiva, the pet-name given by the child's aunt for the reason that he had been born on the night of the festival of Shivratri. I follow here the transliteration system of the Allied Chambers' *Transliterated Hindi: Hindi-English Dictionary* (1993), excepting those names and terms already familiar in different spellings in discourse on popular Indian cinema.

4. This is the same image that Bhoothnath's imagination superimposes on the skeletal remains of the body exhumed from the ruined *haveli*. The lastingly iconic quality of this image is affirmed by its evocation in a recent jewellery exhibition advertisement (Art Karat Gallery), featuring the former filmstar Rakhee (who coincidentally, like Meena Kumari, also reportedly had an alcohol problem. 'Rakhee with other gems', *Times of India,* 20/12/1994). By contrast, Chhoti Bahu's image of Bhoothnath, interspersed in the same sequence, is of a shy, artless and endearingly childish young man.

5. Looking is conceived very much as a two-way process in India, epitomized in the devotee's visual interaction with the deity (see Babb 1981 and Eck 1981: 5). As a film-maker, Guru Dutt was extremely conscious of the communicative power of eyes in close-up shots; as an actor he was always worried that his own eyes lacked adequate expressive power (see Kabir 1996: 45, 71, 73).

6. Comment on BBC Channel 4 programme, In search of Guru Dutt (1989).

7. Available analyses of these films (as Kabir 1996; or Rajadhyaksha and Willemen 1995) do not indicate such an obsession, but on the other hand these critics have also not remarked on the podoerotic and podosemiotic focus of *Sahib, Bibi aur Ghulam*.

8. See for instance the sources cited in Rossi 1977. I am grateful to Veena Das for reminding me of the Freudian reading of the big toe.

9. Rossi (1977: 11) quotes Dr G. Aigremont, a German psychologist and author of *Foot and Shoe Symbolism and Eroticism* (1909) as follows: 'In India, in the art of love, there exists a toe kiss, which serves as an exceptionally

strong and successful erotic arousal. The woman kisses the big toe of the man in order to arouse him to love.' This is one of the few references to Indian podoculture in Rossi's book in which, not unexpectedly, his chapter on 'oriental podoerotomania' is dominated by Chinese examples.

10. Rossi (1977: 69–70) refers to a number of psychological studies whereby respondents, shown only pictures of faces and shoes, succeeded with a high degree of accuracy in identifying the persons' occupations and personalities. Rossi concludes from this that: 'The shoe appears to be a particularly expressive item in the identification of roles and statuses'.

11. Kabir's description of this scene is worth quoting in full:

'The entire sequence of Chhoti Bahu's introduction is seen from Bhoothnath's perspective and because he is terrified of meeting her, his eyes are lowered: the camera takes Bhoothnath's angle of view and follows the patterns of a rich carpet on which he walks to enter the room. We hear Chhoti Bahu, still off screen telling him to be seated. Then we see a pair of feet adorned by *alta* vermilion colour walk across the room; this is as high as Bhoothnath's eyes dare venture. He sits humbly on the floor and is asked his name. Finally when he does look up, the camera tracks in dramatically and holds on a close-up of Chhoti Bahu. Her intense and tragic aura startles Bhoothnath, and from that first look, he becomes her slave—her *'ghulam'* as referred to in the film's title' (1996: 112–13). See illustration, p. 164.

12. Swimming against the tide of popular and feminist indignation, a number of feminists have sought to reinterpret the role and character of the vamp, and to revalorize—positively rather than negatively—the recent collapsing of heroine and vamp roles (see e.g., Mazumdar *et al.,* 1996).

13. The burden of the article quoted here, a piece entitled 'Some women are forever', was that the most 'ethereal' Indian screen beauties, and the most memorable screen performances, have always been by 'women in love', typically, with 'the directors who created them'. Waheeda Rehman's outstanding performance in *Sahib, Bibi aur Ghulam* was seen as animated by her reputed affair with Guru Dutt. Meena Kumari's emergence as a 'tragedienne *par excellence'* through her performance in the same film was similarly seen as coloured by 'the pathos in her life' (presumably referring to the breakdown of her relationship with her husband, Kamal Amrohi, which dated from that time). Public reactions to this film, at the time of its release and in retrospect, illustrate the typical elision of on-screen and off-screen personas and events (see Vasudevan 1995: 103–6).

14. This article was a spoof on the notorious song-dance item, *Choli ke peechey kya hain?,* from Subhash Ghai's *Khalnayak* (1993). Though ultimately banned in response to public outcry, this piece has been immensely popular none the less.

15. This is especially the interpretation of those familiar with Bimal Mitra's Bengali novel, *Sahib, Bibi, Golam* (1952), on which the film, and its earlier Bengali stage and screen versions, were based. (The novel was also, apparently,

available in Hindi translation.) The film's script writer and 'official' director, Abrar Alvi, has recently made the same comment on the BBC Channel 4 Movie Mahal programme, In search of Guru Dutt (1989). See also Rajadhyaksha and Willemen (1995: 348) and Kabir (1996: 115) for the comparison of *Sahib, Bibi aur Ghulam* with Satyajit Ray's *Jalsaghar* (1958).

16. Similarly, Rajadhyaksha and Willemen (1995: 348) see the contrast of the past and the future exemplified in the contradictory attitudes of the two female figures: in Meena Kumari's impassioned plea to her husband not to leave her (i.e., as in the song *Na jao saiyan*), counterpointed against Waheeda Rehman's 'robust and girlish presence'.

17. Pigeon-flying was a favourite pastime of the Muslim nobility, as recalled with considerable nostalgia in both cinema and fiction (for instance, Ahmed Ali's *Twilight in Delhi*). In *Sahib, Bibi aur Ghulam,* the motif of pigeon-flying has rather the same function as an index of feudal indulgence as does chess-playing in Satyajit Ray's film, *Shatranj ke Khiladi* (1977). See also Kesavan (1994 esp. 251–3).

18. For instance, comments by Shabana Azmi on Movie Mahal, BBC Channel 4 (1989); also Kabir 1996: 113.

19. A similar case is argued by Orsini in her paper (1995) on the 'social romance' type of popular fiction of the 1920s and 1930s. She noted that in these social novels, 'the element of romance often came to overshadow the original aim [i.e., of social critique for social reform]. Social critique became part of the plot, a voice, the cause of further *frisson* and of dramatic, extreme situations, while feelings of love and the vicissitudes of desire emerged as the crux of the narration' (p.14). Referring in particular to J.P. Srivastava's novel, *Dil ki ag urf diljale ki ah,* she comments that in this novel 'only a brief mention of [a social] issue is enough to recall the whole argument about it. The thrust of the novel is the multiple romance, the *mise en scène* of desire—meeting, romance, separation (penance) and fulfilment—hindered by family, class and social propriety, or by chance and destiny' (p.17).

20. Of course, such a sweeping characterization of the romantic mode across time and genre needs further substantiation, especially since 'romance' is not usually recognized as an independent genre of popular cinema. *Sahib, Bibi aur Ghulam* is conventionally identified as a 'melodrama', a genre in which Guru Dutt is said to have specialized, and/or as a 'social' film. (See entries under these titles in Rajadhyaksha and Willemen 1995.) In view of its horrific and tragic elements, the film might even be classed as 'gothic', to use a category that is not conventionally deployed in the classification of types of popular Indian cinema. Writing on a similar problem in reference to genres of twentieth century popular fiction, Orsini has coined the term 'social romance' to emphasize the consistent melding of social (reformist) and romantic themes in these novels which, as she notes, 'bear strong resemblances to the "social" of commercial Indian cinema' (1995: 1). Interestingly, and conversely, the romantic element is characteristically downplayed in 'serious fiction' (ibid.: 17–18).

21. See Kapadia (1966: 167ff). These three goals equate roughly with three of the four Hindu aims of life—dharma, artha and kama—these goals being opposed to the highest goal of spiritual liberation (moksha). Liberation implies withdrawal from productive and reproductive roles, and the elimination of desire. For a thought-provoking analysis of the conceptualization of women that each of these goals entails, see Allen (1982).

22. This is a theme that I have explored at greater length in another paper (see Uberoi 1995. (b)); also Singh and Uberoi 1994).

23. See Uberoi (1990: WS45) for a discussion of this opposition in the genre of calendar art, a genre historically closely linked with popular cinema.

24. Hansen (1992: 163, 169–70) has made a similar observation regarding the popular Nautanki theatre of North India.

25. There is some evidence to suggest that self-arranged marriages are increasingly tolerated, so long as they are reasonably caste/class isogamous. In self-arranged marriages, dowry is usually not required.

26. The red powder used by married Hindu women to mark the hair parting, a symbol of the married state.

27. Bhoothnath, who has arrived at the great house barefoot, and in rustic attire, is now dressed out in the garb of a *babu*—*dhoti* and jacket, socks and garters, and shiny leather shoes. He is not only uncomfortable in this new attire, but in the westernized ambience of a tea-party.

28. Significantly, (1) in the domesticated space of the kitchen; and (2) by the sick-bed. It is actually Jabba, not Bhoothnath, who first acknowledges erotic arousal, in flashback, as she watches Bhoothnath leave to take up a new job after the closing of the Mohini Sindoor Factory.

29. This change is signalled in the song that the formerly bold Jabba sings as Bhoothnath departs to take up his new job (see note 28 above):

Meri bat rahi mere man men
Kuch kah na saki uljhan men

(What I wanted to say remained in my heart
In my confusion, I could not utter a word) (Kabir 1996: 118–19).

30. In contemporary films also—for instance, *Hum Aapke Hain Koun...!* or *Dilwale Dulhaniya Le Jayenge*—a romantic commitment marks the end of youthful playfulness and boisterousness, and the beginning of a new restraint, responsibility and seriousness. (see Uberoi 1995a).

In the film narrative, the opposition initially set up between the enlightened and modernizing Brahmo, Suvinay Babu, and the ritualistic and traditional Bhoothnath is also dissolved: Suvinay Babu's factory actually turns out a product—the love-inducing *sindūr*—whose efficacy is shown to be illusory. Bhoothnath, on the other hand, in time becomes a professional engineer, westernized in manner and life-style, and dressed in the costume appropriate to his profession—'safari suit', boots and solar topi, blue-prints in hand. This is how we see him in both the first and the closing scenes of the film.

31. Translation, BBC Channel 4, Movie Mahal, 1987. This is arguably the most famous scene in the film, both summarizing the tragically asymmetrical relationship of Chhoti Bahu and her husband, and demonstrating the considerable histrionic talents of the actress Meena Kumari. In fact, all the songs and song-dance sequences in this film are regarded in nostalgic recall as classics of their type. Guru Dutt was reputed to take unusual pains over the songs in his films, insisting that the songs advance the dramatic narrative (see Kabir 1996: 25–6; 54–5, 57), rather than being opportunistically inserted for mere entertainment value (the charge against most contemporary directors). *Na jao saiyan* was one of the top ten film songs of 1962.

32. This scene is almost repeated when he brings the wine flask to her: her face is invisible as her trembling hand takes delivery of the substance of her self-destruction. The scene of the delivery of the wine flask contrasts sharply with the scene earlier when she receives the pot of love-inducing *sindur*—with the reverence with which one receives *prasad,* or a sacred blessing.

33. Reportedly, in the film as first released, Chhoti Bahu begs her husband to let her take one last sip of liquor. Guru Dutt deleted this scene in response to public disapproval, and instead had the paralysed zamindar repent of his ways, finally showing Chhoti Bahu the sort of respect and affection she had so desperately craved (Kabir 1996: 114).

34. Possibly this ambiguity was the reason for the film's commercial lack of success, despite its starring both the leading female stars of the day, and despite Guru Dutt's formidable reputation as a director following the commercial success of *Chaudhvin ka Chand* (1960).

35. I hope to take this up in another paper. *Pakeezah,* which also stars Meena Kumari (it was released posthumously), is incidentally also a podoerotic/podosemiotic—indeed, if one might coin another such phrase, *podosadomasochistic*—text.

REFERENCES

Allen, Michael, 1982, The Hindu view of women, in Michael Allen and S.N. Mukherjee (eds.), *Women in India and Nepal,* Australian National University, Canberra: 1–20.

Babb, Lawrence A., 1981, Glancing: Visual interaction in Hinduism. *Journal of Anthropological Research* 37, (4): 47–64.

Das, Veena., 1976, Masks and faces: An essay on Punjabi kinship. *Contributions to Indian Sociology* n.s. 10, (1): 1–30.

Eck, Diana L., 1981, *Seeing the Divine Image in India*, Anima Books, Chambersburg, Pa.

Gangadhar, V., 1993, The 'Choli ke neeche' syndrome. *Debonair* (September 1993): 22–3.

Gore, M.S., 1968, *Urbanisation and Social Change*, Popular Prakashan, Bombay.

Hansen, Kathryn., 1992, *Grounds for Play: The Nautanki theatre of north India* Manohar, New Delhi.

Jayamanne, Laleen, 1992, Sri Lankan family melodrama: A cinema of primitive attractions. *Screen* 33, (2): 145–53.

Kabir, Nasreen Munni, 1996, *Guru Dutt: A life in cinema*, Oxford University Press, Delhi.

Kakar, Sudhir, 1978, *The inner world: A psycho-analytic study of childhood and society in India*, Oxford University Press, Delhi.

——, 1986, Erotic fantasy: The secret passion of Radha and Krishna, in Veena Das (ed.), *The word and the world*, Sage, New Delhi: 75–94.

Kapadia, K.M., 1966, *Marriage and family in India*, Oxford University Press, Bombay.

Kazmi, Fareed, 1994, Muslim socials and the female protagonist: Seeing a dominant discourse at work, in Zoya Hasan (ed.), *Forging identities: Gender, communities and the state*, Kali for Women, New Delhi: 226–43.

Kesavan, Mukul, 1994, Urdu, Awadh and the tawaif: The Islamicate roots of Hindi cinema, in Zoya Hasan (ed.), *Forging identities:* pp. 244–57.

Khubchandani, Lata, 1993, Some women are forever. *Debonair* (September 1993): 43–4.

Marglin, F. Apffel, 1990, Refining the body: Transformative emotions in ritual dance, in Owen M. Lynch (ed.), *Divine Passions: The social construction of emotion in India*, Oxford University Press, Delhi: 213–36.

Mash, Melinda, 1995, The audience and the public: Text, context and pretext in a feminist project. Paper presented at the seminar on, Images of women in media, International Institute for Asian Studies, Leiden, 6–8 November.

Mauss, Marcel, 1979 [1934], Body techniques, in *Sociology and Psychology: Essays by Marcel Mauss* (trans. Ben Brewster), Routledge and Kegan Paul, London: 95–123.

Mazumdar, Ranjani, Shikha Jhingan and Shohini Ghosh, 1996, Pleasurable engagements: Bombay cinema and the female spectator. Paper and video screening at the Centre for the Study of Developing Societies, Delhi, 2 February.

Nandy, Ashis, 1980, Woman versus womanliness in India: An essay in cultural and political psychology, in, *At the Edge of Psychology: Essays in politics and culture*, Oxford University Press, Delhi: 32–46.

Oldenburg, Veena, 1991, Lifestyle as resistance: The case of the courtesans of Lucknow, in Douglas Haynes and Gyan Prakash (eds.), *Contesting power: Resistance and everyday social relations in South Asia*, Oxford University Press, Delhi.

Orsini, Francesca, 1995, From social critique to romance: The 'social' in popular Hindi fiction. Paper presented at the seminar on 'The consumption of popular culture in South Asia', School of Oriental and African Studies, London, 19–21 June.

Rajadhyaksha, Ashish and Paul Willemen (eds.), 1995, *Encyclopaedia of Indian cinema*, Oxford University Press, Delhi.

Rangoonwalla, Firoze, 1979, *A Pictorial History of Indian Cinema*, Hamlyn, London.

Rao, Vidya, 1996, Wives, tawaifs and nayikas: Transcending the boundaries of identity. *The Indian Journal of Social Work* 57, (1): 39–67.

Rossi, William, A, 1997, *The Sex Life of the Foot and Shoe*, Routledge and Kegan Paul, London.

Singh, Amita Tyagi and Patricia Uberoi, 1994, Learning to 'adjust': Conjugal relations in Indian popular fiction. *Indian Journal of Gender Studies* 1, (1): 93–120.

Srinivasan, Amrit, 1988, Reform or conformity: Temple prostitution and the community in the Madras Presidency, in Bina Agarwal (ed.), *Structures of patriarchy*, Kali for Women, New Delhi: 175–98.

Trawick, Margaret, 1990, The ideology of love in a Tamil family, *in* Owen M. Lynch, (ed.), *Divine passions: The social construction of emotion in India*, Oxford University Press, Delhi: 37–63.

Uberoi, Patricia, 1990, Feminine identity and national ethos in Indian calendar art. *Economic and Political Weekly* 25, (17): WS 41–8.

——, 1995a. Imagining the family: An ethnography of viewing 'Hum Aapke hain Koun...!'. Paper presented at the seminar on The consumption of popular culture in India, School of Oriental and African Studies, London, 19–21 June 1995.

——, 1995b. A suitable romance? Trajectories of courtship in Indian popular fiction. Paper presented at the seminar on Images of Women in Media, International Institute for Asian Studies, Leiden, 6–8 November 1995.

Vasudevan, Ravi, 1993, Shifting codes, dissolving identities: The Hindi social film of the 1950s as popular culture. *Journal of Arts and Ideas* 22 (3): 51–84.

——, 1995. 'You cannot live in society—and ignore it': Nationhood and female modernity in *Andaz. Contributions to Indian Sociology* n.s. 29 (1-2): 83–108.

Yalman, Nur, 1963, On the purity and sexuality of women in the castes of Ceylon and Malabar. *Journal of the Royal Anthropological Institute* 93, (1): 25–58.

Femininity and its Discontents*
The Woman's Body in Intimate Relationships

Meenakshi Thapan

I

INTRODUCTION

In my work on femininity and culture, it became increasingly evident through interviews with middle and upper class women in New Delhi, that what I was seeking to understand, viz., the cultural underpinnings of femininity, was impossible without an understanding of women's own perceptions of their femininity.[1] Thus femininity is created through both the cultural and the personal. Women's experience of everyday life is closely linked to their notions of their bodies and their sexuality seen in relation to an ideal femininity. Their experience of 'psychological oppression' in intimate relationships is therefore often related to their notions of the 'perfect' female body and their own sexuality. In a sense, then, these women are as much oppressed by the values of a patriarchal society as they are by their partners in intimate relationships.

This paper then, is an attempt to identify and decipher notions of the body and sexuality in urban Indian women's narratives on the nature of physical and psychological oppression experienced by them in the home. On the one hand, the paper examines the different kinds of violence women experiences in the home and on the other hand, it links some of the experience of oppression to women's notions of their bodies and sexuality. At no point in the paper is the argument made that women are responsible for the physical battering and psychological torture they may experience in the family.

The female body, in this paper, is viewed as the lived body or the communicative body through which the woman seeks to both define her life spaces and express herself in different situations and contexts in everyday life, all of which shape her identity as a feminine being.[2] The body is, clearly a medium of culture, in the sense in which we take care of it and maintain it, eat, dress, and adorn ourselves, communicate with others, and so on. However, the body is not only a text of culture, as Susan Bordo points out. It is also more directly, a 'practical ... locus of social control' so that we are in a sense not what we want to be but are made through culture, what Foucault calls the 'docile body' regulated by the norms of cultural life. It is precisely in the pursuit of an ideal femininity, ever-changing and elusive, that 'female bodies become docile bodies' (Bordo 1993: 165–6). Thus femininity 'disempowers us even as it seduces us' and like Sandra Lee Bartky, I seek to understand how 'the values of a system that oppresses us are able to take up residence in our minds' (1990: 2). This brings us to the question of power and, as Foucault puts it, we need an analysis of power 'from below'.[3] For this, Bordo suggests we need to understand the 'mechanisms that shape and proliferate, rather than repress desire, generate and focus our energies, construct our conceptions of normalcy and deviance' (1993: 167). This will help us to understand how women collude with forces which often sustain their own oppression.

As I have already suggested, women's experiences of oppression or violence in the home are closely linked to their perceptions of their bodies and notions of femininity. In this context, the female body often appears no more than as a 'body-for-others', socially constructed, and therefore under the constant gaze of the Other.[4] In John Berger's words,

Men look at women. Women watch themselves being looked at. This determines not only most relations between men and women but also the relation of women to themselves. The surveyor of woman in herself is male: the surveyed female. Thus she turns herself into an object—and most particularly an object of vision—a sight. (Berger 1972: 47.)

The internalization of representations of the female body by women appears to be fundamental to the formation of feminine identity but this does not happen in a straightforward manner. It is only by 'mapping the way in which the body circumscribes subjectivity' that we can begin to understand how 'gender is constitutive of identity' (McNay 1991: 131). In women's narratives, we find that the body is continuously perceived as both defining and limiting a woman's identity by both the perpetrators of the violence and by women themselves. It is in this sense that, in intimate relationships, the Other's definitions of the body are often experienced as painful and oppressive as they are not congruent with women's own perceptions of their bodies and identities.

There is no doubt that the visual and print media in any culture influence women's perceptions through the imaging of the female body as the 'perfect' or 'desirable' body. Images of youthful women with beautiful faces and bodies are presented to the urban Indian woman. With the advent of television and the printed word in an increasingly modern urban India, 'the rules for femininity have come to be culturally transmitted more and more through standardized visual images' (Bordo 1993: 169). Thus, 'we learn the rules directly through bodily discourse: through images that tell us what clothes, body shape, facial expression, movements and behaviour are required' (ibid.). Some of these images are presented to us through advertisements, fashion displays, beauty contests and their icons, fashion models, through women's magazines and so on. Cable television in urban India has brought home the obsession with the perfect female body in the west through commercials, talk shows, soaps, etc., many of which, obliquely or directly, address the desirability of the female body in one way or another. The concern with what is considered excessive weight and with the shapely female body which emerges in the women's narratives is to a large extent a reflection of what Kim Chernin (1981) has called the 'tyranny of slenderness' in the west.

This paper also seeks to examine the different forms of 'psychological oppression' that women experience both in intimate relationships as well as in relations with the extended family in the home. Psychological oppression, or what women themselves refer to as 'mental torture' or 'emotional violence', has not been sufficiently documented primarily due to what is considered 'lack of evidence'. That is, women often do not talk about this aspect of their lives, nor is there any 'proof' of their experience. It is precisely for this reason that I sought to examine notions of the body and sexuality drawn from women's experiences of psychological oppression sometimes accompanied by physical violence.

Women's experiences, based on everyday life, do indeed help us to understand the nature of the oppression and violence women encounter. It is important to stress that it is absolutely necessary to begin, as Smith points out, 'with what we know directly in our lives' (1994: 156), i.e., with experience.[5] However, it becomes important to remember that although experience does not '*ground* knowledge in any conventional sense, ... women's experiences and what women say, make important contributions to the creation of knowledge' (Harding 1992: 185–6). While this paper therefore does not offer any major conclusions on the causes of physical and psychological violence experienced by women in the home, it does certainly seek to provide a mapping of the field, as it were. What is the nature of the violence? What forms does it take? How is it related to women's perceptions of their bodies and sexualities? What do women's narratives on 'oppression', as they experience it reveal to us? These are some of the questions this paper seeks to address.

The analysis is based on material from interviews conducted with middle-class and upper middle-class women in Delhi, belonging to different regional and professional backgrounds, varying marital status, and with a variety of ideological positions on family, marriage, and life in general.[6] An attempt was made to identify women from more or less the same kind of social background, viz., the educated, professional, urban women, for purposes of maintaining a certain homogeneity in the collected material. It might thus appear that there is a commonality in the women's narratives that relates both to their experience as well as to their articulation of it. The narratives of women from lower income groups would perhaps contain somewhat different experiences and their articulation would differ from women belonging to the middle classes.[7] Incidentally, one common thread running through all the narratives presented in this paper is that the women had all entered into so-called 'love' marriages as opposed to the more commonplace 'arranged' marriages. There is no doubt however that women's experience of violence and psychological oppression in everyday life and especially in the home are not random or isolated experiences. If we connect women's experiences, clearly then 'what emerges is a flood of common experiences' (Stanko 1985: 18) and it is this similarity that shows us the extent and the nature of the humiliation and suffering women experience regardless of their education or status in society.

II

VIOLENCE IN THE NUCLEAR HOME

Violence is defined here as *a form of action or abuse intended to inflict physical or psychological harm on another person.* Following Hoff, I would further add that the 'meaning of physical acts of aggression cannot be separated from the acts themselves'. It is therefore essential to understand the 'processes and *context-specific meanings* of violent social interaction including the relationship between verbal and physical aggression' (Hoff 1990: 9). It is in this context that women's accounts of psychological oppression become important.

Violence in the nuclear home takes many forms and is often not visible to an outsider. A woman may be physically battered but continues living life as if nothing was out of place. A woman may also be psychologically oppressed but this is not always perceived by another person. Stanko has argued that women 'learn to define their worlds and thus their experience as less important than men's' and therefore they 'internalize and silence many of their experiences of sexual and/or physical intimidation and violation' (Stanko 1985: 17). It is only when women may need intervention, either through the family or friends or through counselling, that some of these hidden or invisible experiences of violence within the home are revealed. What emerges are narratives by women, with a particular education and status in society, of physical and psychological oppression by their equally well-established and successful husbands. What also emerges are notions of the body that are largely defined by the women's partners and undoubtedly affect women's self-esteem and identity as well as their own perceptions of their bodies.

The Imperfect Body

Leena, a Punjabi, is 33 years old and teaches in a university. She has been educated in universities abroad and in India and married someone of her choice six years ago. They are from different regional communities and have different social, educational and professional backgrounds. Her husband has always 'pampered' her, in terms of giving her a lot of attention and always supporting her physical appearance. So even if she had a 'really bad haircut' or 'wore terrible clothes', he made it a point to appreciate her appearance. Leena thinks they had 'very good communication' and they spoke in a 'private language' always so no one could really understand what they were saying to each other. Much of this private language was 'baby-talk', as Leena puts it, with one partner becoming parent to the other. Sometimes this 'frightened' her as they could not communicate in any other language. He expressed himself a lot as well, cuddling her often and hugging her even in front of friends. All this fell apart about ten months ago when he met another woman. Leena says, 'Maybe now he's grown up, of course at my expense.'

The regional backgrounds of the partners, and the caste, class and community to which they belong would inevitably affect the nature of their interaction despite their educational and professional backgrounds. One outcome of Leena's deteriorating relationship with her husband is the negative nature of his comments about her family and about herself:

He has started criticizing me physically and comments, which are derogatory, about my family. That is, the stereotype of being loud, rotund, money-minded, excessive in every sense. They're non-creative, speak loudly to their wives; they're from a particular social class and background.

In this case, the comments about Leena's family (essentially her brothers and their wives) are really directed at a Punjabi business community, from her educated, westernized Bengali husband. Comments about Leena's body are rather specific:

How I'm not that attractive: I'm short; I have a bigger head [not in proportion to the rest of her body]; I'm fat, and so on. In a relationship, it bothers me that someone who had pampered me so much should switch over so suddenly.

Leena finds it difficult to accept these derogatory comments about her body and her family as she sees them as signs of a marriage gone awry or, in her words, 'a crumbling marriage'. Her husband's interest in another woman is one reason, she thinks, that he tries to continuously denigrate her in his own and in her eyes.

Bartky has argued that both 'fragmentation and mystification' are present in forms of psychological oppression (1990: 23). He defines fragmentation as the 'splitting of the whole person into parts of a person which, in stereotyping, may take the form of a war between a "true" and a "false" self—or in sexual objectification, the form of an often coerced and degrading identification of a person with her body' (ibid). Thus what Leena in fact experiences as 'mental torture' or 'emotional violence' is the attempt to sexually objectify as well as stereotype her. Degrading comments about her body are expressions of an intent to split the whole person into body and mind by focusing on the externally visible physical body. Woman's identity is therefore perceived in terms of the body and women then begin to see themselves in the same way.

Leena defines her body largely in terms of shape and in terms of her own sexuality. The desire for a perfect body is concealed behind her emphasis on her personality.[8] The 'body-for-others' is presented as her personality but underneath lies the 'body-for-myself'

When I see my body in the mirror, I should like it. It should be pleasant for me. I don't like to see sagging breasts or have extra flesh on thighs or hips. So I should maintain my body and eat less. Most men don't talk about my body, that they find my breasts desirable and ravishing, etc. They talk about me as a person. My husband used to talk about my body, before we were married, in letters but not any more. Maybe they don't find it sexy. In my case, it's all hidden but it's all there. I don't dress up to highlight my contours, emphasize my shape, etc. I emphasize more on my personality. ...

Leena works hard at maintaining her definition of the perfect body, by visiting the beauty parlour for facials 'I don't like to see a tired face. I like to see a glowing face in the mirror', by waxing her legs and arms, by bleaching the hair on her face, by hennaing her hair, and by dieting whenever she thinks it is necessary. A 'duality in feminine consciousness' is produced to the extent that Leena has internalized the gaze of the Other and has become at once the see'er and the seen.

As opposed to the different forms verbal abuse may take, there is also the issue of verbal silence which is oppressive for the women who may want to discuss issues and sort out matters. Leena says,

We don't speak about issues that bother us. We never have a fight. We don't throw things at each other. Initially I did but the response was total silence. Total indifference. So I tried to control my anger, to be like him—silent, and not get into confrontations, etc. Then I got out of it. Even now, as he says, he 'does not fight'. No issue is discussed in a raised voice; it has to be discussed 'in a non-hysterical manner'. It's a male point of view. Spontaneity has been taken out of my personality. I've started intellectualizing, theorizing, etc., in the last three years of our marriage.

Leena adopts a strategy that will most likely be acceptable to her husband so she learns to be silent when he is or analyses and theorizes about their relationship when he wishes to do so. She has learnt to cope with the silences in her marriage although she cannot cope in quite the same way with the verbal abuse. She is also emotionally distressed by her husband's lack of interest in her pregnancy or in their expected child:

There is no commitment to my pregnancy. I'm not very sure that this guy is going to be around when I have the baby. He doesn't accept the procreation even though we were *both* not using contraceptives. He should have accepted the baby but he didn't want to take responsibility. So my right to procreate was being questioned. If he was so hassled he should have just used a condom. But he taunted me, 'You've had it your way. you wanted a child and you have it.' But he had a choice to prevent it. Secondly, once the child is there, there is no commitment to the child and especially to the relationship. I don't know if the child will have a father or not. This is also a mental torture. He keeps telling me he will leave after the baby is born. He can't walk out on a pregnant woman. Middle-class values are supporting this relationship as a facade. It can break any time.

There appears to be a relationship between the way women perceive their mothers' experience of 'violence' in the home and their own experience of it. Leena perceives a similarity in the way her mother was treated by her father and the manner in which her husband treats her especially in the context of their sexual relationship. She clearly experiences a dissatisfaction with her sexual relationship with her husband and this becomes another source of distress adding to *her* experience of oppression within the marriage.

My father was an alcoholic and withdrew sexually from my mother .... so a similar experience in my marriage becomes a mental torture. It's ironic that I've felt sexually dissatisfied with my husband due to his preoccupation with work. But I couldn't articulate this then because I thought I was perverse. But now because of the problems we're having, I can articulate it. ... I've had sex [with husband] even when I was tired, etc., but he didn't; it was only at his convenience. ... That's when I started getting attracted to other men very early in my marriage.

Leena's husband is also prone to excessive drinking and she resents the lack of commitment to the home. In her case, it is the repetition of her experience of an unhappy marriage that is the cause of her 'mental torture'.

Mental torture is also not coming home on time, not eating meals on time; a lack of commitment to being home on time. I felt mentally tortured as a child as we *never* had meals together, my father *never* came home on time. ...

Mystification in psychological oppression is defined by Bartky as the 'systematic obscuring of both the reality and agencies of psychological oppression so that its intended effect, the depreciated self, is lived out as destiny, guilt or neurosis' (1990: 23). Women do not however always emerge as victims of oppression but as survivors in a system that views the institution of marriage as the ultimate refuge of a woman. Undoubtedly, women may experience problems related to their physical and mental well-being during the crisis, as we have seen above, but they devise strategies to negotiate their way through the complexities of the relationship and emerge somehow stronger and better equipped to deal with their situation and lives.

The relationship between sex and violence is acknowledged in most analyses of domestic violence. Marital rape is one form of such violence. The female body, through sexuality, then becomes the site for explicit male dominance and control which asserts itself in different ways. Sexuality, for these women, is tinged with fear of the Other's body, and, as one woman told me, she does not move at night as she is afraid she might disturb her partner who might then 'pounce' on her. This issue, important as it is, is however not the central concern of this paper. In the Indian context, Omvedt has pointed to the relationship between violence and sexuality and she argues that 'the everyday reality is that doubts about women's "faithfulness" and efforts to control women's sexuality are major factors in all forms of violence' (1990: 6).[9] Rekha's articulation of the violence she experienced in her marriage, as she put it, in terms of a denial of her sexuality is therefore of crucial significance in understanding the relationship between sex and women's experience of oppression.

Sexuality Denied

Rekha, a Punjabi, is 38 years old, has a Master's degree, and is a school teacher. Her parents are well-educated and successful people with social standing and status. Rekha married when she was fairly young and knew her husband quite well before she married him, and is now separated from him. They were married for many years and have one child. She comes across as an independent, successful, and remarkably content woman considering her unsatisfactory marriage.

Her sexual relationship with her husband was 'almost non-existent' and Rekha sees this as being 'prompted' by him:

This is a form of violence because I wanted it. [This kind of behaviour] is characteristic of a particular generation of men who have changed or altered their moralities, their world-views. This is, on the one hand, the kind of woman they want to relate to, (i.e., one who is) articulate, independent, aggressive. On the other hand, they're scared out of their wits. So, a woman's expression of her sexual rights or her expression of her sexual desire becomes one area of contestation. It's something they can't cope with. It is in part a fear of failure; of an inability to satisfy that [desire] .... Being denied *any* sexual relationship is violence and I experienced this. [The fact that sex] was very occasional and other tensions made it less satisfying. All through our marriage, he did have other sexual encounters so I was certainly being denied a satisfying sexual life. It was a gigantic problem in our relationship.

Rekha does not however see this aspect of the violence she experienced in her relationship as being significant in itself. She endured it because, as she says, 'We shared a great deal, apart from our child. He understood me and I understood him.' The breaking point in her marriage came with the other woman:

His involvement with the other woman for the last year of our marriage broke it up. He inflicted violence on me. I was very hurt by it. It wasn't a moral position I took as he already had other brief sexual encounters. The hurt was heightened because I perceived it as violence. We had a very friendly and interactive relationship in spite of the problems. So the idea that he could continue to do something which was so distressing to me, *that* was the act of violence, the aggression. He was articulating his preference for the marriage but actually continuing the other relationship so I couldn't carry on any longer. .... His other relationship was only against me, not for itself. It didn't last very long. So it was really an act of violence against me. I always saw it as that.

Rekha's analysis of her problem is *her* perception of the situation. Both she and Leena disclose a denial of sexuality in their marital relationships. The question is whether the men did this consciously to negate the women's self-image or because they felt threatened in other ways by the kind of women they had chosen to marry, or simply because they had 'fallen out of love' and therefore sought sexual satisfaction elsewhere. It would seem that women's sexuality is one realm in which men felt they could exhibit their power, as it were, over the women by denying them what was central to their relationship. In both cases, the men did succeed in exhibiting this power which was not however acceptable to the women for different reasons. Controlling women's assertiveness and independence through regulating their sexuality is an acknowledged method of the exercise of patriarchal power. That both these women found such control unacceptable, articulated its experience as a form of violence, and chose to resist the situation is an indication of the possibilities for resistance even in the midst of an experientially oppressive relationship.

At another level, Rekha articulates her perceptions of her body largely in relation to her sexuality. Her ideal femininity is in fact an ideal sexuality, governed however by her body-shape.

My sexuality is related to my body. When it is the shape I like, then I am relaxed. Being a single woman, there is more overt sexual attraction and men are able to express it. So in my attraction to them, one element of sexuality is there, a sexual charge, which I feel able to respond to depending on the shape my body is.

Her husband did not like her weight and as a form of protest, Rekha says, she remained fat all through her marriage. However, she was not immune to his reactions to the extent that she realized that her identity was tied up to this image of being slim. She felt that,

... although I was protesting all the time, I was also succumbing to it. I wasn't relaxed about it and it affected my sexuality. My husband didn't of course realize what he was doing. As a particularly progressive woman, I might say I am not vulnerable to media images of the body but of course one is. A woman's body is pleasing for herself, to have a beautiful body.

Rekha sees herself as being over-weight for the past eight months before I met her. She has cut down on food and does indoor exercises in order to shed weight. She also consciously dresses in a manner that plays down her weight. Rekha has undoubtedly internalized both her husband's perception of her body as well as what she refers to as 'media' images of the female body. This, in turn, has affected her sexuality where an ideal sexuality is defined in terms of perfect body weight. The 'body-for-others' has overtaken the 'body-for-myself' but the two are not perceived separately. That is, 'the body-for-myself' is seen as the signifier for an ideal femininity when in fact it has been subsumed within an overwhelmingly didactic 'body-for-others'.

Doubtless, Rekha has not been traumatized by her experience. On the contrary, she has found a certain independence and joy in living alone:

I find living by myself very liberating. I got married at twenty-two. Before that, I lived with my parents and was shaping my life with others. So therefore shaping my life for myself has been very nice. I got into many sexual encounters to prove to myself that I was sexually attractive. ... It [the marriage] didn't erode my sexuality, my self or identity. Had the opposite effect. I could now assert myself in my other relationships. I'm much more uncompromisingly assertive now.

While women may see themselves as survivors and not victims of their circumstances, clearly, at some level, they are aware of the psychological and physical consequences of their experiences. Rekha perceives these in the form of the 'cynicism' that has developed in her. She says,

The big cost in my break-up was the view that relationships cannot last. A relationship is much more likely to last if you live separately and see a lot of each other. It's not therefore just that violence could be done to me but that I could equally oppress someone else. So it is the nature of *relationships* that this could happen.

Similarly, Leena is cynical about her relationship and about the element of 'love' and 'care' that had earlier characterized their relationship. She has also often imagined pushing her husband 'off a cliff' to be rid of him. It is possible, therefore, that while these women do cope at one level, i.e., in terms of their ability to manage their lives and careers, they do experience the cynicism and bitterness that is a part of a deteriorating or terminated marital relationship. They may also not be able to reconcile their single existence with their own needs, for example, the need for sex and male companionship. While Rekha's uninhibited and liberated lifestyle gave her the freedom to indulge in several sexual encounters, Leena has refrained from entering into sexual relationships with other men.

It is also clear that sexuality is central to these women's definitions of femininity and they appear to depend, to a large extent, on their partners for this aspect of their self-definitions. Lack of sexual interest or desire on the part of the partner is experienced as oppressive and there is no doubt they strive, in different ways, for sexual fulfilment with their partners. It is only when this is denied that they seek fulfilment elsewhere. It would seem that in the nuclear home, women experience a heightened sexuality as compared to the joint family in which their sexuality appears to be viewed differently due to the oppressive relationship with members of the extended family.

III

OPPRESSION IN THE JOINT FAMILY

In the 'joint family', women experience psychological oppression and physical violence from either members of the extended family or the partner, or from both, depending on each situation. The most important point is that, despite the social and educational background of the husband's family, or their progressive outlook, the woman's identity is expected to merge completely with that of her husband and his family: no differences are to be tolerated. Secondly, in certain situations, the woman is seen as no more than a domestic help: someone to cook, to wash, clean the house, and also to earn a living, and sometimes to sleep with. The irony is that in the cases detailed below, the women married men of their choice from caste and regional backgrounds different from their own.

The Inferiorized Body

Saloni, a Punjabi, is from an educated background. She is married into a family in which she considers her father-in-law more educated and from a more cultured family than her mother-in-law who comes from a 'milieu which is more patriarchal'. Saloni suggests that such cultures have 'a distinct notion of how women are to behave and conduct themselves after marriage'. She herself is a bright 39-year-old university teacher who has been married for the past eight years. She had known her husband for many years before they were married. He is from a community and regional background different from hers. She has lived in a joint family for many years and experienced 'oppression', as she put it, from her mother-in-law. She does not however absolve her husband of any responsibility for what took place. The emotional agony she experienced in relating to her mother-in-law is evident in the anguish and despair in her narrative.

The sense of despair I have felt at the way in which she [the mother-in-law] conducted her relationship with me. This has also implicated my husband because I stayed with her, despite my oppression, because of him.

Saloni articulates the manner in which she was oppressed by her mother-in-law in the home:

[I experienced] the feeling of being completely unwanted and unacceptable; in the way in which I dressed, my manner, the fact that I was from the wrong kind of family; Punjabi, middle class, ordinary folk, and therefore the wrong kind of woman. This is not what she wanted for her son. She had no control over me in the sense that I was already there. She had no control over my time as for a large part of the day I wasn't there; I worked. But actually she had a great amount of control over me because of the way she continually expressed her displeasure over the way I ate, dressed, used no make-up. She was constantly chipping away at me, if you know what I mean. There was also emotional blackmail as she used her widowhood as a stick over her own son and me.

Saloni perceives this oppression in terms of what was being done to her as an individual and she decided she could not accept it.

In the first three years of my marriage, I was unsure of myself and they just went along fine. The happiness, the euphoria of marriage was there. Later, the clash is more evident when you become part of the family. I was made increasingly aware of my difference in a way in which I was not earlier. In the next two years, I came to realize that this is the way I am; I can't erase myself into nothingness or be anybody else. So I decided to be much less apologetic about my differences.

The situation was eventually resolved by the mother-in-law moving out and going away to another city. However they continue to meet and spend a fair amount of time together as a family. In the situation of the joint family when the wife experiences violence from the in-laws, the husband is equally involved although he may not be responsible for the oppression. His commitment to his natal family often overrides his commitment to his wife or he experiences a situation where he is emotionally torn between his wife and his natal family. Saloni's husband, she says,

was deeply affected by this tension. He felt hugely guilty on both counts. It affected him physically, he lost weight and suffered insomnia.

The oppression that the wife experiences from members of the extended family often affects the marital relationship. Saloni tends to respond to her husband's comments about her body, which are often made in what she herself calls a 'joking' manner, by worrying whether he is comparing her to the women in his family. She considers these women 'more elegant', what she calls the 'pearls-and-chiffon set' and the complete opposite of her. So if her husband makes a joking reference to her toes, Saloni wonders if he is comparing her feet to his grandmother's feet which are 'very beautiful'. Clearly, what is at stake is the threat to Saloni's femininity by an ideal femininity, as it were, signified by an elegance which she does not possess. She therefore experiences an inferiorized body in the comparison with what she considers a perfect body which is also the body of the oppressive Other.

The nature of the oppressive relationship leaves a taint, as it were, on the marital relationship which is no longer ecstatic as it may have been in the early years of the marriage. Saloni is very sure that her marriage has suffered a certain strain as a result of her relationship with her mother-in-law:

The situation is resolved in that it's not there everyday but its not in the forgotten past either. It's there in the relationship [between husband and wife]. Having experienced head-on confrontations, it does alter things. The initial euphoria is not there . ... We are less caring towards each other; less tenderness and so on. Even now, when my mother-in-law comes to stay or we go there, I'm uncomfortable and apprehensive. The subterranean text is always there. This whole scenario, so prolonged, has not made my marriage stronger. To grow together, you also need to grow apart, so that's what we're undergoing now. If my mother-in-law had been a little more graceful, it would have changed things between us.

The distance between the partners, as a result of the tension in their lives in the joint family, is also reflected in their sexual relationship. For Saloni,

it [sex] is not a predominant thing for me now either for myself or in my marital state. It doesn't bother me if we're in a sexually inactive state. It's not such a heightened experience as it was initially but a more tender and gentler experience. It was altered when I found my mother-in-law's presence all-pervasive and restraining and restrictive. But now it's not there.

The pressures of the joint family existence are such that women tend to feel totally disinterested in sex and their sexuality is not as strongly defined or central to their femininity as it is for women in the nuclear family. This comes out even more clearly in the next case.

The Body in Despair

Sometimes the husband is influenced by his family and their complaints about his wife and in such a situation vents his anger on his wife. In such cases, his anger and the violence against his wife is a result of the frustration he experiences in a situation where he is unable to really manage or handle his own natal family. This is exactly what happened with Sharmila, an upper caste Bengali, who is 45 years old, works for the government, and has been married to an executive in the private sector for fifteen years. They met through a Bengali theatre group in which they are both very active and she says that she married him 'really just to keep the group active' which was falling apart with other people's departures. They lived together with the husband's family and have only very recently moved to a separate, independent home. Sharmila did not hesitate to tell me that the fact that her husband's family belonged to a lower caste (a Scheduled Caste) was probably responsible for their unreasonable and often violent behaviour.

In-laws always tried to play husband against me. Just to make me suffer, in-laws used to encourage him to drink, stay out late, etc. I was forced to cook for thirteen to fourteen people every evening, with separate menus for everyone. Whether I had food or not, no one was bothered. I stopped eating egg and fish so that my husband could eat more. But no one was bothered that I was not eating. *That* was mental torture. In-laws used to complain about me to husband and he used to believe them and start shouting or hitting me. My mother-in-law used to be very happy when he was shouting at me. And later on, I started complaining but he didn't believe me as I had earlier not complained. I asked in-laws to tell one incident in which I actually misbehaved but this could never be stated. My sister-in-law (husband's older brother's wife) abused me and said, 'You have nowhere to go. We'll kick you out', and no one said anything. My mother-in-law was happy that she said it. This hurt me a lot. *Then* I told my husband, 'I'm leaving.'

For Sharmila, physical violence from her husband took the form of 'slapping, pulling hair, shoving me out of the room, shutting the door in my face, etc.' and was accompanied by verbal abuse supportive of the complaints by the in-laws. His abuse, both physical and verbal, is also based on his 'suspicions' about his wife's imaginary relationships with other men. Sharmila finds his suspicions of her infidelity 'very insulting':

He doubts everybody; colleagues, my sister's husband, that I have relationships with them. This I find very insulting. All the time, he is checking on my movements. When we were living with in-laws, then his mother used to give him all the information. When he gets angry, he hits out. ... I had to make him believe that whatever you think is not true or correct.

Her partner's definitions of her femininity as an immoral or promiscuous sexuality undoubtedly affect Sharmila's notions of beauty and self-adornment as well as her ability to interact with friends:

I used to be fond of dressing and my friends used to love that. Now I don't feel like doing anything or going in front of friends. I feel it does not suit me anymore. My husband is suspicious if I dress up too much or if I am underdressed. I want to keep an apparent balance but I don't want to dress up now, for example, *bindi* I've stopped wearing as he always suspects if my *bindi* has got smudged or fell off.

Sharmila's domestic chores in the extended family household, her continuous feeling of exhaustion, and lack of sympathetic understanding from her partner have resulted in her very nonchalant attitude towards sex.

Initially, I used to feel very nice. I was told not to get pregnant by in-laws as their children [i.e., her sisters-in-law's children] were small and they would have had to look after mine as I work in an office. So whenever he came near me I used to feel tense and worried that I should not get pregnant. ... Now, it is mechanical. I am making *chapattis*, it is like that. Most of the time, he is sleeping. Just do it fast and go to sleep. People say it is good for peace of mind, etc., so I do it. But he is out of station a lot and I don't miss that part either.

IV

CONCLUDING COMMENTS

Clearly, violence against women is not only restricted to attacks on her body but, as Ghadially puts it, 'more importantly it is a negation of her integrity and personhood' (1988: 949). In fact, as Bartky points out, psychological oppression is dehumanizing and 'depersonalizing; it attacks the person in her personhood' (1990: 29). The women's narratives show us how their femininity is defined largely in terms of their body-shapes, their sexuality, and their inability to conduct themselves within the dictates of a normative femininity. In Saloni's case, her physical appearance and her conduct, both within and outside the home, was expected to merge completely with what was expected of her by her husband's family. However, Saloni resisted this oppression and no doubt the fact that she is educated, independent and has a career, helped enormously in her resistance. Sharmila's oppression in the joint family was enhanced by her husband's lack of empathy with her situation and his physical battering.

Women too play a role in colluding with their oppressors by accepting prevailing definitions of femininity and the female body which they translate into their own ideal femininity so that its oppressive nature remains hidden even to them. There are two aspects to this problem of women allowing patriarchal notions of femininity to function from within themselves. The narcissist woman, as Simone de Beauvoir points out, sees her body not as an 'instrument of transcendence' but as an object meant for another (1961: 300). She internalizes the gaze of the Other and begins to view her body in the manner in which it is sought to be made desirable and perfect for the other. In other words, she becomes the Other in relation to her body.

The other point is that women are helped in the maintenance and beautification of their bodies, and therefore in the perpetuation of their oppression, by an extremely competent system of cultural norms and practices that seems to exist for this purpose. This is what Bartky calls the 'fashion beauty complex' (1990) with its array of cosmetics, clothes and other paraphernalia which, through aggressive advertising through the visual and print media, address the modern, urban woman. The narcissist tendency in a woman is perhaps enhanced by this system in which women are both unwittingly and willingly trapped. The question then arises whether there is an autonomous, independent femininity that is not geared to the gaze of the Other, but is an expression of a woman's innermost self? Or do women's attempts to adorn, shape, and perfect their bodies reflect a masquerade and therefore suggest a form of resistance to prevailing patriarchal definitions of the female body? Clothing and self-adornment, it is possible, as Baert suggests, are 'positioned not in a closed circuit of self-reflection ... but as a calibrated social act with many possible implications' (1994: 372). It is in this sense that 'masquerade' is seen as a 'strategic mobilization and negotiation of gender self-representation in a *mise-en-scène* of a performativity of gender' (ibid.).[10]

Following Butler, I would argue that '*woman* itself is a term in process, a becoming, a constructing that cannot rightfully be said to originate or to end. As an ongoing discursive practice, it is open to intervention and resignification' (1990: 33). We are therefore continually engaged in the process of shaping, moulding and transforming our bodies and identities in everyday life. The possibilities for negotiation and redefinition of femininity are endless but we must recognize the limitations imposed by social relations and cultural practice. The extreme feminist utopia of an autonomous femininity perhaps does not exist. It is the making and remaking of the complexities of gender identity in everyday life, through engagement and continuous negotiation with the Other, that does prevail.

*This was the title of a paper by Jacqueline Rose that I read some years ago.

ACKNOWLEDGEMENTS

A different version of this paper entitled 'Images of the body and sexuality in women's narratives on oppression in the home' has been published in the *Economic and Political Weekly*, 28 October 1995, Women's Studies Special Issue, XXX, (43): WS 72–80; in Will Wright and Steve Kaplan (eds.), *The Image of Violence in Literature, Media and Society*, Selected papers of the 1995 Conference of the Society for the Interdisciplinary Study of Social Imagery, University of Southern Colorado, USA; and in the Nehru Memorial Museum and Library, Research-in-Progress Papers, 'History and Society', Second Series, No. CIX, January 1996. Revised versions of the paper were also presented at Hofstra University, New York; the South Asia Workshop, University of Chicago; and at the Annual Conference of the Society for the Interdisciplinary Study of Social Imagery, University of Southern Colorado. I am grateful for the encouragement and criticism I received everywhere, all of which helped in the reworking of this paper which is part of a larger study on 'Femininity and Culture' on which I started work when I was a Fellow at the Centre for Contemporary Studies, Nehru Memorial Museum and Library, New Delhi. I am especially thankful to Carol Breckenridge, Pradeep Jegannathan, and Kirin Narayan for their excellent comments and suggestions. The usual disclaimer applies. I am also very grateful to the women who agreed to be interviewed for the project and revealed their lives, feelings and emotions to me.

NOTES

1. The present paper is part of a larger project on the cultural construction and creation of femininity in some urban Indian women in New Delhi. I view the female body as a text of femininity which is culturally coded, socially constructed and inscribed as well as agentially negotiated. In India, the dominant religious discourse and cultural practice has a fairly elaborate set of images and norms for an ideal and largely domesticated femininity. The rules for the presentation of bodily self in everyday life are clearly defined and we are socialized into conformity from very early on in life (see for example Dube 1988). I shall not discuss this aspect of the nature of socially constructed femininity at any length here as my own work is more directly concerned with the construction of femininity through certain forms of visual and textual representation of bodily images in contemporary India.

2. See Thapan (1995: 44–9) for an exploration of the lived body in everyday life. Other contemporary work on different aspects of the female body includes that of Das (1988), Bartky (1990), Davis (1991, 1995), Bordo (1993), Grosz (1994).

3. In this paper, I am not examining Foucault's views on power in any depth and refer to them only to the extent that they inform my perspective on why women experience oppression in relation to their bodies. See Foucault (1975, 1977, 1980, 1982, and 1990) for his discussion of power. See Thapan (1995: 38–44) for a discussion and critique of Foucault in this context. See also Cousins and Hussain (1984), Dreyfus and Rabinow (1982), Diamond and Quinby (1988), Sawicki (1991, 1994), McNay (1991, 1994), for analyses of Foucault's conception of power.

4. The psychoanalytic theory of 'the gaze' suggests that the observer 'objectifies the subject of the gaze in pursuit of scopophilic and voyeuristic pleasures' so that women are always perceived as the objects of male heterosexual desire (Craik, 1994: 12–13; see also Mulvey 1988).

5. Henrietta Moore has argued that experience is 'intersubjective and embodied; it is not individual and fixed but irredeemably social and processual' (1994: 3). It is therefore not an individual's limited perspective but also not a collective phenomenon. It varies across cultures, races, and within a culture, according to class, caste and regional orientation.

6. I am studying middle and upper class women in Delhi for two reasons. First, women in this class are a neglected research category in women's studies in India in the sense that it is often assumed that as they are economically privileged, their experience of violence and conflict in everyday life is less significant than that of women from lower classes. Secondly, these women represent precisely the category of urban Indian women who, because of their status and position in society, are exposed to an array of visual images of femininity which they have internalized and which informs their femininity. For other different kinds of studies of upper class women in Indian society, see Kapur (1970, 1973), Roy (1975) and Singh (1990).

7. Kakar examines the case of lower class women, among other categories in his study on Indian sexuality (see Kakar 1990: 65–84).

8. In an excellent paper on the body in consumer culture, Featherstone discusses the performing self and the attention paid to the shaping and perfecting of the personality as a mode of self-presentation. See Featherstone (1991).

9. Omvedt raises the important theoretical question of whether violence 'necessarily' has a 'sexual character, and is sexuality inherently (biologically) linked to force and dominance—or can we locate social and historical factors that determine the nature of such a linkage today?' (1990: 6). Rekha, the respondent in my research, who experienced psychological oppression when her husband withdrew sexually from her, sought to answer some of these questions in her interview relating her experience to the sexuality and socialization of Indian men today.

10. I have elsewhere examined some forms of resistance and subversion in the context of women's clothing and self-adornment; see Thapan (1995).

REFERENCES

Baert, R., 1994, Skirting the issue, *Screen*, 35(4): 354–73.

Bartky, S.L., 1990, *Femininity and Domination: Studies in the phenomenology of oppression*, Routledge, Chapman and Hall, New York.

Berger, J., 1972, *Ways of Seeing*, BBC Books, London.

Bordo, S., 1993, *Unbearable Weight. Feminism, western culture and the body*, University of California Press, Berkeley.

Butler, J., 1990, *Gender Trouble. Feminism and the subversion of identity*, Routledge, New York.

Chernin, K., 1981, *The Obsession. Reflections on the tyranny of slenderness*, Harper and Row, New York.

Cousins, M. and A. Hussain, 1984, *Michel Foucault*, Macmillan, London.

Craik, J., 1994, *The Face of Fashion. Cultural studies in fashion*, Routledge, London.

Das, V., 1988, Femininity and orientation to the body, in K. Chanana (ed.), *Socialization, Education and Women, Explorations in gender identity*, Orient Longman, New Delhi.

Davis, K., 1991, Re-making the she-devil: a critical look at feminist approaches to beauty, *Hypatia*, 6(2).

——, 1995, *Reshaping the Female Body. The dilemma of cosmetic surgery*, Routledge, New York.

De Beauvoir, S., 1961, *The Second Sex*, Penguin, Harmondsworth.

Diamond, I and L. Quinby, 1988, *Feminism and Foucault. Reflections on resistance*, Northeastern University Press, Boston.

Dreyfus, H.L. and P. Rabinow, 1982, *Michel Foucault. Beyond structuralism and Hermeneutics*, Harvester Press, Brighton.

Dube, L., 1988, Socialisation of Hindu girls in patrilineal India, in K. Chanana (ed.), *Socialization, Education and Women*.

Featherstone, M., 1991, The body in consumer culture, in M. Featherstone, M. Hepworth and J.S. Turner (eds.), *The Body. Social process and cultural theory*, Sage, Newbury Park.

Foucault, M., 1977 [1975], *Discipline and Punish. Birth of the prison*, Routledge, London.

——, 1980, *Power/Knowledge* (ed. Colin Gordon), Harvester Press, Brighton.

——, 1982, Afterword. The Subject and Power, in H. Dreyfus and P. Rabinow (eds.), *Michel Foucault. Beyond structuralism and hermeneutics*, Harvester Press, Brighton.

——, 1990, [1976], *The History of Sexuality*, vol. I, Penguin Books, London.

Ghadially, R., 1988, *Women in Indian Society* Sage, New Delhi.

Grosz, E., 1994, *Volatile Bodies. Toward a corporeal feminism*, Indiana University Press, Bloomington.

Harding, S., 1992, Subjectivity, Experience, Knowledge: An epistemology from/for rainbow coalition politics, *Development and Change* 23(3): 175–93.

Hoff, L. Ann, 1990, *Battered Women as Survivors*, Routledge, London.

Kakar, S., 1990, *Intimate Relations. Exploring Indian sexuality*, Penguin, Delhi.

Kapur, P., 1970, *Marriage and the Working Woman in India*, Vikas, Delhi.

——, 1973, *Love, Marriage and Sex*, Vikas, Delhi.

McNay, L., 1991, The Foucauldian body and the exclusion of experience, *Hypatia* 6(3) (Fall 1991): 125–39.

——, 1994, *Foucault. A critical introduction*, Continuum, New York.

Moore, H., 1994, *A Passion for Difference*, Polity Press, Cambridge.

Mulvey, L., 1988, Visual pleasure and narrative cinema, in C. Penley (ed.), *Feminism and Film Theory*, Routledge, London.

Omvedt, G., 1990, *Violence against Women. New movements and new theories in India*, Kali for Women, New Delhi.

Roy, M., 1975, *Bengali Women*, University of Chicago Press, Chicago.

Sawicki, J., 1991, *Disciplining Foucault. Feminism, power and knowledge*, Routledge, New York.

——, 1994, Foucault, feminism and questions of identity, in G. Gutting (ed.), *The Cambridge Companion to Foucault*, Cambridge University Press, Cambridge.

Singh, R., 1990, *The Womb of Mind. A sociological exploration of the status-experience of women in Delhi*, Vikas, Delhi.

Smith, D.E., 1991, Writing women's experience into social science, *Feminism and Psychology*, 1(1): 155–69.

Stanko, E.A., 1985, *Intimate intrusions. Women's experience of male violence*, Routledge and Kegan Paul, London.

Thapan, M., 1995, Gender, body and everyday life, *Social Scientist*, 23(7–9): 32–58.

The Witch in the Category
A Cultural Approach to Menstrual Symptomatology

Punam Zutshi

I

PRELUDE

From the last years of the nineteenth century, menstruation has come to be redefined in terms familiar to us: a growth of endometrial lining which responds to changes in hormones and sloughs off. The menstrual cycle as we know it today comes to be a specific part of the physiology of the uterus—that is of its innermost lining which grows cyclically and is subject to the process of denidation or desquamation. Prior to this, the history of menstruation is truly part of the discourse of blood: its flows, its 'coction' from food, its purification, its nutrient functions. The break from theories of humours, of fermentation and of reflexes comes with the formulation of the hormonal or endocrinological paradigm, and the microscopic examination of the uterine lining. The quickening in the knowledge about the endometrium and its hormonal correlates is notable in the last years of the nineteenth century. Westphalen in 1896, Walter Heape in 1897, Ludwig Fraenkel in 1903, Fritz Hitschmann and Ludwig Adler in 1908 and Robert Schroeder in 1915 contribute to the knowledge of the cyclic growth and shedding of the endometrium in response to hormones. This culminates in the work of Edgar Allen and Edward Doisy in 1923 which identifies the 'ovarian hormone', later called oestrin, responsible for producing estrous conditions and related uterine bleeding to a fall in the estrogen level in the blood. Between 1929 and 1935, termed the heroic age of reproductive endocrinology by Guy Marrian, all the chief naturally occurring hormones are isolated and described in the work of Alan Parkes, Adolf Butenandt, George Corner, Willard Allen, A. Girard, E. Laqueur and Marrian amongst others.[1]

In 1931 when the hormonal paradigm is being institutionalized, Robert Frank, himself a research worker in reproductive endocrinology, coins the term Pre-Menstrual Tension (PMT) for changes perceived in women before the onset of their periods. Writing in the *Archives of Neurology and Psychiatry*, Frank seems to be engaged in making an endocrinological statement about what has historically been part of the knowledge of writers of medical texts and handbooks. Significantly, the ground Frank covers is largely that of hysteria at a time when Sigmund Freud, following in the tradition of Jean Charcot has transformed hysteria into the psychoneuroses.[2] Frank considers the premenstrual correlates of 'hystero-epilepsy' among other cases, relating PMT to the excess of 'female sex hormone' levels in the blood and urine of suffering women. Endocrinology and Psychoanalysis are both engaged in redefining hysteria and melancholy.

In 1932 Mary Chadwick in her book *The Psychological Effects of Menstruation* is engaging in a dialogue with Anthropology on the one hand and Reginald Scot's 1584 text *'Discoverie of Witchcraft'* on the other, is struck by the similarity between the witch and the menstruating woman. Chadwick is not an isolated example. She works in a tradition that is reading the texts of the Inquisition. In 1897 Freud had read Kramer and Sprenger's *Malleus Maleficarum* of the fifteenth century, and was struck by the parallels between the confessions of witches and his hysteric patients, as also the fantasy of diabolic coupling of witch and devil.[3] Ernest Jones, disciple and compiler of the master, had thought long about the nightmare and the incubus in the context of witchcraft accusations (1910, 1931) and Gregory Zilboorg, historian of medicine had yet to produce his 1935 book *The Medical Man and the Witch during the Renaissance* about the role of the Witch Hunt in medical evolution; *Malleus Maleficarum* providing 'the first clinical pictures of psychopathology'.

If Psychoanalysis and Psychopathology are defining themselves in this debate with the past, Gynaecology and Reproductive Endocrinology, which are becoming modern, scientific disciplines will not engage in this exercise by definition. Nor will histories of medicine; scientific progress requiring the chronicling of disjuncture and pioneering steps into the future. *Lancet* in 1915 and the *American Journal of Obstetrics and Gynaecology* newly restructured in 1920, signal the new era in the study of menstruation and reproductive endocrinology by faithfully chronicling the folklore and customs of savages and pre-modern Europe to remember one last time who we are not.[4]

The figures of witch and primitive will disappear. What archaeology, what genealogy will uncover these?

II

THE MATERIALITY OF SYMPTOMS AND THE PROBLEM OF DISEASE CATEGORIES

This paper attempts to understand what goes into the making of modern western disease categories related to women. It does this through an exploration of pre-menstrual and menopausal symptoms based on archival material and interviews from hospital-based fieldwork that I undertook on the East Coast of USA in 1986 and 1987.[5] While the focus on the cultural forms an intrinsic part of the studies of illness experience in the modern west, it is applied only partially to the study of disease categories as in the study of 'culture-bound syndromes'[6].

While the study of the cultural or social construction of such disease categories offers itself occasionally as a critique of presumed objectivity or scientificity where culture continues to persist as distortion or trace, this paper holds that there is a cultural basis to all categories, different medical systems presenting competing universalities.[7] At the same time it holds medical knowledge is not reducible to its cultural basis. Medical knowledge rests on a classification that is in the first instance socio-cultural, and builds on this to itself become part of the collective representations of a society. In order to understand the birth and transformation of medical categories, one takes methodological recourse to the materiality of signs and symptoms (Barthes 1988: 202–13). One also necessarily goes beyond the medical classification to culturally locate both the phenomenon under study and its classification.

The category of Pre-Menstrual Tension that arises at the very outset of the new endocrinological thinking is an important marker in the history of this new paradigm, as it mediates between the old and new structuring of menstrual cycle-related experience and disease categories. PMT is articulated into the Pre-Menstrual Syndrome (PMS) in 1953 by Dr Katharina Dalton and Dr Raymond Greene accompanying the more sophisticated analysis of menstrual hormones. While Robert Frank had recommended Roentgen rays directed against the ovaries and venesection to relieve the 'tension', Dalton is an early proponent of today's emphasis on hormonal replacement. While menopause is gradually coming to be medicalized in terms of a deficiency disease (Lock 1985), I take both categories together to primarily understand PMT/PMS because both in complementary ways are medical exemplars of the broader cultural argument in USA of 'raging hormones' which render women unfit for public office, being at the mercy of their hormones. As will become evident in the course of this paper they are manifestations of the same logic which historically and culturally unfolds in a particular manner.

PMS and the Menopause syndrome are both represented in the anthropological literature as possible candidates for being 'culture-bound syndromes' bound up with cultural beliefs and bodily conditions that may not be universal (Rodin 1992; Kaufert and Gilbert 1986). Both share in the conversion of perceived symptoms, molimina into 'syndromes' in the second half of this century: PMS mediating between PMT and the new category, Late Luteal Phase Dysphoric Disorder, and Menopause coming to be seen as a Deficiency Disease—both participating in the discourse of Psychiatry and Reproductive Medicine.

Whilst PMS has been characterized variously as progesterone deficiency or, psychosomatic disorder, amongst other descriptions; its symptoms which set in seven to ten days before the menses are characteristically 'mood swings', edema of the lower extremities, abdominal bloating, depression—the patient becoming increasingly 'anxious, restless, irritable and hostile'. Impairment of judgement and episodes of violence can occur in severely affected individuals. Disruption of domestic and professional life are emphasized with PMS now becoming accepted as a mitigating factor in crimes in the UK and in France, becoming the grounds for a plea of temporary insanity (Yen and Jaffe 1991: 296–7).

Characteristically the symptoms which pass with the onset of the period are considered to be part of the PMS. The maintenance of a menstrual calendar is a crucial aid in diagnosis, allowing one to see if the symptoms are generally distributed in the month or clustered in the last ten to seven days of the cycle.

Menopause is described as a time when Follicule Stimulating Hormones are high and estradiol and progesterone levels decline with accompanying vasomotor symptoms. Vaginal atrophy and depression form part of the changing profile of women (Yen and Jaffe: 389–92).

Whilst the presence of psychological disorders complicates both pictures of PMS and Menopause, the problems relating to ageing are seen as complicating the Menopause picture (Yen and Jaffe 1991: 297, 389).

In the next section I examine the embodiment of these categories by women where I do not emphasize something like a pure PMS or Menopause, instead seeing it in and as part of the lives and experience of women.

III

From the Field: The Articulation of PMS and Menopausal Suffering

Lisa Hunt, 26 was my introduction to the western world of PMS. She was a White Anglo-Saxon Protestant divorced single parent living with her mother and daughter. A one-time nurse, she ran an agency of construction workers. She had mentioned being extremely premenstrual to Dr Campion when she came for her first visit. She was suffering from dyspareunia or pain during intercourse on account of Endometriosis. The contraceptive pill the doctor had advised for Endometriosis had also helped her with her PMS symptoms.

When I asked her what her PMS was like she had said 'mood swings, being out of control, irrational'. When I asked her to describe it, she elaborated:

How can I describe it? You're constantly on edge and you feel very, very irritable. Whereas most of the time I am pretty good humoured, easy-going I snap all the time, I yell at my daughter continually. Y'know I notice that I'm yelling at everybody, I'm not even talking in a civilized way. ... I tend to want to be by myself.[8] Stay in bed or stay on the couch, watch TV and be alone. Do things that I can be alone and have very little conversation. And I got severe headaches, terrible lower-back-ache, (retain) incredible amount of water and my feet get very swollen—and hands. I just feel very miserable all over. I feel a great amount of pressure in my head, terrible tension-headaches, terrible and I just feel very snappish. [And this happens how long before your period?] It starts a week before my period and I cry more easily. And another thing I've noticed is I get very suspicious. Almost like a kind of paranoia. Very suspicious of people and motives in different things. ... Mostly to do with relationships. Y'know my boy friend—we would always fight at that time. I would always think he was lying or this or that. I never believed what he was saying regardless of whether it was the truth or not. And you realize after ... when I get my period it's almost like a sense of relief, it releases the tension. Then you realize actually you have been foolish the way you behaved before ... it's almost like being two different people.

[Imagine you were having an attack of PMS—Can you?] I feel very picked upon, people are persecuting you, picking on you, everyone's out to get you. You just feel very sad and lonely. Sort of cranky and isolated. I feel very, very sad. And it's amazing because as soon as I get my period about three days later, I'm ready to pick up and I feel like a new person and I'm happy, and I want to call my friends and I want to go out again. ... My mother has it very severely and I think we sort of shut ourselves off from the world and the only people we really associate with is each other because we know how we are. ... Whereas someone who didn't know you—like when you are dating someone y'know for a month or so—and then all of a sudden you get your period and you're a different person. Like [speaking on boy's behalf] 'Forget it! Who needs this? *She's a witch once a month*' so you tend to isolate yourself.

[You aren't a household kitchen-witch at that time?] No, no I'm not a nice person. I don't even like myself. I really don't. I'm just cross. I feel cross and dumpy and fat and terrible. I could always tell I was getting my period because I felt so terrible. I realized that. Well, people, women, my mother would say 'What is wrong with you?' *Different people, friends who saw me on a daily basis saw me change from this easy-going person to a real witch every three weeks*. I'd get very uptight, more argumentative.'

When you say '*real*' witch what were the specific qualities?

Lisa: Well, you know, *somebody who is just kind of naggy, bitchy; witchy would be taken as losing control, being childish and irrational and not being very civilized.*

She said she could 'build the case' against anybody at this time. It's almost as if you can see very clearly. At that time every thing becomes very clear. Of course you're not (clear) things are distorted. Because you're not being very rational. At that moment ... I know what everybody's motives are, what everybody wants from you.

I'm thinking so much ... you ... take away the blinders, you take your heart away. D'you know what I am saying? When you think with your heart, you tend to look at things differently, the way you want to see them or you want them to really be. When I have PMS I get very ruthless in my thinking and I strip away pretences and illusions. It's almost a jaded feeling. You find very little to like in people. You say 'this is such a terrible world'.

In some cases they (my suspicions) are right. In a lot of cases what you're doing is being too hard on people: Over-analysing and looking for ways and things to fail, that sort of thing. Relationships or whatever. Whereas at other times you're building on it, working, making things work, 'PMS comes, forget it! Nothing matters'. [She mentions that her stepfather used the Dr Jekyll and Mr Hyde metaphor for her mother at the time of her PMS.] Do you get violent?

I can, yes, I can. I have a bad temper anyway but I finally start throwing things, you don't have any patience. I've never got violent with my daughter. That's just a part of maturity.

During her period Lisa describes herself as being at her sexual peak 'all those hormones running around'.

* * *

Jennifer Peters, 53, is a school teacher who suffers from PMS and has pre-menopausal symptoms. She is White Anglo-Saxon Protestant and describes herself as 'working middle class'. She is divorced with adult daughters who live independently while she lives with a man in a stable relationship. She had told her doctor she had always had a troublesome week before her menses, but got relief with the onset of menses. And now no longer does, feeling pre-menstrual all the time. She had been waking up with an almost locked jaw and gritted teeth a week before her periods; having hot flashes in the early hours of the morning, disturbing her sleep. She was seeing Dr Campion for hormonal replacement, for a second opinion since she has a history of breast hyperplasia. The doctor notes in his record that she has 'emotional symptoms' of tearfulness.

She dates her symptoms becoming acute to four years prior to her visit to Dr Campion, when back from a trip across the country; she was finding it hard to cope with the reopening of school. The swelling, the bloating, the weight gain had worsened. She would wake up with clenched teeth as if 'my tongue was pushing up against the roof of my mouth'. 'I had to get to a better place some time before school started. ... I was getting very, very anxious about school starting, and fearful that I was not going to be able to pull off my job.' She was given a tranquilizer for extreme PMS symptoms. Later, hormones had helped, but since she had been at high risk for cancer, she had to review the situation. Describing her menopausal symptoms:

The hot flashes were as if somebody had turned up the thermostat either in the whole house or in your body—I would be awakened out of sound sleep almost as if you have a temperature, y'know. Hot flash doesn't say it. ... you're just burning up and then when that stops, you're immediately chilled because you're so wet. ... Usually you have to change your night clothes. There was a lot of restlessness and a lot of frustration. Somehow y'know, emotionally it made me very tense and anxious. Sometimes I had chest pains ... a great big pressure on my chest and shortness of breath: things I had associated with psychosomatic things. You've been taught to ... you're supposed to think yourself out of those things. And then I had an ECG. It was just an anxiety attack ... I was embarrassed. I was supposed to be having control over an anxiety attack, so that would just add to the whole frustration of having one.

Something was pushing on my chest. I could feel my heart pounding in my throat—I was having numbness in my left arm all the way down. ... I thought, I was having a nervous breakdown. ... My tongue was so numb—it felt big and numb. At that time I would be a running medical bulletin which got to be very boring, then I was embarrassed I was turning neurotic. ... I would visualize it as being this complaining, neurotic crazy lady. ... That was when I went into 'Co-Counselling.'[9]

I was very concerned that women get bitchy and intolerant and complaining around the period—that whole culture of things—this male/female business—men thinking women as unpleasant to be around. Later I started to notice that women were unusually tolerant, have an enormous amount of giving to do as caretakers and tolerating—and if they—child and husband noticed any difference in my disposition, it would in my estimation be the level that they were functioning all the time. ... that I wasn't just that supreme giver, I wasn't that giver of unqualified love. ... *so it wasn't that I turned into a witch so much as that I didn't have that enormous margin of tolerance that I normally had. ... that selfless martyrdom'.*

What they or rather the world at large were calling witchiness. ... if a woman complained then she must be having a period. It would always seem an unfair, unjust assumption.

* * *

Michelle Kent, 28 is also a White Anglo-Saxon Protestant. She is married and works as a secretary. Describing her confusion about the overlay or overlap of her being an 'Adult Child of an Alcoholic' (another very American social phenomenon) and her PMS, she said:

You begin to wonder what is real and what is PMS. It's very frustrating. I'm a very sensitive person and I have many personal problems within my family and dealing with life and so on. So when PMS comes I'm always. ... Is it because it's PMS or because I'm an 'Adult Child of an Alcoholic' or is it because my marriage is not right, is it because of where I live or is it my job? What's the real meaning of the problem? However, immediately after the PMS clears up, if those problems are so great, why is it they seem so small two days later? It would not be like that as far as I'm concerned. I would still be suffering two days later and trying to work my problems out. But they ... it's just ... when I get PMS I usually get very depressed, I don't know why I am alive. I can't figure out why I'm living. What's my purpose here? What if I'm going to suffer like this? Why do I need to be alive? Why don't I kill myself? Why don't I ... I don't feel important. I feel so miserable that sometimes I don't want to be alive, that's how it feels. But then again 'how can I kill myself? I'm a real chicken.

This conversation with the self includes the realization 'It was worse when I didn't realize it was PMS. Now I have something to lean back on Oh! It's my PMS. In a couple of days I'll feel better. So it's a lot nicer that way. Although I still feel the anxiety and everything. At least I know I don't have to kill myself to be rid of it. It'll go away in a couple of days. I'm not going to be like this forever.'

* * *

Jane Atkinson is 52, a White Anglo-Saxon Protestant, middle class and divorced. She works as a psychologist, and describes how she was diagnosed as having endogenous depression at her menopause.

I used to be a runner. I was physically active and found it easy to exercise. I loved exercise. ...When I started to go through menopause, my periods became irregular and there was some diminution of my interest in exercise and I had some depression at that time, but I can actually mark it to the September that my period stopped and like in a heart monitor you know there are the beeps and then all of a sudden [mimes buzzing, humming sound and indicates with a horizontal movement of her hand 'a going flat']. I was just like that ... it was like I switched that tune off and I felt flat and I found it difficult to exercise. I didn't care about exercise and was going into depression ... and nothing changed it. I mean, I couldn't even though I tried to exercise ... it was like someone had turned off the spigot.

She had been put on an anti-depressant and estrogen which had helped her.

It was really the anti-depressant or the combination but it was really like someone turned the light on again. It was really like flicking a switch and all of a sudden, I had the physical stamina.

There had been a problem with palpitations, and growth of the uterine lining which had necessitated a break in the medication. She describes all kinds of difficulties or 'catastrophes' which were also building up. She had found herself a psychiatrist since there was

a sense that the therapy wasn't touching this physical sense of depression. I was also losing functioning. I was losing short-term memory ... I wasn't able to sleep. But the loss of short-term memory was what finally got me to the doctor because in my work I can't afford not to remember and I got very frightened because I can't afford to lose functioning. You know I support myself. ...What is interesting since I've been on the new medication the memory is coming back and it's like from day to day. I can notice it ... it's almost like a physical shift I think ... very strange.

She describes herself as 'actively suicidal' when her symptoms were at her worst but that she would never try it.

IV

THE FIGURES OF THE WITCH, MELANCHOLIC AND HYSTERIC: THE CLASSIFICATION OF SYMPTOMS

The case material presented above serves to draw attention to (1) the specific symptoms and illness experience of women suffering from Pre-Menstrual Syndrome and undergoing Menopause. (2) It focuses on a cultural figure, that of the witch which serves as a vehicle to convey the feeling of anger, being out of control, having an altered consciousness or sense of self. I shall argue that the symptoms women present, classifiable today under the Pre-Menstrual Syndrome and Menopause, overlap with profiles of melancholy and hysteria. This will be shown through a comparative study of the classification of symptoms over time. The figures of the witch, the melancholic and hysteric which adumbrate the experience of PMS and Menopause will be explored and elaborated. We turn first to the medical categories of hysteria and melancholy before drawing the connections with the heretical figure of the witch as it appeared in the witch-hunts and Inquisition to understand what this aspect of disease and transgression said about the nature of womanhood and sexuality in the past and to understand its transformations today.

The discussion of the aetiology of hysteria has been foregrounded in an important paper by Mari Rodin on the social construction of Pre-Menstrual Syndrome (Rodin 1992). Rodin responds to the proposed psychiatric category of Late Luteal Phase Dysphoric Disorder

(LLPDD), the new incarnation of PMS which enters the revised Diagnostic and Statistical Manual III in 1987, by making the case for an examination of cultural beliefs relating to the place of reason, rationality and women in the west. To this end, Rodin suggests that the aetiology of hysteria which provided the prototype for PMT in 1931 is the clue to the persistence of the idea that a woman's sanity was consistently tied to her reproductive system and her role in society. Rodin argues that despite the inconsistencies in the study of PMS: prevalence rates that range from 25 to 90 per cent; disagreement over duration of PMS: six to seventeen days; methodological weakness in the research; the consistency in the conclusions that women can become totally incapacitated because of PMS; and that hormonal changes influence behaviour, are indicative of unstated assumptions about women and the menstrual cycle, rather than of causal relationships or direct hormonal control of emotions. These assumptions militate against giving women important responsibilities in the public world of work, reiterating the preferred role of women as wives and mothers (1992: 49–52).

Rodin's paper makes the case for the persistence of tacit cultural knowledge in medical categories:

... hysteria and PMS may represent different forms or discourses of the same ideology—that in western society it is natural, and therefore imperative, that women confine their interests to the home and to children or jeopardize their health and sanity. In the case of hysteria, we saw the explicit recognition of this relationship in one of the remedies for hysteria—marriage (ibid. 55).

For the purpose of this paper I argue that while attending to the aetiology of hysteria does advance our understanding of PMS it is the figure of the witch that completes the semiology or symptomatology of PMS, and of menopause. The aetiology of hysteria does not provide us an adequate understanding of Frank's 1931 PMT prototype. Rather the symptomatology of hysteria allows us to comprehend the similarities and differences in the classification of symptoms over time. The discourse on blood, it must be recalled, provides the frame in the older paradigm for the understanding of menstruation and menstrual blood. This discourse underlines the discussion on hysteria and melancholy as also the witch figure. It will also explain symptoms experienced by menopausal women, such as hot flashes or flushes.

Let us first turn to hysteria. By hysterical symptoms were usually meant till this century: convulsions, paroxysms, contortions, suffocation, even muteness. Hysteria was primarily conceived as a disease of uterine origin, caused primarily by abstinence from sexual activity (voluntary or involuntary) and the desire for a child; the uterus till the sixteenth century pictured as wandering around the body, pressing on the chest causing 'suffocation of the mother' i.e., the matrix or the womb. This could also be caused by 'retained menses' or amenorrhoea. However retained 'sperm' more than retained menses, could cause this problem. Intercourse was recommended as a cure for the problem, as were methods of 'fumigations' of the parts to tempt the uterus back to its position or the application of strong smelling substances to the nose. Into the Greek discussion of hysteria, the Christian world introduced the machinations of the devil and witchcraft (Veith 1965).

Looking back on the material I have presented, it becomes clear that one can see some traditional symptoms of hysteria in the case of the menopausal Jennifer Peters' anxiety attack: her gritting her teeth, clenching of jaws, pressure on the chest. This is not necessarily explicable by hysterical aetiology. Here it will be simply part of the physiological processes of menopause.

What is important to discussions of both PMS and Menopause, is the experience of mild or severe depression bringing to mind the older debates on melancholy which saw melancholy as causing hysteria. Depression and hot flushes could be also attributed to bloodletting which diverted blood from the womb. These could equally be attributed to the changes taking place at the time of menopause in the blood. Jane Sharp's *The Midwives Book* in 1671 explained, 'elderly women, whose courses were stopt when they were young, are troubled oftentimes with the Spleen, and hypochondriack Melancholy ... when the thin part of the blood is inflamed they grow very hot, and red in the Face, but that lasts not long' (Eccles 1992: 75).

Lisa Hunt and Jennifer Peters' use of the term 'witch' to describe themselves pre-menstrually alerted me to a very different usage of the term 'witch'. The term 'witch' was used in the context of being in a rage, very angry and out of control. Pre-menstrual anger also occupies a central place in Emily Martin's *The Woman in the Body* (1987). The use of the term 'witch', in principle, one imagines may be used in other contexts, but if other informants echoed this usage it was also in the context of menstruation. There are in American literature—both popular and middle-brow—'witches'—Stephen King's witch Carrie in the book of the same name—associated with menstruation, blood, supernormal powers and vengeance; and John Updike's slightly jaded witches in *The Witches of Eastwick*—women no longer young or married, being malevolent, carrying out the intentions of the devilish Darryl Van Horne (King 1974; Updike 1984).

The other 'witches' in America are healers, herbalists and practitioners of alternate medicine both native American and White, seen as and defining themselves against mainstream medicine, claiming to possess wisdom grounded in the relationship between their bodies and the cosmos, self-consciously linked to pre-Christian traditions of the Earth-Mother and the Mother-Goddess, living according to rhythms of time different from those of modern industrial capitalism. Associated with crystals and quartz, plants and music, alternate life-styles, book shops of esoteric and occult wisdom, this 'new' cult of witches provides a very different configuration of religion—even politics.

V

ARCHIVAL EXPLORATIONS

As a figure of speech the 'witch' provides a clue to a different cultural and historical complex which we shall explore through a reading of selected texts: the *Malleus Maleficarum* (The Witch Hammer) by Heinrich Kramer and James Sprenger (1486), *The Psychological Effects of Menstruation* by Mary Chadwick (1932), and Rober Frank's paper 'The Hormonal Causes of Premenstrual Tension' (1931).

The fifteenth century *Malleus Maleficarum* provides us with an important account of the witch as heretic, written by the Dominican Inquisitors Heinrich Kramer and James Sprenger. The question that is central to this text is: why are women more prone to be witches? Pope Innocent VIII who issued a Papal Bull in 1484 to ensure that the inquisitors Kramer and Sprenger would not be hindered in their task, does not focus exclusively on women. In this Bull, the Pope is alarmed by the depravity that has beset parts of Germany in the late fifteenth century which,

Many persons of both sexes unmindful of their own salvation and straying from the Catholic Faith, have abandoned themselves to devils, incubi and succubi, and by their incantations, Spells, conjurations, and other accursed charms and crafts, enormities and horrid offences, have slain infants yet in the mother's womb, as also the offspring of cattle, have blasted the produce of the earth, the grapes of the vine, the fruits of the trees, nay, men and women, beasts of burthen, herd-beasts, as well as animals of other kinds, with terrible and piteous pains and sore diseases, both internal and external; they hinder men from performing the sexual act and women from conceiving, when husbands cannot know their wives nor wives receive their husbands; over and above this, they blasphemously renounce that Faith which is theirs by the Sacrament of Baptism, and at the instigation of the Enemy of Mankind they do not Shrink from committing and perpetrating the foulest abominations and filthiest excesses to the deadly peril of their own souls, whereby they outrage the Divine Majesty and are a cause of scandal and danger to very many (in Kramer and Sprenger 1948: xix).

Kramer and Sprenger however are relentless in their demonization of women. They halt only to invoke the Virgin Mary and the good women Judith, Esther and Deborah as keepers of the faith. Women like the first woman Eve, were deficient in faith 'for *Femina* comes from *Fe* and *Minus*, since she is ever weaker to hold and preserve the faith. But by grace and nature faith never failed in the Blessed Virgin, even at the time of Christ's Passion, when it failed in all men'. Eve is the first temptress which is why the Scriptures have much that is evil to say about women. But as the whole sin of Eve was taken away by the benediction of Mary, Eva becoming Ave, 'preachers should always say as much praise of them as possible' (ibid. 44).

This does not keep the two authors of *Malleus* from agreeing with Cato of Utica: 'if the world should be rid of women, we should not be without God in our intercourse. For truly without the wickedness of women, to say nothing of witchcraft, the world would still remain proof against innumerable dangers' (ibid. 46). It is important to recognize that the Inquisitors are not concerned with Eve's persona as the mother of all the living and do not pay much attention to the Virgin Mary's being the Mother of God 'blessed among women' who ensures the humanity of Jesus. Rather, they rest secure in the maleness of Jesus which ensures that the male sex will not be wizards 'And Blessed be the Highest who has so far preserved the male sex from so great a crime for since He was willing to be born and to suffer for us, therefore He has granted to men this privilege' (ibid.: 47).

Women are more prone to be witches for several reasons: they are more credulous; naturally more impressionable and more ready to receive the influence of a disembodied spirit; when they use this quality well they are very good, but when they use it ill they are very evil, they have slippery tongues and are unable to conceal from their fellow-women the things they know by evil arts; since they are of feeble intellect it is not surprising that they should come more under the spell of witchcraft. *'But the natural reason is that she is more carnal than a man, as is clear from her many carnal abominations'* (ibid.: 44 emphasis mine;). She is by nature quicker to waver in her faith, as was the case of Eve. Also when her love is turned to hate 'She seethes with anger and impatience in her whole soul, just as the tides of the sea are always heaving and boiling' (ibid.: 4). 'The most powerful cause which contributes to their increase of witches is the woeful rivalry between married folk and unmarried men and women. This is so even among holy women, so what must it be among the others' (ibid.: 45). Crucially, the conclusion is *'And indeed just as through the first defect in their intelligence they are more prone to abjure the faith; so through their second defect of inordinate affections and passions they search for, brood over, and inflict various venge-ances, either by witchcraft or by some other means'* (ibid. emphasis mine).

Women will follow their impulses even to their destruction. They may kill themselves either for love or sorrow because they were unable to work their vengeance. The Inquisitors are firm in their stand on vengeance. Further, the question of sorrow and the disease of melancholy where it arises, the Inquisitors are aware, will cause women to have phantastical apparitions occur to them. And to this fact are immediately connected women who are liable to imagine extraor-dinary things: namely that the devil or incubus has copulated with them. This may give rise in some women to think they have been made pregnant by an incubus. But this will not keep Kramer and Sprenger from suspecting copulation with an incubus or Devil as women in their carnal lusts are wont to do this (ibid.: 167).

In women particularly given to witchcraft three vices predominate: infidelity (both in the sacred and secular senses), ambition and lust (ibid.: 47). There are witches of three sorts: those who injure but can-not cure, those who cure but 'through some strange pact with the devil' cannot injure, and those who both injure and cure. Amongst those who injure is one class who can perform every sort of witchcraft and spell and is given to (against every instinct of human or animal nature), eating and devouring children of their own species. This is the most powerful class of witches, raising hailstorms and hurtful tempests and causing harm that they cannot undo (ibid.: 99). She profanes the sacra-ments of the Church in order to work evil and make predictions (ibid.: 197).

The overriding concern, it would appear in the *Malleus*, is with faithfulness, fertility and fructification in the life and world of the members of the faith, in short the life-affirming faculties against which the witch works her powers. She infects

with witchcraft the venereal act and the conception of the womb: First, by inclining the minds of men to inordinate passion; second, by obstructing their generative force; third by removing the members accommodated to that act; fourth, by changing men into beasts by their magic art; fifth by destroying the generative force in women; sixth by procuring abortion; seventh, by offering children to devils, besides other animals and fruits of the earth with which they work much harm (ibid.: 47.)

The priests work to reconcile one, the work of witches to the presence of an Almighty God and two, the work of the devil and the work of nature; and conclude that it is in 'the two divine permissions which God justly allows namely that the Devil, the Author of all Evil should Sin and that our First Parents should Fall, that the work of witches originates' (ibid.: 71). And as we have seen Eve, the mother is cast in the role of the temptress by the authors. However, as the Inquisitors reiterate, matrimony is a work of God, being instituted by Him, but is wrecked by the work of the Devil. Thus it is the matrimonial unit whose procreation is sought to be hindered by witchcraft (ibid.: 47–8).

Thus, while women are conceptualized as prone to being witches, the witch is seen as being in opposition to the matrimonial pair whose procreative faculties and offspring she is out to destroy. The matrimonial pair must obviously be the earthly counterpart of the Holy Family.[10] The figure who is the opposite of the witch therefore must be the Second Eve: the Virgin Mary, the mother who by nature and grace is unfailing in faith, as Kramer and Sprenger point out. It is she as Ave who points the way to the transformation and redemption of Eva. Unlike the witch in whom infidelity, lust and ambition predominate, the Virgin is a model of rectitude 'quintessential motherliness' in the words of Marina Warner. She is obedient, submissive, gentle, forbearing, compliant: the model for the Christian Mother and wife (Warner 1983: 190).

We now turn to Mary Chadwick's early twentieth-century recuperation of the witch figure. Her 1932 publication *The Psychological Effects of Menstruation* is a reading of Reginald Scot, the anthropology of menstrual taboos and Freud in a single frame, coming at a time when the cyclical aspects of menstruation were being formalized in terms of endocrinology. While Robert Frank coined PMT in 1931, Chadwick's work was exploring similar yet different teritory on the basis of her psychoanalytic work.

Chadwick starts by explaining the similarities between the effects that menstruous or menstruating women have on their environment (quoting Pliny, the first-century B.C. natural historian whose 'descriptions' are commonplace in any study of menstruation) and the accusations brought against witches. Establishing her connection between menstruating women and witches as responsible for the harm they bring to neighbours; killing cattle, causing horses to be hag-ridden or miscarry, preventing butter from being made from cream, or turning cream sour, raising tempests and storms, Chadwick argues that *it is because menstruating women were harmful (and in this sense similar to witches) that menstrual taboos were instituted* (1932: 11–25). In trying to psychoanalyse the witch-cult, in seeing Scot's melancholic women in her own cases and in trying to make pragmatic sense of menstrual taboos her conclusions are:

We cannot help feeling that we find in them [sources on the history of witchcraft] evidence enough to supply the theory that the witch-woman was to a great extent the menstruating woman or that she belonged to the type, whom we still find most likely to be disturbed by special symptoms at such times and who repeat in their dreams and phantasies during the monthly flux wishes or obsessions comparable to the actions and behaviour of the witches, that brought so much discredit upon them in former times, and reminds us of the remarks of Dr. Harry Campbell, concerning what he calls the *monthly neurosis* of women, and which Freud describes as the sudden intensification of libido, which leads to an outbreak of recognizable neurosis (ibid.: 11).

In keeping with the general explanatory framework of the time, Chadwick diagnoses the witch as,

the homosexual woman suffering from an obsessional neurosis, a masculinity complex ... connected with an overwhelming mother fixation. ... We notice her belief in the power of her death-wishes, spells and incantations that she can carry out in connection with her belief in her omnipotence of thought, also that her intense wish for power has led her to seek ways of obtaining it through the supernatural methods of Black Art. This allows her an obsolete ritual as the vehicle of her sadistic impulses coupled with an outlet for her hatred and repressed sexuality, as well as an expression of perversion associated with anal and oral stages of development, cannibalism and poisoning. We may find the explanation of many of the activities of witches, which brought them into grave disfavour with their neighbours during the Middle Ages and later in such symptoms. (ibid.: 22.)

Chadwick's version of the 'monthly neurosis' is that at the time of her menstrual period, the woman is temporarily unbalanced. She acts differently from her accustomed habit, her actions are unreliable and it is often impossible to know what to expect from her at this time. Her memory is frequently impaired and she cannot be relied upon to carry out duties which usually she performs perfectly. She feels a repugnance to usual food and has strange longings for curious articles of diet. 'She feels injured by her condition and wishes to obtain revenge in some direction as compensation to her outraged feelings.' *Sometimes her hostile feelings are directed towards parents or other men. This is why others*

fear that she may rob them of their virility, which indeed she might very well like to do, spoil or steal their weapons or clothing; injure their boats, because they are connected with pursuits in which she is not allowed to share. Phantasies of this kind appear in great profusion among menstruating women (ibid.:26; emphasis mine).

Chadwick presents the 'standard witch':

She is usually represented as being an old or ageing woman, unattractive and envious, always ready to destroy the good fortune of all her neighbours and apparently causing havoc among the crops and cattle of men who displeased her.[11] *In those days they tried to gain a more direct gratification for their impulse of aggression and desire for revenge, but not so safely as those of the present day who damage their neighbours by other methods, not so likely to bring them into difficulties with the law.* (ibid.:50 emphasis mine.)

After first having established the similarities between the accusations against witches and taboos against menstruating women, the witch is psychologized as being like the menstruating woman. Then as we see from the quotation above, the witch and the woman who suffers monthly neurosis become one, united in their capacity for aggression and injury.

The appendices to Chadwick's book carry two cases studies and extracts from Reginald Scot's (1584) *Discoverie of Witchcraft.* Under the heading How Melancholie abuseth old women and of the effects thereof by sundrie examples, Reginald Scot differentiates between the 'coosening' witches, i.e., those practising deception or fraud and those 'poore melancholike women which are themselves deceived':

For as some of *these melancholike persons imagine, they are witches and by witchcraft can work wonders, and doo what they list.* ...'*Why should an old witch be thought free from such fantasies who (as the learned philosophers and physicians saie) upon the stopping of their monthlie melancholike flux or issue of blood, in their age which needs increase therein, as (through their weakness both of bodies and brains) the aptest persons to meet with such melancholike imaginations,* with whom their imaginations remains even when their senses are gone. (in Chadwick 1932: 61 emphasis mine.)

Scot's further explanations for 'who are privileged from witches, what bodies are aptest to be bewitched or to be witches, why women are rather witches than men, and what they are' use Johannes Weyer's medical knowledge

Women are also (Saith Vairus) *monthlie filled full of superfluous humours and with them the melancholike bloud boileth,* whereof spring vapours, and are carried up and conveied through the nosethrels and mouth and to the bewitching of whatsoever it meeteth. For they belch up a certain breth, wherewith they bewitch whomsoever they list. And of all other women, leane, hollow eied, old beetle browed women are the most infectious. ...' *'Old women, in whom the ordinarie course of nature faileth in the office of purging their natural monthlie humours, show also some proofe hereof,* namely of being able to through their eyes' gaze upon the other to bring illness either continual or intermittent. (ibid.: 62 emphasis mine).

Chadwick's work can be seen as symptomatic of the modern view of the world of witches—her reading of necessity, an ahistorical and overdetermined one. Yet it has the benefit of recognizing the subliminal or unexpressed aspects of the nature of western culture of history and medicine—and presenting a metonymy of menstruation/menstrual blood-woman-witch which usually is characterized as belonging traditionally to the magical world view. Of necessity, the social and cosmological topos is excised from the picture making for a particular reading of the texts relating to the Inquisition where the witch and the harm she wreaks becomes the central focus of the reading. Chadwick's work has the significance of a cultural text which opens the door to texts of an earlier age. Simultaneously she provides us with a modern evocation of the witch, even while appearing to psychologically explain the witch of the past.

While Reginald Scot is arguing that in fact those accused as being witches are not witches but melancholics who imagine themselves to be witches, he bases this on a theory of melancholia. The causation or aetiology in this case is that those in whom the monthly flow has ceased tend to suffer from melancholia. But the question of witchcraft is not dismissed. On the one hand the ceasing of menstruation leads to imaginings, on the other both during menstruation and after the menopause, women's eyes and breath can bewitch and infect with continual or intermittent disease. Thus women do carry within themselves the power to bewitch. Scot is circumscribing the scope of a witch's activity, not ruling out the existence of bewitchment. However, with regard to melancholia it becomes important to note that age becomes a factor in explaining the delusions of the old 'witches' who were victims of melancholy. Johannes Weyer's countering of 'demonomania' of the witch-hunt had laid the ground for Scot's work for the witch's imaginings of harmful activity. Melancholy or melancholic humours assumed the presence or effect of bile which created the so-called depression and the expression of anger amongst women. The word 'atrabilarious' signifying ill-tempered was used to describe the melancholic humours where bile was the key humour. Melancholy was called in to explain the delusions of those who were not 'in fact' witches but imagined themselves so. Melancholy itself is intimately related to hysteria. Demonic possession forms part of the history of hysteria and it is important to point to the role performed by 'retained menses' or unpurged blood in the aetiology of these hysterical fits or conditions.

The Devil's work in natural disease is a problem that confronted physicians in the seventeenth and eighteenth centuries at a time when the reality of witchcraft had theological sanction; in this paper we only allude to Lester King's study of Friedrich Hoffman who in 1703 reasoned that the Devil insinuates himself in the workings of people's bodies and minds *through a predisposition in blood*. It is important to keep in mind that *historically, menstruation is part of the general discussion of blood—becoming part of the uterine/endometrial cycle much later in the end of the nineteenth century*. Hoffman's work was representative of medical thinking and the medical understanding of witchcraft. It is a pointer to the complexities of the problem of blood as conceived by medicine.

Mary Chadwick's 1932 monograph as we have seen is an account of the internal debates that mark the birth of Psychoanalysis, debates concerning the Inquisition, 'Natural History' and Anthropology. Robert Frank's 1931 paper on the other hand marks the scientific progress that Reproductive Endocrinology, at the time a new paradigm, is making. Taken together they are two modes of understanding, dualist in intent, which may illuminate each other and the past of our present medical categories, if we plot them as a moment on a single trajectory. Thus we can bring the category of the witch to bear on modern discussions in endocrinology. The witch of the Inquisition as a social category exemplifies sin and heresy, a threat to the social body as also the Body of God. Those who argue against the excesses of the Inquisition, as did Reginald Scot and Johannes Weyer, medicalize this figure: the problem of evil is shown to be one of disease. As Scot argues, fraud is to be separated from the melancholic delusions of witches. Later witchcraft must be disassociated from hysterical passions. From the medical space of hysteria epileptic convulsions, psychoneuroses and PMT are differentiated by Neurology, Psychoanalysis and Reproductive Medicine respectively in the late nineteenth and early twentieth centuries.[12] Robert Frank's 1931 paper stands between the worlds which are themselves a creation of the modern paradigm of medicine.

Frank's paper takes as its starting point 'the well known' fact that normal women suffer from varying degrees of discomfort preceding the onset of menstruation. Employers of labour take cognizance of this and make provision for the temporary care of their employees. Frank identifies three groups of women—those who suffer minor disturbances that include increased fatigability, irritability, lack of concentration and attacks of pain. Another group where symptoms are of sufficient gravity require the patient to rest, pain playing the predominant role. There is another group in whom grave systemic disorders manifest themselves during the pre-menstrual period. Two cases from this group are described in great detail—a case of idiopathic epilepsy where menstrual periods were preceded by epileptic attacks, another dealing with severe bronchial asthma. These cases illustrate 'the close connection between the ovarian function and systemic manifestations due to other organic systems'. The third case that is reported in some detail, describes the occurrence of hystero-epileptic manifestations when periods are delayed. Frank then moves to the next group of women: those who complain of a feeling of indescribable tension from ten to seven days preceding menstruation which continues till the time the menstrual flow occurs. The onset of the menstrual flow usually signalled complete relief from both physical and mental tension. Frank argues that excess accumulation of the female sex hormones leads to intense personal suffering, unrest and irritability. This tension can be temporarily relieved by venesection or permanently by toning down ovarian activity by Roentgen treatment directed against the ovaries. Amongst cases of tension that Frank observes, moderate tension manifests in despondency, severe tension in 'becoming impossible to live with', suffering from sexual tension or cardiac irregularities. *The severest tension manifests in suicidal desire, becoming an unbearable shrew, 'almost crazy' or psychoneurotic, these attacks leading to family discord.* In the discussion that follows Frank's paper presentation, it is significant that one of the doctors present is 'reminded of the hysterical patient who shows uncontrollable tension during her pre-menstrual period ...'. In these cases 'overstrong sexual emotions have found an outlet in hysterical symptoms' (1931: 1056ff.).

The presence of hystero-epileptic manifestations, the asthmatic attacks, the epileptic seizures, the severe depression all call to mind hysteria (convulsions, paroxysms) and melancholy of an earlier age. One of the remedies that Frank recommends is venesection which is the bloodletting of yore, an old treatment for hysteria. *The category of pre-menstrual tension (PMT) is obtained by the intersection of two axes: that of the knowledge of hysteria and melancholy, the other, what is known of the periodic symptoms associated with the menstrual cycle, or put another way the pre-menstrual aspect of the cycle in which hysteria and melancholy provide the model for classifying symptoms.* The picture of rage can be discerned from being 'an unbearable shrew' which comes to be symbolized by the 'witch' of the discourse of Lisa Hunt and Jennifer Peters.

Chadwick's and Frank's work are two ways of articulating the problem. Chadwick concentrates on the menstrual period in keeping with the emphasis on menstrual blood and taboos, while Frank operates with the more 'medical' emphasis on the period *prior* to the menstrual flow—as books on midwifery, compendia on women's health are aware of.[13] Chadwick works to make the case about the witch woman really being the menstruating woman in keeping with the Freudian emphasis on taboo, yet moves to include the period prior to the menstrual flow; as also the women whose periods are delayed or who are going through or approaching the climacteric. The twin beliefs about the dangerous and magical nature of menstrual blood and the function of menstruation as a ridding of excess humours; a purification operates within the metonymy of menstrual blood-woman-witch. Historically, if we argue that the witch is a hysteric or melancholic we are still within this larger structure. Once we get to the modern idea of a menstrual cycle in place of menstrual blood, the metonymy moves from the 'witch' (menopausal or pubertal) to 'the witch once a month' the pre-menstrual woman, incorporating symptoms of hysteria and melancholy.

VI

The Witch-Once-a-Month

If we now look at *Once a Month* (Dalton 1979) by the doctor who made the case in 1953 along with Dr Raymond Greene for the Pre-Menstrual Syndrome, we recognize that we are back to 'the-witch-once-a-month' figure of Lisa Hunt and Jennifer Peters. Dr Dalton writes, 'Once a month, with monotonous regularity chaos is inflicted on American homes' (1979: 1). Her first chapter 'The Curse of Eve' couches the problem in terms of an evolutionary process: 'Once a month women are reminded that their reproductive system is still in the process of evolution. But it is no good waiting another two or three million years for mother Nature to iron out the flaws' (ibid.). While the syndrome embraces different symptoms which occur with lesser and greater severity before menstruation, we shall focus on the ones that 'can change a woman from Jekyll to Hyde within minutes' (ibid.: 6). Thus, while pain, water, retention, depression, tiredness, headaches, iritability amd mood swings are part of the PMS, the central images around which this category is organized are those of transformation and excess: from a wonderful wife with a lovely nature to one who spits with rage once a month; from a darling little love bird to a suddenly angry, argumentative, shouting, abusive bitch; becoming a dragon on the war path (ibid.: 11, 80, 91). Dalton clarifies that these changes could be attributed by an observer to a lack of self-control or even evidence of the woman's true character. Rather they should be attributed to the 'natural ebb and flow of the menstrual hormones over which the woman has little control' (ibid.: 11).

Pre-menstrual irritability is commoner in the married woman, Dalton states. The husband naturally has problems trying to calm a supersensitive, edgy, irrational and agitated woman at this time. Too many end up with visits to the marriage guidance counsellor or in divorce (ibid.: 29–30).

The tempests and storms that the 'witch-once-a-month' now raises are personal, domestic and societal. In an ever widening ripple from the domestic sphere outwards, the professional world of work, the public sphere and ultimately it is the country and its economy that pay the price of the periodic transformation of women. At the extreme she can now traumatize and batter her babies, smash dishes, engage in husband bashing, cost him his chances of promotion, bring her marriage to the verge of a breakdown. She is likely to have brushes with the law on account of assault, even homicide or at the very least drunk and disorderly behaviour. She affects her chances of getting employment, holding the job down, receiving promotion and even risks losing her job unnecessarily. She costs American industry 8 per cent of the wage bill on account of absenteeism, lowered mental ability and decline in efficiency. The violence can turn against herself as high rates of suicide during the paramenstruum show (ibid.: 1979: 30–32, 84–100).

Dalton quotes a study that suggests that 60 per cent of married women report their sex urge to be highest before menstruation. She comments that unfortunately for those with pre-menstrual syndrome, this is also the time at which many of them are most horrible to their husbands and when to spite him they refuse his sexual overtures (ibid.: 87).

The norm that the PMS and Menopause sufferer deviates from in her behaviour, is that of the 'Christian' mother/housewife by becoming unable to be the giver of unqualified love and to engage in selfless martyrdom as Jennifer Peters in the earlier part of the paper pointed out. She becomes out of control, demanding and destructive. Thus women otherwise nurturant and vitalizing become angry witches once a month.

To speak of the witch is not to discount the grid or matrix that produces medical categories which consists of modalities of work and social requirements.

Frank's work (1931) to some extent and Dalton and Greene's (1953) shows us a new modality that the discourse on women's bodies must address: the changing world of work. It is crucial to recognize, as Emily Martin does, that it is the entry of women into the work space and its incorporation of a standardized linear time that begins to raise questions about the capacity of women to work. Martin shows that the relationship between menstruation and women's capacity to work had been a central issue in the nineteenth century. She argues that the entry of women into the work force coincides with the largely negative findings of research on women's capacities (Martin 1987: Ch. 7). In terms of the argument we have been formulating, the new focus on women's abilities to work is in consonance with the norm of the wife/mother role being challenged. What has altered profoundly are the changing conditions of all work in the nineteenth century.

Yet, we must point out that the claim that the burgeoning interest in PMS post–1970 is a response to the second wave of feminism

(which saw the greatest incursions by women into the work force
without the aid of a major war) is simplistic. To state that PMS is a
manoeuvre designed to return women to their homes (ibid.: 121) or,
as Rodin argues, that the medical establishment is on the side of marriage and household (1992: 55) fails to recognize the power that
medicine promises over the body. While PMS can be and is the cause
of discrimination against women, as a medical category it is equally
designed to deal with incapacity. The medicalization of the pre-
menstrual phase has been accompanied by the argument that 'x' number of working hours of productive time are lost, once women enter
the public world of work. The question of equality of men and women
uses as yardstick, the body of the male worker and standardized linear
time. This is one part of the rationalization of the modern world, where
the market economy and public space are seen as validating the life
and work of women.[14] Medicine even as it makes the case for incapacity, is on the side of 'fixing' bodies, making them fit specially
for the demands both of home and work space. Medicine tantalizingly
promises full participation and equal rights. What is important to focus
on is not just what PMS says about women's nature but what it is
seeking to do to women's bodies: a project of turning the body into
a carefully controlled environment where cyclicity is muted—a new
way of imposing social order.

VII

MENSTRUATION, SEXUALITY AND WOMEN'S BODIES

The question of sexuality that runs through the discussion on women
implicitly or explicitly through the Inquisition manuals, medical
knowledge and the figures of witch, hysteric and melancholic implicates menstrual blood in its working. The Inquisitors Kramer and
Sprenger refer directly to the menstruation of women only in passing:
to gaze upon a menstruous woman is to render the gaze infected with
witchcraft (1948: 17). Their suggestion that devils are themselves affected by certain phases of the moon acting more on men's minds in
this phase, is made in the context of lunacy and the influence of the
stars. However, more ominously this could be applied easily to the
menstrual flow, since its connectedness with moon phases was equally
part of the common knowledge of the time (ibid.: 31). While mention

of woman's carnal abominations in the *Malleus* is taken as referring to her menstruation by some commentators (Delaney *et al.* 1976: 39), the question of the carnality of women which renders them prone to witchcraft is subsumed by the concern with the Fall of the first Parents, Adam and Eve, that is to say by the Original Sin. The curse that God places on Eve is the sign under which her menstruation and her travails in labour come to be placed. The conditions under which fertility comes into the Judaeo-Christian world are these. While Eve is also regarded as the mother of all living, this function or role is not one the Inquisition will care to consider. Eva is the temptress, redeemed only by Ave. This other mother is the Virgin who has over the centuries been 'cleansed' of all her natural excretions except tears and milk, rendered '*immaculate*' literally free from spot or stain *(macula),* which has been taken to mean not just that the Virgin was herself born without sin, but that the Virgin did not menstruate. Once the Virgin's menstruation and lactation was her necessary contribution to the humanity of Jesus, the eternal son of God (Wood 1981: 718–19). From being the matriarchal Theotokos, or mother of God the Virgin makes a transition to being the Madonna, Our Lady (Illich 1982: 157–60). Under a master symbolic operation which separates unclean, stained, cursed from the pure, immaculate and the blessed, we end with a largely unmediated binary logic: both Eve as the mother of all living and the role of the Virgin's menstruation are lost sight of. While in the Old Testament, the Levitican taboos focus on the unclean nature of women as they menstruate, the promise of fertility ('being as numerous as the stars in the heavens') promised to the tribe of Abraham completes the picture of woman. The earthiness of the Black Virgin counteracts the 'white-and-blue' nun-like Madonna to some degree, but inferential logic by which menstruation can be seen as not in itself being sinful, loses out to the socio-cultural drift of symbols. Part of the curse of Eve applies to desire, which must be to one's husband. Sexuality outside of this matrimonial unit is witch-like. Those outside of this unit will be suspected of witchcraft.

Thus while menstrual blood ought also to evoke the figure of the mother, we find it is the witch that haunts our categories. Surely the argument could be cast in terms of being a mother. This position is formulated by medicine: this would link it with being part of the normal suffering women must undergo to have the capacity to bear children. Then some amount of menstrual trouble would be seen as it has been before the current medicalization, as part of the experience of being a woman, a position that would find little favour with most doctors and patients of the present day. This would be part of the travails of Eve, part of the normal expectations of being a woman. In the scheme where the Christian mother is upheld, the witch is the other face of Eve. Symbolically the witch represents the negative pole of the powers of women's sexuality and fertility. She thus allows sexuality and its projections, frustrations and castrations to be laid at her door. She bears the burden of being scapegoat: after all as the popular wisdom goes, she harms and rages, brings catastrophe where she chooses.

The power to bewitch that Reginald Scot grants to the witch, that is to bring disease and raise inordinate passions, lies as it were in women's blood. Magical powers seen to reside in women's life-cycle crises on account of their menstruation, have always contributed to their sense of otherness, as Mauss has pointed out (Mauss 1950: 27). In times of fear and trouble these magical powers, always awe-inspiring, come to be seen as the sources of evil and malevolence. If till at least the middle of the eighteenth century, the devil's work in natural disease—it was being reasoned—worked, as we have seen earlier in this paper, through a predisposition in the blood, the clustering together of issues surrounding blood must be cataclysmic for women.

Magic lies in the transitions, the nodal points of a woman's life-cycle. The appearance of blood, its disappearance, its migrations invite attention. These flows of blood bode well for the body. Menstruation provides in terms of health, a source of purification of noxious humours, a source of renewal in its periodic return. These features are of medical value, the natural counterpart of venesection and bloodletting which functioned as treatment for varied problems, not the least of which was the easing of sexual passions of celibate monks.

The question of sexuality is explicitly addressed in the older texts we have looked at. Chadwick raises the question of the monthly neurosis which occurs in tandem with the sudden intensification of libido which occurs at or around the menstrual period. The bracketing of the paramenstruum (the pre-menstrual phase combined with the duration of menstruation) is specially equated with an increase in sexual desire. The correlation that Frank finds between pre-menstrual tension and 'excess female sex hormone' in the blood and urine of women thus signals the translation of sexual desire into the language of hormones. Young Lisa Hunt will describe herself as being at her sexual peak with 'all those hormones running around'.

From the hypothesis of excess female sex hormone in the blood (Frank 1931) to that of cyclic changes in sodium and hence water metabolism controlled by the oestradiol levels relative to progesterone that is the oestradiol/progesterone ratio (Dalton and Greene 1953) the question of heightened sexuality can be read through the central focus on the contrast between estrogen and progesterone or the progesterone deficiency hypothesis as it comes to be termed. While today progesterone therapy is being discarded and a more sophisticated explanation in terms of neurotransmitters such as opiods and serotonin is being articulated (Yen and Jaffe 1991: 297), the advocacy of progesterone for at least the last thirty-five years points to the persistence of a logic encoded in it.

Estrogen and progesterone levels come to conceptually stand in a simple binary way for the essential components of women's sexual and reproductive processes.[15] From being hypothesized and isolated as those hormones responsible (1) for sexuality: *estrus* or heat and (2) for pregnancy: *pro-gestation*. At the next level these come to symbolize a condensation of the alternations and complexities of the cycle, to represent woman in her different aspects.[16] Thus in sufferers of PMS as the progesterone levels are proportionately far lower than estrogen levels, progesterone is recommended: a nurturance-inducing antidote to the sexuality-heightening estrogen.

Dalton's text (1979) appears then as an elaborate decoding of the scientific shorthand 'estrogen versus progesterone'. Her contrast between estrogen deficiency as against progesterone deficiency explains the difference between those who suffer pain (spasmodic dysmenorrhoea) and those who suffer PMS respectively. The tables in which this is mapped, the commentary about the women who exemplify both types can be read as a veritable allegory on women suffering along differing modalities. Where the estrogen-deficient suffer pain, the progesterone-deficient suffer from the pre-menstrual syndrome (ibid.: 134–7). This is the hypothesis before other 'substances' such as prostaglandins were posited as the cause of pain in the 1980s.

Significantly, while other therapeutic strategies were advocated for PMS: androgens, Vitamin B and diuretics—both androgen, the male hormone and Vitamin B prescribed to improve the liver's ability to inactivate estrogens are aimed at the opposing of estrogen (Dalton and Greene 1953: 1014). Thus the language of hormones, it will be seen, addresses issues of sexuality and fertility in a new way without having to resort to the language of social life and its arrangements.

Emily Martin's review of PMS connects it to the question of the ordering of time in modern industrial society where no allowance is made for time unconnected to work discipline. She argues that the medical arguments focus on the negative implications of women's altered responses during the pre-menstrual phase. The pre-menstrual phase may be a time of a very different notion of work: creative and building on enhanced sensitivity. Using cross-cultural material Martin suggests that taboos take cognizance of this altered time making for different uses of this time. Freed from routine chores women attend to other activities. Beng women cook special dishes at this time. Martin also refers to the important Yurok Indian case of Thomas Buckley which showed how this tribe had used the menstrual phase for spiritual practices. Contemporary writers such as Shuttle and Redgrove reason that the experience of this phase can also be a moment of truth flaring into the consciousness (Martin 1987: 123–35).

Clearly, the pre-menstrual phase combines in itself both negative and positive possibilities. It is not so much a period of dual potential as in the very nature of potential itself.[17] The medicalization of the pre-menstrual phase masks the truth of this phase. It by definition, fixes the negative pole and offers this as an accurate picture of the nature of women's bodies and experience inasmuch as its reality is dependent on social arrangements of time and symbolic conventions that underlie the highlighting of one face of Eve rather than the other. This phase can be a moment of truth flaring into the consciousness or it can be, in the absence of social or personal recognition and adaptation, evoke just so much noise.

However, when we draw on examples from tribes to establish the truth about the menstrual cycle and its phases we run the risk of decontextualizing these examples from the particular society's modes of thought and codes of conduct that they are embedded in. Perhaps to then talk of truth and noise is to draw conclusions of one sort and not another. For the examples belong to worlds in which nature and environment on the one hand and the human body on the other are mediated by different social practices.

Savyasaachi's account of the Hill Maria of Bastar suggests that in a society where shifting cultivation is practised and fallow periods are built into agricultural practice, both cultivation and menstrual cycles are bound up with the self-regeneration of nature. The menstrual period when women go to live in menstrual huts outside the village is a period of fallow, both periods signifying 'the recuperation of fertility although both create an illusion of barrenness (no crop from the fallow land and no activity on the part of the menstruating woman). But the illusion, in fact, confirms what it negates, i.e., fertility and reproductivity, (Savyasaachi 1993: 65).

VIII

THE WITCH IN THE CATEGORY

This archaeology has traversed the distance from disease to evil.[18] It has moved from PMT through hysteria and melancholy to the heretical figure of the witch. This archaeology has been undertaken not through a Foucauldian archive, but through the different cognitive worlds that can be discerned in it, using the configuration of symptoms and symbols yielded up by fieldwork and texts as our guides into this area.

The three worlds that the witch, melancholic and hysteric, the woman suffering from PMS inhabit are treated ideal-typically. Chronologically they overlap, they are not structural transformations of each other but each one represents the stages and transformations through which the questions of menstruation and womanhood pass.

The witch figure of the Inquisition and *Malleus Maleficarum* disappears. The witch that Sigmund Freud and Mary Chadwick, among others, are able to conjure up after the witch-hunts cease, can only be looked at dispassionately, scientifically after an interregnum of repression, amnesia or simply the passage of time; also, one in which evil has become a medical problem. H.C. Lea begins assembling the materials on witchcraft and the Inquisition as a moral and scholarly task at the turn of the century. The witch that Mary Chadwick resurrects focuses on her menstruation, her sexuality and her aggressive impulses which lead her to injure. The question of blood, desire and destructiveness disappears into the language of monthly neurosis, tension, progesterone deficiency, estrogen and progesterone levels on the one hand and threats to domestic harmony and costs to the economy on the other. Synecdocally, hormones rage.

Yesterday's medieval witch is not today's pre-menstrual or menopausal sufferer. But historically and symbolically she is important to the focus that blood, desire and destructiveness come to have for classification to proceed in a certain direction. To say there is a witch in the category is to recapitulate the historical process and the cognitive shifts by which we come to our present medical categories. It is not to deny a biological basis for the PMS. It is to urge us to examine the direction that medicalization takes and for what subliminal reasons. While Martin focuses on rage and work-discipline and Rodin on hysteria, this paper's focus on the witch provides the missing dimension of the question of woman's blood, sexuality and destructiveness central to this category. The questions of temporary insanity and incompetence in the work place—extremely important to the emergence of this category in the modern period—are ones we have only alluded to in this paper.

When 'witch' is used by men and women to symbolize rage or a temperamental woman, a convention is unthinkingly followed. This convention is the metonymy of menstrual blood–woman–witch that operates when speaking of women 'at that time of the month'. In the modern world the unreflective use of the term corresponds more to the angry witch of the fairy-tale. If the figure of the medieval witch is reclaimed and elaborated consciously it is in the articulation of the Earth-Mother, Mother-Goddess tradition which bases itself on the view that Christianity had demonized these earlier religions. This reading of history forms the grounds for a modern cult looking to 'other' traditions of self-knowledge and healing, contributing to the continuing discourse on the nature of women's bodies and consciousness, opening a new chapter in the history of sexuality and femininity.

ACKNOWLEDGEMENTS

I owe a debt of gratitude to Savyasaachi, Sarbani Sarkar, Anuradha Shah Veeravalli and Srinivas Veeravalli, Tarini Bahadur, Raema Sood and Dr Amrit Srinivasan for their help in the writing and revision of this paper. Fieldwork in USA was made possible by a United Nations University/WIDER grant through the active support of Dr Frédérique Apffel Marglin and Prof. Stephen Marglin, as also by the generosity of 'Dr Campion' and the women in my field. I acknowledge the gifts of my teachers Prof. J.P.S. Uberoi and Dr Mohammad Talib, to my work.

GLOSSARY

amenorrhoea	: the absence of menstruation for two months or more
androgen	: male hormone
denidation	: literally de-nesting, endometrial sloughing
desquamation	: the coming off in scales of skin or in this case of the endometrium
diuretic	: substance or drug that increases the output of urine
dysmenorrhoea	: painful periods
dyspareunia	: pain with sexual intercourse, frequently a symptom of endometriosis
endometriosis	: condition in which cells of the endometrium become displaced on to the outer lining of the uterus, ovary or abdomen; continuing to respond to menstrual hormones, they cannot shed so accumulate as tiny cysts leading to scarring. This causes great pain and leads to infertility
endometrium	: innermost lining of the uterus
estrogen (estrin, oestrin, oestradiol)	: female sex hormone produced by the ovaries. In its natural or synthetic form produces oestrin, changes connected with menstruation and pregnancy. Name derived from *estrus*, the zoological term for heat, from the Latin word indicating gadfly and hence frenzy. *Oestradiol* is a naturally occurring estrogen. *Oestrin* is an earlier name for estrogen
hyperplasia	: abnormal enlargement of part caused by increase in the number of cells
late luteal phase	: of the four phases of the menstrual cycle—follicular, ovulatory, luteal and menstrual, the late luteal phase is approximately days prior to the start of the menses. In the absence of the implantation of a fertilized ovum, a sharp linear decline in progesterone, estrogen and other hormones occurs resulting in endometrial sloughing or menstruation
progesterone	: female sex hormone produced by the corpus luteum in the ovary causing the lining of the uterus to thicken and other bodily changes necessary before conception can occur
vasomotor symptoms	: those which take place on account of the action of nerves on the diameter of blood vessels, e.g. palpitations.

NOTES

1. This section emphasizes the break that denidation makes from menstruation as flow which makes it possible to talk of the menstrual cycle in a strict endocrinological sense. A Foucauldian sensibility is implicit in the reading of material from the history of medicine chronicling both the history of endocrinology and gynaecology which discuss the phenomenon of menstruation. The work of Medvei (1982), Corner (1951) and Parkes (1965) falls in the first category. The work of Freind (1729), Eccles (1982) and Laqueur (1990) falls in the second. Cianfrani (1960) contributes to both. The first set provides information about the key researchers mentioned here. While it is customary to focus on either menstruation as part of the discourse of blood as Laqueur does (1990) or as endometrial sloughing, I focus on the implications of the discontinuities that this definitive break makes for our comprehension of the menstrual cycle. To talk of the differences between theories of plethora, that is the removal of excess blood, and purging, that is the purification of blood, as Crawford does (1981: 50–3) does not detract from the overarching discourse on blood.

2. Ilza Veith's work on hysteria (1965) is an essential text alongside which I have read the birth of endocrinology.

3. Freud's reading of the *Malleus Maleficarum* is taken up in the work of Catherine Clement (1986) who emphasizes the centrality of hysterics and sorceress as figures of women in the western world.

4. I base myself here on Crawfurd (1915) and Wright (1921).

5. I observed over a hundred doctor/patient interactions in the OB/GYN (Obstetrics and Gynaecology) Out-Patient Department and a doctor's private practice in the same specialization and hospital. At the out-patient facility there was a greater variation in terms of class and race, than at the doctor's practice which drew on a largely middle-class and upper-middle-class white population. Of this the White Anglo-Saxon Protestant group was the largest. The same was reflected in the group of women I interviewed.

6. The cultural nature of illness experience is best presented by Good and Del Vecchio Good (1981). The discussion on culture-bound syndromes for instance, in Psychiatry in *Social Science and Medicine* 1992, 35(1) introduced by Charles Nuckolls goes further than other formulations in positing a Durkheimian homology between social structures and classification systems.

7. I follow Press who argues against setting western biomedicine apart from all other systems which are to be labelled ethnomedicine. 'The implication of such usage is that non-Western medicine is culturally generated, while biomedicine is a natural system of some sort, and independent of ideological, cultural genesis' (Press 1980: 45). That modern scientific and rational knowledge presents itself as the self-existent storehouse of truth and it is *sui generis*, the only one of its kind, the rest charmingly called 'ethnoscience' at best and false superstition and darkest ignorance at the worst, has been the burden of J.P.S. Uberoi's argument in *Science and Culture* (1978: 14).

8. In the extracts from my interviews, I use three dots '...' to indicate pauses in the conversation, not my editing of it.

9. Co-counselling is a formal system of reciprocal lay counselling.

10. Historically, the Holy Family comes to be important from the fifteenth century. While matrimony becomes a sacrament only in 1563 through the Council of Trent, it must be remembered that the Church position on marriage and procreation was in direct contradistinction to the Cathars who believed that to beget children continued the Devil's work, in that it perpetuated the material universe. The roots of the Tridentine decision run back deeper in time at least to the twelfth century (Warner 1983: 188, 144–5). In the modern context Lloyd Warner's work focuses on the importance of the family in his chapter 'Sacred Sexuality—the Mother, the Father and Their Family' (Warner, W. Lloyd, 1961: Ch. 7).

11. The witch was originally conceived as old, unmarried or widowed, and post-menopausal. She comes to be the young pubertal girl as well over time. If most, if not all, witches were women, then all women could be witches. Not only the cessation of the menses but their first appearance caused women to be witch-like as also the periodic return of this flow.

12. For Epilepsy and Neurology, I base myself on *The Falling Sickness* (Temkin 1945).

13.See for instance, John Freind's *Emmenologia* (1729) and Eccles for Jane Sharp (1982: 75).

14. This Weberian and Foucauldian synthesis on the rationalization of the body and the world is implicit in the work of Bryan Turner (1984). The question of linearity and cyclicality is addressed in Martin (1987) and Oudshoorn (1990). I draw my own conclusions on the subject.

15. The complexity of the two hormones, their interaction with each other and other hormones is not being denied. The contrast between them is cognitively significant for reproductive endocrinology as for the argument in this paper.

16. Parkes points out that once crystalline progestin was isolated in 1934 the idea of a single female hormone believed in by several endocrinologists, finally disappeared (1965: xxiv).

17. I owe this formulation to Anuradha Shah Veeravalli. This entire section owes a great deal to conversations with her.

18.The journey from evil to disease has been postulated by historians and philosophers of medicine such as Owsei Temkin (1973) and Georges Canguilhem (1966).

REFERENCES

Barthes, Roland, 1988, Semiology and medicine in item, *The Semiotic Challenge*, Basil Blackwell, Oxford: 202–13.

Canguilhem, Georges, 1978, *On the Normal and the Pathological* (trans. Carolyn Fawcett) Reidel, Dordrecht.

Chadwick, Mary, 1932, *The Psychological Effects of Menstruation*. Nervous and Mental Disease Monograph Series no. 56, Nervous and Mental Disease Publishing Company, New York and Washington.

Cianfrani, Theodore, 1960, *A Short History of Obstetrics and Gynecology*, Charles C. Thomas, Springfield, Ill.

Clement, Catherine, 1986, The guilty one, in H. Cixous and C. Clement, *The Newly Born Woman* (trans. Betsy Wing), University of Minnersota Press, Minneapolis: 1–59.

Corner, George, 1951, Our knowledge of the menstrual cycle, 1910–1950, *The Lancet*, 28 April: 919–23.

Crawford, Patricia, 1981, Attitudes to menstruation in seventeenth-Century England, *Past and Present*. 91: 47–73.

Crawfurd, Raymond, 1915, Superstitions of menstruation. *The Lancet*, 18 December.

Dalton, Katharina, 1979, *Once a Month*, Hunter House, Pomona, Cal..

—— and R. Greene, 1953, The Premenstrual Syndrome. *British Medical Journal* 1: 1007–14.

Delaney, Janice, M. J. Lupton and Emily Toth, 1976, *The Curse. A cultural history of menstruation*, E.P. Dutton, New York.

Eccles, Audrey, 1982, *Obstetrics and Gynaecalogy in Tudor and Stuart England*, Croom Helm, London.

Foucault, Michel, 1972, *The Archaeology of Knowledge* (trans. A.M. Sheridan,) Pantheon Books, New York.

——, 1975, *The Birth of the Clinic: An archaeology of medical perception* (trans. A.M. Sheridan) Vintage, New York.

Frank, Robert T., 1931, The hormonal causes of premenstrual tension, *Archives of Neurology and Psychiatry* 26: 1053–6.

Freind, John, 1729, *Emmenologia*, (trans. Thomas Dale), T. Cox, London.

Good, Byron and Del Vecchio Good, Mary Jo., 1981, The meaning of symptoms: a cultural hermeneutic model for clinical practice, *in* Leon Eisenberg and Arthur Kleinman (eds.), *The Relevance of Social Science for Medicine*, Reidel, Dordrecht: 165–96.

Illich, Ivan., 1982, *Gender*, Pantheon, New York.

Kaufert, Patrica and Gilbert, Penny., 1986, Women, menopause and medicalization, *Culture, Medicine and Psychiatry* 10(1) Special Issue on Anthropological Approaches to Menopause: 7–21.

King, Lester, 1974, Friedrich Hoffman and some medical aspects of witchcraft, *Clio Medica* 9(4): 294–330.

King, Stephen, 1974, *Carrie*, Signet, New American Library, New York.

Kramer, Heinrich and James Sprenger, 1948 [1486], *Malleus Maleficarum*. (trans. with an Introduction, Bibliography and Notes by Montague Summers), Pushkin Press, London.

Laqueur, Thoma S., 1990, *Making Sex. Body and gender from the Greeks in Freud*, Harvard University Press, Cambridge, Mass..

Lock, Margaret, 1985, Models and practice in medicine. Menopause as syndrome or life transition? in Hahn and Gaines (eds.), *Physicians of Western Medicine*, Reidel, Dordrecht: 115–39.

Martin, Emily, 1987, *The Woman in the Body. A cultural analysis of reproduction*, Beacon Press, Boston.

Mauss, Marcel, 1972 [1950], *A General Theory of Magic*, Routledge and Kegan Paul, London.

Medvei, Victor, 1982, *A History of Endocrinology*, MTP Press, Lancaster.

Oudshoorn, Nelly, 1990, On measuring sex hormones: the role of biological assays in sexualizing chemical substances. *Bulletin of the History of Medicine*, 64: 243–61.

Parkes, A.S, 1965, The rise of reproductive endocrinology, 1926–1940. The Sir Henry Dale Lecture for 1965. *Journal of Endocrinology* 34(3) Proc. Soc. Endocrinol. xx–xxxii.

Press, Irwin, 1980, Problems in the definition and classification of medical systems. *Social Science and Medicine* 148(1): 45–58.

Rodin, Mari, 1992, The social construction of premenstrual syndrome. *Social Science and Medicine* 35(1): 49–56.

Savyasaachi, 1993, An alternative system of knowledge: fields and forests in Abujhmarh, in Tariq Banuri and F. A. Marglin (eds.), *Who Will Save the Forests? Knowledge, power and environmental destruction*, Zed Books, London: 53–79.

Temkin, Owsei, 1945, *The Falling Sickness. A history of epilepsy from the Greeks to the beginning of modern neurology*, Johns Hopkins Press, Baltimore.

——, 1973, Health and disease. *Dictionary of the History of Ideas*, II: 395-406.

Turner, Bryan, 1984, *The Body and society, Explorations in Social Theory*, Basil Blackwell, Oxford.

Uberoi, J.P.S., 1978, *Science and Culture*, Oxford University Press, New Delhi.

Updike, John, 1984, *The Witches of Eastwick*, Knopf, New York.

Veith, Ilza, 1965, *Hysteria. The history of a disease*, University of Chicago.

Warner, Marina, 1983, *Alone of All her Sex. The myth and the cult of the Virgin Mary*, Vintage Books, New York.

Warner, W. Lloyd, 1961, *The Family of God. A symbolic study of Christian life in America*, Yale University Press, New Haven.

Wood, Charles T., 1981, The doctor's dilemma: sin, salvation, and the menstrual cycle in medieval thought *Speculum* 56(4): 710–27.

Wright, Jonathan, 1921, The views of primitive peoples concerning menstruation. A review of literature. *American Journal of Obstetrics and Gynecology* 1(4): 400–2.

Yen, S.S.C. and Robert Jaffe, (eds.), 1991, *Reproductive Endocrinology, Physiology, Pathophysiology and Clinical Management*, W.B. Saunders Philadelphia.

Prostitution
The Contemporary Feminist Discourse

Jean D'Cunha

INTRODUCTION

The issue of prostitution and trafficking (for the same) has once again caught international attention since the 1980s, generating vociferous and sharply polarized international debate. As women from the South, active in the women's movement and sensitive to the concerns of women in prostitution, it is imperative that we familiarize ourselves with the nuances of this discourse, so as to evolve a feminist perspective from the South on the issue of prostitution and sex trafficking. This will facilitate meaningful action and strategy that is grounded in, and responsive to our realities.

The urgency of this exercise is further prompted by the fact that theorizing on the issue of prostitution has, till recently, largely been a western feminist enterprise, with critical consequences for the lives and practice of women in our parts of the globe.

This working paper is, therefore, an attempt firstly to critically evaluate existing feminist constructions of prostitution and outline elements of a Southern women's perspective on prostitution located within the context of the political economy of women's reproductive labour and sexuality (Sanghera 1990: 22–3) and the inequitous North-South dimensions of the issue. Central to this exercise is the need to grasp the historically specific and interactive processes of (1) incorporation of women's reproductive labour into the sex service sector/industry; (2) the construction of sexuality and its appropriation by the dominant discourse; and (3) the systematic denigration of women and cultures by constructing the 'other', through potent structurally determined ethnic constructs like race, etc.

As the elements of such a perspective have largely been based on the reality of prostitution in parts of South and South-East Asia and not primarily on India specifically, indigenous structural categories like the prostitution-caste linkage have not been explored here, which constitutes a limitation of this working paper.

I

THE CONTAGIOUS DISEASES ACTS

Public opinion and debate on prostitution and trafficking today is far from new, shaped in many ways as it is by the Repeal Campaign and the Social Purity Crusade pioneered in nineteenth-century England, in opposition to England's Contagious Diseases Acts (CD Acts). It is, therefore, necessary to briefly plough back into history to grasp the significance of these Acts and the kind of resistance they generated, for this in a sense informs contemporary constructions of the prostitute and prostitution, in Present legal systems and the contemporary feminist discourse on prostitution.

England's Contagious Diseases Acts of 1864, 1866 and 1869 were introduced to control prostitution and the spread of venereal diseases (VD) among enlisted men in English garrison towns and ports. The acts legalized prostitution, while simultaneously subjecting women in prostitution to a system of compulsory registration with provincial authorities and mandatory health checks for VD (Walkowitz 1980: 1–2).

The pragmatism that underscored the CD Acts was, however, simultaneously grounded in and undermined by a set of moral and ideological assumptions. For in demanding the medical examination of women in prostitution, without imposing periodic genital examinations on enlisted men, i.e., the clients, architects of the Acts reinforced a double standard of male sexual morality that (1) upheld the patriarchal belief in a naturally active male sex drive; (2) set aside a class of public women to contain this 'irrepressible' sexuality; (3) sanctioned male sexual access to a class of 'fallen' women, who provided 'sanitized sex'—all in the interests of reconciling 'male sexual drive' with military efficiency and the preservation of male institutions (D'Cunha 1991). Ironically, women in prostitution were discriminatorily penalized for this while clients were not. It is pertinent to observe that an earlier attempt to introduce periodic medical examination among soldiers had failed, as enlisted men violently objected to this and officers feared that compulsory examination would whittle down the morale of their men. Evidently male bonding and a shared male identity cutting across class, ethnic and rank divisions played a major role in determining attitudes to male sexuality and official policy towards the military man's sexuality (Enloe 1983). By contrast it was contended that such objections could not apply to prostitutes, who were presumably bereft of 'self-respect' and powerless to protect this intrusion (Walkowitz 1980: 3).

In any case targeting the woman in prostitution, to the exclusion of the client, did not help achieve the medical goal of controlling the spread of VD (Walkowitz 1980).

The significance of this cultural interpretation of the Acts notwithstanding, it is of paramount importance to understand them in specific time-space coordinates, for the Acts were instituted at a nodal juncture in English history that coincided with the 'spreading web of capitalist relations of production and exchange, the formation and consolidation of new classes and the class tensions that this engendered; bourgeois concern over the political mobilization of the underclasses and obsession over the forms of family organization, sexual standards, medical care and moral instruction by which they would safeguard their property and profits and reproduce the social structure; the politics of nationhood and redefinition of the citizen in the nation'. (Cooper and Stoler 1989: 610–11.)

The class politics of late nineteenth century Europe resulted in a profusion of debates by scientists, social reformers and State agents over the biological and moral nature of the rapidly expanding European working class populations (ibid.). Against this backdrop, the concern with prostitution, and women in prostitution reflects another crucial ideological component of the regulationist position—decisive State intervention into the lives of the unrespectable poor. As Judith Walkowitz puts it,

both women in prostitution and enlisted men were members of the "social residuum"—the casual labouring poor who inhabited the "nether regions" of society. A source of cheap labour and illicit pleasure for middle class Victorians, this social under-world was also the focus of deep seated social fears and insecurities most vividly expressed in the images of the filth and contagion associated with "Great Unwashed". Pollution became the governing metaphor for the perils of social intercourse between the "two nations". It assumed heightened scatological significance in a society where the poor seemed to be living in their own excrement, and where the first programmatic attempt to deal with urban social problems was in the realm of sanitary engineering. Literally, and figuratively the prostitute was the conduit of infection to respectable society. She was none the less, the object of class guilt and fear, a powerful symbol of sexual and economic exploitation under industrial capitalism. (Prostitution in Victorian Society 1980: 3–4.)

The CD Acts thus reflect a view of the socially under-privileged as degraded and powerless, yet potentially threatening and disloyal. As military reforms, the Acts were linked to a deliberately designed policy creating a professional bachelor army and navy without family ties or local identities. This, it was hoped, would foster single-minded devotion enhancing efficiency, as well as to help contain military budgets. Military authorities additionally hoped that providing enlisted men controlled outlets for heterosexual activity, would act as a brake on homosexuality in the ranks as well. For their part, local civilian officials enthusiastically endorsed the Acts as a means of controlling street disorders and disciplining the unrespectable civilian poor in the community (ibid.: 4).

Through the control of sexuality, the Acts reinforced patterns of class and gender domination. They demonstrate the obsessive preoccupation with and modification of sex that according to Michel Foucault,

distinguished Victorian sexuality from the official sexual code of earlier epochs. The modern debate over sex, was a strategy for exercising power in society. By ferreting out areas of illicit sexual activity, a new technology of power and "science of sexuality" were created that facilitated control over an ever widening circle of human activity. The "new sense of sexuality" identified sex as a public issue; rigidly differentiated male from female sexuality; focused attention on extra-marital sexuality as the primary area of dangerous sexual activity; and "incorporated" perversions in individuals who, like the homosexual were now accorded an exclusive and distinct sexual identity'. (ibid.)

The CD Acts embodied and related these shifts in focus and concern, for under them, extra-marital sex became a question of State policy and national importance. A complicated 'technology of power' was established to oversee and manipulate the social lives of the unrespectable poor. Special controls were placed on the female body, in that women in prostitution, not their male clients were identified as the primary source of disease and pollution. This medical and police supervision in turn created an outcaste class of 'sexually deviant' females, forcing women in prostitution to acknowledge their status as 'public' women and destroying their private associations with the general community of the labouring poor (ibid.: 5).

However, while the CD Acts created a 'technology of power' they also unleashed mammoth social and political resistance, in the form of the Repeal Campaign and the Social Purity crusades that drew the struggle against licensed brothels and 'white slave traffic' for prostitution into the ambit of international debate and action (ibid: 5). It eventually resulted in the formulation and adoption by the United Nations of the Convention of the Suppression of Traffic in Persons and of the Exploitation of the Prostitution of Others in 1949. United Nations member States who subsequently ratified the convention and were signatories to it, framed national and local laws, in conformity with the convention, to deal with the suppression of traffic for prostitution.

II

THE REPEAL CAMPAIGN

The Repeal Campaign, which by 1880 grew into a formidable force to reckon with, was far from monolithic in its composition and ideological orientation—constituted as it was by middle-class women organized into the Ladies National Association, middle-class males and working-class radicals. While the campaign did make the prostitute, thus far invisible, the focal point of international discourse on sexual politics; and while the more liberal within the movement defended women in prostitution as victims of social injustice rather than as criminal miscreants; and protested against male sexual licence as an expression of the double standards of male sexual morality, and opposed police repression of solicitation by women in prostitution as a dangerous extension of State power and a discriminatory measure directed solely at women rather than male profligates (ibid.: 140), the movement was not without its contradictions, couched as it finally was within a moralistic and victimology perspective.

For while women Repealers defended women in prostitution at a certain level, and women's larger right to a legal, political and economic identity beyond the family, they failed to fully challenge fundamental Victorian assumptions related to women's sex roles and separate spheres. Emphasizing women's purity, moral pre-eminence and domestic virtue, they eulogized women as sacrosanct wives and upheld a single standard of chastity (ibid. 117). In fact the principal female spokesperson for repeal came to be a wife and mother, though mature single women of prominence were time and again invited to join (ibid.: 120).

Stories of instrumental rape, false entrapment, pitiful suicides were widely publicized to appeal to public sentiment. Registered women were projected as innocent victims of male lust, medical and police tyranny. Women in prostitution thus came to be treated as objects of solicitude, even by middle-class moralists who condemned the Acts for legitimizing vice (ibid.: 1980: 140).

Male and female repealers did advocate certain legal measures restricting trade in vice, like increasing the age of consent and punishing seducers and third-party managements (ibid.).

As sensational stories of prostituted children and traffic in white women had propagandist value and as it was found politically expedient to depict 'fallen women' as inert victims of evil machinations, Repealers failed to address the socio-economic and political bases of prostitution. They consequently stressed the casual nature of prostitution as a stop-gap measure for women in dire financial straits. It was the regulationist system, they argued, that deemed women to a life of sin by publicly stigmatizing them and preventing them from finding alternate employment. 'Voluntary prostitution' had no place in this perspective. It is not surprising, therefore, that women Repealers were often indignant when confronted with women in prostitution who refused to be rescued or reformed (ibid.: 132).

Though the Repeal Campaign was largely able to structure the public discourse on sex and arouse popular ire at male sexual licence, it was appropriated and rechannelled into repressive anti-vice campaigns. The history of the Repeal Campaign does not end triumphantly with the removal of the CD Acts from statute books in 1886, but more ominously with the rise of Social Purity crusades and police crackdown on street prostitutes and brothel-keepers (ibid.: 145, 146–253).

III

THE SOCIAL PURITY MOVEMENT

The Social Purity movement that emerged towards the end of the nineteenth century in England, The Netherlands, Imperial Germany and the USA was trapped within the confines of a moralistic perspective on prostitution constructing the issue in terms of the immorality of traffic, promiscuity, vice and emotional indifference (Chauvin C. 1982). Its primary concern was to restore public morality and combat the social evil of prostitution. It perceived the prostitute as the repository of vice, placing the moral burden and onus of action on the individual women in prostitution.

Moreover, the Social Purity Movement initially addressed itself solely to trafficking in western women, between countries in Western Europe and USA and from here on to the colonies. While colonial administrators generally agreed on the evil of traffic as a means of supplying sexual services in prostitution, they perceived traffic in local women and children for prostitution as a product of cultural backwardness of the colonized population (Commission of Enquiry into Traffic in Women and Children in the Far East—1933). This artificial distinction between international and local traffic in women and children for prostitution was marked by cultural chauvinism and racism. So too colonial governments' positions on prostitution in licensed brothels varied.

Some United Nations member States like the United Kingdom and The Netherlands, which signed and ratified the Convention for the Suppression of Traffic in Women and Children, 1921, did so on behalf of their colonies as well. They adopted the abolitionist line and shut down licensed brothels in their colonies. Brothel-keeping and soliciting in the street for prostitution were consequently penalized under the crimes of immoral earnings and vagrancy respectively. Other United Nations member States like France pursued the regulationist system in colonies like Indo-China, permitting licensed brothels and enforcing compulsory registration of prostitutes (while imposing penalties on traffickers), for by and large licensed brothels were still considered to be a more humane means of treating women in prostitution, who were assumed to have rationally and consciously entered the profession. (ibid.).

Needless to say, the treatment of prostitutes—protective measures against their exploitation and against trafficking for prostitution—differed sharply along racial lines, in favour of white women. State control of traffic was advocated against traffickers who brought white women to the colonies for prostitution, but not at traffic within colonies. Further, the refusal by colonial administrators to recognize the relationship between the traffic in women and children and licensed brothels, as a safe burgeoning market for traffickers, only increased the vulnerability of local women in colonies who were trafficked in for prostitution. The equation of prostitution with promiscuity by consent resulted in ,stringent State control, being exercised only over the women in prostitution, while the role of client, who was an active participant was ignored. The criminalization of women for soliciting in the street, drove them into brothels where they were subject to further control and exploitation by brothel managers, pimps and the colonial State.

The situation today remains relatively unchanged for there exists an avalanche of evidence that establishes that national laws framed, in conformity with the UN Convention 1949 have largely failed in suppressing the practice of prostitution or 'immoral' traffic in women and children for prostitution (D'Cunha 1991).

Further, predominantly based on the world view of the Social Purity Movement, these laws rest on the following patriarchal assumptions:

(1) that prostitution is the oldest profession, whose universality, inevitability and necessity as a social evil is lodged in a static biological construct of sexuality, viz., male sexuality as naturally active and irrepressible, satiated in the institution of prostitution, rendering the latter functional to male biology.

This system of law designated as the tolerationist system of law, consequently does not seek to abolish prostitutes or prostitution *per se*, but is only targeted against traffic in women and children for prostitution.

(2) that prostitution is a female phenomenon (a definition that results from patriarchal socio-cultural constructions of manhood and womanhood).

(3) that prostitution emerges from the contradictions of the moral system alone and is offensive to public moral sensibilities.

(4) that the onus for such offence rests with the women in prostitution, perceived as an embodiment of promiscuity.

(5) that consequently deviance of such women from prescribed cultural standards (which are largely sexual), elicit criminal sanctions against them for soliciting publicly for prostitution.

(6) that deviance through criminal sanctions can be combined with 'rehabilitation and reformation of offenders' through protective homes and corrective institutions.

To begin with, criminal sanctions against the women in prostitution contradict the declared spirit of the Act, that does not seek to penalize prostitutes or prostitution *per se.*

Further, while the act of prostitution is legal, penalties for loitering and soliciting render it difficult to work. For a woman cannot make contact with her client legally. Even more discriminatory is the fact that while both women in prostitution and clients are active participants in the act of soliciting, it is only the woman who is subject to the legal process.

Criminalizing women in prostitution constricts and reinforces their subjective identity as social deviants, reinforcing a prostitute subculture which is morally outcaste. This drives many a woman to operate more discreetly and clandestinely, using fictitious names and addresses. One can only speculate on the effect of constant shifting between real and work designated identities or between restricted and open activity, on those who remain in the profession for long. The value extracted from women in prostitution, facilitated by a process of making it invisible, renders the woman even more dependent on and vulnerable to the exploitation of commercial enterprises and vested interests who appropriate gain from the trade of sex and women's bodies. The woman's physical mobility and bargaining powers too are severely restricted. The invisibility of a woman's oppression and exploitation behind closed doors is thus ensured (D'Cunha 1992).

Other controversial trends have also been observed over the last few decades. Research on prostitution laws point to distinct class, ethnic and gender biases in enforcement of criminal sanctions in prostitution. While women in prostitution are overwhelmingly penalized, clients, brothel managers, pimps and procurers remain relatively untouched (D'Cunha 1991).

Secondly, while prostitution is illegal in several countries, the same countries permit the simultaneous coexistence of a variety of legally endorsed sex-related services and establishments, in the form of escort service agencies, 'eros' centres and the like, for the contribution that this sector makes to the economies of these countries is enormous. In the meanwhile, traffic in women for prostitution continues through legally sanctioned overseas employment agencies, international mail order bride agencies and the like (personal discussions with Thai and Filipina activits, 1991).

Quite evidently the issue of prostitution and more specifically trafficking for prostitution cannot be framed within the narrow confines and concerns of the morality perspective, for such a perspective fails to distinguish between the social institution of prostitution and the individual woman in prostitution, thus concealing the economic and ideological base of the institution and its interaction with the wider socio-economic political and ideological processes. Also concealed are the individual and collective vested interests grounded in the economic system underlying prostitution.

The static and ahistorical assumptions of the moralist point of view are unable to capture the processes of social transformation that impact women as a group and result in changes in the institutional manifestations of prostitution. The failure to recognize the hierarchical structure and organized nature of the sex industry also conceals the heterogeneity and fragmentation within the prostitute population itself.

The moralist and institutionalist perspective that resonate in our prostitution laws, inevitably result in placing the onus of social blight and invisibility on the individual woman in prostitution, compelling her to resolve the contradiction between social necessity and social unacceptability.

Critical of such a moralistic perspective on prostitution is the contemporary feminist discourse on prostitution of which one such construction is an understanding of prostitution as an expression of sexual politics.

IV

PROSTITUTION AS AN EXPRESSION OF SEXUAL POLITICS

This view treats the socio-cultural constructions of gender as an extension of biological sex differences and is grounded in the assumptions of the primacy of antagonistic contradictions between the sexes, that stands disconnected from class analysis. These contradictions, characterized by a relationship of male domination and female subjugation, derive from male control over female sexuality, operationalized through patriarchal sexual norms, practices and social institutions like the family and prostitution, that either deny woman's sexuality or sexually objectify and violate women (Mackinnon 1982; Millet 1971). Patriarchal cultures by and large deem sex a male right, thereby legitimizing sexual violence and aggression against women.

This violence and aggression against women inheres in a variety of locales including prostitution. Prostitution is thus perceived as another form of male violence against women, on a continuum of other forms of violence and abuse of women such as wife bashing, rape, pornography and the like and is functional to male cultural hegemony (Mackinnon 1982).

By thus asserting a condition of oppression common to all women, this formulation challenges the artificial divide between 'Madonna and Whore'. Moreover it views a woman's entry into prostitution in terms of force and violence—the product of well-designed strategies employed by individuals and organized trafficking networks, taking optimum advantage of women's economic impoverishment and emotional vulnerability (Barry 1981). Finally as male control and manipulation over female sexuality is seen as the basis for male domination, violence and aggression against women, this view advocates a determined struggle against any and every practice or institution sustaining the same (ibid.).

The strength of this approach lies in its female-centreness; its foregrounding of male sexual promiscuity and violence against women as male constructions and expressions of patriarchy. However, the focus on patriarchy as the single analytical framework to understand prostitution to the exclusion of the economic, political and ethnic bases of the phenomenon renders this approach inadequate. The economic basis of prostitution and its interaction with wider social processes and transformations including the inequitous North-South relationship and its impact on women remain concealed. Also consequently, masked are the newer forms of deprivation and impoverishment and the increasing diversification of the institutional manifestations of prostitution, that accompany socio-economic transformations and the ordering of global relationships. Further concealed is the heterogeneity and hierarchy of interests within the sex service sector between its organizers/controllers and women in prostitution on one hand and within the prostitute population, on the other. Why and how female sexuality comes to acquire a value also goes unaddressed.

There is consequently no space in this approach to understand prostitution as a form of labour. Moreover, all women in prostitution are designated as victims of patriarchal oppression and all forms of prostitution are simplistically and uniformly reduced to conditions of force and violence. Finally, at the level of political praxis, adherents of this position are confronted with the following dilemma: how does one support and work with women who for a large spectrum of reasons continue to operate within the sex service sector, without at the same time supporting the institution of prostitution? Yet another feminist construction of prostitution, that has emerged partly in response to an understanding of prostitution as an expression of sexual politics, is an analysis of prostitution as an expression of relative self-determination for women.

V

PROSTITUTION AS AN EXPRESSION OF RELATIVE AUTONOMY AND SELF-DETERMINATION

This position is framed within the contours of the sex role theory and liberal feminism. It asserts that patriarchal oppression and female sexual objectification are conditions common to all women (Truong 1990: 48). This position points to the similarities in the role and position of 'straight women' and women in prostitution, arguing that the madonna-whore divide is an artificial construction. For ultimately prostitution utilizes the same attributes of the female sex role towards the same ends (Rosenblum 1975: 169–85).

In the context of a patriarchally structured and operative job market marked by male preference in jobs and a limited range of gender-stereotyped, poorly paid, low-status occupational choices available to women, women's entry into prostitution is understood as an entrepreneurial or conscious-rational choice (Rozenblum 1975; McLeod 1982).

Given the prevailing socio-economic structure, wherein most occupations for women reflect the patriarchally defined female role, grounded in marriage, prostitution and various forms of sex-stereotyped wage work, women in prostitution must not be castigated as the only women opting for work that in some ways endorses male dominance.

Taking sexual discrimination against women and their consequent marginalization as its point of departure, this view frames the issue of prostitution in terms of double standards of male sexual morality designed to repress and control female sexuality and discrimination in the job market. Viewing the operationalization of this discrimination informally through patriarchal norms/practices and formally through the mechanism of the legal system, it makes a strong case against the stigmatization of women in prostitution as the social residuum (World Charter for Prostitutes Rights; 1988).

Against this background, it asserts that our struggle should be directed towards demanding legal reforms, that recognize prostitution as a valid form of labour and at safeguarding women in prostitution against discriminatory and exploitative practices. This view conse-quently defines the struggle for rights of women in prostitution and the right to prostitute, as an expression of a prostitute's basic right to self-determination, liberty and autonomy of all kinds, including sexual (ibid.).

Thus while traffickers in persons for the purpose of prostitution must be prosecuted through specially formulated trafficking laws, delinked from other laws governing prostitution, 'free choice' pros-titution must be decriminalized, i.e., totally removed from the pur-view of criminal sanctions or State regulation through zoning laws and mandatory registration, the breach of which incurs penal sanc-tions against prostitutes. Prostitution businesses must, in fact, be subjected to the same labour laws (and not criminal laws), that other businesses are subject to (ibid.).

Constructed within the framework of liberal feminism, this perspec-tive views sexual discrimination as given and operative through formal and informal socio-cultural practices. As the political economy of gender discrimination and for that matter prostitution is left unex-plored, it can at best only address itself to reform of unfair legal prac-tices against women in prostitution and a challenge to their moral stigmatization (Truong 1990: 49).

The inability of this position to draw the connection between the economic base of prostitution and wider socio-economic and political processes and transformations, as a determinant of chang-ing institutional manifestations of prostitution, has resulted in posit-ing the rigidly dichotomous categories of 'free choice' and 'forced prostitution'—categories disassociated from the institutional arran-gement within which the act of prostitution takes place and the socio-economic background of the woman in prostitution. It is, therefore, necessary to deconstruct the structural factors and mechanisms conditioning a woman's entry into and continued operation in prostitution, before we define 'free choice'. Further, empirical reality points to greater complexities in terms of degree of choice on a continuum, rather than a static mechanistic 'free-forced' dichotomy (8th ISIS—WICCE Programme on Poverty and Prostitution, 1991).

Moreover the 'free-forced' dichotomy which is largely a construct of countries of the North, attempting to normalize prostitution there as a woman's free choice, not only ignores the existence of prostitution as a result of force of economic circumstance or the use of blatant force and violence in the North, thus distorting the prostitution reality there; it also ignores the fact that the principal impetus for women and children of the South to be drawn into prostitution, in fact entire communities to be plugged into the prostitution—trafficking nexus, is linked to extreme conditions of poverty, growing indigence and an abysmal lack of alternatives that are the result of imposition of western paradigms and models of development on our realities. In view of the globalization of the world order and the predicted trends of development, more communities will find themselves dispossessed and entering the circuit of poverty and shrinking choices—a situation for which this perspective contained within the liberal feminist frame work, claims no responsibility, rendering prostitution a Third World problem. Also unaddressed by this view is an existing prostitution reality in the South, characterized by greater degrees of freedom (8th ISIS—WICCE Programmes on Poverty and Prostitution 1991).

Further, the demand to recognize free-choice prostitution as an acceptable form of labour (ensuing partly from the desire to protect the individual woman in prostitution), collapses the distinction between the individual in prostitution and the social institution of prostitution. The exploitative and patriarchal basis of the institution of prostitution thus remains unchallenged (Barry, *et al.*, ed., 1983).

Moreover, whether or not prostitution is characterized by choice, the very condition of commodification of sex and women's bodies, and of distancing of the sexual experience involving the most personal and erotic parts of one's physical and psychic being from the total person, is indicative of the alienation and dehumanization of the woman in prostitution (Barry 1981). So too, even in institutional arrangements affording greater degrees of freedom to women in prostitution, a woman is subject to blatant and insidious forms of management, client, State violence. Neither are women within such institutions always totally free to determine the choice of client, their pace and rates of work or the nature of sexual activity.

The experience of Marilyn Montgomery, a Bombay-based call girl exemplifies the point. Montgomery was flung down from the sixth floor of the Yugoslavian Embassy building, Bombay by her Yugoslavian client for refusing to engage in anal sex with him (Slides by Forensic Expert Pritam Phatnani, Bombay).

Similarly discussions with German women in prostitution operating in high-grade German clubs in Frankfurt, revealed that there was a limit to the number of clients that one could refuse, before being fired by the club management. Also while many women working in the club used to refuse sadomasochistic sexual activity, they were gradually being forced to comply as a result of a loss of clients to young Asian and black women being trafficked into Germany and being forced to engage in kinky sex, in conditions of confinement and bondage, at lower rates (Personal discussions with German women in prostitution 1986).

Moreover, the proposal to introduce laws against trafficking, delinked from other laws governing prostitution, is problem-ridden in its application, for it is difficult to clearly distinguish between, 'forced' and 'free choice' prostitution. While trafficking is the principal means by which a steady supply of women's sexual labour is maintained to the sex service sector and is often related to conditions of confinement and bondage, women once induced into prostitution may later acquire internal upward mobility within the sex service sector along the free-force continuum, rendering it difficult to discern where and how to apply trafficking laws.

What is more, the decriminalization of third-party managements only legitimizes the exploitative core of the sex service sector and allows traffic in persons for prostitution to flourish. For historically there has been a link established between increase in trafficking and legalized prostitution including legalized brothel prostitution (Barry 1981).

As important to the recognition of prostitution as a form of work, is the discourse around whether it is an acceptable form of work for women, the varied social relations of work in the different institutional manifestations of prostitution, how labour is supplied for this kind of work and how we can concretely address ourselves to the concerns of women operating within the sex service sector without endorsing third-party managements and prostitution as an institution.

VI

UNDERSTANDING PROSTITUTION WITHIN THE CONTEXT OF THE POLITICAL ECONOMY OF WOMEN'S REPRODUCTIVE LABOUR/SEXUALITY AND NORTH-SOUTH RELATIONS

Against this background it is necessary to frame the issue of prostitution within the context of the political economy of women's reproductive labour and sexuality and the North-South dimensions of the phenomenon. Crucial to this enterprise as mentioned at the outset is the need to grasp:

(1) the process of incorporation of women's reproductive labour into the sex service sector/sex industry;
(2) the process of construction of sexuality and its appropriation by the dominant discourse, and
(3) the process of systematic denigration of women and cultures by constructing 'the Other' through powerful structurally determined ethnic constructs—like race, for instance (Sanghera 1990: 22–3).

Each of these three processes interacts with and feeds into one another, constituting the terrain of the problematic. Each encompasses concepts like sexuality, racism, reproductive labour—which are historically specific, dialectically and materially constituted, conditioning in turn the processes that encompass them (ibid. 23).

In examining the process whereby women's reproductive labour is incorporated into the sex service sector/industry, it is further necessary to highlight the role of ideology, the State, economic agents and the means they employ in the process. Women's sex work is examined as a specific aspect of reproductive labour and the social relations that govern and organize it. The obvious point of departure, therefore, is that women in prostitution or sex workers are not morally depraved, but the reproductive labour they engage in within the sex service sector/industry is historically specific and materially rooted.

VII

REPRODUCTIVE LABOUR

Reproductive labour is that category of labour that derives from the use of the body—particularly its sexual dimensions—as an instrument of labour. At a very general level, the value of this labour is anchored in the necessity of human beings to routinely recuperate and renew their physical, emotional and social energies so as to enhance their productive or labouring capacities (ibid). Reproductive labour embodies two principal constituents: the sexual aspect wherein biological sex is seen as a source of life (Foucault 1978: 25) and the social aspect. The sexual further encompasses two dimensions:

(1) biological procreation or reproducing the species through the physical process of birth and
(2) provision of bodily pleasure through sex.

The second dimension of women's reproductive labour—the social, covers a wide spectrum of functions for physical and emotional sustenance, such as cleaning, cooking, laundering, nurturing etc., popularly subsumed under the label 'domestic work'. The aggregate of the social and sexual dimension constitutes women's reproductive labour.

Historically, as well as currently, women's reproductive labour, or the use of women's bodies to provide various services pertaining to the physical, sexual and emotional reproduction of labour power has occurred under a diverse range of social relations of production.

Thus under slavery, in the context of master-slave relations, women were directly and blatantly coerced into being biological breeders. Under capitalist relations defined by market forces, surrogate motherhood or the notion of the 'womb for rent' are conceivable (Sanghera 1990: 24).

Reproductive labour, as an aggregate of its two facets can be organized solely within the domain of the household, as in the case of the housewife who performs both sexual and social labour, or it can be disaggregated with one or both of its components organized under wage relations. Thus in the case of prostitution or sex work, the sexual aspect of reproductive labour is detached from its procreative adjunct and subject to a network of commercial relations. However, under a dominant mode of production, characterized by capitalist relations, the exigencies of the productive process, the pressure to maximize productivity, the altering division of labour, the process of reconstitution of gender relations in the capitalist core has drawn the social aspect of reproductive labour into wage relations as well, in the form of cleaning/laundering services as packaged domestic services. Under sex tourism in South East Asia for example, reproductive labour is forced into the commercial area in dissected segments or as an aggregate. In the 'hired wife', sex tour package, both dimensions of reproductive labour as performed by the housewife in the household placed under the purview of market forces. Here wage relations dominate, to ensure capital accumulation, and patriarchal relations coincide to sustain ongoing capital accumulation (ibid.).

In its disaggregated form segments of reproductive labour are marketed in various combinations to clients. How and under what conditions does this disaggregation of women's reproductive labour get exacerbated under capitalism?

The patriarchal monogamous family has traditionally been the most important site for women's reproductive labour for reasons related to norms of descent and transmission of inheritance through the male line. Though the process of disaggregation (particularly the sexual aspect) has existed prior to capitalism, this intensification is partly related to capitalism's disruption of kinship and family relations, wherein sexual and emotional needs or the need for a social identity are fulfilled. This disruption entails a disruption of the provision of reproductive services, including the social and biological aspects. Large-scale production separating the work place from home, urbanization and migration for jobs, militarization, trade and commerce—all products of capitalist, political, economic and cultural expansions—result in large-scale spatial mobility and the concentration of predominantly male labour in new sites. This mobility and concentration dislocates relations of human bonding and reproduction through kinship relations. In this context, old relations are replaced by new ones. New forms of sexual needs, desire and social significance are governed by the dictates of the market. As a result a plurality of sites mushroom—the brothel for example—beyond the household through which sexual and social aspects of reproduction are organized to facilitate the process of reproduction and production. These sites are often organized on class, ethnic lines (Truong 1990: 196).

This intensification of the disaggregation of reproductive labour, specially its sexual aspects and its operation through a variety of locales, is connected to the process of capital accumulation under capitalism, facilitated by the exploitation of sex and women's bodies as commodities, by controllers of sex service sector/industry, to make the enterprise possible in the first place. Fiscal benefits, the earning of huge foreign exchange reserves by nation-states and the social necessity of organizing reproductive labour in the above manner result in collusion between the larger State apparatus and the immediate controllers of the sex service sector/industry (Personal discussions with Thai and Filipina activits, 1991).

Beyond and above this, structurally induced material factors such as poverty, deprivation and its interaction with patriarchal cultural settings that marginalize women from access to education and the job market for instance, render commercial provision of sex services a survival strategy for large masses of women.

The plurality of sites of reproduction is associated with a plurality of discursive elements on sexuality and social control, the plurality being by and large expressed through the manipulation of female sexuality. Social constructions of sexuality have by and large distinguished the male and female body and sexuality through the mechanism of attribution of specific qualities or denial of these; as part of their natural or normal biological functions (potency vs. receptivity; purity vs. pollution; creativity vs. functionality). Such a differentiation results in the notion that males and females have essentially different sets of naturally and biologically determined sexual needs, desire and significance—a notion that has come to be popularly regarded as a scientific truth, warranting no further exploration. (Truong 1990: 195.)

However, while the functionality of female sexuality in procreation and in providing male pleasure is particularly emphasized, its significance is simultaneously denied through the denigration of the female body. Moreover, within the female populace itself there is another level of inter-subjectivity and fragmentation that has been created, viz., the polarization between sexual pleasure and procreation. This creates dually opposed mutually exclusive categories of women, i.e., the home bound wife responsible for social and biological reproduction and the public woman, the sexual temptress and provider of sexual pleasure. 'From the perspective of intra-subjectivity, these rigid role and trait stereotypes act upon the human body, its ideation, perceptions and consciousness and create a narrow, restricted and distorted human understanding of what is pure and sacrosanct, natural and offensive about sex' (ibid.).

This discourse underscores State structure, law and the like, as exemplified in prostitution laws, where women in prostitution are defined as sexual offenders for threatening as they do, the norms of conjugality and prescribed cultural and sexual codes for women as chaste and faithful wives and mothers (D'Cunha 1991).

It must be emphasized that while wage labour under capitalism is considered productive labour, the productivity of sexual services for reproduction under wage relations is not considered so and is rendered invisible by ideological mediations and institutional structures governing sexuality.

This invisibility and the legal and moral isolation of women in prostitution facilitates the intensification of accumulation of capital from sex and women's bodies, rendering the women even more vulnerable to and dependent on the employer. Furthermore legal and social persecution of women in prostitution reinforce rigid standards of what is moral and immoral that impinge negatively on the self-identity and consciousness of women in prostitution. Legal persecution also limits space for resistance or discounts resistance where the space is created (Truong 1990: 197).

VIII

THE NORTH-SOUTH DIMENSIONS OF THE PROSTITUTION REALITY

The alarming increase in the magnitude of prostitution, the increasing diversification of the sex service sector and forms of trafficking, especially in countries of the South make it imperative to contextualize the issue of prostitution and the sexual imaging of women from these societies, within the framework of North-South relations; because the prostitution reality in our societies is in a sense very much a North-South issue.

The alarming increase in the magnitude and dimensions of poverty and prostitution in our societies is largely the outgrowth of our colonial histories which ushered in capitalism—private property, commodity production, socio-economic and political inequalities. The organic unit of the household, the unit of production was broken up with each individual becoming a separate unit of labour, feeling fragmented and entering the labour market independently for economic survival (8th ISIS—WICCE Programme on Poverty and Prostitution 1991).

While most of our societies have attained formal political independence from colonial powers, we continue to be subordinated economically, politically and socio-culturally by newer and newer forms of domination and control by the centres of capitalism.

The poverty thus resulting from these structurally induced inequities, and intrinsically linked with capitalist relations of domination and subjugation between the 'Centre and Periphery', interfaces with our patriarchal cultures, where gender discrimination against women at all levels, renders poor women even poorer than men, within the general culture of poverty, rendering prostitution a survival strategy for large masses of women in our realities.

It is necessary at this juncture to view poverty not just as an economic category with a relative dimension, differing in terms of degree from one country to another or from region to region within a country, but to also reconceptualize poverty, broadening its scope from economic poverty to political and socio-cultural poverty and a general 'poverty of spirit'. For though the North has attained higher levels of material prosperity, it has a growing and ever-increasing poverty of spirit, not to mention the growing consumerism and commodification of human relations and human beings in countries of the South as well. This is becoming more and more evident, with women from the South, who have gone beyond survival needs, entering the sex service sector, as a result of the dictates of a capitalist consumerism (ibid.).

Within this context of the commodification of every aspect of human life, sex and women's bodies have also been commodified. Prostitution has now become a lucrative market and a booming industry; differentially tiered with profit accruing to the organizers and controllers of this sex service sector/industry while the women are by and large exploited. The distinction between women's reproductive labour performed by the wife and women's sexual labour incorporated into the sex service sector/industry and engaged in by women in prostitution becomes sharper and more pronounced.

In the context of the internationalization of capital the sex service industry has also become internationalized, with the demand for and supply of women in prostitution crossing local, regional and national boundaries, acquiring borderless dimensions, the manifestations of which are prostitution around military bases; sex tourism; and overseas trafficking in women for the entertainment industry in the centres of capitalism (personal discussions with Thai and Filipina activists 1991).

The consumers of women's sexuality in this internationalized sex industry are largely rich, middle-class and working-class men from the North; whose greater purchasing power has the capacity to buy countries of the South, their cultures and their women. Alienating work conditions; high levels of consumerism, greater inability in dominating assertive western women; the fragility of human relations including man-woman relations; high divorce rates; difficulty in meeting socially prescribed standards of sexual imaging in western societies, resulting in the inability to find partners—are factors pulling together in a particular configuration to create an alienated self that also breeds an alienated sexuality. This results in changes in sexual needs and demands to include the exploration of different female sexual partners and newer forms of sex including perverted and kinky forms. It is women and increasingly children from the South whose sexual labour is incorporated into the sex service sector/industry, that cater to such men from the North (ibid.).

Thus large scale production of sexual services and eroticism implies a continuous supply of sexual labour into the sex service sector/industry, for the extraction of surplus value. The effect of this process has been an increase in the use of violence, utilizing relationships of sexual domination, gender inequalities and conditions of economic domination, to locate and supply this labour—a supply effectively maintained by international criminal networks constituted by recruiters, agents and middlemen both from the North and the South. The principal means used to supply this labour is trafficking through kidnapping, abduction, deceit or lure of good jobs, fake marriage contracts, befriending and sale into prostitution. Women and children thus trafficked in may be sold into a range of sex service-related establishments governed by varied social relations, such as confinement and bondage in a brothel, to relations that are more loosely linked. National governments of both the North and the South, in not taking decisive action against these networks and in formulating policies that directly or indirectly result in prostitution of women, create conditions for and reinforce the institution of prostitution in our societies (ibid. D'Cunha 1991).

Interacting with the economic and political system to further keep alive and perpetuate the institution of prostitution are patriarchy, religion and racism, for instance.

The most fundamental patriarchal assumptions of the institution of prostitution are 'sex is a male right' and 'sex and women's bodies are commodities to be bought and sold in prostitution' (Barry 1981). The fragmentation of women's reproductive labour into that engaged in by 'madonnas and whores' is yet another ideological dimension of the institution of prostitution.

Religious ideology, by its support to patriarchy indirectly supports prostitution and generally discriminates against women in prostitution. In some cases it may even blatantly sanction and legitimize prostitution, as in the case of the *Devadasi* system in India.[1]

Interfacing with patriarchy and religion is racism, for racism especially between the North and the South has resulted in a racist sexual imaging and construction of women's sexuality, with alienated men from the North searching out the 'exotic docile Asian women of the South' to cater to their sexual demands. This 'exotic sexual imaging' is simultaneously coupled with a denigration of these cultures and women, exemplified in the cultural imaging of Thailand, for example, as the 'brothel of Asia' or the sexual imaging of Filipina women as 'small brown fucking machines' (Personal discussions with Thai and Filipina activists 1991). This inter-subjectivity established between the South and the North emphasizing the 'Otherness' of the South, the sexual availability of Southern women and their cultures of poverty is a phenomenon related to two processes:

(a) creating a distinct national identity to attract consumers from the centres of capitalism; and (b) legitimizing oppressive practices by relating them to the culture of a particular ethnic group, helping to ease the consumer's conscience. A new legitimacy—'national development' especially of the South—is resorted to for intrusions of local and international capital and consumers into the realm of sexuality. (Truong 1990: 200.)

IX

CONCLUDING REMARKS

While it is necessary to understand prostitution as a form of labour, though not an acceptable one, in view of the institutions' patriarchal and exploitative basis; while trafficking is condemned as a form of force and violence and a human rights and women's rights violation; while a distinction is made between the individual and institution of prostitution, the following issues and dilemmas arise at the level of political praxis.

There is the need to concretely and actively address in practice the concerns of individual women in prostitution, especially those who continue to operate within the sex service sector, without legitimizing the institution of prostitution and third-party managements. Another important issue is whether or not we make a distinction between the rights of women in prostitution and the right to prostitution and how this translates ideologically and practically. We also need to consider the implications of a position critiquing the institution of prostitution and trafficking with respect to prostitutes' rights groups defending the institution, and our linkages with them. These are issues that beg sustained ideological and action-directed exploration, that is sensitive to the needs and concerns of women in prostitution.

ACKNOWLEDGEMENTS

This is a revision of an earlier paper on 'Prostitution and Sex Trafficking', presented at the International India-Canada Conference on 'Violence Against Women: Women Against Violence', Canadian Studies Program, SNDT Women's University, 13–17 December 1993.

NOTES

1. Amrit Srinivasan provides an account of the structure of the *devadasi* tradition in the Province of Madras in nineteenth-century India. The *devadasi* or 'slave of God' was a term applied to a category of females who were ceremonially dedicated at an early age to the deity of the local temple, for temple services. 'This ceremony resembled in its ritual structure the upper caste Tamil marriage ceremony. Following this the *devadasi* was set apart from her non-dedicated sisters in that she was not permitted to marry and her celibate or unmarried status was legal in customary terms.' Although denied the customary ceremony of marriage, she was *Nityasumangali*, the auspicious one, who could never be widowed. 'Significantly however, she was not prevented from leading a "normal" life, involving economic activity, sex and child bearing. The very rituals which marked and confirmed her incorporation into temple serivce, also committed her to the rigorous emotional and physical training in classical dance, her hereditary profession.' In addition, this served to publicly advertise her availability for sexual liaisons with a (usually upper caste) patron and protector. Very often in fact, the costs of temple dedication were met by a man who wished to have a sexual liaison with the *devadasi*. 'It was crucially a woman's "dedicated" status which made it a symbol of social prestige and privilege to maintain her. The *devadasi* thus came to represent a badge of fortune, a form of honour managed for civil society by the temple' (Srinivasan) 1985).

REFERENCES

Ballatchet, Kenneth, 1980, *Sex and Class under the Raj. Imperial Attitudes, policies and their critiques, 1793–1905*, Widenfield and Nicolson, London.

Barry, Kathleen, 1981, *Female Sexual Slavery*, Avon Books, New York.

——, Bunch Charlotte, Castley Shirley (eds.), 1983, International Feminism—Networking against Female Sexual Slavery. Report of the Global Feminist Workshop to organize against traffic in women, Rotterdam, 6–15 April.

Chauvin, C, 1982, *L'Eglise et les Prostitutée.*, Editions du Cerf, Paris.

Commission of Enquiry into Traffic in Women and Children in the Far East, 1933, Report to the Council, Geneva, League of Nations.

Cooper and Stoler, 1989, Introduction: Tensions of the Empire: colonial control and visions of rule, *American Ethnologist*, 16(4): 610–11.

D'Cunha, Jean, 1987, Prostitution in a patriarchial society: a critical review of the SIT Act, *Economic and Political Weekly*; 7 November.

——, 1991, *The Legalization of Prostitution. A sociological inquiry into the law relating to prostitution in India and the West*, Wordmakers, Bangalore.

——, 1992, Prostitution laws—ideological dimensions and enforcement practices, *Economic and Political Weekly*, XXVII(17), 25 April.

Elements of a Southern Women's Perspective on Poverty and Prostitution developed by participants (including author) and resource person Jyothi Sanghera at 8th ISIS Women's International Cross Cultural Exchange Programme on Poverty and Prostitution, at Thailand, the Philippines and Geneva, September–December 1991.

Enloe, Cynthia, 1983, *Does Khaki Become You? The Militarization of Prostitution*, Pluto Press, London.

Foucault, Michel, 1978, *The History of Sexuality, Vol. I, An Introduction* (trans. R. Hurley), New York.

Leonard, Eileen B, 1982, *Women, Crime and Society: A critique of theoretical criminology*, Longman, New York.

Mackinnon, Catherine, 1982, Feminism, Marxism, method and the State. an agenda for theory, in N.O. Keohane *et al.* (eds)., *Feminist Theory. A critique of ideology*, Harvester Press, Sussex.

Mcleod, E, 1982, *Women Working. Prostitution now*, Croom Helm, Kent Millet, Kate, 1971, *Sexual Politics*, Hart Davis, London.

Personal discussions with German women in Prostitution at the 2nd World Congress on Prostitution, Human Rights and Feminism, 1986, European Parliament, Brussels.

Personal discussions with Thai and Filipina Activists during ISIS Women's International Cross Cultural Exchange Programme 1991.

Rosenblum, K.E, 1975, Female deviance and the female sex role. A preliminary investigation, *British Journal of Sociology*, 26: 169–85.

Sanghera, Jyoti, 1990, Creating international brothels (Dissertation proposal), Department of Sociology, University of California, Berkeley.

Slides by Forensic Expert. Pritam Phatnani, Bombay.

Srinivasan A, 1985 Reform and revival. Devadasi and her dance, *Economic and Political Weekly XX(44) ()2 November):* 1869–70.

Truong, Thanh-Dam, 1990, *Sex, Money and Morality. Prostitution and tourism in South East Asia,* Zed Books. London.

Walkowitz, Judith, 1980, *Prostitution and Victorian Society. Women, class and the State,* Cambridge University Press, Cambridge.

World Charter for Prostitution Rights, February 1988, International Committee for Prostitutes Rights, Amsterdam.

The Impossible Subject
Caste in the Scene of Desire

Susie Tharu

I

'YOUR FUNERAL IS ALSO PART OF YOUR LIFE AS A LIVING MAN'[1]

No reader familiar with the canonical texts of modern Indian literatures needs to be told how large the figure of the Hindu widow looms there, and in what unexpected places it makes an appearance. Indeed—and I discovered this to my surprise while working on *Women Writing in India*—from about the middle of the nineteenth century this figure has held a more-or-less centre-stage position in the national imagery. It could be argued, and I am going to do so, that when a writer features a widow as a protagonist he or she is, consciously or unconsciously, making an intervention in a debate centred on this figure; a debate whose history is a history of Indian humanism and its intimate yet troubled relationship with Indian feminism. It is only when we frame widow-narratives in this way that other crucial dimensions of the genre become apparent. The widow is a figure whose very life is marked by a specific death. She is *vidhava* (without husband) and consequently in need not only of public protection, but also of regulation, governance. Widow stories therefore are invariably also subtly modulated historical engagements with questions of governmentality and citizenship.

A close reading of two contemporary short stories that feature the widow as protagonist provide the basis for this paper on gender, caste and citizenship. The figure provides one story with its title: 'Mother'. This widow is a young woman. In the other she is a visitor from three generations ago, a great-grandmother. Both stories devolve around the widow's relationship with a younger person in the family. Death is thematic. The questions raised therefore are of reproduction and in-heritance—of life itself and the possibilities of its continuity.

II

'A SOLID RELIABLE THING: A WONDERFUL RESILIENT MACHINE'[2]

I shall begin with the more recent story, Gita Hariharan's 'The Remains of the Feast' taken from her 1992 collection, *The Art of Dying*, because it is a story about a Brahmin widow. After all, when one thinks of a widow, one thinks of a Hindu widow, and when one says Hindu widow, in the last century no more than now, one means Brahmin widow.

The story, very briefly, is about a Brahmin woman who was widowed young and has lived the prescribed life of austerity. She has outlived her only son and his wife, and is now with her grandson, a retired bureaucrat, his wife, and their medical-student daughter. Suddenly at 90 when she is dying of cancer, a new life bursts forth in a hitherto controlled appetite that declares its scandalous self. It desires everything that it has been forbidden: cakes with eggs in them, from the Christian shop with a Muslim cook, Coca-Cola laced with the delicious delight that it might be alcoholic, *bhel-puri* from the fly infested bazaar, possibly touched by untouchable hands, tweezed eyebrows, shaven legs; and finally, in the flourish of death, a sari of bridal red. Years of deprivation pale into insignificance against the grandeur of this feast in which the flesh reasserts its primal authority. Hariharan's plot is minimal; the pleasure of the tale invested in the dry, ironic tone and in the tension set up between narrative and narratorial accounts. The story is a finely etched and mischievously framed cameo. It presents itself as that—a jewel in a minor genre, to be enjoyed in passing. In that sense, the seriousness with which I approach and stay with this text is a misreading. Yet, to my mind it is precisely the apparent lightness of this text, the ease with which the reader passes over its objects, the understatement and the non-violence with which authorial voice can affirm its common sense, its logic, its taste, it is precisely these that mark the story out as a significant text of our time.

In some ways the widow in this story is the costumed, nineteenth century subject of the colonial social reform movements. Her head is tonsured, she wears white cotton, eats only the prescribed daily meal of non-heating foods and lives as an appendage in a household organized around its active 'householder' subjects. But unlike her predecessor, this widow is not the victim of a cruel and superstitious society. Far from it. She is a being with a joyous, child-like relationship to her body which is the secret of her health, her self-sufficiency, her longevity—perhaps also because she has escaped the government of the post-independence socialist decades. Her resilient embodiment is the basis of her primitive, enduring personhood, and her irrepressible force as a subject-agent. With it she survives the twentieth century, quite, but undefeated. Literally of course, and also as we shall find, politically. Hers is a body-personhood that exceeds discipline (she makes farting a musical event, she laughs indecorously, her body odours rampage through the house and survive even her death). This body-person has a native wit that can play social injunction off against injunction like a fish in post-structuralist water (caste-gender taboos as well as the secular norms of middle-class propriety are forced to move aside, when the demand is the gratification of a desire expressed in the face of death) and laugh subversively in the very face of authorities that would control her. This is a body-person that can compel the reiteration essential to its maintenance. As a result, while two intervening (Nehruvian?) generations may have lost touch with this strength which displays itself, heightened and stylized like an art-work, in the dying woman's grossly irreverent appetite, the great-granddaughter has the ability to recognize the appetite for what it is and affirm/indulge it, despite the disapproval of her proper middle-class parents. It is the great-granddaughter who smuggles in tabooed goodies and finally even makes an attempt to draw the most sacred of traditional rites—the funeral—into the old woman's new life by draping the body in red silk. She is also the fictional narrator.

Positioned as a mirror-image to the narratorial mediation in this neatly structured story is another mediation—that of the great-grandmother's desires, which function as a lens through which the young woman's own more contemporary appetites and deprivations come into focus, and may be recognized for what they actually are. A medical student who must live up to her gold medal, she pores over her books late into the night. She experiments with the options open to the modern woman: 'greedily' she flips through the 'new-smelling' pages of her 'hard-bound' anatomy book. But she can feel it is not there, or as 'a big doctor-madam' that she will find satisfaction. The illustrations in the medical text reduce the body to lurid colour-coded parts, all labelled and numbered. These pleasures and their promised futures are no match for the nights she has spent in the soft warmth of her grandmother's bed, surrounded by the 'safe, familiar, musty, smell' of the old woman's flesh.

The body that Hariharan's story affirms, firms, re-firms in its citation is 'a solid, reliable thing ... a wonderful, resilient machine' (p. 10). Nothing seems to have the power to corrode it—neither the violence of a tradition that decrees asceticism and denial, nor that of a modernity which would discipline it in other, multi-coloured yet no less ascetic, terms. The canonical authority of this body, the stigmata that proclaims its sainthood, however minor and secular-modern that may be, lies in its ability to survive and to resurface, and in its power to effect reiteration across generations and across a social map that includes the young narrator, the author and the reader, a social map that is also a map of new India.

I began this discussion by saying that 'The Remains of the Feast', can be read as an intervention in a long-standing debate in Indian feminism; indeed that the flaunting of the Hindu-widow protagonist suggests that the author herself might well regard it as a statement of that kind. But what exactly is the feminist statement that the story makes? To the extent that the body that is reaffirmed in the narrative is only incidentally a female body, it is also a feminist body. Let me explain. The narrative does not present widowhood, and the paraphernalia of ritual and taboo that attends it, as gender oppression. The enemy here is not patriarchy, but a social world that fails to sustain the spirit. The victim is fleshly nature itself, not woman. The fact that both the characters happen to be female, or that they belong to separate historical times, seems incidental to the main thrust of the narrative which asserts the claim of a natural appetite for life—be it male or female—against an order which seeks to deprive or discipline it. All the same, to take for granted the equality of male and female so completely as to assume that the universal body may be represented by the female as adequately as the male is, I submit, a feminist stance, as is the old woman's rebellion and her bid for liberation and fulfilment. However—and this is a consequence of its particular feminism— it is also a stance whose impatience towards historical and actually existing Indian feminism (an excess given the resilience of embodied humanity) is evident in the structure of the plot as much as in the narrative tone. Thus while the suffering and the degradation of the

Hindu widow (*sati*, incarceration, tonsure, the prohibition of remarriage, the denial of her sexuality) were issues that provided the nineteenth-century social reform movements with their· mobilizing force and in fact shaped their feminism, in this story all that, and indeed widowhood itself, becomes unimportant. We encounter the familiar shaven-headed figure, but search as we will for the pain that roused protest, we will not find it since the victim-widow has been replaced by a body whose robust appetite and Rabelaisian humour is a capable substitute for feminist struggle, then and now. Its good sense is one that can resist both the follies of tradition and the enthusiasms of modernity more effectively than a hundred and fifty years of feminist fanaticism has managed to do.

There are crucial differences that mark off the embodied individual of Hariharan's story from the ascetic, even anti-consumerist widow-figures that emerged in the early years of the twentieth century with the Swadeshi movement and found a new stint of life a couple of decades later in Gandhian nationalism. These strong, self-reliant figures were emblematic of a culture and society capable of effective counterpoint to colonial ideologies and western notions of the good society. There is much, however, that they share, including the fact that for these figures too reform was largely irrelevant.

I turn to the caste politics of this text. It is singularly easy to forget that the feminist salience of the story is based on the fact that its protagonist is not just a Hindu widow but a *Brahmin* widow. Her upper caste status comes into play in a variety of ways. The family own, and continue to own, property in the village which they now manage from the city. For two generations they have been part of Indian officialdom, the new Brahmins who also have a stranglehold on the professions—the old woman's son was an administrator, the grandson an accountant. The great-granddaughter is studying to be a doctor. The desires and appetites that drive the plot are structured by the proscriptions that govern a Brahmin widow's life. In this story those predictable hungers are updated to include others excited by the more modern pruderies of a colonial middle class (alcohol, street food, body noises, make-up, female desire) that transform the lot into a metaphor for human appetites, whetted perhaps by denial, but simple human appetites all the same. The family are exemplary in their modernity. They practise nothing that can be called serious discrimination based on caste or gender. The prescriptions of the law are not forced on to the widow; rather, her traditional life in the household signifies the scope of an Indian modernity that can accommodate tradition without compromising its humanism. When the old woman is about to die, they call the doctor, not the priest. There appears to have been no opposition to the young woman studying medicine. In fact there is such a close fit between tradition and modernity, brahminism and secularism, that they signal a natural continuity in the new and altogether persuasive frame that the narrative sets up. The initial terms in both pairs are designated as unnatural and as excesses—whether they be the excesses of ritual proscriptions, secular-modern ambitions (including feminist ones)—which then become the lack or the disorder that drives the narrative.

Theoretically the question of caste is figured into the argument of this story in two distinct, but related ways. First, and perhaps most important, it makes an appearance as the caste *system* and not as caste discrimination, oppression or expropriation. The older woman can therefore break the hold of caste (which is by now residual, a frail psychological object) by consuming the proscribed foods. Fit (and indeed the only) agent for this revolution in brahminism is the modernizing Brahmin herself. Secondly, the transition from brahminism-tradition to secularism-modernity seems so smooth that there is no reason to presume any substantial conflict there. If the task of the mid-twentieth century *avant-garde* was the shaping of a modernity that would select the best from tradition and maintain India's distinct cultural genius as it moved into a scientific future, what seems required now is the setting up of a third category, premised on embodied nature and political moderation, that must repudiate the ascetic excesses of ritual brahminism as well as those of a puritanical, work/production-oriented spirit of national capital. I do not think it is insignificant, that the late-capitalist, fund-bank widow *consumes* her way to freedom.

If we push beyond the self deprecating gestures with which the story presents itself we are confronted with a cultural politics seriously engaged in the making of a new moment in the genealogy of the Indian citizen as agent-self and as humanist individual. It is a moment in which, a citizen-subject beleaguered by the challenges to its authority that have arisen from the struggles of dalit-bahujans, feminists, socialists and a host of others, and drawn by the offer of equality that is held out by a global (free market) liberalism, re-notates those struggles to enable their absorption into its body. As it recasts the grievances of women and of dalits to present itself as answer, it renders their historical and present-day struggles redundant. The reverse effect is the more significant one; what surfaces in this story as a feisty and irrepressible nature is in fact a body meticulously fashioned as response to movements that threaten its 'identity' and its interests.

To what extent has this embodied and agentive self—or a very similar one—also been the body-self unwittingly affirmed and renewed by historical feminism? What does that norming cost the feminist movement? How might it affect possibilities of egalitarian and democratic alliance or initiative? These are chastening questions and ones that we might learn how to ask as we find our way through the second text I want to discuss: Baburao Bagul's 1969 story about a dalit widow. Not, however, before observing that the brahminical-modernist formation of the citizen-self may be one reason why it has taken me a quarter of a century to learn how to read the feminism of this dalit story.

III

'NOT A SINGLE DALIT WOMAN IS EITHER HAPPY OR CONTENTED FROM THE HEART. SHE IS ALWAYS WORRIED.'[3]

The mandatory summary to begin with. This is a difficult task, because unlike a well-made short story which is pared down to a single focus, the plot here is layered like that of a novel and is bustling with character and event. The time-span of the story has a classical brevity (one evening, seven pages), yet the narrative is structured as a series of episodes that cut from location to location, flashback from the immediate present to the recent and the more distant past, and shift focus from the private world of the subject-self to the outer world of power. I think the only possibility might be to risk brutalization of the structuring of time in Bagul's narrative and present a chronology of events. I hope that the scope and texture of the story can be regained, partially at least, in the discussion.

Some time before he was born, Pandu's mother and father leave their village and come to the city after the father, in a fit of jealous anxiety, 'almost kills his brother with an axe.' Things are only worse in the city. The mother has to work all day at construction sites to feed the family and pay for milk and medicines. Her husband, drunk and tubercular, is too weak and overwrought with resentment and suspicion of his wife to find work himself. The sexual tension between them builds up and spills out into their already tense world in which abuse and attack are the everyday texture of life, not only for them but for everyone. He accuses her of selling herself for favours, tries repeatedly to deface her, makes an attempt to brand her body with hot tongs; she turns on his dying body in vengeance demanding her 'conjugal rights', hoping to hasten his death. When he dies, she feels she has killed him. Ten years elapse. She has continued to work, resisting, for her son's sake, the advances of several men, despite desperate need for the material benefit that would accrue. Pandu is at school, but he is miserable. He never smiles, never responds, either to the teacher or to the taunts of other children. His body, Bagul writes, is lead. One evening, back from a usual schoolday of attack and abuse, sitting alone in his empty hovel waiting for his mother, hungry yet unable to stomach the cold gruel left for him on the hearth, the small changes in their everyday life begin to 'make sense' to him. He reads them, indeed reads himself in them: new Diwali clothes, a new tilt of his mother's head, a new drape to her clothes, a fresh intensity to the taunts at school and on the street. His mother is a whore. He the son of a——. When she returns from work, braving that day as everyday the sexual attacks and the moral reprobations of the street through which she must walk to reach the relative safety of her home, Pandu turns on her the full force of his pain and resentment. He shouts at her and runs out of the house. I quote:

The room now seemed to her like the cremation grounds. ... She heard the sound of the dogs in the distance, and thinking he had come back, joyfully opened the door.
'Come son, forgive this old sinner.'
The door opened and the overseer stood in the doorway. His massive frame seemed to dwarf everything else in the room. 'What's happened? Why do you look so scared? You are sweating.' He hugged her, pretended to wipe the sweat off her face, and started caressing her arms and her breasts. She slowly responded, and out of the hunger of the past ten years of widowhood flared an uncontrollable desire. And that was why she failed to hear the timid knock at the door, the faint, hesitant cry, 'Mother!' He saw them, his mother and the towering figure of the overseer in a tight embrace. His last hopes seemed to crash about his head; broken-hearted, he wildly rushed towards the door. She saw him then, strained after him, calling his name, but the overseer, already blinded with lust, refused to let her go; he was pulling her into the room with his strong brown arms. Pandu was running away at great speed; his fast falling tears had almost blinded him, the stray dogs ran at his heels, snapped at him and now he was screaming, shouting with terror, afraid of the dogs. ...

She was trying desperately to escape from the bear-like hug of the overseer. But like a person stuck fast in the quagmire, she found release impossible. ...

A summary of this kind necessarily scants detail and structure. It also excludes from its scope one of the most stunning aspects of the story—what I will call, following Walter Benjamin, a 'linguistic air'. A few comments on this air. For those normed by its procedures, the everyday use of language assumes, indeed can assume, a fit so close between the sign and its referent that the referent saturates the domain of signification. In 'The Task of the Translator', Benjamin refers to this mode in which language is used as the linguistic air, arguing that translation rises to (but also exists in/has the bearing of) a higher and purer linguistic air than the original, since a translation is concerned less with the transfer of meaning or information and more with essaying a mode of signification.[4] The linguistic air in Baburao Bagul's story is related to that of a Benjaminian translation, though it is not identical. The linguistic air of a translation draws attention to the signifying system that is another culture. In the nether world of Bagul's story, on the other side of the border in which sign and referent have a natural fit, language does not just thematize another process/mode of signification. In that air reality is self-evidently an effect of the symbolic whose logic is apparent everywhere. Signification is a full-scale materializing and de-materializing force. Events, bodies, persons, objects and selves are signs that have to be cautiously investigated and deciphered if they are to make sense.

In this linguistic air, which is as much the air of real life as it is of the art work, bodies are so wayward that they must be branded; tuberculosis is a caste-mark, memory an aspect of present time and public location: it rushes in from the world to habilitate a personal past; a body-subject whose 'life' is not affirmed by another spirals rapidly back into insignificance. There can be no leisure in this world that must move to the busy beat of an elsewhere, no time for pause, no occasion for consolidation for reader or story-teller. Nothing holds, nothing stands still, nothing may be taken for granted. It is the symbolic that gives birth to subjects, and tempts their dreams with agency while it watches ceremoniously over their many and rapid deaths. A single death would indeed be a comfort.

In addition, the subject in this nether world is not 'impossible' simply because agency is an effect of discipline, or because it is in-process, or because it is not affirmed in citation-reiteration, or indeed because one and one can never actually make a One, an integral whole, and there is always a remainder. It is impossible because it is constantly annihilated.

Gita Hariharan's widow-story is about the assertion of life that makes death itself a sort of fruition, a celebratory feast. 'Mother' could well be read as the drama of life and death in the scene of the untouchable family. The narrative turns us into witnesses as mother, son, husband, wife, lover, suitor, man, woman and child give birth, one to another, and die, kill, desire or imagine the death of the other in a series of overlapping acts of affirmation and denial. Indeed the story opens with a longish account of one such coming-to-life and its death. Normally indifferent and listless, 'backward' children thrill to 'a new joy of being' as they listen to a teacher read out a poem about a mother who is a river of life, a *Vatsalya Sindhu*. The poem 'transports' them into another realm and their 'muddy faces shine with a strange wonder' as they smile 'happily through their unkempt hair'. Enabled by the poem to map those mythic proportions on to memories of his own mother, the young protagonist, Pandu, magically comes to life as 'a child'. A body, stooped with the load of his living, straightens into normality. It returns to him, rather, it returns him to himself: he wants to shout, to wave his arms about in joy. The new propriety also finds this untouchable housing in a community: 'the hostility he usually felt towards his classmates abated somewhat. He sat watching them at play and a benign smile slowly came to his face.'

Sealing the contract of reconciliation between secured self and habitable world is the high point of Pandu's newfound happiness and vitality; the assertion of his own ability to exclude another. 'Snotnose', he and Lakhu shout out at another boy in spontaneous consolidation of their exuberant togetherness. The poem he listens to in class literally has the power to inspire Pandu. It breathes him into brief life as son, as child and as 'touchable' member of a community. It gives him a mother. But the imaginary interpellation is hardly born before its life is snuffed out by another more compelling one: 'Don't touch Pandu, any of you. My mother says his mother. ...', Kishan's yell and the laughter it elicits from the class drains Pandu of life: he slowly returns to his seat and sits down 'woodenly'.

It is a double murder this—of child and mother—and one that will be insistently re-enacted, elaborated and related to other dramas of life and death in the story. The domain of the symbolic sustains all life and demands merciless maintenance of its extraditions and death sentences of which there are many kinds. There are those rehearsed in the desperate masquerades that play at and endorse power in the very face of powerlessness (Bhaga the school-rowdy, Dagdu his community role model, the jealous husband, the sexually demanding wife). Thus,

Bhaga put up his shirt collar ... like a street rowdy, squared his lips and told Pandu, 'You bloody pimp. Just come out. I'm going to murder you.' He removed a rusty old blade from his note book and threateningly placed it at Pandu's throat.

More characteristic of this world, however, are the real murders, not these make-believe ones. Those involve the actual or desired elimination of a killer(s) and are posthumous acts of self-defence in which a murdered person must kill in order that he or she may live again. Thus, orphaned by Kishan's remarks, Pandu feels a 'demonic, murderous rage rising within him. He could have killed them, murdered them all in cold blood. It was good to think of them lying together in a pool of blood.' Walking back from school that evening Pandu encounters a drunken Dagdu. He is scared, but when Dagdu, jealous and depressed, insults his mother, Pandu loses 'his childlike feelings as the murderous fires continued to haunt him; he felt like hurling a heavy rock at Dagdu's swaying, retreating form and his mind's eye was luridly coloured by the spraying blood that he imagined would gush out of Dagdu's head.'

Structurally analogous to the many deaths, murders, births and rebirths that constitute Pandu's life, is the coming-to-life and new death of Pandu's mother, the murder she commits, the ones she dreams of committing, the ones committed on her. For a man in this world, a wife's youth or her beauty are not sources of joy but of anxiety and emasculation. Beauty is the property mark of the world across the border, a branding. A beautiful woman is one who has been picked out by its laws, one whose life is held by its designs and its assumptions. To make a beautiful woman his wife, to hold her in that esteemed position and thereby to affirm his own proper masculinity, his status as husband, a man must erase those marks which are also the marks of his emasculation, his dispossession, the impossibility of personhood. Pandu's father's

blows, therefore, were always aimed at destroying [his wife's] full-blown beauty. He hoped she would lose a lot of blood, become lame, deformed, ugly and so in spite of his ebbing strength, he would aim at her face, nose, head, eyes. Then he threatened to kill her when she was asleep. He blamed her entirely for his disease, his failing strength, his joblessness.

For similar reasons, he would rather 'die, allow this child to die', than let his brother, who looks at his wife with 'lust in his eyes' anywhere near them. For Pandu's father, this brother is the most dreaded of mirrors, one into which he cannot bear to look, for he sees there the image of his own utter degradation/death in one who is his own flesh and blood. To survive he must break that mirror—kill, even his brother.

For the woman who is Pandu's mother, the memories that haunt are those of the 'most degrading act of the day' when her husband would strip her and scrupulously check out her body and its clothing for marks of her infidelity. The break point comes when she wakes up one night to find him heating tongs to brand her body, to mark it indelibly, to burn into it the sign of his possession. It will be a mark of power, indeed of patriarchal power, but it is at the same time a mark of his desperation. It is she now who turns to the kill. She will demand—and like the demands that he makes on her, this too is an excessive, impossible demand for his failing tubercular body—she will demand that he husband her, and in the process push him into death. She will want to murder her son too when she recognizes in his eyes the 'same dark suspicion' she has seen before—in the eyes of his father.

Like Pandu, who momentarily comes alive in the promise of the poem, she too glimmers into brief life in the arms of the overseer at the construction site. With the affirmation he provides she can walk straight, 'secure in her new found love.' Her mirror now refracts a different light and she grows desirable in her own eyes as much as in his. But for this dalit to find bodily life thus, as woman-self, she must die as mother. 'Whore, I spit on your clothes', Pandu shouts in a desperate, last-ditch attempt to conserve his ethical identity before he runs out of the house into his death as son-child.

IV

CASTE IN THE FEMINIST SCENE OF DESIRE

For a feminist reader hitherto secured in her well-made upper caste world, the story is epiphanic. It eases open and displays totally different logic to a violence that has hitherto been described to her only in terms that distance and repudiate it as—and I can think of no better example than the comment by the celebrated playwright Vijay Tendulkar, cited in his foreword to

Bagul's book—'uneducated, uncultured, abnormal.'[5] It is a logic that
(1) implicates both her and her world anew, since it replaces the mark
of this extradited 'Other' on the many institutions, familial, psychic,
ethical, that ground her personal, and therefore as a feminist also her
political, life and (2) renews her understanding of patriarchy and the
subjugations that structure and sustain it.

For the widow-mother protagonist—and for the dalit feminist—
nothing comes so easily, yet there is in the story the stirring of a new
kind of movement: from the never-ceasing shuttle between the extraditions and deaths that comprise her impossible life, to a struggle to
leave, and in that single act to renotate the world. It is a movement,
not so much to demand entry into the many temples of the contemporary world, but to re-designate and rework those institutions. The
beginnings of a movement, possibly, from untouchable-harijan to dalit.

But what exactly is untouchability in this dalit story? I think it is
significant that Baburao Bagul refers to each of the interpretative
frameworks that address the caste question, but takes issue with all of
them. Thus, both *varnashramadharma* (and untouchability as it is con-
figured in that brahminical-colonial-Gandhian scheme of scholarship
and politics) and sanskritization (Indian sociology's attempt to mod-
ernize brahminism by transforming it into a question of consent and
aspiration and not bigotry or exploitation) are noted emblematically.
It is easy to provide examples: the Hindu (?) widow is the central
figure, the move from the village to the city sets the plot in motion,
the narrative opens with the child's desire for a mother who is a *Vatsalya Sindhu*, 'Don't touch Pandu, any of you', Kishan yells out. The
question of consent, more specifically the question of what exactly
constitutes consent for a subject that stands thus, askew, in the grids
of citizenship—is thematic in this story which might well be read as
an extended discussion of the dynamics of that single issue. However,
in the citation-re-theorization occasioned by this story each of these
classical objects of political theory are so transformed that they are
virtually, yet not totally, unrecognizable. In contrast, the question of
political economy is addressed, and its effects insistently documented.
We are told that the children in the community are backward and
ill-nourished, the family immiserated, the father tubercular and jobless,
the mother slaves at a construction site for the pittance that will put
a meal a day into their bellies, lower caste women live in constant
fear of sexual attack, the unemployed hang around the basti, drunk
and depressed, or move around in lumpen-rowdy gangs. Here too
the objects are emblematic, but they are recognizable as those of a

Nehruvian/socialist scheme of things. Structurally however, the narrative accords neither political economy nor history the status of an interpretative horizon. Work, wages, property, expropriation all figure here, as does the aspiration for a wholesome humanity. But they are drawn into a frame that reworks the discursive logic of untouchability as it proposes a theory of caste as (1) extraditions that are revised and renewed by a brahminism that is constantly updating its patriarchy, (2) desire in the scene of the family, and (3) bodies that are compelled by, but disallowed contract into the feminine or masculine; bodies, therefore, that shuttle, always deficient, always in excess. In brief, as terror in the domain of the citizen-subject.

V

If in modern Indian literature the choice of the widow as protagonist should be read as an announcement that the text is an intervention in feminist theory, how might we describe the political/theoretical moves that are being made by the texts that we have been discussing? It seems to me that the stories represent two of the most powerful contesting forces within feminism today. On the one hand the pressures of a re-empowered middle class whose Fund-Bank aspirations are global, and who must remake its humanism to suit. On the other the questions raised by the dalit movement, terrifying and full of promise.

ACKNOWLEDGEMENTS

Different versions of this paper were read at Columbia and Cornell Universities, SUNY at Syracuse, the Universities of Pennsylvania and Michigan and the Central Institute of English and Foreign Languages. I am grateful to each of these audiences as well as to other members of the Subaltern Studies editorial collective and my research students for stimulating discussion. Special thanks to Satish Poddval and Mary John for their detailed and extremely useful comments.

NOTES

1. Jean Genet, *The Screens*, (trans. Bernard Fretchman), Faber and Faber, London, 1963: 57.

2. Gita Hariharan, *The Act of Dying, and Other Stories,* Penguin, New Delhi, 1992.

3. Kumud Pavde, at the Fourth World Conference of Women, Beijing, September 1995.

4. Walter Benjamin, *The Task of the Translator*, (trans. Harry Zohn), Schocken Books, New York 1968: 69–82.

5. Vijay Tendulkar's 'Foreword,' in Baburao Bagul, *Maran Swasth Hoth Aahe* (Death will be Comfort), Continental Publishers, Pune, 1969.

Femininity and Sexual Difference
A Critical Reading of Helene Cixous

Vidhu Verma

I

INTRODUCTION

In this paper, I explore a reading of sexual difference as found in the
work of Helene Cixous, a French feminist writer. Born in Oran,
Algeria, in 1937, she had a mother of European Jewish descent and
a father of Mediterranean descent. She was brought up in Algeria and
lived there until 1955 when she left for France. Her family background,
her birthplace, her exposure at an early age to several languages, and
political upheavals such as the rise of Nazism and the Algerian war,
have been determining factors in her writing. Beginning with her doctoral thesis entitled 'The Exile of James Joyce, or the Art of Replacement', she has explored in a variety of fictional works, the themes of
loss, exile, death and origins. What interested me most and, finally
motivated me to write this paper, is the way her works address and
explore the relations between sexuality and writing. She claims, in a
move which defies the laws of literary genre, the need for the author
to be the 'lightest and most transparent' in order to talk of the Other,
and 'to create the other's space'.[1] Assuming an epic dimension, her
texts repeat characters, their stories, events and conflicts which travel
from one text to another without ending or beginning.

Given the range of questions she raises I would like to specify,
right at the beginning, that this paper deals with only one aspect of
her writing—the part played by writing in the construction of sexual
difference. She has written innumerable political tracts, plays and
literary works which are unimaginable in their sheer intensity. I have
focused on a relatively smaller number of texts published till 1990.

Much of her recent writing has been concerned with theatre. Recent plays include 'The Terrible but Unfinished Story of Sihanouk' and 'India of their Dreams'.

In India, many scholars are familiar with the American and British feminist tradition but the work of French feminist theorists has not been very influential. However, the involvement with women's writing has rapidly developed over the years and it has focused on the stereotypical ways in which women have been represented. I was, therefore, keen to investigate Cixous' approach towards writing; the way it questions the dominant traditions in the philosophy of language in which the contrasts between logical discourse and experience have been foundational. Like Cixous, I believe, we need to examine the attitude towards language that has confined women's knowledge and expression. I make no claim, in this essay, to examine the entire gamut of ideas she has covered. I will only try to set forth a few points of interest to us, which arise out of her research.

In this paper, I present Cixous as a feminist philosopher whose work should be seen as representative of a feminine practice of writing, known as *ecriture feminine* (henceforth EF) but also as being distinctive enough to be treated separately. Her explicit focus on the relationship between writing and sexual difference sets her apart from contemporary French scholars.[2] Her approach is also distinctive in that it informs us about the theories concerning the place of women in language that has no counterpart in Anglo-Saxon literature.[3]

I first examine the basic tenets of a 'feminine' practice of writing as practised and formulated by Helene Cixous in the context of the contemporary debate on sexual difference (see Phillips 1987; Barrett and Phillips 1992). By moving away from the abstract universal categories of the enlightenment, she questions the prevailing readings of sexual difference. The present analysis will focus on whether she is successful in attacking the universalizing pretensions of previous traditions. I then look at the challenge and paradox central to EF: it purports to subvert the patriarchal order, but is bound up in the very system or reading it claims to undermine. It is argued by some scholars that EF does little more than emphasize women's basic anatomical differences with men. Does EF perpetuate and recreate stereotypes about women as sexual and biological by celebrating them? To what extent is this a regressive move informed by the same concerns of a patriarchal tradition it claims to eventually dismantle? As I hope will be demonstrated, the answers to these questions are extremely complex. The transformations in Cixous' writing over the last twenty years cannot be reduced to one position. Her essays on the transformative and political dimensions of writing indicate conflicting ways of defining what feminine writing is. Moreover, there is a contradiction in Cixous' work rising out of those statements which affirm the cultural and historical aspects of the body and those which fail to explain how such aspects manifest themselves.

II

EQUALITY AND DIFFERENCE

What reading of the history of sexual difference is made possible in the existing philosophical space? What space does the work of Helene Cixous occupy?

A common space for a discourse on the difference between the sexes begins by presupposing the immutability of the relation—a belief in the ahistoricity of their difference. Sexual difference is seen as a conflictual transaction whose terms have been defined once and for all. But this imaginary philosophical object is problematic (see Fraisse 1994). When we talk about the history of sexual difference, there is no single philosophical criterion that testifies to its presence in its own right. The criteria for establishing differences change historically and within each society. Neither sexuality nor the female body can be taken as fixed and universal. The nature and extent of variation in gender relations across time, cultures, and social divisions is difficult to establish.

For example, the reading of SD in any society includes the impact of culture on the construction of the Self. According to some studies of Hindu culture, as far as male psychological development is concerned, the 'ultimate authority in the Indian mind has always been feminine. It is this authority that the traditional Indian male propitiates or makes peace with ... (Nandy 1993: 38; see Kakar 1991).

Further, if we turn to study history as an event like the national movement, it appears as an occasion for a redefinition of sexual difference. History presents itself as the site of new discourses which justify changes. We can see how the relation between the sexes is reformulated when society adopts a new political agenda, as we did, in India, by adopting the constitution. Such examples make it implausible for us to view sexual difference as a transaction which has been defined once and for all.

A second reading of sexual difference is by examining it in opposition to the debate on equality. In the past several years, the equality vs. difference debate has been used to characterize conflicting feminist positions. The question of whether men and women differ other than in reproducitve capacities, and whether such differences account for distinctions in social role and status, has generated heated arguments over the past two decades.

What are the central issues involved in the debate on equality?

Juridical equality as a fundamental value provides a major inspiration for many feminist writers sympathetic to the liberal tradition. It does not deny sexual difference but neutralizes it in favour of a representation of non-sexed individuals with identical juridical roles. But equality in its formal aspect fails to highlight many kinds of discrimination against women and to note specific biological differences between men and women (for example, women have a different set of needs like maternity leave related to their body whereas men can demand paternity leave only on the basis of their social role).[4]

Another version of the equality debate claims that the basis of women's subordination to men lies in their reproductive biology. Science and developments in technology make it possible to transform and control reproductive and procreative practices. Therefore, the specificity of the reproductive body must be overcome if sexual equality is to be realized (see De Beauvoir 1983; Firestone 1970).

Yet another version argues for eliminating and transcending traditional distinctions of masculinity and femininity even if biological differences are retained. This belief is based on the assumption that human beings are not necessarily constituted by society but instead are capable of withdrawing from society to redefine their own identity. A commitment to abolition of sex roles is taken to imply a commitment to androgyny. Androgynous people would remain biologically male or female but socially and psychologically they would no longer be masculine or feminine. In short, according to this version there should be no characteristic, behaviour, or role ascribed to any human being on the basis of her/his sex.

The difference response has several versions amongst which is the one inspired by Marx's theory. Socialist feminists locate the fundamental cause of gender differences in the organization of production or sexual division of labour. Women's natures are formed by the interaction between their biological constitution and their physical and social environments. In order to understand women in a given society, 'we must examine the kinds of labour they perform, the ways in which this labour is organized, and the social relations that women form with each other and with men as a result of their labour and its mode of organization' (Jaggar 1983: 83).[5]

In contrast to the above version, some feminists advocate the affirmation and celebration of women's bodies and their capacity to recreate and nurture. In its most extreme form this view argues that the specific capacities and powers of women's bodies imply an essential difference between men and women, where women are presented as essentially loving and caring, and men as aggressive and selfish. These scholars argue that there is an essential difference which should be retained, not eroded by scientific intervention.

An exponent of this version, Carol Gilligan, claims that the ethics of justice and ethics of care are two different moral orientations. The ethics of care indicate how women's moral judgement relies on relationships and narratives instead of obligations, rights, and impartiality (see Gilligan 1982: 19).

Helene Cixous rejects both these readings of sexual difference. She proposes a reading which challenges sexual difference as an eternal transaction and aims to move beyond the equality vs. difference paradigm.

In her writings, Cixous draws our attention to the way binary oppositions operate in western political thought. Her critique involves reversing and displacing the hierarchical construction rather than accepting it as self-evident. Such hierarchical structures also dominate the formation of female subjectivity and thus of sexual difference (see Shiach 1991: 6–7). Moreover, sexual difference is locked into a structure of power, where difference, or otherness, is tolerated only when repressed. This view is illustrated in her writings on equality and more specifically on EF.

Two arguments figure in Cixous against the versions of equality I mention above. First, in insisting on equality as something women claim despite all differences, they have been encouraged to deny aspects of themselves and to conform to some unitary norm. Second, that this norm was never gender neutral. Like other proponents of EF, Helene Cixous believes that the way forward for women does not lie in achieving equality within the system. Equal rights fail to indicate how the patriarchal system embodied in our language has repressed and made use of women's difference (see Cixous 1984a: 55). Instead of a search for equality in which we are as 'phallic' as they are, Cixous feels the need to conceive of processes in which,

upon entering society one does not identify with men but that one works on other possibilities of living, on other modes of life, on other relationships to the other ... in such a way that one also brings about transformations in oneself, in others and in men (ibid.: 56, 60).

The equality versus difference paradigm cannot structure choices for feminist theory and politics: the oppositional pairing misrepresents the relationship of both the terms. Both responses are caught up within the same paradigm by understanding the body as a given biological entity which either has or does not have certain ahistorical characteristics and capacities. To this extent the equality versus difference debate is located within a framework which assumes a body/mind or nature/culture dualism. Therefore she argues, instead of framing analyses and strategies as if such binary terms were timeless, we need to ask how the dichotomous pairing of equality and difference works. Instead of remaining within the terms of existing political discourse, we need to subject these terms to critical examination.

In the next section, I look at Cixous' attempt at providing an alternative to the equality vs. difference paradigm. There is nothing self-evident about difference even if sexual difference is seemingly apparent. The questions she raises are: What qualities or aspects are being compared? How is the meaning of difference being constructed?

III

AN ALTERNATIVE PRACTICE OF WRITING

In this section, I examine Cixous' claim that the categories of patriarchal language created and maintained by the contemporary masculine order cannot express women. She studies the relationship between writing as a means of reformulating the principles of the present masculine order and as a generative force capable of expressing sexual differences through EF. The passages I have selected for this exploration are cogent examples of the strengths and weakness of this dominant concept.

In the final section I examine whether Cixous' work marks the beginning of a space for interrogating the feminine or it is a retreat into conventional ways of understanding the world. Some questions are raised: If the current order defines and obliterates women, how can we conceive ourselves in ways which escape its schema? Is our task to refuse existing power altogether and to formulate a new language derived from a different experience and desire? Is it plausible for women to analyse their own experience—inscribe in writing a new order not defined by the masculine?

The first element of Cixous' theorization of a practice of feminine writing can be found in her discussion of alternative representations of sexual difference. She rejects the Freudian and Lacanian models which privilege the phallus in the formation of sexual identity (see Shiach 1991: 16–17). Secondly, the subject of EF offers an opportunity for change. Writing with the body has the following two components. The first is that women's bodies including our sexual experiences have been determined by men. She urges women to break the parameters of masculine definitions and to express themselves in writing. Second, for her, speaking and writing involve the translation of thoughts through a complex network of chemical messages and movements. A writing, which is close to the rhythms of the body, and which infuses life into the text, reconstitutes subjectivity in new ways.

In what follows, I examine evidence to support the view that despite Cixous' claim to go beyond the binary distinctions of the enlightenment tradition, she seems to put forward an essentialist view of woman's body and language in her earlier writings such as 'Sorties', 'The Laugh of the Medusa', 'Castration or Decapitation?'. I shall argue that a 'movement', a visible transformation, is noted only in her recent writings (see Shiach 1991). These later writings constitute a yearning toward and almost a grasping of, an alternative practice of writing.

In one of the better known texts, 'The Laugh of the Medusa', Cixous urges us to dismantle patriarchy through the exploration of a unique women's language, created by and manifesting women's sexual difference. Women must 'come' to writing in order to explode the dominant masculine text and to replace it with a feminine counterpart. She then argues for the possibility of understanding such sexual difference, at the level of sexual pleasure, of *jouissance*. Female pleasure is superior to the phallic single-mindedness it transcends, since woman's 'libido is cosmic, just as her unconscious is world wide' (1976: 889). Here she opposes a definition of sexual difference based on anatomical/body parts and instead focuses on physical drives: sexual pleasure.

Although Cixous argues against the notion of a female sexuality which is 'uniform, homogeneous, classifiable into codes—any more than you can talk about one unconscious resembling another', she is of the view that until now women's writing has been controlled by a masculine economy. Hence, the need for a woman to write 'herself', which will allow her to carry out the transformations in her history (ibid.: 976). In order to become taker and initiator,

woman must write her self: must write about women and bring women to writing, from which they have been driven away as violently as from their bodies. ... Woman must put herself into the text—as into the world and into history—by her own movement. (ibid.: 875)

In an attempt to avoid a narrow definition of EF, Cixous maintains that it is 'impossible to define a feminine practice of writing and this is an impossibility that will remain, for this practice can never be theorized, enclosed, coded—which doesn't mean that it doesn't exist (ibid.: 883).

But in this text Cixous accepts a certain level of essentialism when she writes of the 'false woman' who is 'preventing the live one from breathing'. Again she describes woman's speech as one which 'passes into her voice' as opposed to a speech marked by logic (ibid.: 881). I shall discuss this point later.

In Castration or Decapitation Cixous offers a practice of writing that is akin to 'flying' in language. She aims to do this by providing multitudes of meanings against single fixed meanings. She puts forward a text that has neither origin, nor end, a text with several beginnings, a text that goes on and on (see 1981: 53).

This position is reiterated in her later writings like *The Newly Born Woman* (1985). The feminine practice of writing resists enclosure in conceptual frameworks:

At the present time, defining a feminine practice of writing is impossible with an impossibility that will continue. ... But it will always exceed the discourse governing the phallocentric system (see Cixous 1990: 36).

In these texts Cixous also maintains that the nature of femininity cannot be determined once and for all, but that we can hope for a 'glimpse' of a different economy of sexuality.

What distinctive aspects can be identified as important for construction of more representative women's writing? Cixous implicity acknowledges features of EF by viewing women as determined by the masculine economy even as writers. According to her, most women who write have for the most part, considered themselves to be writing not as women, but as writers. Such women may declare that sexual difference means nothing, that there's no attributable difference between masculine and feminine writing. ... Most women are like this: they do someone else's—man's—writing and in their innocence sustain it and give it voice, and end up producing writing that's in effect masculine ... to be signed with a woman's name doesn't necessarily make a piece of writing feminine. (1981: 51–2; see 1987: 1; 1988b: 25).

She goes on to claim that femininity can be found in writings by men. But this claim is validated only if Cixous has an idea of what feminine writing is.

On closer examination we have evidence that Cixous' adoption of the term 'feminine' derives from the description of a particular type of response to the laws which govern patriarchy. For example, biblical patriarchs might blame Eve for the eviction from paradise. But Cixous interprets Eve's decision to follow her desire as feminine and her response as arising from a different process of communication. In a very engaging text, 'Reaching the Point of Wheat, or A Portrait of the Artist as a Maturing Woman', she explains:

I think it is true that her decision must have been determined by something 'feminine' in her structure, particularly her desire and her non-fear of knowing what is inside ... Taste is the first act of knowledge, for women and for all men who are women. (1987: 3.)

In her essay 'Tancredi Continues', Cixous cites the example of the famous lovers who were absolutely faithful to their own being—not as man or woman (see 1988b: 42). Despite their diversity, the subtext of many of these essays is the emphasis on fractionated identities; gender identities are not fixed to one another, but mediate with each other over a wide range of possibilities.

Given this rough idea of a feminine practice of writing, we can then look for texts which appear to be women texts. According to Cixous, a feminine textual body can be defined as a 'female libidinal economy, a regime, energies, a system of spending not necessarily carved out by culture .... it is always endless, without ending: there is no closure, it does not stop. ... These are texts that work on the beginning but not on the origin. The origin is a masculine myth ...' (1981: 53).

She describes the feminine texts as being close to the voice, 'very close to the flesh of the language, much more so than masculine texts, '... there's tactility in the feminine text, there's touch. ...' (ibid.: 54). The works of Clarice Lispector, a Brazilian writer, are seen to possess a 'peculiarly female attentiveness to objects', the ability to perceive and present them in a 'nurturing' rather than a 'dominating' way. Cixous' work may also be considered as an example of feminine writing. She speaks of other male writers such as James Joyce, Kafka, Kleist, Genet and Shakespeare, who have produced antiphallocentric texts, and which show a great deal of femininity. But how do such men overcome the differences based on sexual pleasure which are emphasized by Cixous?

Although she fails to answer this question, in the journal *Boundary*, Cixous attempts to clear some of the misconceptions that have arisen concerning her work. Elaborating her position, she describes 'feminine writing' as a 'dangerous and stylish expression full of traps which leads to all kinds of confusions. First of all words like masculine and feminine which circulate everywhere and which are completely distorted by everyday usage, words which refer, of course, to a classical vision of sexual opposition between men and women are our burden'. She chooses to speak of a 'decipherable libidinal femininity' which can be located in a writing produced by a male or female (1984a: 51).

Libidinal femininity, in principle, remains the most thoroughgoing and compelling example we have of confrontation with the idea of sexual difference. All that is ultimately left behind by Cixous, as soon as she attempts to convey its meaning. She asserts that the economy said to be feminine would be characterized by features, traits, which are more adventurous, more on the side of spending, riskier, on the side of the body, is more livable in women than in men (1984: 54). Or more explicitly, a feminine libidinal economy stands for the Other's freedom—it is an economy which tolerates the movements of the Other, 'the comings and goings' (see 1990: 38). Unlike the masculine, which is associated with appropriation, the feminine is about taking the Other into oneself, and being taken into the Other—'the art of receiving' and the 'art of giving' (see 1987: 19).

I should clarify that Cixous doesn't believe that a man and a woman are identical. Sexual differences exist even if the binary distinctions do not make any sense. In her conversations, she argues that 'men and women have the whole of humanity in common', and that

at the same time there is something different, I consider a benediction. Our differences have to do with the way we experience pleasure, with our bodily experiences, which are not the same.... The way we make love—because it isn't the same—produces different sensations and recollections. And these are transmitted through the text' (Sellers 1988b: 150; see ibid.: 15).

What is repeated in most of these essays is that biological differences between the sexes give rise to different bodily experiences, different perceptions, and thus create different sources of knowledge.

Such unambiguous statements on sexual difference are followed by those that point out the difficulties in asserting it in the first place. In some articles, she modifies this position by introducing the term 'libidinal economy' which I mentioned above. She sees the body sometimes as distinctly cultural as caught up in representation. In these she argues

it is not anatomical sex that determines anything here. It is, on the contrary, history ... the cultural schema and the way the individual negotiates with these schema, with these data, adapts to them and reproduces them ... if we resign ourselves to keeping words like 'feminine' and 'masculine' it is because there is an anchoring point somewhere in a far distant reality. ... Let us try as quickly as possible to abandon these binary distinctions which never make sense. (1988: 18.)

Given the discussion above we may argue that instead of ignoring women's biological and cultural history, Cixous maintains that we must take account of it and demonstrate how women's special features make possible a different form of writing. In these texts, there is a hint at uncertainty as well as the interweaving of the two libidinal economies.

This is evident again in her later writings such as 'Difficult Joys'. She adopts a position against constructing sexual difference around pleasure. While discussing the 'quarrel' of sexual difference in writing, she admits it is not simple: 'I don't believe that women are sheerly women and men, men' (1990b: 23).

IV

SEXUALITY AND WOMEN'S WRITING

From the above discussion we find the idea of a 'shuffling' gender identity in Cixous' work. I have also argued that she wavers between affirming sexual difference and denying any definition of that difference. In Cixous' work there is a hint of a writing which is 'feminine' and yet which goes beyond the limitations of gender (see Still 1990b: 49). What is of particular interest to us is the way she favours texts that undermine the fixed categories of sexual identity. But because Cixous has described the different experiences of a male or female body as entailing different sensations and perceptions and offering different sources of metaphor for understanding these, she seems as being close to an essentialist position (ibid.). She suggests, for instance, that the female potential for 'pleasure' and the ability to give birth to another human being may contain the basis for an alternative Self (see Jones 1981).

This has given rise to several interpretations of her work which represent a range of political positions. Two interpretations which I examine above, can be found directed both against Cixous in particular and against *ecriture feminine* in general. Some call her a biological essentialist while others try to locate her idea of the feminine. The first charge of biological essentialism implies that she assumes an unmediated causal relation between biological sex and sexual identity based on pleasure (see ibid.). In addition, she takes the feminine to be a pregiven libido, prior to language, in which specific female drives are grounded, thus positing two distinct libidos. This charge is illustrated by various passages from her early writings, which we examined above. Cixous defines a woman's language as closer to the body, to sexual pleasure and that this closeness to the body and to nature could be subversive (see Marks and Courtivron 1981: 219).

This critique is based on the fear that she is offering an ahistorical and therefore essential definition of female specificity and thereby positing a femininity which is not constructed by society. She reduces the diversity of women to a falsifying unity by ignoring social divisions such as racial and class differences. Some writers also criticize her for a preoccupation with the text, a lack of political analysis and for omitting any materialist analysis of power (see Moi 1985).[6]

This challenge is also directed against her idea of the 'feminine'. Cixous evades defining a feminine practice of writing but she alludes to that notion in most of her writings. Very roughly, to speak or write like a man, is to assert mastery, to be in control of meaning, to claim truth, objectivity, whereas to speak like a woman is to allow an outpouring of meanings.

But it would be a mistake to attribute to Cixous a static notion of 'woman' or 'femininity' whether it is woman as essence, or woman as outside history. The originality and the limits of Cixous' project are strictly linked and difficult to disentangle. The originality consists in her introduction of 'woman' as a concept implicated in the male/female oppositions of patriarchal metaphysics. What Cixous tries to do is to subvert the discourse of patriarchy and reveal its contradictions. The project involves challenging the masculine monopoly on the construction of femininity, the female body and woman. These constructions prevent women from expressing their sexuality. EF claims to offer ways in which institutions and signifying practices (speech, writing, images, myths) belonging to masculine culture can be resisted. For this reason it is inappropriate to reduce her project to an essentialist strategy. Instead it is plausible to see her quest for an exploration of an individual feminine subjectivity in the earlier writings *shifting*, towards an understanding of history as a struggle between two competing economies (see Shiach 1991).

Occasionally Cixous advances questions of political identification, specially those related to her Arab childhood (see 1984a: 59). In 'Poetry is/and (the) Political' she explains, 'receiving is a woman's science. Knowing how to receive is the best of gifts... is the poetic-political practice (see Cixous 1980: 36). Certainly the self predominates in her narrative. But she explains the self's centrality historically and politically as in 'From the Scene of the Unconscious to Scene of History', where she writes explicitly of the 'Self' as one 'that has come to be reconciled with the difficulties of the world. But it is not given, it must be formed' (1989: 9). She asks, being aware of the dangers of essentialism, 'Of whose History am I the witness? How to unite History and text?' (ibid.: 11). The self exists here as part of an interdependent network between the biological and other material factors. Hence it is incorrect to propose the thesis that she is preoccupied only with the text.

The strength of Cixous' reading comes from her attention to the equality vs. sexual difference paradigm. She wants us to recognize that human identity is sexually differentiated and exists in bodily form, whereas the debate on equality tends to deny the body, and to deal only in the abstraction of the individual or the citizen.[7] Difference, as presented by her, however, is not concerned with privileging an essentially biological difference between the sexes. Rather it is concerned with the unsteady and unattached space, in which bodies are recognized as different only in so far as they are viewed as possessing or lacking some socially privileged quality or qualities. More important, her work also involves a yearning towards an alternative practice of writing. But to what extent this form of writing succeeds in constructing an alternative symbolic order cannot still be answered in a definite way. I cannot see any firmly constructed theory here since her writings beg us to imagine an entirely different social order.

That brings us to two limitations present in Cixous' work. In politics, she challenges the theory of assimilation which implies the transcendence of group difference. This ideal assumes equal social status for all persons treating everyone according to the same principles, rules and standards. In contrast, a politics of difference argues for equality, and the participation and inclusion of all groups, which requires different treatment for oppressed or disadvantaged groups. Therefore, the principle of equality should not rest on how similar we are or how closely we approximate the norm. What we need is a multiple plurality in which being different matters. Such a formulation will focus attention more on other forms of oppression and thus link up the politics around sex, class and race. The politics of difference suspects all universal standpoints including the feminist one and dislocates the centrality assigned to theoretical categories like patriarchy through which we can challenge gender oppression. If Cixous acknowledges a politics of difference, it rests uneasily with her ideas on sexual difference which privileges the libidinal economy (see section II).[8]

In arguing as such, my aim is both to remind us of the continued relevance of her reading of sexual difference and to emphasize the political importance of attending to the historical context. One reason why Cixous' construction of an alternative symbolic order is incomplete, I suggest, in that it is located within the contradictory space of these two claims—that have essentialist references to woman and those statements in which the historical/cultural is admitted (see Still 1990: 51). On the one hand she admits important contributions to the history of feminist thought which have been made by men. Obviously neither the ability nor the willingness to contribute to feminist understanding is a sex-linked trait. Here 'masculine' describes not a biological category but a cognitive style. On the other hand she believes that certain female traits give rise to literary modes which emerge from the libidinal sources rather than social and cultural sources. There is radical potential in her emphasis on the body as the place where we engage with and understand the world. But that potential is limited if the body is sometimes presented in essentialist terms.

The manner in which Cixous claims that gender differences have significant historical implications is, however, misleading. In some essays, she seems to ignore these features, privileging the private body at the same time as she denies its role in public history. For example, on the historical novel, Cixous writes,

if I were to write a historical novel, what would it matter if I were a man or woman? But if I write about love, then it does matter. I write differently. If I write letting something of my body come through then this will be different, depending on whether I have experience of a feminine or masculine body. (Sellers 1988b: 150; see 1988c).

In 'The Two Countries of Writing' Cixous writes of this dilemma again:

I write as a woman. So as a woman I can write of women. As a woman, I can use my body to inscribe the body of a woman. But I can't do that for a man. So if I wrote a novel, I would have on the one hand a complete woman and on the other hand semi-real men. This I can't do. (1988a: 10; see 1989: 15.)

It is due to such contradictory claims that feminist research has found Cixous' work as being ahistorical or essentialist.

To conclude on the questions raised in the beginning of this paper, it is in its most formal sense that we can say that a feminine practice of writing, proposed by Helene Cixous, is based on an essentialist position. Such an interpretation arises because, in her eagerness to defend women as women in order to counteract patriarchal definitions of women, Cixous' concern is to identify a female identity and specificity. In her early writings, the feminine text is described in biological terms—as close to the flesh (see 1981: 54). She rightly points to the need to deconstruct the various symbolizing procedures that hold the patriarchal vision in place. Later, in the concept of libidinal femininity, Cixous is positing that the oppositions might relate to each other, that is, each sex might be able to assume each other's characteristics. The problem is that of the conditions under which women might be able to write. She believes that women have always been writing in the way masculine economy has wanted them to. Either we are speaking a masculine language and hence are inarticulate as women or we are outside the symbolic structures of language. But to assert that women have been caught in a web structured by masculine concepts implies that women are incapable of analysing their oppression unless they devise a new writing unfettered by the masculine order. Recent research, however, invalidates such claims. There are numerous examples of women writing in a language of their own and sometimes in a prose which is 'not gender-marked' (see Sarkar 1993: 59). Many feminist scholars suggest, while retrieving past narratives, that gender poetics are not always monolithic male constructs, and allow women to present positive images of the Self, images that we can recognize and value (see Tharu and Lalita 1991).[9] I suggest that the dismantling of metaphysical oppositions, a task Cixous ably performs, is only part of a long journey. We need a framework, for understanding women's writing which allows access, not only to the subversive, but also to the female voices struggling to be heard in our patriarchal tradition.

ACKNOWLEDGEMENTS

I wish to thank the Maison des sciences de l'homme (Paris) for allowing me to collect research material for this paper in 1994. I am grateful to Madame Gentot and Monsieur Racine for giving me a peaceful and stimulating academic home for several weeks, and to Danielle Maase-Dubosc, Genevieve Fraisse and Francoise Picq for introducing me to French feminist scholarship. I owe a special debt to Helene Cixous who gave generously her time and published material.

NOTES

1. See her conversations in Susan Sellers, ed. (1988: 153).

2. She has been identified with a group of feminists such as Kristeva, Irigaray and Derrida and Barthes. Here I am referring to the way her approach is different from eminent French feminists like Christine Delphy, Michelle Perrot and Colette Guilluimme.

3. The intellectual background of French feminism differs sharply from the American and British feminist traditions. Anglo-Saxon literature has generally focused on the material oppression of women and the power relations between men and women, a task ignored by the French feminists I refer to. But the emphasis on women's experience tends to overlook the relation between language and writing, reading, and texts.

4. See Phillips, ed. (1987).

5. According to Holmstrom, the differences between men and women can be explained by the 'sexual division of labour institutionalized into sets of practices and social and cultural institutions' which is further 'subsumed under a theory explaining the sexual/social division of labour'. Cited in 1984: 465.

6. For instance in 'The Laugh of the Medusa' she writes of woman as 'the taker and initiator' in every symbolic system, in 'every political process', without explaining what the political is, see 1976: 880.

7. Carole Pateman (1988) argues that the citizen is based on the male image. To extend to women the 'masculine' conception of the individual, is to sweep away the intrinsic relations between the female owner, her body and reproductive capacities.

8. In a recent paper Cixous (1993) raises questions of a very different kind— of literary and political commitment—which I have not taken up.

9. For a critique of recent women, writing in India see Rajeshwari Sundar Rajan (1993).

REFERENCES

Allen, Jeffner and Iris Young's, (eds.), 1989, *The Thinking Muse: Feminism and Modern French Philosophy*, Indiana University Press, Bloomington.

Barrett, Michele, 1987, The concept of difference, *Feminist Review*, 26 (Summer).

——, and A. Phillips (eds.), 1992 *Destablizing Theory, Contemporary feminist debates*, Polity Press, London.

Benhabib, Seyla and D. Cornell (eds.), 1987, *Feminism as Critique: Essays on the politics of gender in late-capitalist societies*, Polity Press, Blackwell.

Bordo, Susan, 1986, The Cartesian masculinazation of thought, *Signs*, (11) 3.

Braidotti, Rosi, 1986, Ethics revisited. Women and/in philosophy, cited in Pateman and Gross (eds.).

——, 1989, The politics of ontological difference, in Brennan (ed.).

Brennan, Teresa (ed.), 1989, *Between Feminism and Psychoanalysis,* Routledge, London.

Butler, Judith and Joan Scott (eds.), 1992, *Feminists Theorize the Political*, Routledge, New York.

Cixous, Helene, 1984a, Interviews with Verena Conly, *Boundary*, vol. 12, no. 2.

Chodorow, Nancy, 1978, *The Reproduction of Mothering. Psychoanalysis and the sociology of gender,* University of California, Berkeley.

Conley, V.A. and William Spanos, 1984, On feminine writing: Boundary symposium, *Boundary*, (12) 2.

De Beauvoir, Simone, 1983, *The Second Sex*, Penguin, London.

DeLauretis, Teresa, 1984, *Feminist Studies/Critical Studies*, Indiana University Press, Bloomington.

Derrida, Jacques, 1974, *Of Grammatology* (tran. Gayatri Chakravorty Spivak), John Hopkins University, Baltimore.

Duchen, Claire (ed.), 1987, *French Connections. Voices from the women's movement in France*, Hutchinson, London.

Eagelton, Mary., 1986, *Feminist Literary Theory. A Reader*, Basil Blackwell, Oxford.

Faure, Christine, 1981, The twilight of the goddesses or the intellectual crisis of French feminism, *Signs* 7 (11).

Firestone, S., 1970, *The Dialectic of Sex: The case for feminist revolution*, William Morrow, New York.

Flax, Jane, 1987, Post-modernism and gender relations in feminist theory, *Signs*, 12 (4).

Fraisse, Genevieve, 1994, *Reason's Muse. Sexual Difference and the Birth of Democracy,* Chicago Press, Chicago.

Gilligan, Carol, 1992, In a Different Voice. *Psychological Theary and Women's Development* (Harvard University Press, Cambridge)

Griffiths, Morwenna and Margaret Whitford (eds.), 1988, *Feminist Perspectives in Philosophy*, Macmillan, London.

Harding, Sandra and M.B. Hintikka (eds.), 1983, *Discovering Reality: Feminist Perspectives on Epistemology, Metaphysics, Methodology and Philosophy of Science*, Dordrecht, Reidel.

Holmstrom, N., 1984, A Marxist theory of women's nature, *Ethics*, 8 (3).

Jaggar, Alison, 1983, *Feminist Politics and Human Nature*, Harvester, Brighton.

Jardine, Alice, 1981, Introduction to Julia Kristeva's women's time, *Signs*, 7 (11).

Jones, Ann Rosalind, 1981, 'Writing the Body. Towards an understanding of 'Ecriture feminine', *Feminist Studies*, 7 (2).

Kakar, Sudhir, 1991, *Intimate Relations, Exploring Indian sexuality*, Penguin, Delhi.

Kuhn, Annette, 1988, Introduction to Helene Cixous's 'Castration or Decapitation', *Signs*, 7 (11)

Lovibond, Sabina, 1989, Feminism and postmodernism, *New Left Review* 178 (November-December).

Marks, Elaine and I. de Courtivron (eds.), 1981, *New French Feminisms*, Harvester, Brighton.

Miller, N., 1986, *The Poetics of Gender*, Columbia University, New York.

Mitchell, Juliet, 1975, *Psychoanalysis and Feminism*, Penguin, London.

Moi, Toril, 1985, *Sexual/Textual Politics. Feminist literary theory,* Methuen, London.

—— (ed.), 1987, *French Feminist Thought,* Blackwell, Oxford.

Nandy, Ashis, 1993, *At the Edge of Psychology. Essays in politics and culture*, Oxford University Press, Delhi.

Nicholson, Linda J. (ed.), 1990, *Feminism/Postmodernism*, Routledge, New York.

Niranjana, T., P. Sudhir, V. Dhareshwar (eds.), 1993, *Interrogating Modernity. Culture and colonialism in India*, Seagull, Calcutta.

Pateman, Carole, 1988, *The Sexual Contract*, Polity Press, Cambridge.

Pateman, Carole and Elizabeth Gross. (eds.), 1986, *Feminist Challenges. Social and political theory*, Allen & Unwin, London.

Philips, Anne, (ed.), 1987, *Feminism and Equality*. Blackwell, Oxford.

Ray, Bharati, (ed.), 1995, *From the Seams of History*, Oxford University Press, Delhi.

Sarkar, Tanika, 1993, A book of her own. A life of her own. Autobiography of a nineteenth century woman, *History Workshop Journal*, 36.

Showalter, Elaine, 1986, *The New Feminist Criticism. Essays on women. Literature and theory*, Virago, London.

Stanton, Domna C., 1986, Difference on trial. A critique of the maternal metaphor in Cixous, Irigaray and Kristeva, in Nancy K. Miller (ed.), *The Poetics of Gender*, Columbia University Press, New York.

Sunder Rajan, Rajeshwari, 1993, *Real and Imagined Women. Gender, culture and post-colonialism*, Routledge, New York.

Tharu, Susie and K. Lalita. (eds.), 1991, *Women Writing in India. 600 B.C. to the present*, vol. 1, Oxford University Press, New Delhi.

Selected Bibliography on Helene Cixous

Primary Sources

1976, The Laugh of the Medusa, *Signs*, 1 (4): 875–99. Reprinted in Marks and Courtivron, (eds.) 1980, *New French Feminisms*, Schocken, New York.

1979, *Vivre l'orange*, Paris, des femmes.

1980, Sorties (tran. A. Liddle), in Marks and Courtivron (eds.).

1980,' Poetry is/and (the) Political' (personal copy).

1981, Castration or Decapitation?, *Signs* 7 (1): 41–55.

1984a, Interview with Verena Conley, *Boundary* 2 12 (2).

1984b, Reading Clarice Lispector's Sunday Before Going to Sleep, *Boundary* 2. 12 (2): 41–8.

1986, Interview with Susan Sellers, *Women's Review* 7: 22–3.

1987, Reaching the point of wheat, or A portrait of the artist as a maturing woman, *New Literary History*. 19 (1).

1988a The two countries of writing: Theatre and political fiction (personal copy).

1988b, Extreme Fidelity, and Trancredi Continues' (tran. A. Liddle and S. Sellers), cited in S. Sellers (ed.), 1988, *Writing Differences: Readings from the Seminar of Helene Cixous*, Open University Press, Milton Keynes.

1988c, Conversations in Sellers (ed.).

1989, From the scene of the unconscious to the scene of History (tran. D. Carpenter), *Future Literary History*.

1990, Difficult joys, cited in Wilox, McWatters, Thompson, and Williams (eds.), *The Body and the Text. Helene Cixous, reading and teaching*, Harvester Wheatsheaf, London.

1991, *Coming to Writing* (tran). A. Liddle and D. Carpenter-Jensen, Harvard University Press, Boston.

1993a. *Three Steps on the Ladder of Writing*, Columbia University Press, New York.

1993b, Without end no state of drawingness no, rather: The executioner's taking off, *New Literary History*, 24 (1).

1993c, Bathsheba or the Interior Bible, *New Literary History*, ibid.

Secondary Sources on Helene Cixous

1988, Sellers, Susan (ed.), *Writing differences Readings from the Seminar of H. Cixous*, Open University Press, Milton Keynes.

1990, Still, Judith, A Feminine Economy: Some Preliminary Thoughts, in Wilcox, Helen *et al* (eds.), *The Body and the Text,* Harvester Wheatsheaf, London.

1991, Jenson, Deborah (ed.), *'Coming to Writing' and other Essays by Helene Cixous,* Harvard University Press, Cambridge, Mass.

1991, Shiach, Morag, *Helene Cixous. A politics of writing*, Routledge, London.

Women and Work
From Housewifization to Androgyny

Susan Visvanathan

In this paper I shall first briefly review the literature on housewifization, which shows that capitalism and the market at first reduce the woman to passivity, and then as she enters the career and professional world, imposed on her a double burden of work. I shall also look at the concept of androgyny in the Jungian sense in order to understand the positive quality of breaking sex-role stereotypes. In the second part, I attempt to understand Sr Philomena-Marie, a trade-unionist of the fishing struggle in Kerala. Finally, in the third part, I compare Sr. Philomena-Marie to another androgynous figure, Joan of Arc.

I

WORK AND LABOUR, AUTHORITY AND POWER

Carolyn Merchant, Claudia Von Werlhoff, Maria Mies and Ivan Illich have argued very forcefully that capitalism had rendered woman a captive of the house. The labour of housewives goes unnoticed as shadow work, they are not seen to be part of the economy.[1]

These authors have argued that in capitalism, women were seen as belonging to the domain of Nature, and were to be broken, tamed, cultivated and civilized. Women who experimented with healing, agriculture, emotion and war were punished. Science and exploration were male domains; women could not innovate. Notions of order were defined for them, the subduing of women's nature was the greatest expression of the hierarchy of gender. The housewife is the transformation of the creative energies of women into one systematic type of labourer, one who is concerned primarily with reproduction, i.e., the birth of new members for the labour force, and their sustenance and nature. This labour does not create surplus or capital, it cannot be sold on the labour market. It is, as one feminist has argued, love and responsibility.[2] These are not in capitalist patriarchal ideology things of value, for value only arises from profit in the market. So the histories of men are visible (Joan of Arc and the Slave Queen dress as men) while women constitute simply, a sex.

In a plea for return to motherhood *and* work, feminists like Sylvia Hewlett tried to handle the question of what gender neutrality actually entailed. While women enter the professional world (or the labour market) on an ostensibly equal footing with men, the domestic space still represented traditional hierarchies and differences. Women bore children, cooked and cleaned, while men controlled property, women and children. Both men and women went out to work, but women's earnings were a 'second' salary. Their official roles were continuing in a gender-defined way, but their commitment to the codes of work had to be neutral. Their actual involvement in the powerful roles in a society were seen to be negligible. What one required as a concomitant to gender neutrality of social roles at the work space, was gender neutrality in the domestic space. This would involve the socialization of young children, so that work allocation was not gender-specific. Boys as well as girls had to be trained to cook, clean, wash, shop, rear children and earn. This was work, not 'women's' or 'men's', but work that needed to be done in a shared and reciprocal way.

Why were women alienated from the control over productive processes although it was they who sustained the manpower required for the market? Women were seen to be objects of nature to be dominated rather than worthy of egalitarian interaction. They were the bearers of children, they made things grow, they understood the cycles of nature within their own bodies. By excluding women, men externalized that from which they themselves were born, that which had to be a part of them.

Michelle Rosaldo underlines the fact that in most societies women may have power, but men usually have authority.[3] Authority becomes a veil which separates and distances men so that they can control interactions as they wish '... by avoiding certain sorts of intimacy and unmediated involvement they can develop an image and mantle of integrity and worth.' The 'natural' attributes of womanliness (ascribed status) are contrasted to the achieved status of 'becoming a man'. Because women are excluded from the domains of rationality and power by cultural stereotyping, they appear as Other. Women's status,

Rosaldo argues, is achieved from their stage in a life cycle, from their biological function, and in particular from their sexual or biological ties to particular men. For Rosaldo, the two extremes of this position can be seen in the witch, who sleeps with the devil, and the nun who is the bride of God.

Carolyn Merchant in *The Death of Nature* (1979) shows how western Science domesticated Nature (and women) through the questions and methods of science. The earth was transformed from the image of a nurturing mother into a source and potential for economic interest. The disorderly elements of female nature would be subjugated, and women became passive dependants in both production and reproduction. Even today, the exclusion of women from knowledge about their bodies, their isolation in labour as if pain was demeaning and infectious is representative of a scientific objectivity as opposed to empathy and subjectivity as experienced in traditional assistance at childbirth.

Nature and culture in such a perspective were no longer categories in relationship, but were now dual, external, divided and antagonistic. It was a fair description of the relationship between the sexes. Women, being identified with nature, became associated with animality, just as were indigenous people in the colonies. Thus women, the enslaved and animals all belonged to one class. Hannah Arendt writes that women and slaves were homologous because they were hidden away, belonged to someone or another, and their life was 'laborious' and devoted to bodily function (Arendt 1958). Arendt argues that the chief function of 'labour' is the production of life and therefore labour is associated with procreation. However the least durable are those things which are needed for consumption, for life itself. If not used immediately by men they perish. Therefore, the daily labour of women which contributed to subsistence was not inscribed in memory. Arendt says that work—what men did—was different, for it transformed things from matter into material, from nature *into culture*, and was associated with the hands, with skill and knowledge, rather than with the body.

Why then is labour, life generating as it is, associated with passivity? Carolyn Merchant for the history of the West, and Leela Dube for India (Merchant 1979; Dube *et al.* 1986) have shown that women are associated with the earth who bears and nourishes the seed, which is the vital, life generating active principle. Corporeality, substance and matter thus, in patriarchal societies derive from the female—therefore also putrefaction and mortality, but quickness, the mind, the soul, cerebrality is passed through the male. The passivity of women is continually reconfirmed through men's language. Leela Dube argues that a woman is alienated from her productive resources (like land, she belongs to someone) and has no control over her offspring. Illich would call gender neutrality fatal to the women's issue (Illich 1992). What is required is complementarity, argument, conversation and understanding; where in Buber's terms the 'I-it' relationship characterizing the subject as masculine and dominant, the object as female and passive should be substituted for an 'I-Thou' or 'I-You' relationship whose language is tempered by dialogue (Buber 1970). As Anna Kingsford, one of the early feminists maintained, women when kept back from articulating and achieving this were deformed, and in this, the men lost out too, for one sex cannot be handicapped without the other suffering.[4]

II

THE THEME OF ANDROGYNY

Virginia Woolf's novels became an interesting exercise in articulating the theme of the suppression of women's work capacities. In *The Voyage Out*, Rachel's passion and proficiency in music while acknowledged may not be professionally used. Hewet, the most sensitive and gentle of men believes that Rachel becomes 'less desirable as her brain began to work.' Hewet argues that women see men as horses do, 'They see us three times as big as we are or they'd never obey us.' (Woolf 1982a). In the end, Rachel must die—she represented the classic constraint upon individuality and being that masculinist societies imposed upon their women: talented and unprofessional, dying in the small cabin spaces that society provided for them. *A Room of One's Own* became a symbol of private space and autonomy, where women could find their own sense of being, write a new history of actions and events (Woolf 1995). I shall not go into an analysis of Woolf's work here, except to mention that in *Orlando* (1928) Woolf (1979) destroyed this conception of women's being as conventional, peaceful and consensually embedded in patriarchy. She substituted a male-female figure who so light-heartedly, so brilliantly destroyed and ravaged all notions of women's being, transformed roles and rules, work and custom.

Woolf's work explored two central ideas about women and consciousness. One was the idea of androgyny. In A *Room of One's Own* she playfully and poignantly sketched a mythical account of Shakespeare's sister Judith, as talented as her sibling, but fated to die and remain anonymous for she was a mere woman. As in this lecture she also spoke of the only possible way for women's emancipation—it was a plan for the soul. 'In each of us two powers preside, one male, one female, and in the man's brain, the man predominates over the woman.' (Woolf 1995). Where there was harmony between the two forces, spiritual cooperation, a fusion, the greatest creativity is possible. While Woolf herself was housewifized and sanatorium-ized, through the character of Septimus Smith, in the novel *Mrs Dalloway*, she tried to show that God and nature speak in many voices and some have the gift to hear and understand. Her portrayal of Orlando became a powerful exegesis of the concept of androgyny.

June Singer in her valuable interpretation of Jung's work (Singer 1993) argues that there is a natural biological opposition between men and women which is the basis of creativity. She develops Jung's notion of the *anima* and *animus* to underline that every man has a feminine side, and every woman a masculine side, which are rendered unconscious by culture. The repression of the *anima* (in men) and the *animus* (in women) creates both the longing for the Other, as well as the awe, fear and incomprehensibility associated with the Other (ibid.: 234).

The cultural stereotyping of emotions would then possibly end. Jesus, for instance, as a man, had no dilemmas about articulating a theory of love and care. Interestingly, though, C.F. Andrews who imitated Jesus in many ways, was thought to be effeminate by some. June Singer writes, 'I think it must have been the *anima* of Christ that urged him to seek out that one lost sheep.' (ibid.).

Further, Singer writes that 'unless we are partners with that contrasexual side of our nature, the soul that leads us to our own depths, we cannot become full and independent partners with a beloved person in the world outside.' (ibid. 268). It allows us identification with others and what Jung called the Self.

In her later work *Androgyny* Singer (1977) distinguishes between various terms in order to define what androgyny really is. Neither hermaphroditism, which is a lack of physical differentiation, nor bisexuality which is a lack of clarity in gender identification, the Jungian concept of androgyny expresses 'a natural unforced and uninhibited (male or female) sexuality'. Yet neither tends to extremes. Men do not need to exude *machismo*, or women to pretend a naive and

dependent character. 'Excessively polarized personality types' according to her thrive in cultures which demand repression of natural tendencies. Androgynous individuals lift these repressions 'not in order to
prepare a way of living out sexual impulses so much as in order to
permit what has been repressed to return and to be reintegrated into
conscious awareness.' (ibid.:19). Consider Virginia Woolf's classic experience of an androgynous state, which Clarissa Dalloway feels, 'a
match burning in a crocus, an inner meaning almost expressed.' It is
a revelation which allows her to 'then feel what men felt.'[5]

The androgyne consciously accepts the interplay of the masculine
and feminine aspects of the individual psyche (Singer 1977: 21).

In a stunning critique, 'Against Androgyny' Jean Bethke Elshtain
demolishes arguments in favour of the concept showing how
androgyny in feminist discourse has removed the mythic frames of the
term. (Elshtain 1987). She believes that the presence of difference
within the human frame has always been a cause of vexation (!) but
that in the feminist discourse on androgyny, the fused body disappears.
I think Jung's basic contribution is to reorganize the body in terms of the
conscious and the unconscious which Singer celebrates and Elshtain completely ignores.

Androgyny clearly has a long and complex history of usage which
I am not in a position to elaborate here. Why it becomes useful as a
concept is because it so clearly negates gender neutrality. The latter
does not allow for biological spaces to appear or to be clarified.
Androgyny is more elastic, and that very flexibility also questions
basic stereotypes which *fix* gender attributes in one way or another.

Like any term, androgyny can be put to different uses, for different
purposes.

I shall now look at a specific case in order to understand how
androgyny is a useful term for understanding women and creative
work. I take the specific case of a woman, a Christian nun called
Philomena-Marie who led the fisher people's struggle in Kerala in
1984. I shall also show the ambiguity of the term: at one level
Sr. Philomena-Marie functions at an androgynous level, at
another level she sees her commitment to the struggle in a gender-
neutral role as an official in the fishworkers' union.

III

THE FISHING STRUGGLE AND A NUN'S BIOGRAPHY

In Kerala, the fisherfolk's struggle against capitalistic ravaging of the sea had drawn tremendous strength from Christianity. (Some of Jesus' best friends were after all fishermen—Peter, for instance. Many of its leaders today are drawn from the Church, though there are many internal contradictions. The struggle itself is about the opposition between capitalists and their trawlers which ravage the sea, over-fishing the waters, using destructive purse-seine and trawl nets without any regard for spawning seasons or ecological balance. In this sense, the sea is merely a commodity base. The fisher people contest this indiscriminate fishing and have been organizing protest after protest without much success.

Sr Philomena-Marie begins to stand out in this struggle by her sheer insistence that she was ready to martyr herself, that she would fight until the cause was won. In this determination she took on the State, the capitalists, the Establishment Church. She was jailed in the summer of 1984, and soon after she began her twenty-three day fast.

The bishops of the state after studying the participation of the radical members of the clergy in a trade union movement resolved that fast to death was not permissible, nor participation in protests culminating in violence. They were to be warned about supporting radical slogans, warned against dangers to their faith.

Sr Philomena-Marie was forced to call off her fast, but she never lost her will to help the fisher people, to lead them in their agitations and to coordinate their work for them. In a speech in 1991, she said,

When human rights are trampled, no one can stay neutral. Neutrality on such occasion is equal to a crime. From the experience of the struggle we learn that justice is not given but taken by the concerted effort of the people concerned. The Church by her neutrality is supporting the existing political and economic system. When we struggled with the people ever ready to give up our life, the bishops could see only disobedience, violence, entering into politics. The boat (trawler) owners go with the blessing of the bishop. When poor people fight for their rights, they will be characterized as communists and Naxalites. The Church can only understand charity and distribution of bread.[6]

How does one understand the power of this woman, and her active involvement in the fisher people's struggle? I went to Valiyathura, a fishing hamlet close to Thirnvananthapuram on 9 June 1994. Sr

Philomena-Marie helps to coordinate the work of the KSMTF (*Kerala Swatantra Malsya Thozhilali Federation* or the Kerala Fish workers' Union) at its headquarters there. Sr Rose, her associate, showed me around the narrow margin of the village, hemmed in by large houses. The sea had eroded the coast very recently, so many of the fisher people were staying in the village school. Malaria was on the rampage, and the children were unable to attend school, because these were the three hungry months; torrential rain, no work and no food. I could well believe Sr Philomena-Marie's comment that illiteracy predominates, for when school starts in June, the fisher people are incredibly impoverished. Not surprisingly, I was told that several pockets of Valiyathura were well-known for their illicit distilleries and the hire of wives and daughters as prostitutes.

It was eleven o'clock, a strangely bright hot day in the monsoon. The sea was sky-blue. Some fishermen were looking out at the surf, others were playing cards; some just stared at Sr Rose and me through eyes wretched and drunk. This is *Panna-Massam*—the bad months when the Arabian Sea is usually turbulent and storm-trossed, and fishing is by traditional discipline almost nil. Sr Rose has been with the Valiyathura community for eleven years and had begun embroidery classes for the girls 'in order to distract them from prostitution.' She uses a house on the beach, austere and old, with a desk near the window, from which you can hear the sea.

Sr Philomena-Marie came to this house and took me to her own KSMTF office: a bleak room overlooking a disused courtyard where the only thing of any interest was the existence of a scavenger cat looking for food under dry rustling heaps of palm leaves. We sat and talked for three hours. I report some of that conversation. She was born sixty-four years ago, she is small and slight and frail today, with an untidy greying bun, intense ardour for her work, and eyes strangely innocent.

Many reasons brought her to the path that she is on. Like daughters of many traditional families she was educated in a convent in Athirampuzha, near Kottayam, and then decided to serve God, through involvement with the sick and wounded.

She joined the Medical Missionaries in 1948, and understood the nature of professionalism where her work as a pharmacist became an end in itself. As she rose along the bureaucratic ladders of the order, she went to Delhi in the early 1970s and got an MBA degree at the university. It was then that she learnt about trade unionism, and sitting in a class which was geared to the 'other' side of union politics (i.e., management-biased) she understood what capitalism was. She learnt her union politics from capitalist texts, by reading between the lines.

At the same time those of her companions who were working in Latin America spoke of their encounter with liberation theology. Sr Philomena-Marie was forced to reflect on the dichotomies that faced her as an administrator, and as a religious person whose actual vocation was to work with the poor. ('When I was a child I wanted to be a saint, I wanted to give my life to the poor.')

The safety of the interior of the convent felt too much like an upper middle-class home. So in 1978, she went to Anjengo, a fishing village near Thiruranananthapuram. There she met Fr Thomas Kocherry who was the priest for the local community, but often went out to sea with the fishermen. This was her first experience of 'enculturation'—instead of bringing an Institution to them (the Established Church) they lived with the poor and could identify with them. Life was simple here. They ate like the people, frugally, and lived ascetically in the small houses by the sea. Yet, what was most difficult was 'the feelings of superiority'. Sr Philomena-Marie said, 'It was a struggle, both theoretically and ideologically. We battled to be like them, not superior to them. Yet it was we who had all the answers, we had education and money, we were the leaders.'

The Medical Missionaries at Anjengo ran creches, and like Sr Rose in Valiyathura, did all that they could to alleviate the terrible poverty of the fisher people, and the consequent violence of their lives— the excess of alcohol, the illiteracy, the fatalism. The Christian fishers were proud of their heritage, of the traditions linking them to Sr Xavier. They were pious and felt chosen in their life, to live alongside the beautiful sea. The very existence of the sea took away the squalor of their lives.

In 1979, there was a flood on the lake where the coir-workers, who were Hindus lived and worked. The Anjengo religious team helped them and worked with them. The fishermen who lived across the road on the seaside saw that the religious helped everyone regardless of what religion they belonged to. Then, soon after, the Boat Workers' Union was formed, because Fr Thomas Kocherry and Joeychen Antony decided that they had to take on the responsibility of asking for audited accounts on behalf of the boat owners who had taken loans from the government. This nucleus joined with parallel unions in Kerala to become the larger group called the KSMTF.

This was how the priests and nuns working with the fisher people slowly became part of the unions. They had to help with the bureaucratic structures, the accounts, the paperwork. The several cupboards in the KSMTF office symbolized the universality of bureaucratic order—the files, stationery, ledgers. 'We were not separate, we were part of the movement', the nun kept reiterating. The relevance of power however was subtle and to Philomena-Marie frightening, as if there could never be true egalitarianism even in a movement like theirs.

In 1981, the trawler owners bypassed the enacted law. Fr Thomas Kocherry and Joeychen Antony (he died at sea aged 38) went on an indefinite fast. That year P.M. (as she is called) discovered the power of the people, of the federation. The years that followed, with the many commissions, brought the struggle to its logical climax in the fast of 1984.

In that year, when the struggle was at its peak, Sr Philomena-Marie volunteered to fast. She said, 'I don't believe in indefinite fast. That means nothing. One must fast until one gets what one is so desperately seeking, or fast to death.' Her superiors objected, but she was steadfast. She would stand beside the fishers, not behind.

First, she joined the picketers in order to be imprisoned, 'Jail is the only recourse.' Thirteen of them, three nuns, six other women and seven men, by union decision were chosen to picket the Directorate and go to jail. They spent six days in jail in the company of prostitutes and distillers.

We became friendly with them, though there was a hue and cry in the local press about nuns locked up with *veishyas*. Still they told us their stories and we created a community through prayer and conversation. We had to have courage, specially to encourage the lay women who were in the jail on behalf of the fisher people's struggle. The publicity was advantageous for us. While we were there we learnt a lot. Some of us pretended to be sick and got a good view of the jail health services. After we came out, the union asked me if I would go on fast. Sr Alice, who was already fasting, was growing weak and had to be hospitalized. I was glad to fast. My father and mother and my brother came. My father was very angry. He said, 'You do exactly what you want all the time.' A long while ago, when I was a child, he had said, 'If you join a convent you'll only jump the walls.' My mother was sad to see me fasting. She said, 'Do you have to do this much.' I said, 'You have no right to ask this question. It was you who dedicated me to the people.'

After that she stayed by my side all the time, going home only when she was forced to. After the nineteenth day I was forced into the hospital by the police. There they physically forced me on to the drip, but I fought with tremendous strength. I don't know where the strength came from. They said, 'It is our duty to save you for your future work, for the people.' I resisted and continued my fast although my condition was fast deteriorating. The union asked me to stop. It was the fifty-fourth day of the struggle, the twenty-second day of my fast. The movement was running out of resources—human and financial. Some of the leaders felt that they could not handle the situation. If I died, the people would go out of control. Besides if I died the union would be held responsible for my death. So I stopped.

Sr Philomena-Marie reached into the recesses of those bureaucratic stores and took out several reports of the KSMTF for me. The struggle goes on.

In the last part of this essay I shall look at androgyny, celibacy and dress to understand how a woman becomes an active leader, a symbol of the fishing movement which cuts across religious divides and becomes a forum for human rights issues, and for the safety of the sea.

IV

DOES ANDROGYNY NEUTRALIZE GENDER?

Sr Philomena-Marie is a woman who has given her life to Christ. The complexity of the relationship is implicit. She is certainly one of the 'wise virgins'. This is one of the most poignant stories that Jesus told: it was of women who waited for their bridegroom in a state of preparation, and the parable highlights their joy in comparison to the anxiety and trepidation of the virgins who were disappointed because they were not ready to meet the Lord.[7] However, marriage—spiritual marriage is about the meeting of the soul, and the understanding of the self and Other. The metaphor of a marriage is used in order to understand the intensity of desire, but when we say 'Virgin' and 'Bride' we are speaking of a consummation that is yet to come. In this sense, Death presents the face of virtue, for it has lost its sting, and offers only the vision of resurrection and the union with the beloved.

The complexity arises, not with the love metaphors of religious union, for these are found in all societies, but with the concept of androgyny. For Jung, it represented the fusion of characteristics associated with masculinism and feminism in such a manner that it would create the whole being.[8] It articulated the idea quite familiar to us now that psychological characteristics had social and archetypical undertones, and that the focus and development of one or the other was the basis of gender typing. How then could one use one's energies, psychic or religious in the most creative way? One sees this very clearly in the life of Jesus. I shall not consider physiognomy, because the face represented is the desired face of western heterosexual norms: he is always poignantly beautiful. But let us look at the androgyny of his nature—a child who is presented with gifts of perfume and gold, who is identified with the gentleness of pastoralism, and the careful art of carpentry, which combines both physical strength and contemplative concentration. This Jesus grows up to be friends with fishermen and prostitutes, rich men and tax collectors, he is often with women and children, light enough to walk on water, capable of great and ferocious anger, he weeps quite openly, and teases his mother, he cannot bear pain and humiliation, and asks the God who is another form of his own self to take away the bitter cup. Weak and defenceless as he is before his father, he is quite different at the courts. This Jesus cannot then be stereotyped, because from one moment to the next we do not know how he will behave. What are the sources of his strength, his imagination (for he is always telling stories) and his courage?

Perhaps it lies in the body of his mother from whom he is corporeally constituted, since apocryphally Joseph is only his foster father. If Jesus is physiologically and perfectly created, but in a godly way—for 'in the beginning was the word' and then 'the word became flesh'—we clearly are at a loss if we search for him merely corporeally.[9] The androgyny of his being does not question the right he has to his manhood; it only states that while being a man he could understand and empathize with women as much as with the Centurion's daughter or Lazarus, or the lepers, the blind or Zachariah, who was always so ashamed. For centuries, this empathy, this understanding of the Other in the essence of his being or her being, has come down to us as the concept of love. This love however was culturally specific—it was not sexual (though the intensity of desire communicates itself in the story of Mary Magdalene) but appeared in the form of wisdom and peace. Jesus would, through the symbol of his life and death, and the visions his friends had of him, define the intensity of spiritual existence and experience.

When Philomena-Marie leads the fishers she symbolizes the fact that she is a woman, a follower of Jesus, a Bride of Christ. However she also leads them in another way, not *because* she is a woman or a man but because she understands the rules of parapolitics, of capitalism and profit, of the servitude of the declassed. In that sense, she does not stand in for the bride of Christ—she is an office member of the KSMTF. She understands her job, she is highly qualified in management theory, her rhetoric does not carry any of the tones of gender or religion. She could be either male or female, nun or priest, Hindu or Christian. (Visvanathan 1994).

One of the greatest problems of understanding work is in the terms which neutralize gender. In the unbridled years of feminism, when women pitted themselves against male bastions it was important to believe that same is equal to equality. Yet, in recent issues of *Feminist Review* and *Signs*[10] some of the most poignant reviews have been about lost identity—what happened to motherhood, what happened to being and celebrating womanly selves; did being a woman mean hating the 'Other'; how would one then look at complementarity and the division of labour? In a brilliant indictment of maleness and the right to die in war, Genevieve Lloyd[11] argues that heroism is for men, and in war they transcend their love of life for the rationalist ideas of justice and freedom. Women, however, it is believed, cannot overcome nature, or transcend death, because their role is to reproduce. Freedom and consciousness then are male preserves, but when a woman sacrifices her sons, she overcomes nature and becomes a citizen (like the Spartan Mother who does not weep for slain sons, but rejoices in the victory of her country at war).

Androgyny means overcoming the cultural parameters of what it means to be a man or a woman, but raises the problem of a *common humanity*. Work then is defined in terms of ability and interest, and the distinctions between men's work and women's work would at once be devalued. Androgyny, then, is about fearlessness, and role choices which are not biologically defined. Anthropologists are familiar with instances of role reversal which augment clearly enough the *cultural* reasons for demarcating work as gender-specific. Trying to explain this in evolutionary terms would be as trying as asking why penguins and sea horses have gentle, loving nurturing fathers, while cats are so oedipal-fixated that the tom sometimes kills his offspring.

Androgyny as we saw is not about bisexuality or about hermaphroditism. It is not about transvestism, though we shall see that the latter becomes an important code by which androgyny often articulates itself. One of the complexities of androgyny *could* be substitutability, which sociologically is not a problem when applied to role behaviour. Substitutability is usually about roles and not persons. It argues that the case for resemblance is so high in tribal society that one tribal is alike another, one factory worker like another, though levels of skill or biographical characteristics may hugely vary.

So if Jesus is acceptably androgynous in the Jungian sense he only articulates in his person and his character true consanguinity. Biologically we too are of cognatic descent, but socially we may be patrilineal or matrilineal in our societal and individual self-definitions. Each of us is composed of father and mother in a genetic composition that is structurally universal, except in the case of mutation. Androgyny celebrates the differences and similarities that involves being human.

The case of Jesus is problematic only because his relationship with his father is philological, with his mother corporeal. His father is God, but his mother only a saint. It is this cultural hierarchy that allows Fr Tom Kocherry (another KSMTF leader) to be like Jesus, but Sr Philomena-Marie cannot. She must remain (an androgynous) woman.

V

JOAN OF ARC

The most interesting thing about androgyny is that it does not necessitate gender neutralization. In this context, let us look at Joan of Arc.[12] I shall draw my story from Marina Warner, Tom Keneally, Bernard Shaw, William Shakespeare, though Joan specialists know that this is a small cluster in the Milky Way of Joan researches.

Joan constantly refers to herself as The Maid or The Virgin. What she conveys most stridently is the preparation for consummation, the Virgin Sacrifice by Fire. She must die so that her country may be liberated. What is most significant is that Joan does not menstruate—her 'womb is dead'—therefore she may not conceive, but conceive only the deed or word or value. In this sense Joan, Mary the Virgin Mother and Sr Philomena-Marie are homologous. Sr Philomena-Marie achieves the fertility and power of the word through celibacy.

The works of celibacy are well-known to us through the lives of the saints in all the religious traditions, and specifically the life of Mahatma Gandhi. Sexual energy, in Jungian terms, is transformed into the energy required for self-realization or political battle. Celibacy, like androgyny is about the consciousness of one's own sexual identity, and the pain or the glory that arises from transcending or overcoming one's biological and psychological and social drives. Joan understood this well: she was, for one side, a Saint, the Maid, the Virgin. For the English, she was a whore who led a dissolute life, who lay side by side with soldiers unafraid, a transvestite who used a war to glorify herself. Most of the stories about Joan were about the fact that men were afraid to touch her, that they never wanted to touch her. Her virginity, her celibacy, her virtue, her 'integrity'[13] became the symbol which could heal a ruptured France. No wonder then that celibacy and androgyny can together combine, as in the case of Joan of Arc and Sr Philomena-Marie. It combines so powerfully, that they are able to lead the workers, and be noticed only for the power of their vision. Charismatic authority, as, therefore, the least socially allocated grace, is an idea that settles upon a person, its power lies in the eyes of the beholder.

Any reader of the texts of Jesus would immediately understand the *advaitic* power of 'I am the Way, the Truth and the Life.' It is as Ivan Illich says 'I is never gendered' because 'I' is from the oral tradition. (Cayley 1992). The listener knows immediately from the voice what the gender of the speaker is. In this sense, Christ's sayings do become patriarchally defined. Thus Sr Philomena-Marie knows that she can be a friend of the fisher people as much as Jesus. But patriarchy as established conventions will not allow her to take the place of Christ.

Not surprisingly, when she is locked up in prison for trade union activities, it is with the prostitutes. 'We prayed with them, made friends with them, shared their troubles.' That is a symbiosis of role identity with Jesus, impervious of gender. The newspapers scream that, 'Nuns have been locked up with *veshyas*' (prostitutes). For Philomena-Marie, 'the courage and love of Magdalene is the unarticulated theme of her compassion, which links celibacy with profligacy and makes the latter redeemable.'

Joan, on the other hand, hated prostitutes and chased them out of the camps. Legend has it that the sacred sword that won her victory at Orleans broke on the back of one such prostitute, and then there followed her defeat and capture and death. For Philomena-Marie, prostitution, like alcoholism, is an occupational hazard arising out of the frequent economic crises in the lives of the fishers. What is important is to provide alternative modes of employment to women.

Joan dressed as a boy and was burnt at the stake for it, because this was a role reversal, contrary to Nature and so heretical. Yet dressing as a boy meant that she could ride a horse, and ride to war. Sr Philomena-Marie dressed in indistinguishable fawns, dull browns—neither does she merge with Nature nor does she stand out. This is in contrast to the brilliant hues wom by the fisherfolk. Her clothes mitigate her gender (they do not neutralize it or transmute it) because these are the colours one would associate with renunciation, but also with bureaucracy.

So in a world of men, Sr Philomena-Marie plays out her vocation. She is unafraid of prelates, capitalists, governments and death. She is of course thin (anorexic in the new equations between fasting and visions) and overworked. She oscillates between many roles. She nurtures a boy (married at eighteen), his wife and child because they cannot quite manage on their own. She races between one village and another providing medical help. She keeps the KSMTF office in order. Earlier she stayed with a woman whose husband had died at sea, and helped her reorient her life. Sometimes she gets thrown out of a Sunday school classroom because the visiting prelate sees her trade unionism as a bad example to young children. She eats her food with co-workers (nuns from a nearby convent) or with an office bearer at the KSMTF. And she has to cope with that abstraction—called a reputation—sometimes out there in the blazing limelight; at other times completely forgotten and marginalized as another Joan of Arc emerges in another part of India, taking the question of water in a different direction. She says, 'We are networking with other movements. We are in touch with Medha Patkar.' There can be no competition or jealousy in the emulation of saints, there can only be patience and reservoirs of heroism which sees martyrdom as the true androgynous term. This paper is not oriented towards asking for martyrdom for that would be a terrible act of lassitude and irresponsibility on our part, but asks to listen to the voice of the potential martyr and respond to the commitment to the cause, to be sensitive to the person who fasts, has visions, rebels, hears voices, and see in the androgyny of his or her being questions we need to really ask ourselves about what it means to be human.

Acknowledgements

Fr George Keeran, SJ; Fr T.K. John, SJ; Fr Gispert-Sauch, SJ; Fr Raja, SJ; Fr Paddy Meagher, SJ. I must also thank Harish Trivedi and Shiv Visvanathan. The first part of the paper was written at length for an Inaugural Lecture at the Jesuit Scholasticate, Vidyajyoti in 1990. A section of Part II appeared in *Seminar*, November 1994.

NOTES

1. Susan Visvanathan (1992), a review of literature; Ivan Illich (1981, 1982), Carolyn Merchant, (1979); Maria Mies (1986), Maria Mies *et al.* (1988)

2. Sylvia Hewlett, *A Lesser life*, 1986.

3. Michelle Rosaldo, *Woman, Culture and Society: A Theoretical Overview*, 1974.

4. Cited in Maitland (1896).

5. How terrible is the envy that Woolf feels for those male citadels into which women had no entry. In *Jacob's Room*, the contempt for women is well recorded. 'No one would think to bring a dog into church, a dog destroys the service completely. So do these women—though separately vouched for by the Theology, Mathematics, Latin and Greek of their husbands' (Woolf 1984: 30). *Night and Day* chronicles a greater resolution of the conflict between women's roles and work, between marriage and occupation. Work cannot yet be a career, but there is a greater celebration of cerebral endeavour and to some extent masculine adaptation to feminist strivings. Katharine Hilberry, in this novel, is a secret mathematician. 'No force on earth would have made her confess that. Her actions when thus engaged were furtive and secretive like those of some nocturnal animal.' It is Jacob, of *Jacob's Room* who is the inheritor of history, architecture and learning—also of war and death.

6. Speech at Hyderabad, 1991, cited in Visvanathan, (1994).

7. Gospel of Matthew 25: 1–13.

8. C.G. Jung *et al.*, *Man and His Symbols*, 1978.

9. The sources of this interpretation are people's narratives amongst a practising Christian community in Kerala. Visvanathan (1993).

10. Ann Snitow, in *Feminism and Motherhood*, has paradigmatized the shifts in feminist thinking, from the separatism of the 1960s to the anti-motherhood manifesto of the 1970s. Finally, she says, 'In the 1980s we have apologised again and again for ever having uttered what we now often name a callow, classicist, immature or narcissistic word against mothering. ... We have embraced nurturance as an ethic, sometimes wishing that men would share this ethic without much hoping they will' (Snitow 1992: 42).

In a completely different vein, Prue Chamberlayne analyses the emergence of *The Mother's Manifesto* and disputes arising out of it. The Manifesto was issued by women who were a part of the West German Greens in 1987. Their demands 'include collective provision for child care, a revision of urban design, pay and pensions for home careers, flexible employment, in- creased leisure time and the facilitation of political activity for mothers'. According to Chamberlayne, many feminists believed the Manifesto was reactionary and could even mean a return to Nazism, presumably to kitchen, church and kindergarten. The Manifesto reflected the disenchantment with individualistic, capitalistic, competitive values which deny biological spaces to women. The debates on caring have become centre space. German feminists echo the anguish of Ivan Illich, that gendering has led to greater inequality, that participation in the labour market, has led to greater violation and loss of autonomy for women (Illich 1982; Chamberlayne 1990: 10–11). The sadness of the Manifesto, it seems, lies in that it wages an assault on non-mothers, in a way that was waged by women against men, or men against women in earlier years. German feminists like Giselda Erler say that as mothers they feel 'marooned', relegated to a reserve as guardians of a dying culture. Mothers must be returned to the centre of societies, the quality they impart to life of sharing, intimacy, uniting of body and soul, which have been destroyed by 'reason' must be valued once more. In the same way, such feminists do imagine the development of a new male tenderness and responsiveness through intimacy with babies, as well as a rediscovery and extension of eroticism in experiences surrounding reproduction (Chamberlayne 1990: 11).

There is therefore the possibility of the transcendence of existing gender roles; and yet the retention of differences.

Joan Tronto analyses Carol Gilligan's famous theory of care as being both situated in women's experiential morality as well as transcending difference. Care, therefore, centres around responsibility and relationship, rather than rights and rules, it is concrete rather than abstract, it expresses itself in activity rather than in theory, engaging in 'daily' experiences and moral problems of real people in their everyday lives (Tronto 1987: 648).

What about 'caring' or pro-feminist men? Lynne Segal, in her essay 'Femininism, Socialism and the Problem of Men' (1989) quotes Jonathan Tonstram, who was an active participant in communities centring around socialism and women's rights. 'I feel it is vital for men to be more closely involved in child care if patriarchy and male violence is to begin to crumble. And that, however, bleak our immediate political prospects, one thing that can happen now is that men can change' (cited in ibid. 1989: 3).

Segal urges an analysis of masculinity which she feels is an area of conceptual deprivation. 'There are many different kinds of men and masculinities—gay, straight, gentle and tough, democratic and authoritarian—and these are all cut across by race, class, ethnicity and religion' (ibid.: 1989: 15).

That feminist experience contributes to theoretical wholism is a point made over and over again (Haug 1992: 16). But Mary Louise Adams in her essay, 'Identity Politics' (1989) argues that personal experience was used in the feminist cause as a means to liberation, but it should not cut feminists off from larger struggles. Similarly, Sally Alexander (1991) states that the first wish of feminist history was to uncover new meanings for femininity and women, to propel sexuality 'to the forefront of the political mind' and was very similar to the goal of psychoanalysis. The latter attempted the discovery of a subjective history through image, symbol and language. She asserts that psychoanalysis and feminism arose together. (I would even assert that early critiques of Freudian psychoanalysis came from feminist novelists like Virginia Woolf, as *Mrs Dalloway* and *Orlando* clearly show.) Alexander argues that psychoanalysis preferred to focus on the mother-child relationship while feminism went into the debates about the rights of 'workers' and 'citizens', the rights of women in the public sphere (Alexander 1991: 128–33).

In this pursuit of questioning 'normality' feminists like Shiela Rowbotham have critiqued the concept of the good or 'normal' mother in an essay called 'To Be or Not to Be' (1989). She asserts that feminism's main contribution was to show that happiness could come from other things than mothering. Feminists came out honestly with their feelings, to show that motherhood could be both: oppressive or liberating; it was feminists who articulated the belief that 'motherhood must be freely chosen and socially transformed'. Yet by the 1980s she concedes, with Liz Heron, that feminists were 'melting into motherhood' (ibid.: 84).

11. Genevieve Lloyd, Selfhood, War and Masculinity (1986).

Virginia Woolf argued in *Three Guineas* shortly before World War II, and her own despairing suicide that 'as a woman, I have no country. ... As a woman my country is the whole world' (Woolf 1986: 125). She insisted on a policy of non-participation where women would refuse to endorse war celebrations, activities or even discussion. She could only do this if she was economically independent, and further Woolf even pressed for wages for housewives. Marriage and motherhood, she argued, is a profession. She stated that women's work was as sacred as that of the clergyman who is paid without derogation. It is interesting to note that Woolf saw housewifization and motherhood as creative possibilities of women's self-expression. She never excluded it as a profession. Mrs Ramsay in *To the Lighthouse* is a very powerful person. It is in a seemingly corrupt and yet intensely intelligent figure like Clarissa Dalloway (1915, 1925) that housewifization with its boredom, its tragic loneliness is handled. The deprivation from work—the elite and languid body—is expressed here as the broken and diseased female body. Yet there is something resilient in Mrs Dalloway. What seems like corruption, an idleness enforced by society, becomes almost contemplative.

Mrs Ramsay, in *To the Lighthouse* on the other hand, merges with things. When she dies, everything becomes empty. The house, representative of an order that she sought in the world and in human relationships becomes the symbol of emptiness. For Mrs. Ramsay, the world was a hive, which captured the intensity and intimacy of conventional family relationships, where women were indeed so dominant and central.

See also Gilbert (1989). Gilbert shows how during World War I, women began to play an unusually important part. Earlier they had been powerless, but now they were the great sacrificers—sacrificers of fathers, brothers, sons, sweethearts and husbands. She quotes D.H. Lawrence, 'Why do the women follow us, satisfied/Feed on our wounds, like bread, receive our blood/Like glittering seed upon them for fulfilment.' Further she argues that the war meant that the women could join the labour force, and this was the first rupture with a socio-economic history that had heretofore denied most women chances at first class jobs. ...

12. Marina Warner's fascinating account of Joan of Arc focuses on her marginality in terms of social and political roles, and her clarity regarding her female biological identity. Warner writes that 'the state of suspension, of indifferentiation achieved by a transvestite girl was confirmed by the Christian tradition as holy. Sexlessness is virginity's achievement and a metaphor for martyrdom, as hagiography bears out'. Warner disclaims the 'disorder of the androgyny of the neuter' in Joan's case (Warner1991: 157). She says that 'in holiness, androgyny is not neither this nor that, it is the fusion—and Joan belonged to this order—the absoluteness of the way, the impregnability to relativism, which means their sovereignty over time' (ibid.: 158). Warner asserts that Joan is the symbol of mobility, accepting neither her peasant birth, nor her female condition, or the limitations that would be a consequence of this (ibid.: 151). Having dressed as a boy, and while cutting her hair in the latest masculine fashion, Joan, yet, 'never proclaimed herself a boy. Indeed she never once pretended she was male, since she referred to herself in the feminine gender, as La Pucelle, the Maid' (ibid.).

13. Marina Warner's term.

REFERENCES

Adman, Mary Louise 1989, There's no place like home or identity politics, *Feminist Review* 31: 22–3.

Alexander, Sally 1991, Feminist history and psychoanalysis, *History Workshop* 33 (Autumn). 128–33.

Ardener, Edwin 1986, The problem of power, in Dube *et al.*

Arendt, Hannah, 1958, *The Human Condition*, University of Chicago Press, Chicago.

Buber, Martin, 1970, *I and Thou*, Charles Scribner, New York.

Cayley, David, 1992, *Ivan Illich, In Conversation*, Anansi Press, Toronto.

Chamberlayne, Prue, The mothers' manifesto and disputes over Mutterlichkeit, *Feminist Review*, 35 Summer 1990.

Cobbe, Frances Power, 1895, *The Divine Law of Love*, Victoria Street Society, London.

Dube, Leela, *et al.*, 1986, *Visibility and Power*, Oxford University Press, Delhi.

Elshtain, Bethke Jean, 1987, Against androgyny, in Anne Phillips (ed.), *Feminism and Equality*, Basil Blackwell, Oxford.

Ferguson, Moira, 1989, Mary Wolstonecraft and the Problematic of Slavery, *Feminist Review*: 82.

Gilbert, Sandra M., 1989, Soldier's heart, in Elaine Showalter (ed.).

Haug, Frigga, 1992, Feminist writing. Working with women's experience, *Feminist Review*: 16.

Illich, Ivan, 1981, *Shadow Work*, Marion Boyars, London.

——, 1982, *Gender*, Pantheon, New York.

Jung, C.G., 1973, *Memories, Dreams, Reflections*, Vintage, New York.

——, 1978, *Man and His Symbols*, Picador, London.

Joseph, Cherian and K.V. Easwar Prasad, 1995, *Women, Work and Inequity* National Labour Institute, Delhi.

Keneally, Thomas, 1991, *Blood Red, Sister Rose*, Hodder and Stoughton, London.

Lloyd, Genevieve, Selfhood, war and masculinity, in Carol Pateman and Elisabeth Gross (ed.), *Feminist Challenges: Social and Political Theory*, Allen and Unwin, London.

Maitland, Edward, 1896, *Anna Kingsford,* George Bedway, London.

Mani, Lata, 1991, Multiple meditations. Feminist scholarship in the age of multinational reception, *Feminist Review* 35 (Summer).

Managena, Oshadi, 1921, Against fragmentation, *Journal of Gender Studies,* 1(1) (May).

Merchant, Carolyn, 1979, *The Death of Nature*, University of Calfornia Press, Berkeley.

Mies, Maria, 1986, *Patriarchy and Accumulation on a World Scale*, Zed Books, London.

——, V. Bennholdt-Thomsen and C. von Werlhoff, 1988, *Women: The Last Colony*, Zed Books, London.

Rosaldo, Michelle, and Louise Lamphere (eds.), 1979, *Women, Culture and Society*, Stanford University Press.

Rowbotham, Shiela, 1988, To be or not to Be: The dilemmas of mothering, *Feminist Review* 3 (Spring): 83.

Segal, Lynne, 1989, Slow change or no change. Feminism, socialism and the problem of men, *Feminist Review*: 5.

Shiva, Vandana, 1988, *Staying Alive*, Kali, New Delhi.

Showalter, Elaine (ed.), 1989, *Speaking of Gender*, RKP, New York.

Singer, June, 1973, *Boundaries of the Soul*, Anchor-Doubleday, New York.

——, 1977, *Androgyny*, Anchor-Doubleday, New York.

Snitow, Ann, Feminism and Motherhood, *Feminist Review:* (spring).

Tronto, Joan C., 1992, Beyond gender difference to a theory of care, *Signs* (Summer).

Visvanathan, Shiv, 1995 Unravelling human rights.. Paper for the Beijing Summit on Women.

Visvanathan, Susan, 1992, Housewifization and Women's Rights, Occasional Paper, NMML

—— 1993, *The Christians of Kerala*, Oxford University Press,Madras.

——, 1994, The fishing struggle in Kerala, *Seminar* (November) 1994.

Vyvan, John, 1969, *In Pity and in Anger: A Study of the Use of Animals in Science*, Michael Joseph, London.

Warner, Marina, 1991, *Joan of Arc*, Vintage, London.

——, 1933, *Alone of All her Sex: The Myth and Cult of the Virgin Mary*, Vintage, New York.

Woolf, Virginia, 1966, *Mrs Dalloway*, Penguin, London.
——, 1979, *Orlando*, Triad/Panther, London.
——, 1982a *The Voyage Out*, Granada, London.
——, 1982b, *Night and Day*, Granada, London.
——, 1984, *Jacob's Room*, Granada, London.
——, 1986, *Three Guineas*, Hogarth Press, London.
——, 1988, *To the Lighthouse*, Granada, London.
——, 1995, *A Room of One's Own*, Penguin, London.

Shame and Control
Sexuality and Power in Feminist Discourse in India

Kalpana Viswanath

I

INTRODUCTION

This paper seeks to analyse the discourses of the women's movement in India from the specific perspective of their understanding of the female body. The women's movement includes within its fold a variety of groups with different ideologies and agendas of action.[1] Here I shall focus specifically on those actors that locate themselves as part of the autonomous women's movement within contemporary politics. These groups were formed in the latter half of the 1970s in many cities in India.[2] They initially mobilized around the issues of dowry and rape. They located themselves as autonomous from the State and from political parties. These groups were also unique as they raised issues that were earlier not considered political, such as rape and domestic violence. An understanding of the personal as political was central to their feminist politics.

In common with feminist discourses elsewhere, the women's movement in India too has privileged the analysis of the forms in which the female body is constructed in societal discourses as an important source of women's oppression. However the specificity of cultural practices in India has given a certain direction to the manner in which the women's movement in India has addressed this issue. Hence the relation between the theoretical formulations of feminism and the specificities of the place from which the women's movement articulates its concerns will be the focus of this paper.

There are two different registers on which theories of the female body and sexuality are conceptualized in the following sections. The first is the understanding of the anthropological contribution on women in India which has generated some central ideas about how the female or the feminine is viewed in Indian culture and society. These have looked at the female body and sexuality within symbolic systems. Unfortunately they have not taken women's lived experiences as the base from which to conceptualize these symbolic universes that structure women's lives. In these theories one can find a way to look at women's sexuality within a cultural universe but without being able to connect the representation with the experience. The women's movement, on the other hand, begins with women's experiences. The aim of the movement is to translate these experiences into social texts that would provide the basis for political action. But we shall see that the movement often focuses on women's experiences and politics without a strong understanding of cultural and symbolic systems.

In this paper I shall focus on the notion of shame which has been analysed in depth within anthropological literature on India and has also been central to a feminist understanding of women's bodies and sexual politics. Though there is an overlap in how the two discourses have discussed the notion of shame and its implications on women's sexuality and movements, there are differences in their understanding of how it structures and controls women. The women's movement which is also looking at this within the context of power and patriarchy could sharpen its politics if it incorporates an anthropological understanding of shame and honour as centrally defining women's sexuality.[3]

II

SHAME AND HONOUR: THE ANTHROPOLOGY OF WOMEN IN INDIA

Anthropological work on women in India has studied the cultural and symbolic contexts within which women's lives are circumscribed. There are certain key ideas which anthropologists have seen as important for understanding how women's bodies and their sexuality have been defined and given meaning. Purity and pollution, honour and shame and *purdah* are cultural ideologies that play an important role in controlling women's behaviour and the spaces they can occupy. All these concepts have been extensively studied by anthropologists, but for the purposes of this paper, I shall only concentrate on how these notions affect women's sexuality and their movements in society.

Purity and pollution are central categories that determine social relationships in Hindu society. Within the caste hierarchy, there are certain castes which are considered inherently more or less pure. There are also different states and conditions which are more polluted, such as association with death. These categories provide the basis for social interaction as, pollution is transmitted by contact.[4]

Within the context of women's lives, purity and pollution take on a further dimension as these are closely linked to their sexuality and fertility. Women's bodily experiences of menstruation, childbirth, lactation are also seen to define them as polluting or impure (Allen and Mukherjee 1982; Das 1988; Fruzetti and Ostor 1982; Ferro Luzzi 1974). Menstruation and reproductive functions are directly linked to women's bodies and their sexuality. Female sexual desire, menstruation, and childbirth are independent feminine functions that can have dire consequences for men if not controlled. Female sexuality therefore has both a negative and dangerous connotation (Gatwood 1985; Bennett 1983).

Caste and gender work together to circumscribe women's sexuality in further ways. Men are often directly dependent on women for their status. It thus becomes imperative to protect women's sexuality so that they do not bring dishonour to the family (Allen and Mukherjee 1982; Mandelbaum 1988). Women are not allowed to marry men of a lower caste and it is in fact seen as a crime, but may marry a man of a higher caste. Women are seen as 'gateways' to the caste system, as points of entrance and thus the sexuality of a higher caste woman becomes more important to maintain (Yalman 1963; Das 1979). Central to these ideas is the construction of women as wives and mothers. In their role as the mothers of sons, it becomes most important to guard women's sexuality as it is integral to the maintenance of patriarchy and patriliny.

The married woman is seen as auspicious and women wear many different symbols of marriage (Dube 1988). In opposition to her is the widow who is inauspicious and not allowed to wear any symbols of marriage and there are severe restrictions in her dress, eating habits, participation in rituals and in social life. It is true that the state of widowhood is differently defined among upper and lower castes, which gives direction to the manner in which the widow's body would become available for societal manipulation and the link between caste and gender.

Women are also restricted from moving around freely in public as they are seen to be dangerous and in danger. Women's presence in public spaces threatens the male social order (Ram 1992; Papanek and Minault 1971; Sharma 1980; Ganesh 1989). There are rules on their visibility and invisibility. *Purdah* delimits the spheres that women can legitimately occupy. The ideology of segregation and of purity and pollution serve to define women in terms of the spaces that they are allowed to occupy and the limits of their social relations.

But why are women seen as needing control? This is linked to the idea of female sexuality as wild, uncontrolled, insatiable and dangerous (Wadley 1977; Bennett 1983; Gold 1994). It is seen as being capable of devouring the male if not kept under control. They are seen as being unable to control their own sexuality and unless under the control of some man, they may bring shame to themselves and the family. The honour of the family is centrally located in the behaviour of women.

It is believed that women have more sexual energy than men and if it is not kept under control it will sap men of their energies and bring shame to themselves and their families. Women's uncontained sexuality is a potential threat to society (Tapper 1979; Bennett 1983). This understanding of female sexuality as threatening is inferred from the fact that there exist so many rules to enforce it. The need for rules points to the existence of something that always remains threatening.

Thus the ideology of honour and shame has at its centre the control of women's sexuality and allowing its expression only within legitimate spaces. It becomes imperative both for the men of a family to control women's sexuality and for women to do so themselves. These discourses all place the honour of the woman and the family upon the behaviour of women, especially in terms of their movements and in the control of their sexuality (Mandelbaum 1988).

It is important to stress that these are male discourses. They look at honour and shame from the point of view of men and women are merely the sites or the symbols. Though women's bodies and their sexuality are central to this discourse, they are never the subjects of it. Literature does not explore women's own understanding of their sexuality or how they experience shame. This is because the focus is not on shame as an individual emotion but as a principle of social organization and relationships.

Thus though women's bodies define their identity within the discourses of shame and purity, we don't know how this structures their lives other than in terms of male and family honour. Women's bodies and sexuality are circumscribed within these discourses which delimit the spaces that they can legitimately occupy and define the good and the bad woman. This idea of shame is located within the body, within how the female/feminine is viewed within Indian culture—as simultaneously impure and dangerous.

Anthropological discourses have been able to posit the links between women's sexuality, the family and society. They point to how a woman's sexuality is circumscribed within notions of purity and pollution, auspiciousness and inauspiciousness, shame and honour. But anthropological work has focused more on women's lives within cultural and symbolic systems and not so much on women's actual experience of these ideologies in their everyday lives. There has not been much examination of how women's identities and a notion of their self is constituted within these categories.

III

FEMINIST UNDERSTANDINGS OF SEXUALITY

The women's movement in India has examined women's lives and experiences in order to understand their subordinate position and oppression. The starting point has always been women's experiences which feminists have attempted to translate into a social text. This is based on the belief that women's experiences can provide the fabric from which their lives can be understood as meaningful. Thus women's experiences of their bodies, sexuality and their self can be the basis upon which a feminist understanding can be built. It is through the issues of rape and sexual violence that the women's movement has centrally dealt with sexuality.

In dealing with these issues feminists are constantly faced with the nature of shame that is located within women's bodies and that forms an important part of their identity. This has come up whether it has been rape trials where women are shamed within the space of the court, or that they fear taking a case to court because of the knowledge of the inevitability that they will have to face a shameful situation and answer shameful questions within a public space. Similarly in dealing with victims of domestic violence and other forms of violence, women's groups are forced to act within ways to protect both the honour of women and their families. During workshops and other such spaces where women come together to share their experiences, notions of shame are often central to the perceptions of their bodies and of sexuality. These will be looked at in more detail in the following sections.

The feminist understanding of shame arises directly from women's experiences of their own bodies and their self. We shall see that this differs from the anthropological understanding that we saw in the earlier section, both in terms of the perspective and in locating it within a discursive formation. I shall argue that within feminist work, the understanding of shame is one that locates it within the framework of patriarchal power that needs to be challenged as part of a political movement.

Ever since the early 1980s, legal reform has been central to the agenda of the movement. Simultaneously, feminist energies have also been directed at exhorting women to challenge the meaning that sexual violence has been given in a patriarchal society.

Women have been seen as vulnerable because of their bodies. They are seen as being in danger of violation, especially of sexual violation by men. Feminists have specifically questioned the assumptions underlying the fact that women's bodies are vulnerable to male violence and linked it to patriarchal constructions of male and female sexuality. Western feminists have debated at length about sexuality, repression, control and how these are central to women's liberation.[5]

Feminist theory has focused on the constructedness of the notion of the body, of desire, of notions of femininity, of compulsory heterosexuality and all the other ways that the body and desires have been organized and prohibited. It has sought to show how the body has been controlled and regulated, both at the level of the individual and the social body and how patriarchy rests on the foundation of the controlled female body.[6]

Different feminist theories have adhered to different notions of the body. Some have posited that we cannot speak of a biological or a body in nature. These have sought to uncover the constructedness of the body and to show how it has functioned to oppress women and to deny them full expression. This tradition may be seen as exemplified in the work of Simone de Beauvoir in *The Second Sex* which is an attempt to look at women's lives and experiences and the nature and causes of their oppression. The famous statement 'one are not born but rather becomes a woman' suggests that it is society and culture that create women and not some inherent sexual difference (1988: 295). Thus the female body and the experience of femininity is seen as a social construction.

Much of the work within the socialist feminist tradition also looks at female sexuality as having been constructed to have certain meanings within a patriarchal and capitalist society. Allison Jaggar sees that men have throughout history controlled the labour and reproductive power of women. Within a capitalist society women are alienated from their bodies in various ways. Through sexual harassment and objectification, they are alienated from their sexuality; the conditions of their motherhood are not decided by them and modern gynaecology has turned pregnancy and childbirth into an illness and taken control away from women (1983).[7]

Radical feminists, cultural feminists and ecofeminists have an understanding of the female body and experience as essentially different from the male body (Millet 1970; MacKinnon 1989; Shiva 1988). They have created discourses where women's experiences are valued and where women are taught to understand their bodies and its pleasures (Rich 1976; Daly 1978). They have sometimes asserted that women's bodies are essentially different from men's and therefore their experiences are different. There is an underlying notion that women's sexuality has been repressed and that we need to search for ways of expressing sexuality that is not patriarchal. Radical feminists condemn sexuality in patriarchal institutions and forms—institutionalized heterosexuality, pornography, prostitution and sexual objectification of women.[8] They argue that women have to look outside these institutions in order to discover their true sexuality. Beyond the underlying notion that women's sexuality has been repressed, there is also a belief that there exists a 'natural' female sexuality which is inherently subversive and liberating (Martin 1992).

Feminist theories have concentrated their analyses on uncovering the constructedness of female sexuality and to uncover non-patriarchal modes of sexual expression. Sex is seen as a natural construct that has been written upon by patriarchal constructions. There is a strong belief that women need to reclaim their sexuality and redefine desire. Power is seen as represented in 'male dominated heterosexual institutions whose elements are crystallized in the phenomenon of pornography on the one hand, and all discourses and institutions which distinguish legitimate from illegitimate sexual practice thereby creating a hierarchy of sexual expression, on the other' (Sawicki 1991: 227).

These feminist understandings have not been at the centre of the discourse of the women's movement in India, because sexuality has largely been focused upon within the context of sexual violence or the oppression that women face within the family, marriage and the like.

Sexuality has not been looked at as central to women's liberation but as linked to other relations of power within society.

IV

CHALLENGING SEXUAL VIOLENCE

The campaign against sexual violence has been central to the movement ever since the late 1970s when the Mathura rape case became a rallying point around which the movement gained tremendous momentum.[9] Since then there have been various cases of rape which have been pursued by the movement. It has demanded changes in the law and issues like marital rape and child sexual abuse have become part of its agenda. In this section I would like to look specifically at the way this issue has been addressed over the past ten years, how it has been conceptualized from women's experiences and how it provides a frame from which sexuality has been looked at.

In their campaign against rape, women's groups have been divided on whether to focus on rape as a violation of an individual woman or to look at it as a structural problem that all women have to face in a patriarchal society. At a national meeting on rape held in Bombay in 1990, discussions centred around whether to locate rape more as an act of violence or stress its sexual nature. It was felt that emphasizing it as related to the nature of sexuality would be effective if rape was seen from the point of view of the individual woman. But this would not be an effective way to work out strategies with the legal system, or to deal with 'structural violence'—custodial, institutional, political, communal, state (Rape Report 1990).

What we concluded was that though it was necessary for us to redefine rape, we should locate this redefinition in the larger socio-legal context rather than view it in isolation. In other words we move from the individual woman's violation to the rape of women in general, so that the issue always remains in focus. (ibid. 10).

Rape is one area where sexuality, violence and danger are seen to have clear linkages. It is also seen as linked to the power relations in society, gender, class and caste. In a pamphlet on rape brought out by the women's movement in 1980, the question is asked 'What is rape?' and an answer attempted.

Rape is not only a man physically violating a woman. It is an invalidation of a woman's right as an individual.
Rape is a man looking upon a woman as a piece of property. A possession to do with as he wishes to do.
It is an assertion of male power and authority. It is a way of intimidating women.
Rape is a crime continuing relentlessly against women and society. (International Women's Day Pamphlet, 1980.)

The approach of women's groups towards the State and to notions of power has not been simple or unproblematic. At the 1990 meeting, ten years since the campaign for legal changes, women's groups realized that they all faced various problems. A lot of feminist energies had been put into campaigning for changes in the law over the past ten years, yet there was also a feeling among women's groups that they needed to review their strategies.

At the very outset, it was felt that we should try to define rape, this time, beginning with women's experience of violation, not only of their bodies but of their very being in order to reconceptualize the issue and review strategies. (Rape Report 1990: 7.)

Legal strategies that have been adopted by the movement were debated at length, as also the way women's groups have dealt with individual women and their sense of identity. It was felt that the movement has to continue giving energy to both these areas—addressing the State and trying to work out an understanding of how sexual violence affects women's lives and identity.

All disabilities notwithstanding, it was felt that the importance of challenging the legal system is symbolic as well as strategically necessary. ... They [the laws] embody the power of men over women and if we are challenging the assertion of this power in other domains, how can we not do so in law. (ibid.)

Women's groups have tried to provide spaces where women can collectively attempt to define how they perceive rape, both in terms of what it means to their identity and how they perceive men. In a workshop held in 1991, participants were asked to define rape. Some of the answers were:

'Rape is an act of power'.
'It can be done by any man. Every man is capable of rape'.
'Rape should not be seen as an act of lust'.[10]

Feminists locate the dominant patriarchal discourse as portraying male sexuality as aggressive, that men are driven by the need for sex and will therefore seek it out. This is why a rape trial focuses so much on the female body, what the woman was wearing, whether or not she was alone, etc. There is an implicit belief that men are driven to fulfil their sexual needs and will naturally be tempted by women, especially if they dress provocatively, are out alone, are out at night. Being able to define a woman as bad, as not conforming to the norms or roles that patriarchy provides for them, shifts the blame back on her in the public mind and in the eyes of the law. Feminist discourse has tried to challenge this by locating rape and sexual violence as an issue of power.

Our position was: rape is an instrument of power used by all men to keep all women in their place, all women are potential rape victims, irrespective of age, manner of dressing or conduct, rape is not a spontaneous outburst of lust and passion but a preplanned, premeditated action of violence and humiliation, it is an extreme manifestation of the unequal power relationship between men and women. (Agnes 1994: 132.)

The feminist campaign has centrally focused on rape and other forms of sexual violence as an issue of power, of control over women's movements and their sexuality. Women's groups have tried to link up the structures, institutions and practices that seek to control women— the family, the State, marriage, etc. The debates have also centred on the strategies of the movement and the nature of the feminist challenge. Sexuality is not looked at in isolation but within the context of other relations of power in society.

What do we mean by control over our own sexuality: We want to be free to decide how we physically, emotionally and intellectually relate to others, men and women, and our whole social environment, and we want also to be free to determine how others relate to us, we do not want to be made into objects or mindlessly follow prescribed roles. (Bhate 1987: 102.)

...there has been a constant attempt to clarify that understanding sexuality has little to do with free sex and more with power relationships. (Gandhi and Shah 1992: 158.)

Sexual freedom cannot be the freedom of the consumer society which makes sex a commodity and human beings, objects. (Dietrich 1992: 51.)

The aim of looking at sexuality and sexual relations within such a framework is to place it within relations of power and politics that the women's movement has sought to challenge. Central to it is the idea that the personal is political which has been an important slogan of the women's movement. Sexuality thus cannot be seen as merely an issue related to the private lives of women but has to be seen as linked to the institutions and practices that structure their lives and experiences.

V

SEXUALITY AND SHAME: THE VIEW FROM THE WOMEN'S MOVEMENT

The women's movement has also sought to address issues relating to women's perceptions of their bodies, both within the context of sexual violence and more generally as well. In this they have had to encounter shame as women themselves experience it in different contexts and spaces. The aim of the women's movement has been to place this within the context of patriarchal constructions of femaleness and femininity and to empower women to define their own experiences. Women's feeling of shame at their bodies is located within certain discourses that allow men to violate a woman's body and throw the blame back upon women. What feminism has tried to show is that there is a link between shame and sexual violence.

In a booklet entitled 'Have you been sexually assaulted?', the authors state:

Shame is the power with which society represses women and permits sexual violence. Refuse men that power. Do not feel ashamed. (Purewal and Kapur 1990: 17.)

By sexual assault, men assume power over the most private aspect of a woman's life; her body. *We must deny them that power.* (ibid. 9.)

In both these passages, there is an assumption that the feeling of shame is something that is imposed upon women by society and women need to challenge it. Rape has always been seen as something that completely violates a woman and her self. In Hindi though there is a word for rape (*balaatkaar*), it is very rarely used by women. Instead they say i*zzat lootna* which translates as 'losing one's honour'. A woman who has been raped is seen as having completely lost her honour, and the honour of her family. In this fact lies the power of shame. Though the law may claim rape to be a crime, the social and cultural discourse already puts woman's body and her self at the centre. Thus the rape trial is centred around the woman's body, her conduct and her sexual history.

We have to fight rape within ourselves and outside. It is not like theft and burglary, we know it is no ordinary crime. How do we define rape in law and for ourselves, for society. (Rape Report 1990: 7.)

Society expects you to feel ashamed and guilty because the assault was a sexual one. But ask yourself *why* this must be so.

Remember sexual assault is a crime: It has been committed against you. You have the right to demand justice. You have no reason to feel guilty or ashamed. (Purewal and Kapur 1990: 7.)

What is being stressed is the fact that the woman has been wronged, that a crime has been committed against her and thus the fault lies outside her, and she is exhorted not to succumb to a feeling of shame by placing it within the politics of sexual violence.

Anthropological studies have shown that shame is linked to notions of the body, of sexuality and of the good and the bad woman, though mainly from the male point of view. Feminist discourse on the other hand locates shame as a form of patriarchal power that seeks to control women's sexuality and their freedom. Therefore it is seen as power that needs to be and can be resisted as we shall see in the strategies that are used to address it.

Feminists locate women's experience of shame in relation to their bodies as repressive and a mode of controlling their sexuality. Power is located within key institutions and practices like the family, State, heterosexuality. Notions of shame are seen as imposed upon women from outside and therefore need to be resisted. In the anthropological literature, shame functions as a normalizing discourse, as exerting power through positing the normal and the abnormal, the shameful and the honourable (Foucault 1978). Feminists, on the other hand, are speaking about shame not as a productive discourse, but as a form of repressive power (ibid.) Power as repressive is seen to have three central postulates—that power is possessed, that it flows from a central source from top to bottom and that it is primarily repressive in its exercise (Foucault 1978).

Power when seen as productive is everywhere and comes from everywhere (ibid.: 93). It is not imposed from above as a law or rule but rather functions through relationships and through practices. Thus the notion of shame becomes part of each woman's perception of herself. Foucault speaks of power as that which is directed against the body. It works to regulate the body through institutions and practices which are internalized by the body. If we look at the way the power of the discourse of shame functions, we can see that it touches woman's body from various points, whether in the way that a girl is taught to sit, to talk, the messages she receives from her family and her community, from the media, from ritual practices, etc.

Power is 'coextensive in the social body and relationships of power are interwoven with other relationships, like production, kinship, family, sexuality' (ibid.). There is not a central source from which it emanates and causes effects in everything else. Rather it is a cluster of relations. The anthropological discourse of shame and honour can be seen to have an understanding of this form of power. There is no central institution that controls but rather it is spread through the social body and serves to control women's movements and sexuality from various points. The discourse itself produces notions of good and bad women, of what is shameful and what is honourable both for the individual and the family.

Feminist discourse in India, on the other hand, has located shame as a form of sexual politics, as a patriarchal mode of exerting power over women. Since the aim of women's groups is not just to understand, but also to effect change, they have strategized ways to challenge shame as a meaning given to the body. As their understanding of female sexuality locates it as passive and vulnerable to an active, male sexuality, the strategy has been for women to assert their rights to sexual expression and freedom of movement. It has been a complicated process as sexuality is so closely linked to notions of the self and identity. But they have challenged ideas of visibility and women's right to occupy public spaces.

Since women are seen as sexually vulnerable, there has been a focus on women's right to live without this danger in various campaigns of the movement. In 1992, many women's groups in Delhi participated in a march to 'take back the night'. Women dressed in black to protest their lack of safety in public spaces, took out a march at night with candles and torches. The aim of the campaign was to raise a voice against the increasing sexual violence that women have to face in public spaces and to demand the right to move around freely anywhere and at any time.

The question today is where are women safe. Harassed in the bus, beaten at home, fear of moving at night. We have safety neither during the day nor the night.[11]

Again in September 1993 in a letter declaring 22 September 1993 as a national protest day against violence against women, women's groups in Delhi and Jaipur write:

All over the country sexual violence is increasing phenomenally. We live in terror of sexual violence. We are not safe in the streets, at our workplaces, nor in our homes. The violation of our human rights is ignored, trivialized and dismissed. ... The only answer is to collectively take to the streets again, nationally, to say *NO* to sexual violence.

These protests serve the purpose of claiming for women the right to public space and challenge the ideas of *purdah* and of good and bad women. The violence that women face in public spaces is of a sexual nature and it is aimed at controlling women's movements. By challenging this, feminists are laying a claim for women to define their movements.

Another strategy has been to get individual women to share experiences of their bodies and provide them with ways of questioning those in their own lives and a perspective from which to understand the nature of power. For example, a women's group in Delhi, *Jagori* has been bringing out a diary for women for the past five years.[12] Each year this diary explores a theme related to women's lives. The diary takes up a specific theme and it is brought out as a collective effort. The themes have included exploring women's identity, friendships among women, journey into their selves, literacy, experiences of single women and experiences of the body. It is brought out in simple Hindi, with illustrations and is seen as a space where women can reflect and write down their thoughts. The diary is seen not to be just the experiences of the women in *Jagori*, but a larger stratum. Sometimes they have used material from workshops, somtimes they have held meetings in different *bastis*. It was intended to reflect the experiences of women from different backgrounds, social strata and age groups. In 1993 the theme was *tan se man tak* (from the body to the mind), and it explored women's experiences of their bodies at different stages of their lives. From the following passages we can hear some women's voices about their body at different stages of their lives.

When I first started menstruating no one spoke about it much. We were forbidden to go into the kitchen or to touch food, especially the pickles. No one told us why. But when I grew up, I decided to test this, so I not only touched it but I made some pickle and nothing was wrong with it. We were not allowed to go to the temple either. Everyone knows that menstruation is a dirty thing. My body. There's so much shame and disappointment linked with it. It is all wound up like a ball of wool with thousands of knots. I feel scared to look at or touch my own body. Where has this fear come from?
The same body is now giving me new messages—fear, hope. This time I missed

my periods. I too am going to be a mother. I wonder what's happening inside me. I feel a shiver. (*Jagori* notebook 1993.)

During workshops, women are often asked to do certain exercises or play games.[13] For example, some begin with a game where each participant is asked to write her name on some part of her body and then everyone comes together to look at it. It is seen as an ice breaker and simultaneously brings women directly to their bodies and the emotions linked to it, because in looking for the name, they will have to touch another body. Sometimes women are asked to discuss which parts of their bodies cause them pain and pleasure and this is then discussed in the group. The aim is to get women to talk about shame and other feelings that they have about their bodies in order to get them to understand its politics and be in a position to challenge it.

It has been perceived that one reason why they feel shame at their bodies is that they lack knowledge about it. This lack of knowledge is part of the patriarchal design to keep women out of touch with their bodies and sexuality. It is thus seen as a central feminist task to provide women information about their bodies. This is carried out through workshops and literature that is written simply and with illustrations. In a booklet brought out by *Jagori* titled *Hamara sharir hamara haq* (Our bodies our right), written for neo-literates with illustrations, they state,

We women should take decisions about our lives. But how? We don't have information. How does our body work? How are children born? When do women face danger during childbirth? (Jagori 1986: 4.)

Sharir ki jaankari (knowledge about the body) is another booklet that was brought out as a collective effort by the women of *Mahila Samooh*, a women's group in Ajmer and *saathins* (women workers) of the state-run women's development programme. It begins:

We realized that our experiences were similar. The following questions were in all our minds,
Why are there so many restrictions on me?
Why do I get beaten?
Am I dirty (polluted)?
Is menstruation dirty?
If I can't have children, why am I deserted?
Is it because of me a girl child is born?
Do I always have to suppress my desires? (1989: 1.)

There are discussions on the menstrual cycle, with menstrual calendars for women to chart their cycle, illustrations of the male and the female body, about what happens at intercourse and the fact that the sex of the child is determined by the male and not the female. Apart from discussing the normal body, there are also discussions on menstrual disorders, vaginal and cervical infections. Along with this are also discussions of inequality between men and women, and restrictions on the female body.

Why is my energy restricted by society? Why are there so many controls on me? (ibid.: 7).
Why don't I get paid equally? Why is housework not valued? Why do I get less food? Why are my desires never fulfilled? (ibid.: 25)

We can see that it is a combination of understanding the body as a physical body (menstruation, childbirth, etc.) and looking at it within the picture of the larger society, of women's position in the family. Women's bodies and their health can only be understood within the framework of how their lives are structured and located in different institutions.

Whose body are you talking about? I was sent to my *sasural* at the age of 11. When my stomach hurt I ... I didn't realize till five months that I was pregnant. When we don't even understand our bodies, how can we talk about taking decisions about how many children and when to have them. (Jagori 1994.)

Hamara sharir hamara haq discusses in detail the different contraceptives available, how to use them, the dangers of certain contraceptives.

We must make decisions after getting all the information and thinking things through. (*Jagori* 1986: 9.)

The emphasis is on both teaching women about the functioning of their bodies, especially the reproductive functions (though *Sharir ki jaankari* does speak about fulfilling their desires); and locating their lack of power and control over any aspect of their lives, especially within the family. Thus they are trying to get women to understand their bodies, and take control of it. But it cannot be done in isolation as they lack control in all other aspects.

We feel very strongly that the question of women's health must be linked to women's status in society. It is essential to focus on the inherent ideology of women's role in society and its implications on health, health programmes and health education. (Bhate 1987: 84.)

Sexuality and reproduction are not seen as isolated since women perceive themselves as sexual beings within the context of all their relationships and other aspects of their daily lives. There is a belief that if women have more knowledge, they will have access to more power over their lives, to their own self-determination. The strategy being used here is to address women directly, to ask them to speak about their experiences and to help them understand the links between sexual violence, experiences of their bodies and thereby challenge the meanings put on the body by patriarchal discourses.

Women's groups build their understanding of sexuality and the body from women's own experiences of it. They build upon these experiences in order to have a theoretical understanding from which to strategize for change and reclaiming spaces. The significant point is that it is located within the politics of institutions and practices in society, and that sexuality itself is not the only or the main arena of struggle.

In India until very recently, feminist discourse has limited its analysis of sexuality to a critique of patriarchal control over women. Sexuality has never been seen as the main issue for women's liberation at any point by feminists in India. Thus there has been a critique of violence, pornography and other ways that women's sexuality has been controlled linking this to other structures of society. But over the past few years there have been feminist voices that have tried to raise issues of sexuality, desire, and lesbian sexuality as issues that need to be looked at in themselves.[14]

If we look at sexuality, its contents and discontents within the discourse of shame and honour, we see that it is necessary to understand how women themselves are implicated in power and how power and resistance are linked. If power is seen as located in the arms of the State then resistance is also directed at the State. But as we have seen, the power of the discourse of shame lies in the fact that it becomes part of a woman's understanding or definition of her self. Shame cannot be merely seen as an imposition on the female body but has to be seen as the way that the female self is defined. A sexual assault is not just an act of violence like a physical assault, but one that violates a woman's being and her own notion of her self. Thus if women are able to challenge the meaning of a sexual assault in their own lives, if they are able to question the notion of shame, then they are in fact searching for new ways of creating relationships between the body, desire and the female self.

ACKNOWLEDGEMENTS

This paper is part of a Ph.D. dissertation on the contemporary women's movement in India. I would like to thank Professor Veena Das, Dr Patricia Uberoi, Dr Radhika Chopra and Dr Meenakshi Thapan for their comments on various drafts of this paper.

NOTES

1. The contemporary women's movement consists of a wide spectrum of groups including radical left groups of the Marxist-Leninist variety, groups linked to left political parties, NGOs with a commitment to women's issues and feminism, trade union groups, mass movements, autonomous women's groups. They work on many different terrains using different strategies and modes of working, but often come together on certain platforms and issues.

2. For more detail about the autonomous women's movement see Gandhi & Shah (1991) and Kumar (1993).

3. This is not to suggest that the anthropological discourse is better or more encompassing. The point is that the focus of this paper is the feminist perspective and the discourse of the women's movement. Also my involvement in the women's movement motivates me to find ways to sharpen our politics.

4. See for example Dumont (1971) and Babb (1975).

5. For an overview, see Ferguson *et al.* (1984).

6. This we can see in the works of de Beauvoir (1988); Millet (1970); Rich (1976); Chodorow (1978); Rubin (1975).

7. For other feminist theories with a Marxist or socialist perspective, see Kuhn and Wolpe (1978) and Barrett (1988).

8. See Vance (1984). This is a collection of papers from a conference on sexuality. Both the libertarian and radical feminist points of view are elaborated.

9. This was the case of a young woman who was raped in a police station by two policemen who were acquitted in a Supreme Court judgement. The case came to light because four law teachers wrote an open letter which set in motion a nationwide campaign. For more details, see Gandhi and Shah (1992).

10. *Towards Conceptual Clarity*, report of the workshop. This was a workshop held in 1992 which was attended by women activists from all over the country to give them a chance to collectively reflect on their work, on the movement and to share theoretical developments in the area as very often, activists do not get the time to keep up with theoretical issues. This particular workshop was attended mostly by middle-class and English-speaking activists, with one or two exceptions.

11. Pamphlet brought by *Jagori* for the march' to take back the night', March 1992.

12. *Jagori* is a feminist group based in Delhi. It is a training, documentation and communication centre which was started in 1984 by a group of seven persons who felt the need for groups in cities to reach out to smaller towns and rural areas to share the knowledge and information that was available to them using various media, like workshops or booklets, plays, etc.

13. These workshops are held by *Jagori* and many other groups (my experience has been with *Jagori*) where the participants would include women from different women's groups and NGOs. *Jagori* has also worked for a couple of years with the *Mahila Samakhya* programme of the Government of India to provide training workshops on issues of feminism and women's empowerment. These workshops would mostly include women of the lower classes—village, small town and urban slum women. But some workshops have also been with more middle-class women. The women who conduct these workshops are not always members of *Jagori*, but *Jagori* organizes them and sometimes requests other women activists to take some sessions.

14. The Northern Regional Conference of women's groups in Kanpur in 1992 and the National Conference of women's movements in Tirupati in 1994 both had full sessions devoted to the issue of sexuality.

REFERENCES

Agnes, F., 1994, The anti-rape campaign. The struggle and the setback, in C. Datar (ed.), *Violence Against Women*, Stree, Calcutta.

Allen, M. and S. Mukherjee., 1982, *Women in India and Nepal*, Australian National University, Canberra.

Babb, L., 1975, *The Divine Hierarchy. Popular Hinduism in Central India*, Columbia University Press, New York.

Barrett, M., 1988, *Women's Oppression Today. The Marxist/Feminist encounter*, Verso, London.

Bennett, L., 1983, *Dangerous Wives and Sacred Sisters. Social and symbolic roles of high caste women in Nepal*, Columbia University Press, New York.

Bhate, K. *et al.* (eds.), 1987, *In Search of Our Bodies*, Shakti, Bombay.

Chodorow, N., 1978, *The Reproduction of Mothering. Psychoanalysis and the sociology of gender*, University of California Press, Berkeley.

Daly, M., 1978, *Gyn/Ecology. The metaethics of radical feminism*, Beacon Press, Boston.

Das, V., 1979, Indian women. Work, power and status, in B.R. Nanda (ed.), *Indian Women. From purdah to modernity*, Vikas, Delhi.

———, 1988, Femininity and the orientation to the body, in K. Chanana (ed.), *Socialisation, Education and Women*, Orient Longman, New Delhi.

de Beauvoir, S., 1988, *The Second Sex* (tran. by H.M. Parshley), Penguin, London.

Dietrich, G., 1992, *Reflections on the Women's Movement*, Horizon, New Delhi.

Dube, L., 1988, On the construction of gender, in K. Chanana (ed.), *Socialisation, Education and Women*, Orient Longman, New Delhi.

Dumont, L., 1971, *Homo Hierarchus. The caste system and its implications*, Weidenfeld and Nicholson, London.

Ferguson, A. *et al.*, 1984, The feminist sexuality debates, *Signs* 10(1): 106–35.

Ferro Luzzi, G., 1974, Women's pollution periods in Tamil Nadu, *Anthropos* 69: 113–161.

FAOW, 1989, *Report of the National Meeting on Rape*, Bombay.

Foucault, M., 1978, *The History of Sexuality*, vol. 1, Allen Lane London.

Fruzetti, L. and A. Oŝtor, 1982, *Concepts of Person. Kinship, caste and marriage in India*, Harvard University Press, Cambridge, Mass.

Gandhi, N. and N. Shah, 1990, *The Issues at Stake*, Kali, New Delhi.

Ganesh, K., 1989, Seclusion of women and the structure of caste, M. Krishnaraj and K. Chanana (eds.), *Gender and the Household Domain*, Sage, New Delhi.

Gatwood, L., 1985, *Devi and the Spouse Goddess: Women, Sexuality and Marriage in India*, Manohar, Delhi.

Gold, A., 1994, Gender, violence and power: Rajasthani stories of Shakti, in N. Kumar (ed.), *Women as Subjects. South Asian histories*, Stree Publications, Calcutta.

Jaggar, A., 1983, *Feminist Politics and Human Nature*, Rowman and Allanhead, New Jersey.

Jagori, 1986, *Hamara Sharir Hamara Haq*, New Delhi.

——, 1991, *Towards Conceptual Clarity*, New Delhi.

——, 1992, *Aao Mil Jul Gayen*, New Delhi.

——, 1993, *Tan Se Man Tak*, New Delhi.

——, 1994, *Mera Sharir mere Faisle*.

Kuhn, A. and A.M. Wolpe, 1978, *Feminism and Materialism*, Routledge and Kegan Paul, London.

Kumar, Radha, 1993, *The History of Doing*, Kali for Women, New Delhi.

Mackinnon, C., 1989, *Toward a Feminist Theory of the State*, Harvard University Press, Massachusetts.

Mandelbaum, D., 1988, *Women's Seclusion and Men's Honour*, University of Arizona Press, Tucson.

Martin, B., 1992, Feminism, criticism and Foucault, in Crowley and Himmelweit (eds.), *Knowing Women*, Polity Press, Cambridge.

Millet, K., 1970, *Sexual Politics*, Ballantine Books, New York.

Papanek, H. and G. Minault, 1971, *Separate Worlds: Studies of Purdah in South Asia*, Chanakya Publishers, Delhi.

Purewal, J. and N. Kapur, *Have You Been Sexually Assaulted?*, New Delhi.

Ram, K., 1992, *Mukkuvar Women*, Kali, New Delhi.

Rich, A., 1976, *Of woman Born. Motherhood as experience and Instititition*, W.w. Norton, New York.

Rubin, G., 1975, The traffic in women. Notes on the 'political economy' of sex, in R. Reiter (ed.), *Toward an Anthropology of Women*, Monthly Review Press, New York.

Sawicki, J., 1991, *Disciplining Foucault. Feminism, power and the body*, Routledge, New York.

Sharma, U., 1980, *Women, Work and Property in Northwest India*, Tavistock, London.

Shiva, V., 1988, *Staying Alive: Women, Ecology and Development in India*, Kali for Women, New Delhi.

———, 1989, *Sharir ki Jaankari*, Kali, New Delhi.

Vance, C. (ed.), 1984, *Pleasure and Danger: Exploring Female Sexuality*, Routledge and Kegan Paul, Boston.

Tapper, B.E., 1979, Widows and goddesses. Female roles in deity symbolism in a South Indian village, *Contributions to Indian Sociology*.

Wadley, S., 1988, Women in the Hindu tradition, in R. Ghadially (ed.), *Women in Indian Society*, Sage, New Delhi.

Yalman, N., 1963, On the purity of women in the castes of Ceylon and Malabar, *Journal of the Royal Anthropological Institute*: 93.

Index